QUIETLY EXPLODING

THE LIFE OF
MEDAL OF HONOR HERO
CHARLES DENVER (STAFFELBACH) BARGER

A biography by
MSgt (Ret.) Joseph P. Bowman
with Chris Kraft

QUIETLY EXPLODING
The Life of Medal of Honor Hero Charles Denver (Staffelbach) Barger
by
MSgt (Ret.) Joseph P. Bowman
with Chris Kraft

Copyright © 2018 by Joseph P. Bowman

All rights reserved.

Background cover photo courtesy of Australian War Memorial
https://www.awm.gov.au/collection/C46038

Cover and interior design and layout by Clint and Carole Hayes

Publisher's Cataloging-in-Publication Data provided by
Five Rainbows Cataloging Services

Names: Bowman, Joseph P., author.
Title: Quietly exploding : the life of Medal of Honor hero Charles Barger / MSgt. (Ret.)
Joseph P. Bowman.
Description: Garland, TX : Del Hayes Press, 2018. | Includes bibliographical references.
Identifiers: LCCN 2018948103 | ISBN 978-0-9822706-8-4 (pbk.)
Subjects: LCSH: Soldiers--United States--Biography. | World War, 1914-1918--Veterans-
-Biography. | Medal of Honor--Biography. | Police--Missouri--Kansas City--Biography.
| Post-traumatic stress disorder. | Serial murderers--Family relationships. | BISAC:
BIOGRAPHY & AUTOBIOGRAPHY / Military.
Classification: LCC U53.B37 2018 (print) | LCC U53.B37 (ebook) | DDC 940.4/0092--
dc23.

Published by Del Hayes Press, 3009 Cross Timbers Lane, Garland, TX 75044. Visit our
website at www.delhayespress.com for information on bulk orders.

First edition.

Printed in the United States of America.

Dedicated to the memory of my cousin,
Charles Denver Barger
(1894-1936)

With special thanks to
Joseph Arnold Barger

TABLE OF CONTENTS

PREFACE

Charles Denver Barger does not have the name recognition of, say, Alvin York or Eddie Rickenbacker, his World War I Medal of Honor colleagues, but his exploits are every bit as comparable for their daring and bravery. Three trips, 500 yards into No Man's Land, with a withering barrage of machine gun fire following him all the way in and all the way out, he manifested no hint of fear. This feat of supreme heroism was not a one-time occurrence, for he earned three French Croix de Guerres for other actions, and very likely performed lesser degrees of heroic conduct that we never recognized or recorded.

I happened onto Charlie's story several years ago while conducting genealogical research on my father's line. Charlie's father, George, was my four-times great-uncle and a member of the notorious Staffelbach gang. This gang included George's brother, my three-times great-grandfather, Ed, George's mother, my four-times great-grandmother, Nancy, and another of George and Ed's brothers, Mike. These cold-blooded serial killers rank up there with the Bloody Benders, another family of serial killers from Kansas, but the Staffelbach story has never been accurately told ... until now.

When the Staffelbachs went to prison in 1897, Charlie ended up in an orphanage in St. Louis, Missouri, from which he was adopted by Sidney and Phoebe Barger. I found Charlie in the 1900 census under the name "Denver Staffelback," and then as Denver Barger in 1910. Additional research led me to the Find-a-Grave website, where there was a photo of Charlie wearing the Medal of Honor.

Initially, I thought that there had been some mistake. After contacting Charlie's grandson, Joseph A. Barger, however, I learned that Charlie was indeed my cousin through my Staffelbach line, and that he was a Medal of Honor recipient. Piecing together his tumultuous biography, it crossed my mind many times that our violent bloodline may have played as much of a role in his fearless nature as his chaotic upbringing. Killing another human being, after all, is killing another human being, regardless of the circumstances.

Another person researching Charlie's ancestry was Chris Kraft, Charlie's cousin on his mother's side. As I was piecing together the Staffelbach history, I shared it with Chris to help her along with her research. Soon, she returned my material with a number of changes and recommendations for moving the story along. Moreover, she suggested that I eliminate all subjectivity and not get caught up in writing what I "think" happened. No one likes to have their writing criticized, and I am no exception, but once I overcame my initial indignation, I revisited her comments and realized that she was absolutely right! That, as they say, was the beginning of a beautiful friendship.

I went to work drafting this story, from beginning to end, and then submitted each chapter to Chris for her input. We hashed out the details, disagreed on occasion—but not in a negative way—and two years later we finalized this book and prepared it for publication. This book has come a long way from when we started, but I am proud of what we have accomplished. We kept it factual, with as little bias as possible, and made every effort to ensure accuracy. As with any book, however, there will inevitably be errors, and in those instances, I assume all responsibility.

Charlie's biography is unique in many ways, as I have not found a Medal of Honor recipient born into a similar situation. Many, however, grew up in extreme poverty and with few prospects of rising above their dire circumstances. Charlie had every reason to enter upon a life of crime, but, to his credit, he made a herculean effort to become a productive member of society, until his mental faculties diminished. Unfortunately, his struggle to become a productive member of society was one battle in which he would not emerge victorious.

In the aftermath of World War I, veterans' issues were politically partisan rather than an earnest effort to "care for him who shall have borne the battle," as Abraham Lincoln so eloquently stated. President Warren G. Harding appointed the corrupt and scandalous Charles Robert Forbes as first Director of the Veterans' Bureau; President Calvin Coolidge proclaimed when vetoing a bill granting bonuses to World War I veterans, "... patriotism ... bought and paid for, is not patriotism"; President Herbert Hoover was marred by the Bonus March scandal; and President Franklin D. Roosevelt sought to cut veterans' benefits by 40 percent.

There was no Congressional Medal of Honor Society at that time to lobby on behalf of our nation's supreme heroes, and the U.S. government and Veterans Administration ignored repeated appeals to assist Charlie when he needed it most. One can only imagine how these entities turned their back on servicemen of lesser distinction. During the Great Depression, after all, even the smallest compensation would have eased the financial hardship of thousands of downtrodden veterans, many of whom resorted to suicide.

Post-traumatic stress was called "shell shock" during and after World War I, and had such a negative connotation to it that no one with Charlie's reputation could be considered a victim of such an affliction. During World War II, "shell shock" was called "combat fatigue" and those who suffered with it were likened to cowards. Veterans of the Korean War and Vietnam were virtually ignored for years, and it wasn't until after Desert Storm where a renewed respect for veterans emerged. Now, finally, post-traumatic stress is getting the attention it deserves, although a lot of work and research must still be done.

It would have been interesting to see how Charlie's life would have transpired had he had the help he needed for post-traumatic stress, compensation from the Veterans Administration, and a stipend from the government, which Medal of Honor recipients merit today. He certainly wouldn't have met such an untimely and horrific death. The past, of course, cannot be changed, but, as a society, we can learn by past mistakes and prevent recurrence. The service and sacrifice of our veterans justify as much.

Joseph P. Bowman, MSgt, USAF (Ret.)

ACKNOWLEDGEMENTS

Q*uietly Exploding* could not have been written without the cooperation and assistance of many individuals, but the single-most contributor to this book was Chris Kraft, to whom I am eternally indebted. Her insight, encouragement and resolve throughout this process has been nothing short of phenomenal. Upward and onward, my friend!

My cousin, Joseph A. Barger, and his lovely wife, Euleta, were also instrumental in verifying facts and events, and were my inspiration for writing this book. They generously provided photos of Charlie, before and after the war, and newspaper clippings, which aided materially to the final product. Other family members who contributed photos and/or biographical details were James C. Barger, June Buccina, Lisa (Staffelbach) Duitman, Barbara (Lake) Williams, George W. Grokett, and Donnie Hewlett.

There were also several relatives of key figures in this book who went out of their way to provide me with photographs and other material, namely: Linda Brzezinski (relative of Ernest G. Rowell); Georgette Guernsey (relative of Jesse Funk); and Ann (Reed) Scileppi (relative of Robert Reed). Johnny Thompson, a close personal friend of my cousin, James Barger, provided a rare photo of Charlie right after the Armistice; Don Morfe permitted me to use photos of Charlie's headstones; and John H. Bratt authorized the use of photos and biographical information posted on a website dedicated to the service of his grandfather, Martin Verhage, who served in the same regiment as Charlie.

My longtime friend, Stan H. Smith, has been my primary resource of Medal of Honor historical information for 40 years. His role and impact regarding this book cannot be overstated, and to him I owe a debt of gratitude that I could never adequately repay.

Eric Caubarreaux, with whom I catalogued the awards and decorations of General of the Army Douglas MacArthur, was instrumental in verifying Charlie's awards and decorations. For years, his entitlements were erroneously depicted, and even the family believed what was printed in books, newspapers and magazine articles. Eric's expertise, coupled with his association with subject-matter experts, aided immeasurably in accurately representing Charlie's awards and decorations, which are included in the appendix.

The following individuals and organizations were instrumental in obtaining photos, official documentation, or other material, which, collectively, filled in many gaps that would have otherwise been omitted: Gayle Alvarez, President, The Medal of Honor Historical Society; Chris Baker, fourteeneighteen/research; Fred Borch, President of the Orders and Medals Society of America; Det. (Ret.) Clarence Gibson, Kansas City Police Department Historical Society; Joanna Legg, www. greatwar.co.uk; Lori Miller, Redbird Research; and Stacie Petersen, Registrar, National World War I Museum and Memorial. To them, I extend my profound thanks!

Show me a hero and I'll write you a tragedy.

F. Scott Fitzgerald

Chapter One

THE NOTORIOUS STAFFELBACHS

Spawned from a family of cold-blooded murderers, Charles Denver Staffelbach grew to become a legendary warrior, possessing qualities rarely encountered on the battlefield. A quiet country boy, unimpressive by most accounts, he was considered by some to be a little slow, owing as much from a lack of innate intellect as formal education. He was unpretentious and unsophisticated, downtrodden and dirt-poor, mistreated by those a notch up on the societal hierarchy, and possessing every reason to go bad. Nonetheless, with sheer grit, and against all odds, he overcame enormous obstacles to become a productive member of society.

When the United States entered WWI by declaring war on Germany in April 1917, Charles Denver Staffelbach—by then Charles Denver Barger—responded to his country's call, taking to the rigors of the military lifestyle without opposition or complaint. On the battlefield he was fearless, intentionally exposing himself to machine gun fire, as if he were invincible or possessed a death wish. One has to wonder if the disreputable traits of his grandmother, father and uncles were inherent, enabling him to kill without hesitation or remorse, even though he did so for a noble cause.

By war's end, Charlie had earned the Medal of Honor and garnered international acclaim. France, Great Britain, Belgium, Italy and Montenegro bestowed medals upon him to recognize his repeated feats of heroism, and his division commander cited him as the greatest hero of the 89th Division. In fact, the decorations of Alvin C. York, who was certainly more celebrated, dwarfed in comparison.

Charlie returned home to a hero's welcome. An honest man with demonstrated integrity, he eventually became a police officer. The police department retained his services for a decade before discharging him without a pension or compensation. By that time his mind was failing him due to mustard gas exposure during the war, and the Veterans Administration repeatedly denied him benefits. Charlie had risen to his greatest feats in the Army; now he was to experience, slowly and painfully, a very sad fall from grace.

Charlie's biography cannot be adequately conveyed without providing at least a brief historical account about his paternal kinfolk, for their story had a direct bearing on his formative years and, consequently, the trajectory of his entire life. This book, in effect, incorporates two compelling narratives, each of which demands their respective levels of comprehensive research.

Charlie's direct paternal ancestors provide a long line of honorable and successful people, including the famous Swiss goldsmith, Hans Peter Staffelbach (1657-1736). Even his paternal grandfather's siblings made their mark in their respective fields. Their descendants included Charles and Louis Traung, the West Coast lithograph magnates, and the esteemed educator, Dr. Elmer H. Staffelbach. Charlie's parents and grandparents, however, introduce a dark side of the family history.

Charlie's grandfather, Michel Staffelbach, was born in Sursee, Switzerland, on February 2, 1823, and immigrated with his parents and siblings to Highland, Illinois, in 1835. He evolved into a decent farmer, but farming was not his forte. Therefore, when his brother, Joseph, opened a confectionary in St. Louis, Missouri, in 1847, he eagerly partnered up. Although not as gifted a businessman and entrepreneur as Joseph, Michel was passionate about his work and became a first-rate confectioner.

On a visit to his sister's home in Dubuque, Iowa, in the early 1850s, Michel met a young lady named Nancy Chase who was born on August 16, 1832, in Allegany County, New York. They married in Dubuque on June 4, 1852, and through the years they would divorce and marry one another two more times. During their turbulent union, they had fourteen children, but only seven lived to adulthood: Ed, Lon, Louisa, Mike, Emma, George and Mary. George Staffelbach was Charlie's biological father.

During the 1850s, Joseph Staffelbach purchased a farm in Rockingham, Iowa, leaving his brother, Michel, to keep the confectionary afloat. The business folded shortly thereafter, and Michel was compelled to work for the competitor that drove him out of business. In 1861, Nancy talked him into relocating to Jamestown, Wisconsin, to be near her aging parents. The family remained there an entire decade before settling in Rockingham where Joseph was then a very wealthy farmer. Michel had done well while working as a confectioner with his brother, and may have felt that teaming up with him in farming would similarly boost his position in life.

In the early 1870s, new lead deposits were discovered in Lawrence County, Missouri, where prospectors soon amalgamated, and a plethora of mining companies organized. Michel understood that wherever a large influx of people settled there was an opportunity to cash in, so a few months after Charlie's father, George, was born in Rockingham on May 19, 1872, the family returned to Missouri where Michel resumed his profession as a confectioner. T.F. Millard, a reporter with the *St. Louis Republic,* authored the most credible accounts of the Staffelbach family. He described their Mt. Vernon home as "a miserable 40-acre strip of land where the buildings were rotten and in a state of all-around degeneracy."[1]

Millard, who became involved in researching and reporting on this family in 1897 due to their criminal activities, also went into some detail about an incident in 1876, wherein Nancy claimed that Michel molested their eleven-year-old daughter, Louisa.   Michel vehemently denied the accusations and counterclaimed that Nancy "preferred the society of her grown sons" and "rejected his rightful attentions."[2] The charges and countercharges were ultimately dropped, and Michel and Nancy reconciled, but even then, their marriage was unstable.

"For some time after this incident," Millard reported, "the family lived together on the Lawrence County farm, shunned by all neighbors and practically ostracized. But such a state of affairs could not continue. Fearful for his life, as his sons more and more openly espoused the cause of their mother and hurled their threats at him, old man Staffleback [sic] went his way. Mrs. Staffleback [sic] then sued for a divorce, and secured it by default."[3]

Michel moved to Joplin, Missouri, which had once been the world's hub for lead and zinc. In a section of town called Swindle Hill, he purchased a rundown house, which was part boards and part canvas. Millard writes: "This locality of Joplin was inhabited by the scum of the town's population; a cluster of shanties that harbored bum, criminal and prostitute alike; where a man's life was not safe after dark, and where even the police never went singly."[4]

Within a year after divorcing, Charlie's grandparents, Michel and Nancy, remarried, perhaps out of necessity. Michel needed his sons to maintain the farm in Mt. Vernon, and Nancy needed the financial security in which even an unstable married life afforded. Despite every effort, however, their marriage was as turbulent as ever, and in February 1887, he evicted her from their home in Mt. Vernon. She immediately filed a petition for divorce.[5]

Nancy claimed, through her attorney, that she had been a faithful and loving wife, but that Michel had treated her with such indignity that living with him became intolerable. She went on to state that he often declared in the presence of others that he preferred the company of other women. Moreover, she felt obligated to work as a "common domestic" for others to provide for herself, as "he has long failed and refused to provide plaintiff with proper food, clothing and the necessities of life." According to her attorney, Michel would then appropriate part of her paltry wages and use it for his own purposes.[6]

For the second time, Charlie's grandparents divorced. Michel alternately resided in his home on Swindle Hill and his farm in Mt. Vernon. Meanwhile, Nancy was forced to rely upon the income derived from the shiftless labor of her sons, Ed, Mike and George. They would occasionally be arrested for stealing a hog or robbing a smokehouse, which suggests that their introduction into criminal activity was due to necessity. In time, however, Nancy encouraged all her children to turn to more devious and abject means to support her and her family. "The boys were frequently arrested and jailed for short terms," discovered Millard, "and the girls indiscriminately accepted the attention of miners to 'swell the family revenue.'"[7]

Charlie's grandparents married for the third and final time in Mt. Vernon on September 22, 1889. Michel and Nancy remained together until December 1893, when she tried to poison him with "Rough on Rats," an arsenic used to kill vermin. Just after Christmas she filed for divorce, citing charges similar to those in her previous complaints. This time she retained the legal services of John Turk and Norman Gibbs, and resided with the latter until the case went to court.[8]

"Mrs. Staffelback [sic] was stopping at the residence of her counsel, Mr. Gibbs," writes a reporter with *The Springfield Democrat,* "and the husband was jealous of Gibbs, doubtless without the shadow of cause, for there is no snowy contribution from the loftiest peak of the icy and sunkissed [sic] Alps more pure and chaste than the tall blackjack of Chigger Hill. Besides, whatever the old man's memory of the past charms of the plaintiff, she now bears on her face the wrinkles of years, crowsfeet [sic] are about her eyes, and her mouth looks like the stem end of a tomato after a drought. It would be doing gross injustice to Col. Gibbs to assume that his taste reached no higher than this."[9]

This reporter also asserted: "Whatever the charms of Mrs. Staffelback [sic] in the halcyon days of her maidenhood, time has left the tracery of his fingers upon her face and marred the contour of her other physical charms, while the male party in the case is so ugly it must hurt."[10]

When Charlie's grandparents convened at the Lawrence County Courthouse on February 20, 1894, for what became their final divorce, Nancy was put on the stand and testified with startling particularity to the allegations in her petition. Upon cross examination, Michel's attorney, W.B. Skinner, questioned Nancy about the rat poison, to which Gibbs vehemently objected. "Did you furnish Mrs. Staffelbach with the poison?" Skinner brazenly questioned Gibbs.[11]

"Mr. Gibbs came near rending the empyrean vault with a barbaric war whoop of rage," revealed *The Springfield Democrat.* "A shout of laughter went up from the people who crowded the courtroom and the sheriff had to command silence. Some of the children were put on the stand, and while part of them were for the mother, the others were for the father, and they proceeded to relate the most disgusting details of immorality committed by the girls, the mother and the old man."[12]

In the immediate aftermath of this court appearance, Michel resided in his home in Joplin, and Nancy and the children inhabited the farm in Mt. Vernon. Their divorce became official one year from their court appearance. It goes without saying that Michel was not the ideal father, but as long as he remained with the family, his sons were charged with nothing more than trivial offenses. Now they ran amok, and their escapades were about to take a deadly turn.

Charlie's grandfather opened a wholesale and retail candy store in East Joplin. With all the crimes in which Michel's family was mixed up, the deviant accounts of molestation were all but forgotten. When he succumbed to stomach cancer in Joplin on May 15, 1899, his obituary called him "an honest old man and had had nothing to do with his former wife and sons for several years past."[13] Yet Michel died knowing that his line tainted his honorable family name, and for that reason he died disgraced.

Charlie's parents, George Staffelbach and Cora Victoria Lake, married in Mt. Vernon on July 2, 1893. She was born on September 14, 1878, in Verona, Missouri, to William J. and Margaret E. (Ham) Lake, and became a principal player in 1897 as the crimes of the Staffelbach family came to light. She was the firstborn of William's marriage to Margaret, but both of her parents had prior marriages and had children from those marriages.[14]

When Charlie's maternal grandparents, William and Margaret Lake, married on October 14, 1877, in Christian County, Missouri, William was fifty-three and Margaret was twenty-nine. Besides Cora, they had two sons: Robert Harrison Lake and George "Walter" Lake. In the late-1940s, Robert's granddaughter had a homework assignment where she had to ask her relatives about their heritage. That evening at the dinner table, she asked her grandfather about his roots and Robert told her that his ancestors originated in Scotland.[15]

As Robert went into his history, he revealed that his father, William, once sent his sister, Cora, to live with another family to settle a debt he incurred, even though she was too young to be used as "slave labor." The retelling of this story upset Robert so much that he couldn't finish. He abruptly arose from his chair and stormed out of the house to cool down.[16]

Charlie's grandmother and grandfather Lake divorced in 1891 over a dispute regarding Cora—quite possibly due to William sending her to settle this debt. They remarried in Mt. Vernon on September 19, 1892, but the damage to their daughter was irreversible. Although it is unknown where Cora was sent or how long she stayed there, it appears that her time with that family might have given her entrance into the Staffelbach clan.[17]

Robert's granddaughter, Barbara (Lake) Williams, related that William forced Cora's marriage to George Staffelbach when he discovered that she had been "violated." Another of Robert's granddaughters, June Buccina, said that Cora first became pregnant when she was 12, and had never menstruated prior to her first pregnancy. June heard that Cora had a miscarriage with her first baby.[18]

Cora gave birth to Charlie on June 3, on the Staffelbach farm in Mt. Vernon, Missouri. He was presumably delivered by his paternal grandmother, Nancy, who was a midwife. There is some question regarding the precise year of his birth. It is widely accepted that he was born in 1892, which coincides with the 1930 census and his death certificate. If he was born in 1892, his mother would have been thirteen when she had Charlie, and that would have been a full year before she married George in Mt. Vernon on July 2, 1893. That theorem is possible, but doesn't hold up under close scrutiny.

There is significant evidence that points to 1894 as Charlie's birth year, which seems more feasible. Census records in 1900, 1910 and 1920 indicate that he was born in 1894, and his World War I Draft Registration Card, for which he personally provided the information, lists his birthdate as June 3, 1894. The author is convinced that 1894 is accurate, yet absent an official birth record, uncertainty will always exist.

On June 1, 1894, just two days before Charlie was born, police made a carefully planned raid on the Staffelbach's shanty and discovered a large amount of stolen property. Charlie's Uncle Mike was arrested and charged with burglary, which he allegedly committed three months earlier near Clarkson, Missouri. When Mike was caught in Pierce City, Missouri, on June 3, he was wearing a suit of clothes that he stole during the burglary.[19]

Authorities returned Mike to Mt. Vernon and placed him in jail to await trial. Evidently, he didn't much care for the accommodations, for on the evening of July 23, 1894, he made a failed escape attempt with two other prisoners, Bony Cox and Harry Mitchell.[20] On August 16, 1894, Mike was indicted for burglary and larceny, but charges for the former were dropped in exchange for a guilty plea to the latter. He was sentenced to two years at the Missouri State Penitentiary in Cole County.

Charlie's father, George, soon joined Mike in the Missouri State Penitentiary for an unrelated theft, and by then the family had worn out its welcome in Mt. Vernon. According to Mike, a mob of a hundred or more angered citizens, wrecked the place and drove the family out of town.[21]

Charlie's grandmother, Nancy Staffelbach, moved to Joplin after the family's expulsion, and with the financial assistance of her children she purchased a small lot at 1101 Ivy Street (now Conner Avenue), on the corner of W. 11th. The house, situated on the west side of town, was hastily and poorly constructed out of rough lumber and was only intended for temporary habitation. Residing in the small dwelling with Nancy was Ed and his wife (also named Cora), plus their young daughters, Sarah and Samantha. For the time being, Charlie and his mother, Cora, also stayed at Nancy's house while George was incarcerated.*

T.F. Millard reports that Nancy had begun consorting with a Civil War veteran in Joplin named Christopher "Dad" Rodabaugh, who left his wife for her. Over the months, their affair became public knowledge and was scorned throughout the community. On New Year's Day, 1895, Rodabaugh visited Nancy's home on Ivy Street and told her that he had just drawn his pension, amounting to $35. She tried to con him out of a portion of the money, but he didn't give her a dime.[22]

Charlie's uncle, Mike Staffelbach, who obtained an early release from prison, was also at the house that day, and after a while he called his mother aside and told her he needed money. They talked for a few minutes, and a little while later he went outside to converse with his brother-in-law, Billy Martin. Charlie's mother, Cora, overheard Mike tell Billy that he knew where they could get some money if he wasn't afraid and wouldn't tell. Billy assured him that he was game, and then they left. Rodabaugh stayed at Nancy's house awhile, and then started out to visit his sister-in-law. As he walked toward the door to leave, Nancy told him to be careful and not to lose his money. That was the last anyone ever saw of him.[23]

"The next morning they came back," related Cora to Millard in 1897. "Mike, Ed and Billy came in together. I had not got up, and pretended to be asleep. They all went outside and gathered at the corner of the house, near the window. I got up and slipped over so I could hear every word they said. They poured out some money and counted it. I heard them say there was $31.50. Then they divided it.

"Mike told his mother he had got his shirt bloody and had had to steal another. The old woman asked him what he did with it, and he said he burned it. They wanted Martin not to tell, and told him they knew where they could get some more money the next night if they were slick. Mike told Martin that they would kill him if he peached [snitched]. Then I heard them coming, and jumped back into bed and pretended to be asleep.

"The old woman [Nancy] never suspected anything and called me to come help her get breakfast. While they were outside, I heard the old woman say, 'Did you see Dad [referring to "Dad" Rodabaugh]?' Mike answered, 'No, nor I never will unless I look down a shaft.' A week or two after that I left Joplin and went on a visit to my folks."[24]

One can presume that Cora probably took baby Charlie with her.

---

* To clear up any confusion, the reader should understand that Ed's wife, Cora, is not mentioned again in this story, and the Cora referred to going forward refers to George's wife/Charlie's mother.

The Staffelbachs became so disreputable in Joplin that the police warned Nancy that they were watching her family and were going to make it difficult for them to live there. One evening, she quietly gathered a few meager belongings and stole over to Galena, Kansas, a naturally hilly boomtown about seven miles west of Joplin. She retained ownership of her home on Ivy Street in Joplin, and occasionally returned there, yet from that time she resided in an old long-abandoned cabin she found near the southern extremity of "Pickers Point."[25]

T.F. Millard writes: "'Pickers Point' is the name commonly given to that outlying part of Galena, in the midst of her thousand shafts and gray dumps, where congregate when night falls the worst element of the town. Not in all the slums of St. Louis, Chicago or New York could Pickers Point be duplicated for depravity, for vice reached a depth there that startled even those familiar with its habits and ways. Vile brothels abounded on every side, but the houses were, as a rule, so isolated that the inhabitants of one did not know what transpired in another. Lead and zinc miners of the roughest class on earth visited there when they drew their pay, passing the hours gambling or in the company of women even more lowly and degraded than themselves. Disturbances were so common that they attracted little or no attention."[26]

Visiting Galena today, one gets a flavor for the neighborhood at the time in which Charlie grew up there. A typical small Kansas town, Galena has a main street of old commercial buildings and tree-lined residential streets. But, the old Picker's Point is now a large expanse of mostly vacant land, gently rolling hills and mostly treeless. One can still see remnants of abandoned mining operations on site, but with none of the primitive housing that once populated the area. Pathways wind around over the vacant land expanse and one can imagine shanties standing along the paths.

According to Millard, the 12-by-14-foot cabin inhabited by the Staffelbachs sat on a hill, exposed in the winter by icy blasts that swept down the valley, and in the summer, stood unprotected from the sun. It was said to be too small for even two people, and yet it was necessary for this family of eight to eat and sleep there together. The one door was so narrow and low that a child would have to stoop to enter, and the roof was a crazy patchwork of shingles and boards. The single window, completely shattered, consisted of a hole about two feet square.[27]

Inhabiting the tiny dwelling with Nancy were her children, Ed, Mike, Louisa and Emma. Their spouses remained in Missouri, away from the unscrupulous lifestyle the family led in Galena, and were as horrified as the rest of the community when the news of their abominable deeds broke. Cora, who left Joplin with Charlie to stay with her parents a week or two after Rodabaugh disappeared, also resided with the Staffelbachs in Galena once George secured his release from prison.

"At first the incoming created little comment," Millard writes of the Staffelbachs' arrival in Galena, "for in appearance and general make-up Mother Nance and her children did not materially differ from their neighbors. Hovels almost as miserable surrounded them on every side, and their reputation was no worse than that of the locality."[28]

Soon, Nancy opened a house of prostitution that was fronted as a restaurant, seeking to profit from the plethora of miners, prospectors and businessmen passing through the city. Nancy, Emma and Louisa kept the place maintained, while Ed, Mike and George kept it stocked with women. They habitually traveled across the border into Missouri and visited local fairs to prey upon naïve young country girls seeking money, excitement, or a place to live. The bordello soon came to be called Staffelbach House and, according to news accounts, it was quite popular with local miners.[29]

In Carthage, Missouri, on October 5, 1896, Nancy married Charles H. Wilson, a small man of dark complexion, born in Kentucky in May 1837, to an Irish father and German mother. Newspapers reveal that Charles and Nancy knew each other for nearly ten years, and in an effort to besmirch Nancy's reputation even further, they reported that the couple had never actually married. Not surprisingly, they had their altercations, and one time when Charles was in jail for a petty offense, he made the remark, "Just wait until I get out of this and I'll have the whole Staffelbach family in jail!"[30] After his release, however, he did nothing.

Charlie's aunts, Emma and Louisa, were known to engage in prostitution, so it is not surprising that Nancy expected Charlie's mother to participate as well. However, when Cora discovered what was expected of her, she claimed that she grabbed Charlie and ran back to her parent's home in Missouri. She further reported that George summarily wrote a letter pledging that if she returned to him they would live separate lives away from the bordello, and that she ultimately agreed.[31]

In January 1897, just ten or twelve days after her return, Cora witnessed a series of events that led her to believe someone was murdered by the family. After that, she said, she was afraid to run away again.[32] In his *St. Louis Republican* article dated September 19, 1897, Millard recounts the following details given by Charlie's mother, who was around 18 at the time he interviewed her.

An Italian peddler visited Staffelbach House with a pack full of jewelry, pencils, linens, laces, etc. He soon hooked up with a girl named Trixie, who was reportedly from Springfield, and they eventually adjourned to an area in the house where they could be intimate. He gave Trixie a breastpin, some beads, and a scarf pin, and then took out his pocketbook, wrapped it in his coat, and placed it under his pillow.[33]

Charlie's uncle, Mike Staffelbach, happened to notice cash in the peddler's pocketbook and remarked, "You've got a lot of money."[34]

"About $15," the peddler responded.[35]

After a while everyone went to bed, except Ed, Mike and George. Mike kept looking at Cora to see if she was asleep, and she noticed him watching, so pretended to be. "Then Mike slipped over and caught hold of the coat under the peddler's head and tried to pull it out," Cora recalled. "But he woke the man, who jumped up and drew a pistol. Mike knocked it from his hand."[36]

Mike and George assaulted the peddler with a pistol and a club, respectively, while he ran from the house in his underclothes. Mike, Ed and George gave chase, and a minute or two later Cora heard a gunshot.[37]

"In about an hour they came back," Cora revealed. "They had the pocketbook. They stood around the table and divided the money. They had a quarrel over it. When they got through quarreling, Mike said, 'What did you do with the pack? They'll find it and we'll be arrested.' Ed said that he had put the pack in a safe place. Mike said they had better throw it in the shaft. Then they took the pack away and did not come back until nearly morning. Pretty soon after that Trixie left. She said she was going before anyone else was killed. I think the boys sold what was in the pack."[38]

The peddler's corpse was dumped into a mineshaft about ten yards north of Staffelbach House. The other girls were similarly frightened by this vile murder, but they were silenced by death threats.[39]

Among those living at Staffelbach House at the time were two young German girls, judged to be between fifteen- and seventeen-years-old. They arrived in September 1896, and were close friends. "I remember that the weather was warm," stated Charlie's mother, Cora. "Mike and Ed had found them living in a tent over to the north of town, and persuaded them to come to our house. I can't remember the names of the girls. One had dark hair. She was called Alice. The other girl had light hair. Lilly Langston, a girl from Aurora, was boarding with us at the time."[40]

According to T.F. Millard, Mike selected Alice as his mistress and Ed chose the other girl, even though both men were still married. They warned the girls repeatedly that if they ever found them in the company of other men they would kill them. But a week or ten days after the peddler was murdered, Charlie's grandmother Nancy and his father George were minding the Staffelbach bordello when several men entered for drinks and a good time. Charlie's uncles, Ed and Mike, arrived soon thereafter, and everything was fine until Mike saw Alice sitting on the lap of one of the men.[41]

Mike jumped up cursing, and moved to assault the man, who quickly ran for the door and disappeared into the darkness. Mike pulled Alice aside and the two began arguing so loudly that Lydia Daniel, a woman who lived nearby, heard the commotion and watched the remaining clientele flee. It was Cora's recollection that Alice was lying on a bed after the guests departed, and that Mike ordered Alice to get up. She evidently didn't move fast enough to suit him, so he struck her with a blow to the cheek.[42]

Alice attempted to retaliate, and then threatened to leave. According to Cora, Mike feared that she would tell about the peddler, so he seized her by the throat and commenced to strangle her. The other girl valiantly came to her aid when Mike began banging Alice's head against the hardwood floor. Just then, Ed entered the room and began to chastise "his girl" for interfering. When she argued back, he grabbed her and threw her hard upon the bed. Clutching her throat with one hand and drawing his six-shooter with the other, Ed simultaneously choked her and crushed her skull with the butt of his gun until blood flowed from her ears and nostrils and life became extinct.[43]

Mike rolled Alice's body in a sheet and placed it under the bed, and Ed covered the body of the other girl with quilts and left her where she died. Leaving the house, they returned about midnight and took the corpses to a secluded shaft near where they had dumped the peddler. To keep the bodies from surfacing, they covered them with loose dirt and rocks that were piled at the mouth of the shaft.[44]

Charlie's parents slipped outside and watched them dump the bodies, squatting on the edge of the dump from twenty feet away while it began to rain. Thereafter, George instructed Cora to return to the cabin and keep quiet. He ventured off, presumably to meet up with Ed and Mike, although Ed and Mike returned without him about an hour later. At that time, Lilly was pleading with Nancy to allow her to leave Staffelbach House, but the boys feared that Lilly would go to the authorities. Fortunately, she escaped that evening, leaving behind everything she owned. Lilly was never heard from again.[45]

"We all sat up awhile," stated Cora, "and then went to bed. After Mike and Ed came in I overheard them tell the old woman that they had better take the bodies out, that somebody might see them floating. I never knew whether they took them out or not."[46]

For too long, Millard noted, the original dwelling was "too small to accommodate the family and such other immoral women as from time to time lived there. This motley crowd huddled into a dwelling which would by a sanitarian be deemed too small in air space for the healthful accommodation of two persons."[47] To rectify the problem, Ed, Mike and George built a board addition to the original log hut shortly after the girls were murdered. This addition more than doubled the size of the house, and added four rooms in which the occupants lived and worked.[48]

Charlie's grandmother Nancy would be credited in the media with masterminding all the horrendous activities that occurred at Staffelbach

House, but as Millard points out, there appears to be little or no planning that went into the murders that they orchestrated. They were a tough bunch and had no qualms about using physical violence against rowdies and drunks, no matter how disorderly they became, and if pushed too far and circumstances were rife, they would relieve their clientele of their money...and their lives.[49]

In early June 1897, for example, a one-eyed ex-soldier who had "considerable money" visited Staffelbach House looking for Charles Wilson. He said he knew a fellow named Hatfield who knew Charles, and then stayed overnight at the bordello to wait for him to return the following day. Early that morning, he left with Ed, believing they were going to a special place to pick strawberries in nearby Sarcoxie. Soon after they left, Cora reported to have heard Nancy saying that nobody would ever see the man again. A few days later, Ed returned alone without strawberries, but with plenty of cash.[50]

Charlie's family had avoided suspicion up to this time. Killing their victims with little or no justification, the Staffelbachs went about wasting lives with apparently little concern about what they were doing. They found easy access of disposal in abandoned mineshafts as they quietly tossed bodies out of view and out of reach of the authorities. The cash rewards from each murder and a growing sense of control over others, emboldened them to seek new victims. Hungry for money, power, and probably thrills, the family had stumbled upon murder as a fitting means to reach their goals. After a while, however, the Staffelbachs began to get careless. Complacency set in. Their luck began to run out.

Chapter Two

THE MURDER OF
FRANK GALBREATH

Thirty-two-year-old Francis Marion "Frank" Galbreath was the oldest of nine children born to George and Lenora (Isenhour) Galbreath in Illinois on December 10, 1865. In early 1897, he left the family farm in Fort Scott, Kansas, to try his hand at mining. It didn't take long for him to earn a reputation in Galena, Kansas, for being a friendly drunk, and City Marshall Milford Parker threw him in jail a few times to allow him to sober up. Nonetheless, Galbreath was not considered too bothersome, as he only tended to stagger into the way of other people.[51]

Galena mines paid their workers on Saturday, when an estimated $40,000 went into circulation about town. On payday, men came to Galena from miles around, ready to spend their money and have a good time participating in the festivities. Restaurants, saloons and bordellos would be at maximum capacity, and some places would still be open at daybreak on Sunday.[52]

For months, Galbreath routinely visited Staffelbach House on paydays to see Charlie's aunt, Emma (Staffelbach) Chapman, with whom he was infatuated. She provided her services in exchange for a fair portion of his meager wages, which amounted to seven to ten dollars a week. This routine made him an easy mark for the Staffelbach family.[53]

In June 1897, young Charlie's family was about to commit another murder, and Galbreath would become their victim. Charlie's whereabouts during this timeframe is not known, as it was undisclosed in any of the news accounts about the incident. One can assume, however, that he was at Staffelbach House when the incident occurred, because his mother and father were present. Information about the murder, following, is drawn from multiple newspaper articles published in 1897, shortly after the incident took place and in the immediate months that followed.

On the Saturday afternoon of June 19, 1897, Charlie's Aunt Emma sent a boy with a note, written by her, to Stanley Mines, with instructions that the note was to be delivered to Frank Galbreath. If he was not available, the boy was to leave the note with a coworker. In the note, Emma invited Galbreath to come over to see her that evening at 10:00 p.m.[54]

Galbreath was underground when the boy arrived, so the boy left the note with a coworker, as Emma had instructed. When Galbreath emerged from underground, he got the note, read it, and became very eager to act on the invitation. The day labored on, way too slowly for Galbreath's liking, but the thought of seeing Emma at ten o'clock that night kept him plugging away.[55]

After work and after supper, Galbreath and a mining friend named Jesse Jacobs whiled away the hours at a local saloon until after nine. The two then departed for Staffelbach House. As they stepped out of the saloon and into the street, they encountered City Marshall Parker, who realized that Galbreath already had had too much to drink. Parker suggested to Galbreath that he quit for the evening and return home, but he had a date with Emma and he intended to keep it.[56]

The night was unusually dark for that time of year, but the moon would occasionally peep through the clouds and cast a pale glow over Picker's Point. The inebriated miners followed the snake-curved road that wound amid the many shafts and dumps to arrive at Staffelbach House at the appointed hour. Nancy, who had just had an argument with Annie McComb, one of her working girls, was angry upon answering the door. She tersely told Galbreath he could not see Emma that evening and slammed the door in his face.[57]

Disappointed, Galbreath and Jacobs hiked back to the saloon for a few more drinks. About 1:30 a.m., June 20, 1897, Galbreath suggested that they have one more beer and then return to Staffelbach House to see Emma. Jacobs had had enough to drink by that time and said he was calling it a night, to which Galbreath declared that he was returning to see Emma with or without him.[58]

Galbreath arrived at Staffelbach House alone about 2:00 a.m., and woke the entire household by banging on the door. Nancy responded while the girls sleepily gathered in the background, curious about the commotion. When Galbreath demanded to see Emma, Nancy told him that Emma did not want to see him. Galbreath protested, and handed her the note from Emma stating the contrary.[59]

Nancy glanced at the note, dismissed it, and reiterated that Emma did not want to see him. But Galbreath was persistent. Maintaining that he was going to see Emma whether Nancy liked it or not, he declared, "Emma could tell me herself whether she wants to see me!" He then forced himself inside and traded harsh words with Nancy as he made his way to Emma's room.[60]

Emma was lying on a bed with Josie Beck, another one of the girls. Also in the room was Charlie's father, George Staffelbach, and Nancy's second husband, Charles Wilson. Charlie's mother, Cora, was in the house at the time, but not in that particular room. It was likely that young Charlie was there, too, perhaps asleep, although the news articles don't mention him.[61]

Ed Staffelbach, Charlie's uncle, slept in the summer kitchen, housed in a shed near the residence. When he heard the ruckus, he ran to see what was happening. Meanwhile, Nancy grabbed a corn knife that she always kept handy and made her way towards Galbreath. "I'm going to cut your damned head off!" she yelled, but it is uncertain if she drew blood during the ensuing scuffle.[62]

Galbreath knew at this juncture that he was in serious trouble. Ed Staffelbach and Charles Wilson grabbed their pistols as Galbreath left the house, staggering as fast as he could toward Seventh Street, which led out of town. "I'll get him," Charles yelled, and then fired a shot that missed. Ed, a much better marksman, fired a shot from his revolver that struck the miner above the hip. Galbreath slapped his hand over the wound and fell to the ground near a trash dump, but got right back up and continued to flee for his life.[63]

"He couldn't run very fast," recalled Annie McComb, "and Ed ran alongside of him, put his gun to his head, and fired. Frank threw his hand up to his head and fell by the side of the road. Ed took the knife from the old woman [Nancy] and started to finish Frank by cutting his throat. All this time me and Cora had been running along after them."[64]

Annie grabbed Ed's arm and pleaded, "Don't! You'll kill him!"[65]

"Let me alone, or I'll slit your throat!" Ed bellowed, but she continued hanging onto his arm while he slashed the right side of Galbreath's face and neck. Blood from the miner's severed jugular spurted onto the assailant's shirt and pants as his victim slumped to the ground.[66]

"Now you've killed him!" Annie cried.[67]

"Why the hell don't Annie leave Ed alone?" George remarked to Cora, who was then standing by his side.[68]

Ed turned to Annie and warned her that if she ever said a word about the incident he would kill her. Annie, a young widow with a twelve-year-old daughter named Ethel, knew him well enough to know he wasn't bluffing. Meanwhile, Nancy walked over to Ed, took back the corn knife, and casually wiped the blade off on her apron. Then, in compliance with Ed's instructions, she led the women back into the house while the men proceeded to sanitize the crime scene. Cora and Annie, however, slipped away.[69]

Ed, George, and Charles dragged Galbreath's body to an abandoned mineshaft by the side of the road, about 50-feet south of the bordello. The shaft was 60-feet deep, half-filled with water, and appeared to be the perfect place to dump a corpse. To ensure that the miner was dead, or just out of pure maliciousness, Ed placed his pistol behind Galbreath's left ear and fired a final shot.[70] George then rifled through the decedent's pockets, taking about $15 in cash and whatever other valuables he could find.[71]

"I felt sick," Annie revealed, "and me and Cora laid down in the weeds so that we could see them and they couldn't see us. They thought we had gone to the house. I was afraid to look until Cora whispered, 'They're pulling his clothes off.' Then I looked. I saw Ed take him by the shoulders, and George took one leg and Wilson the other. They carried him to the old shaft and threw him in. I heard the splash."[72]

Annie turned to Cora and exclaimed, "For God's sake, what kind of a mess have we got into?"[73]

"This is nothing," Cora replied with a laugh, and then proceeded to tell her about the murders of Rodabaugh, the Italian peddler, and the two young German girls.[74]

After a long pause to take in what she had just heard Cora tell her, Annie asked, "Is that all they did?"[75]

"That's all I know of," said Cora, "but God knows how many more there is, for there has been terrible doings in this house since we came here."[76]

By this time, Annie was frightened and started for the house, but her knees became so weak that she could hardly walk. "The smell of the hot blood turned my stomach," she recalled.[77]

As Cora assisted Annie to the house, they encountered three men that they knew. Frightened as to the events that they had witnessed, they asked the men to stay with them through the night.[78] The men agreed to accompany them home and "... in fact, did spend the night in the McCombs apartment of the Staffenbach [sic] House," according to an article in the *Joplin Daily Herald*, July 31, 1897.[79]

Charlie's Uncle Ed, who ran a tamale stand, returned home sometime after the incident with a pale of chili. Instead of taking it to the dining room, he went directly to his room in the cabin and asked his mother to bring him a clean set of clothes. The entire time, he remained in the shadows where no one could see his appearance, but one girl later testified that by the light from the door she saw large bloodstains on his hands and shirt.[80]

While Ed waited for Nancy to return with his clothes, he called out asking the girls if they wanted something to eat. Charlie's aunts, Emma and Louisa, responded to the dining room with another working girl named Rosie Bayne. After Nancy handed Ed his clothes, she took the pale of chili to the dining room and consumed it with the girls.[81]

Charlie's father, George, returned home before morning, and Charles Wilson, Nancy's husband, came in about sunrise. Charles had Galbreath's light-colored hat, which he cleaned with soap and water and claimed as his own. George and Charles sat at the table and cavalierly talked with Nancy and Ed as if nothing had happened that night. Annie McComb and Rosie Bayne, who watched from a distance, were mystified over their behavior, having just murdered a man.[82] It is particularly unsettling to ponder that three of the four murderers sitting at that table that morning were blood relatives of young Charlie: his father, his grandmother and his uncle.

About 11:30 on the morning of July 19, James L. Passwaters of Hilltop, Kansas, happened into Galena via Seventh Street. As was the habit of strangers entering mining towns, he was looking down the abandoned shafts, and it wasn't long before he came across the shaft where Galbreath's body had been dumped. The sight of his remains floating on the water thirty feet below was, as one might imagine, harrowing.[83]

Passwaters ran two blocks to Main Street to summon the police, and soon returned with Deputy Sheriff Charles L. Rains and Constables Lafayette Roe and L.M. Radley. A large crowd gathered around the mineshaft while the officers hauled the badly decomposed body to the surface. Thomas Lamar, W.J. Weens, William Parnell, Lys Carney and several others believed the body to be that of Frank Galbreath, and some tax receipts in the trousers pocket confirmed their suspicion.[84]

Finding bodies in mineshafts was not an anomaly in Galena, but this was the first time there was unmitigated evidence of foul play. News of Galbreath's murder spread like wildfire, and the State offered a reward for the capture and conviction of the party or parties involved. At that time, lawmen could claim such rewards, and Rains, Roe and Radley were determined to collect it.

The following morning, July 20, 1897, a Coroner's Inquest was held to determine the cause of death. This inquest, while essentially a criminal proceeding, was not in itself a trial, but an investigative tool. An inquest calls witnesses to provide testimony, but suspects are not permitted, at the inquest, to defend themselves. If the inquest finds strong evidence for murder charges, criminal prosecution may follow. Suspects are then able to defend themselves at trial.[85]

Presiding over the inquest into the death of Frank Galbreath was Dr. C.S. Huffman, who elected to keep the proceedings secret. Three bullet wounds and a sliced throat provided mute evidence as to the manner in which death had come, and now a large number of witnesses who lived near Staffelbach House were questioned. Many claimed to have heard shots fired near the bordello in the early morning hours of June 20. These witnesses reported that they did not think much of the explosive sounds, however, because gunshots were so commonplace.[86]

Galbreath's friend, Jesse Jacobs, having been seen with Galbreath the evening before he disappeared, was also called to testify at the Coroner's Inquest, and his deposition implicated the Staffelbachs. Of course, Nancy and Ed denied all knowledge of the affair. Ed even went so far as to say that he was "probably not at home" at the time the murder occurred.[87] Their stories revealed such discrepancies as to excite suspicion, yet Nancy and George left the inquest believing that they had once again outsmarted the law.

Charlie's father, George, was not questioned during the Coroner's Inquest because he was sitting in the Galena Jail at the time. He had been arrested shortly after Galbreath's murder for petty larceny in Baxter Springs, one town away from Galena. Constable Frank Hemstreet was detailed to escort him to Columbus, Kansas, the county seat, for preliminary trial for the petty larceny charge.[88]

While waiting for the train at the Galena depot, Hemstreet was engaged in conversation with County Attorney Charles Stevens, and George saw this as a perfect opportunity to escape. The constable didn't realize that his prisoner was gone until George darted around the corner of the depot. George had probably gained a distance of forty feet east of the depot when he heard the officer's baritone voice commanding him to halt. Glancing back, he saw Hemstreet's gun leveled at him and wisely acquiesced. George laughed off the incident, quipping that he only wanted to get a little exercise.[89]

From the Coroner's Inquest, the lawmen knew that the Staffelbachs were now the prime suspects, and several inquiries led to a tip that Cora Staffelbach, Annie McComb and Rosie Bayne were hiding out in Joplin. On July 27, Rains, Roe and Radley proceeded to Joplin and located the girls. Rains summarily extracted damning information from Annie, which gave him enough probable cause to arrest Nancy and Ed for the murder of Galbreath. The officers returned with the girls to Galena that evening and placed them in jail.[90]

Seeking to arrest the Staffelbachs before they learned that the girls were being held, Rains, Roe and Radley raided Staffelbach House that very evening about 10:00 p.m. A search of the premises turned up the corn knife, which was seized for evidence, and Nancy was placed under arrest for suspicion of murder. Ed was taken into custody at his tamale stand on Main Street for the same offense a short while later. Also arrested was a fellow named Curtis Carpenter whose implication in the affair remains a mystery.[91]

Sitting in the Columbus jail with Charlie's dad was Charlie's Uncle Mike, who was arrested and held more than a month earlier for breaking into a boxcar. Being in jail for that petty crime when Galbreath was murdered, effectively exonerated him for the murder of Galbreath.[92] Ironically, Mike would stand trial for a minor crime on the same day as his mother and siblings were tried for murder. The only murder suspect to have escaped the authorities in Galbreath's demise was Charles Wilson, who wouldn't be found and arrested until the following spring, in Missouri.

Possessing written confessions from Cora, Annie and Rosie, plus considerable tangible evidence of a somewhat circumstantial nature, Rains, Roe and Radley were prepared to present their case in Galena at a preliminary hearing scheduled for the morning of July 29, 1897. Seeking to avoid the publicity and fearing a lynch mob, however, Nancy and Ed waived their right to a preliminary hearing and were transferred to the Columbus County Jail. Here, they were confined along with George and Mike until the September term of court convened.[93]

Annie and Rosie remained in custody, as witnesses, until after the legal proceedings, but Cora posted bond on August 3, and was released on her own recognizance.[94] That same month, officers conducted a more thorough search of Staffelbach House and found additional evidence, including Nancy's white apron, which was stuffed in a hole in the wall. In the center of the apron was a head-size blotch of blood; there was also blood on the embroidery. The apron was taken to Kansas City to be examined by experts to ascertain if the blood was human. It was.

Nancy, George and Ed all pled poverty before Judge Andrew H. Skidmore. Attorney Jesse Forkner and his son, Henry, were appointed to defend Nancy and George, who chose to be tried together. Ed chose to be tried separately, so his trial would take place immediately after the conclusion of the trial of his mother and brother. Ed's attorneys would be J.P. Perkins and Judge Skidmore's half-brother, Charles Skidmore. Attorney Ed Tracewell and County Attorney Stevens would prosecute all three cases on behalf of the State.

The prosecution's job was made a lot easier when Cora, the mother of three-year-old Charlie, turned state's evidence against her husband and his family. Cora told Deputy Roe that she had contemplated escaping from Staffelbach House with Annie and Rosie a number of times, but that all three women were terrified of being killed. Now that her mother-in-law, Nancy, her brothers-in-law, Ed and Mike, and her husband, George, were at last helpless in the meshes of the law, Cora said she finally felt safe to tell what she knew.[95]

On Monday, September 13, 1897, Nancy and George went on trial in the District Court in Columbus, Kansas, with Judge Skidmore presiding. After the jury was seated, Annie McComb was called to the witness stand. She told her blood-curdling story without Cora or Rosie in the courtroom. Her testimony was so damning and detailed that it consumed the attention of the packed courtroom all morning.[96]

That afternoon, Cora took the stand without Annie or Rosie in the courtroom. Without knowing what Annie had said, Cora quite possibly felt alienated as she gave her testimony. She broke down on the witness stand and fully corroborated Annie's story. Then she took it a step further by spilling out details of other murders committed by her husband and in-laws. The jury heard Cora go into detail about the killings of the Italian peddler and two German girls. That revelation sent shockwaves throughout the courtroom ... and there was even more to come from the next witness.[97]

Rosie took the stand without Annie or Cora in the courtroom, and corroborated all the murders that Cora had just testified to. But Rosie also claimed that the Staffelbachs habitually killed their guests for money and dumped their bodies in nearby mineshafts. The courtroom had to be called to order a number of times after Rosie made that disclosure. Even then, murmuring continued as the attendees discussed amongst themselves who had gone missing in the past couple of years. In fact, the Staffelbachs "seemed the most unconcerned persons in the courtroom, frequently laughing at blunders of the witnesses," a reporter for the *Kansas Semi-Weekly Capital* observed.[98]

The following morning, George Staffelbach took the stand. Even his account of the Galbreath murder was detailed and repulsive. During direct questioning, he was easily rattled. His deposition was inconsistent, but it did essentially coincide with the testimony provided by Annie, Cora and Rosie. When asked, he even gave details about the Italian peddler and two German girls.[99]

The small-town media in those days practiced "yellow journalism," brutally prejudging newsworthy characters in newspaper reports. The media was prone to draw conclusions even before judgments were handed down by the courts. In this media frenzy, reporters were quick to label George a coward, and gossiped that in order to lighten his own sentence, or hoping for immunity, he willingly testified against Ed and tried to lay the whole crime at his feet.[100]

When Charlie's grandmother, Nancy, took the stand, strong circumstantial evidence was introduced to support direct testimony garnered from the witnesses by the prosecuting attorneys. The bloodstained knife and the bloody apron were produced and shown to the jury. In total denial, she refused to take any responsibility, wept visibly on the stand, and did not deviate from her story. One minute she was audibly crying, and then the next she appeared stoic. At one point, Attorney Tracewell called her an old hag, which clearly offended her. In the end, none of the "faces" that she presented to the jury seemed to help her gain their sympathy or their trust of her side of the story.[101]

The defendants presented no witnesses but themselves; however, there were enough admissions wrung from George's testimony alone to convict them. When the trial ended, the jury was out less than three hours before they returned with their verdict. George was found guilty of murder in the first-degree and Nancy was found guilty of murder in the second-degree. Immediately after the adjudicators retired, Ed was arraigned for trial on the same charge.[102]

It is not known if Nancy or George were offered a plea deal, but it is known that prosecutors offered Ed the opportunity to plead guilty to second-degree murder, for which he would receive a fifteen-year prison sentence. He refused. Ed insisted that he was innocent and said he would not enter a plea of guilty even if they offered him a deal of only one years' confinement in the penitentiary. So, the day following the guilty verdict of his mother and brother, Ed faced his own courtroom trial.[103]

Very similar testimony that was introduced by the State during George and Nancy's trial also prevailed in Ed's trial. On the witness stand, Ed vehemently denied ever seeing Galbreath and continued to insist that he wasn't even home the night of the murder. However, he was not able to provide a positive statement of his whereabouts that night, which didn't help his case. Moreover, his testimony contradicted that of George, Cora, Annie and Rosie. The jury was out only a few minutes before returning with a verdict of murder in the first-degree.[104]

While Charlie's grandmother's and father's trials were underway, Charlie's mother, Cora, led investigators to the mineshaft where the girls' bodies had been dumped. Excavation commenced immediately. For three weeks that shaft and one other, situated north of Staffelbach House, was excavated and carefully examined for remains. Those working at the shaft were hedged in by a crowd ranging in numbers from 200 to 500, and anticipation that bodies would be found grew with every passing moment. When a bucket yielded something, it would be handed to the medical experts for examination and the crowd would almost hold its breath while the doctors shook their heads over the gruesome find.[105]

Onlookers passing the shafts insisted that the water smelled "very strongly of human bodies." The place took on a circus-like atmosphere. Venders set up lemonade stands, sold cigars, melons, apples, peanuts and lunches, and offered "ice cold cider—all you can drink for five." Charlie's mother thoroughly enjoyed mingling with the crowd, and said she would stay until the skeletons were found. It seemed like everyone wanted to talk to her.[106]

"Cora is only 19," wrote T.F. Millard. "Her appearance would be termed attractive by a Galena miner. A retroussé nose, large gray eyes and regular teeth that would be white did she not chew tobacco. Cora's weaknesses are tobacco and whiskey, to say nothing of her morals. She frankly told me that she has lived a life of shame since her twelfth year. Her manner is inclined to be kittenish, or a wretched attempt at it, and she is rather too familiar. But she had an interesting story to tell, and I braved the filth of the hovel to listen. After I had bribed her to talk—for she has been pumped of late to the verge of an unnatural reticence—with a piece of plug tobacco and a flask of whiskey, she told the story of the murders of the two girls, the old peddler and old man Rodabaugh."[107]

Cora also revealed that she overheard the family talking from time to time about killing a Mr. Moorehouse in Joplin in 1892, a fellow named Frank Smith from Galena, and a man named Brooks.[108] These disclosures, coupled with her detailed and specific deposition, led to the Staffelbach family being blamed for every person that went missing in Joplin and Galena during the respective timeframes that they lived in those cities. It didn't much matter whether the disappearances could be attributed to foul play.

"While confessions are being wrung from Cora Staffleback [sic]," a Joplin newsman proclaimed, "it might be well to learn the fate of old man Brooks, who so mysteriously disappeared from this city before the Stafflebacks [sic] move to Galena, and whose fate now apposed to be known by them. Add this one to their already long list of supposed victims and their fame will rival that of the Bender family who had only nine lives to their credit."[109]

Charles Wilson would tell of yet another murder to Sheriff W.O. Sparks while awaiting trial in Columbus in 1898. Fred George, and his wife, Rebecca, were longtime residents of Galena. Fred was partially disabled, but ran a job wagon and supplemented his meager income by taking in a border named James Chase. Chase, a street peddler who sold powders for headaches and other ailments, sent a letter to *The Galena Evening Times* shortly after Ed's arrest and claimed that Ed had it in for him, so he moved out of the George's home.[110]

Wilson told Sparks that Ed Staffelbach and Rebecca George collaborated to kill Fred George, and maintained that they carried out their plan in early June 1897. Ed and Rebecca then took Fred's horses to Oklahoma, sold them, and split the proceeds. According to James Chase, Ed and Rebecca were to be married the night after Ed was arrested.[111]

While there is a high probability that more victims were attributed to the Staffelbachs, an accurate count is impossible to determine without a confession from the principals...and *they* weren't talking. Thirty to fifty was the popular estimate, but that number was unquestionably exaggerated. When one carefully scrutinizes the newspaper accounts, there appears to be 10 victims, certain and suspected, namely: (1) Mr.

Moorehouse, 1892, Joplin; (2) Christopher Rodabaugh, January 1, 1895, Joplin; (3) Frank Smith, 1896, Galena or Joplin; (4) Mr. Brooks, 1896, Galena; (5) the Italian Peddler, January 1897, Galena; (6) Young Girl #1 (Alice), January or February 1897, Galena; (7) Young Girl #2, January or February 1897, Galena; (8) Fred George, Summer 1897, Galena; (9) the one-eyed ex-soldier, June 1897, Galena; and (10) Frank Galbreath, June 19, 1897, Galena.

From the likes of Cora's testimony, one would conclude that the Staffelbach brothers were comfortable with killing, robbing, and disposing of bodies. It challenges one to believe that the number of their murders was limited to those specified in court. The modus operandi provided by Cora, Annie and Rosie closely resembled the manner in which the Italian peddler met his fate … and that was likely the common method used.

At the mineshaft, workers did not come up empty-handed, but presumably they expected much more than they found. In the first shaft, they discovered a lady's white shirtwaist; a portion of a corset containing blood stains; a woman's gown spotted with blood; a woman's wallet; bunches of human hair; bone fragments, which included a rib believed to be that of a child; a short, heavy wooden club (part of a pitchfork handle) with a clump of hair still affixed; several pieces of human bone; a portion of a human skull; and the large bone of a human arm, clearly showing the formation of the elbow.[112]

The bones were considerably decomposed and softened by alkali water, which did not go unnoticed by authorities.[113] They understood that the bodies may have been consumed by a slower but similar process to a then-recent Chicago murder wherein a man dissolved his wife's body in a tank of caustic solution.[114] Nothing of any significance was found in the second shaft, and the search eventually fizzled out.

In August 1897, the Staffelbach property was advertised for sale by Constable Davenport to satisfy a judgment in favor of one W.C. Foster.[115] Foster removed the majority of the Staffelbach's household goods from the house during the week they were on trial, and for several days thereafter authorities searched Staffelbach House for more evidence. In the lining of the ceiling of one room, Ed's bloody coat was discovered, and they also found a set of dies used for counterfeiting. It is unknown if these dies were ever put into circulation.[116]

At some point, souvenir-seekers began rummaging through Staffelbach House, nearly tearing the place down and carrying off everything of value. The bordello continued to attract the attention of onlookers and would have undoubtedly become a valuable tourist attraction but for a vigilante group, calling themselves the Committee of Public Safety, who had other plans. About 11:00 p.m., on September 22, 1897, forty vigilantes quietly made their way to the house, doused it in kerosene, and simultaneously applied torches in several places. Witnesses say there was no excitement or confusion, but "the most perfect organization was manifest." The Committee successfully exacted their revenge.

There has been some recent speculation that the Staffelbach's bordello was separate from the small cabin and wood addition in which they resided. The *Engineering & Mining Journal of 1899, Volume 67,* page 273, mentions leasing eight lots, known as Staffleback [sic] lots, on land owned by the Galena Lead & Zinc Company. Period newspapers suggest, however, that Staffelbach House was the same place where prostitution and the murders occurred.

In one T.F. Millard article published in the *St. Louis Republic* on September 19, 1897, there are two sketches of Staffelbach House, one showing the original cabin and the other depicting the addition. The caption under the first photo states, "Staffleback [sic] House: View showing the log cabin which was the original house where the girls were murdered." The caption under the second photo states, "The Staffleback [sic] House: A view of the now notorious den in Galena, where four murders were committed."[117] If Millard's account is correct—and Millard's article is one of the few written during this time that followed a more professional writing style, giving the reader a more object viewpoint—Staffelbach House *was* the house in which the family lived, worked, and carried out their gruesome murders.

After Staffelbach House burned to the ground, the danger of lynching subsided. The Committee of Public Safety—and the townspeople of Galena—cooled down. A more rational attitude with a "wait and see" approach settled in, thereby permitting the law to take its course. The *Joplin Herald* opined: "The passions of a mob are quickly kindled and quickly cooled, and if the Galena avengers ever had any idea of lynching the Staffleback's [sic], they have no doubt abandoned it."[118]

On September 26, 1897, the *Daily Tribune* of Salt Lake City, Utah, reported: "The statements of a girl of Cora Staffelback's [sic] character are hardly sufficient to satisfy the committee, and before the people take the law into their own hands to wreak summary vengeance upon these fiendish murderers, they must be satisfied beyond doubt of the guilt of these people."[119]

Charlie's grandmother and father, Nancy and George, were sentenced in the Columbus Courthouse on October 1, 1897, in a courtroom full of spectators' eager to catch a glimpse of the murderers. Nancy, convicted of murder in the second-degree for her part in the Galbreath killing, was sentenced to twenty-one years in the Women's State Prison in Lansing. George, having been found guilty of first-degree murder in Galbreath's death, was sentenced to the State Penitentiary in Lansing for a period of one year; at the expiration of that time, if the Governor of the State of Kansas so directed, he would be taken out and hanged by the neck until dead.[120] Without the Governor's signature to direct a "hanging," George's sentence would be commuted to "life."

Shortly after Ed's arrest, he was reported to be crying a lot in jail. During the interim between the trials and sentencing, he was said to have gone insane through fear of lynching at the hands of a mob. Others said it was just a ruse, for when he first heard of the possibility of a lynching he allegedly remarked that they would hardly hang an insane man. As the legal system moved things along, Ed began to show more and more signs of insanity.[121]

For three days after being convicted of murder, Ed refused to eat or sleep. Day and night, he raved about the murders and said he could save his life if he had a gun and a corn knife. At times, he jumped about his cell singing or swearing and calling for the jailer. He claimed his brothers were guilty and wanted them to pay the penalty, and even went so far as to butt his head repeatedly against the concrete walls to prove mental instability.[122]

About 11:00 p.m., on September 23, rumors circulated throughout the jail that Ed had committed suicide by eating fine glass. When Sheriff Forkner responded, he found Ed in a stupor from "utter bodily exhaustion." A doctor was summoned and administered a vile of morphine. After that, jail staff spent some time attempting to constrain him and eventually got him into a straitjacket.[123]

On the question of sanity being raised, the court appointed Doctors E.A. Scammon, C.S. Huffman and J.H. Baxter as a commission to examine Ed on September 27. They reported, in substance, as follows: "We, your committee, find Ed Staffleback [sic] to be insane. As to the permanency, we are unable to state."[124] Thus, they left the door open for Ed's eventual recovery.

Following the commission's finding, an insanity hearing was scheduled for October 1—the same day that Ed's mother and brother were to be sentenced. On the eve of this hearing, Ed spent the entire night praying and preaching so loudly that it kept everyone in the jailhouse awake. If he were bluffing, he was playing it to the hilt; if he wasn't, he had the good fortune of not understanding the gravity of the situation when he appeared before Probate Judge Edward E. Sapp.[125]

After an entire day of proceedings in an overcrowded courtroom, the jury returned a verdict declaring Ed, in fact, to be sane. It is unknown whether the jury ignored the commission's finding that Ed was insane, or whether the jury just ignored the commission's conclusion. Nevertheless, when Ed appeared before Judge Skidmore the following morning, October 2, he was handed down the same punishment as that received by George.[126]

Puzzling, and impossible to explain, is why George was charged with murder in the first-degree when all he did was rifle through Galbreath's pockets and help dump his body into the mineshaft. He was an accessory, certainly, for he actively participated in the commission of the crime, but Nancy and Charles took a more active role in Galbreath's death and they were only charged with murder in the second-degree.

Charlie's Uncle Mike, who had pled guilty to, and was convicted of, grand larceny, was sentenced on the same day as Nancy and George. He received six years in the State Penitentiary at Lansing for his crime.[127] Charles Wilson would stand trial in the death of Galbreath the following spring. On April 22, 1898, he was convicted of murder in the second-degree and sentenced to twenty-five years in the State Penitentiary.[128]

Although George and Ed were sentenced to death, they were aware that this most certainly meant life in prison, as a Kansas Governor had not signed a death warrant for twenty-five years. "The general opinion in Cherokee County is that Kansas needs a Governor who will sign a batch of death warrants," proclaimed a reporter for the *Topeka Weekly Capital* after the Staffelbach trials. "Opinion is somewhat divided as to the probability of a lynching bee. Public sentiment is undoubtedly in favor of it, but concentrating and leadership are necessary to bring about results."[129]

Governor John W. Leedy also addressed the case, stating that he was not against the death penalty. He went on to say that life imprisonment does not tend to prevent crime. He voiced the opinion that prisoners, with plenty to eat and little to do, planned escapes or studied how to secure pardons. "Our law is at fault, too," he argued. "It is not provided that after a man has served one year in the penitentiary, he may be hanged upon the order of the Governor. Our law should be so amended as to require the district judge to fix the date of the hanging, at which time it should take place unless the Governor interferes."[130]

The governor maintained that Ed and George Staffelbach should hang, but he would not sign their death warrants in the face of the unbroken precedent to the contrary for fear of misconstruction. In fact, he believed nearly all of the forty-seven convicts then under sentence in the penitentiary ought to be hanged; however, he would not so order it because the hanging of so many would seem inhumane.[131]

That, of course, meant that Ed and George would spend the remainder of their lives in prison and not meet death at the end of a hangman's noose. In fact, there were federal and military executions in Kansas, but it wasn't until Ernest Hoefgen was hanged on March 10, 1944, for murdering a student hitchhiker, that the State again invoked capital punishment.

A reporter for the *Modern Light* of Columbus, Kansas, who saw Nancy, Ed and George after sentencing, described them thusly: "The old lady

Staffleback [sic] is a brown-skinned, pinched up, wizened old hag, with two sharp little eyes that glitter like beads. She is absolutely devoid of emotion and when the prosecuting attorneys referred to her in the bitterest of terms, she seemed to enjoy it. George is a young man with a narrow sloping forehead and evasive eyes. Ed is a big man with grey eyes and an ugly look in his countenance."[132]

T.F. Millard observed: "The old woman is by far the most interesting character. No one can see the gang and doubt for a moment that she furnished the brains on which it operated. Mother Nance is crafty and keen. Under a mild demeanor—acquired principally since her arrest—and a soft, plaintive voice, she conceals the fury of a witch and the tongue of a devil. In her sixty-sixth year, she cannot hope to ever live to see the expiration of her term in the penitentiary, as a sentence of 21 years is the lightest she can get.

"The Staffleback [sic] boys—Ed, Mike and George—are common types of the low desperado. Ed is the eldest child. He is heavy of countenance; slow of speech. He would stick a knife into your back, but would cringe at your face. No planner or plotter he. He could stupidly obey orders, but no more.

"George, also, is not bright mentally. He is a coward, and could not restrain his tears when told he must die. He is a notorious liar. He has the ambition to delve deep into crime, but lacks the nerve. To these two sons Mother Nance imparted her viciousness, but not her intelligence and nerve.

"Mike is the nervy one of the boys—cold-blooded and heartless. The fact that he was in jail at the time of the Galbreath murder probably saved his neck for a time. But when he serves his term for burglary he may find a more serious charge awaiting."[133]

In Mike's case, the district attorney would have to prove murder of the family's earlier victims—previous to Galbreath—based upon a few severely decayed body parts, a club, and bloody garments that could not be positively associated with the victims in question. Testimony from Cora, Annie and Rosie would be crucial to conviction, but their credibility was questionable, as Cora was the only eyewitness. Lastly, prosecutors would have to wait for the culmination of Mike's prison sentence before new criminal proceedings could be brought against him.

By that time, the evidence against Mike would be aged and witness's memories would have diminished. And Cora, Annie and Rosie—seeking to start a new life elsewhere—would not be easy to track down. So, Mike, who was implicated by Cora's testimony in the deaths of the peddler and two girls, was the luckiest one of the Staffelbach bunch. He was never prosecuted for the murders for which he was accused.

On October 2, 1897, Sheriff William T. Forkner and six of his deputies made their way to the train depot with the Staffelbachs and eight other prisoners, all bound for the State Penitentiary at Lansing. Ironically, Sheriff Forkner's father, Jesse, and brother, Henry, had defended Nancy and George at trial. Although authorities kept quiet about the Staffelbachs leaving for Lansing that day, news that they would be taken to the pen somehow seeped its way into, and spread throughout the community. More than 500 people gathered to see the convicts off, and while sentiment against the family was still quite hostile, it wasn't as bad as anticipated— until their arrival at Fort Smith, Kansas.[134]

The reader will recall that Frank Galbreath was from Fort Smith. Standing among a crowd gathered for the Staffelbach's brief layover was Galbreath's parents and brothers. Not surprisingly, Charlie's grandmother, Nancy, his Uncle Ed, and his father, George, did nothing to win their sympathy. After the noon meal, Nancy sat stoically fanning herself with no trace of emotion in her face, no show of weakness, no hint of tears. Mike, who was also being transferred from the Columbus Jail to the State Penitentiary for his crime of theft, sat smoking a cigarette and appeared completely free from worry.[135]

Suddenly, something stirred in Charlie's grandmother and she became eager to talk to the large crowd that had gathered at the windows. A deputy raised a window for Nancy, and someone in the crowd asked if she still proclaimed her innocence. She maintained that she never saw Frank Galbreath. "I have never harmed a hair on anybody's head," she insisted, "and they are sending an innocent woman to the penitentiary. They will not keep me there long, as it is not the will of God that it shall be so."[136]

George Galbreath, father of the murdered miner, stood in the middle of the crowd and lifted his youngest son, Alva, above his head. With tears in his eyes, he cried out, "Here is a brother of the boy you and your sons murdered! You dirty villains have robbed me of my son! Does he look anything like Frank?"[137]

At that juncture, Nancy became loud in her demonstrations and the crowd was getting riled, so the deputy prudently closed the window and locked the doors.[138]

Upon arriving at the penitentiary, Ed, in frail health, was assigned the lightest duties in the yard. It was soon evident that he had genuinely gone insane. He settled into the monotony of prison life with his brothers, George and Mike, but they were not permitted to communicate with each other. Prisoners at that time were governed by what was known as the "silent system." In 1899, Ed contracted tuberculosis and passed away in the prison infirmary on November 17.[139] The following day, at 2:00 p.m., his mortal remains were buried in the Cox Cemetery in Joplin, Missouri, which, today, is not accessible to the public.

Nancy never received a pardon, although not for lack of effort on her part. By 1907, her health had deteriorated to the point that she was quite feeble. On Monday, March 8, 1909, she was taken ill with pneumonia and the attending physician announced that she would not last through the day. Realizing that she was dying, she requested that her son, George, and husband, Charles, be at her bedside in her cell in the Women's Ward. The deputies graciously granted her request, even though they didn't have to. Charlie's paternal grandmother died in Lansing State Prison at 3:00 p.m., on March 9, 1909, and was also interred in the Cox Cemetery, where his Uncle Ed had been laid to rest.[140]

Charles Wilson presumably died in prison sometime between 1910 and 1920. Charlie's Uncle Mike lived eight years beyond Charlie's own death in 1936. On September 2, 1944, Mike visited his sister, Emma, in Piedmont, Missouri, and on his way home, near Poplar Bluff, he was killed in an automobile accident. As for Emma, she married Anestis S. Doxis in 1929, and passed away in Piedmont on February 5, 1953.

In these early years, when young Charlie's life was just taking off, his father, his grandmother, and his uncle were ordered to prison for murder, never to experience their freedom again. Now what was to happen to Charlie? Who would take care of him? In the months following, young Charlie's parents would divorce and catapult him into completely new circumstances that would alter the entire course of his life.

Chapter Three

ALONE AND FORSAKEN

The last time Charlie saw his father, George Staffelbach, would have been prior to George entering prison, when Charlie was three years old. And Charlie had little, if any, memory of his mother as he grew up, though he may have been with her until he was four or five. Piecing together his life between 1897 and 1900 is problematic, as no records or newspaper reports have been discovered to pinpoint his whereabouts or circumstances during that time. Based upon family accounts and Charlie's own statements some years later, however, we get some idea of what transpired.

Cora quickly secured a divorce from George after the trial, and it is presumed that she settled in Joplin, the town that she frequented while living in Galena. We know that in August 1901, she remarried to a miner named Casper "Ed" Rolleg. Cora's grandniece, June Buccina, born a year before Charlie died, never knew him, but she heard stories about him from her mother, Ida Lake, who was raised by Cora and Ed.[141]

Sometime between 1915 and 1920, when Cora would have been in her mid- to late-30s, she retrieved Ida and Ida's older brother, Robert Lake, Jr., from an orphanage where Cora's brother, Robert, had placed them after his divorce from their mother. Cora and Ed took the two children into their home to raise them. As a result of this act, Ida came to call Cora "Mother" throughout her life. June, Ida's daughter, came to call Cora "Grandma" and Ed "Grandpa."[142]

June was told by someone—she can't remember who, and it may have been more than one person—a story about how Cora came to lose track of her son, Charlie. The story went that after leaving Galena with Charlie, Cora found a job with a mercantile store to support them, but that she had to leave Charlie unsupervised while she went to work. One day when she came home from work, Charlie wasn't there. Cora never knew what happened to him. Descendants of Charlie may have surmised that he had been taken into custody by the authorities and placed into the orphanage from which he was adopted by Sidney and Phoebe Ann (Owens) Barger around 1900.[143]

Growing up, Charlie was told by his adoptive parents that his father had died, and that his mother had given him up because she couldn't afford to provide for him. Apparently, neither of these stories were true. George, in fact, would not die until 1911, the year Charlie turned 17.

We know that Charlie's father, in July 1898, wrote to then ex-sheriff Forkner to get Forkner's opinion in regard to securing executive clemency from the governor. It had been less than a year since George Staffelbach's conviction, and he was concerned about the community's attitude toward him. In his correspondence to Forkner, Staffelbach maintained his innocence of the crime for which he was then serving a life sentence. Not surprisingly, Forkner offered him no solace.[144]

"The people of this county will never agree to a pardon for such a cold-blooded murderer as he," declared the *Galena Daily Republican* on July 27, 1898, "and he had just as well resign himself to the fact that he will have to spend the remainder of his days behind the prison bars."[145]

Indeed, George remained in prison, never to gain his freedom again. For thirteen years, he was employed in the prison mine where each day more than 10,000 bushels of coal were extracted. Then, on January 8, 1911, at the age of 38, he succumbed to a condition called pyelonephritis, having suffered a kidney ailment since childhood. It is believed that he was buried alongside his mother and brother in the Cox Cemetery in Joplin, Missouri.

Several months after Charlie entered the orphanage, he went to live with Sidney and Phoebe Barger. Sidney, born in May 1837, in Adair County, Kentucky, was in his late 50s when Charlie came to live with them; Phoebe, born in January 1844, in Indiana, was in her early 50s. Phoebe and Sidney had been married since December 12, 1860. Although they bore no children of their own, they had raised his niece, Nancy Ann Bybee, as if she was their daughter. Nancy was only one-year-old when she came to live with them, after the death of her mother in 1867.

Sidney, a lifelong farmer, owned a farm on the outskirts of Harmony, Kentucky, and toiled hard for meager pay. When he could afford it, he would hire a farm boy to help plant and collect his crops, yet for the most part he had performed all the chores alone. Phoebe kept the house in order and had prepared the meals, and when Nancy was old enough, she helped. In 1878 (the same year that Charlie's mother was born), Sidney sold his farm Harmony and moved to Creelsburgh, Kentucky. Despite Sidney's best efforts at farming there, however, farming had not panned out for him.

Phoebe had been particularly close to her widowed aunt, Nancy (Owens) West, who lived in Vineyard, Missouri. Phoebe had pressed Sidney to move to Vineyard where they could assist her Aunt Nancy as she aged. Sidney knew the prospects for farming in Missouri were slightly better than Kentucky, based upon letters received from Phoebe's kin, so he had agreed to the move.

Situated in the Ozarks, which covers much of southern Missouri, Vineyard is a farming community in Lawrence County, about 40 miles east of the Kansas border and seventy miles north of Arkansas. Today, it is difficult to locate on a map, but in 1845, Vineyard was one of the first townships organized in that region due to its agricultural potential and mineral assets that were peculiar to that part of the state.[146] According to *Goodspeed's Lawrence County History,* the countryside was "a perfect blend of flat, marshy and swampy terrain, sufficiently elevated to give pure mountain air without the extreme cold to which mountain regions are sometimes subject."[147]

Vineyard, an all-rural community located in the western tract of Lawrence County, even today lists agriculture as its principle industry. The closest railroad to Vineyard at the turn of the twentieth century was in Stotts City, a main trading center, situated about two-and-a-half miles south and slightly east of Vineyard. In 1900, the population of Vineyard was 1,797, and Stotts City peaked at 902; a century later, Vineyard's population had dropped below 1,000 and Stotts City claimed just over 200.[148]

For the first few years that Sidney resided in Vineyard, he had rented a farm and made a living under the most austere circumstances. Even when his niece, Nancy, moved out of the house in 1885 to marry, thus eliminating a mouth to feed, Sidney barely made enough money to keep a roof overhead and food on the table for himself and his wife. Hunting and fishing, for Sidney, were not recreational sports, but a means of survival.

Through hard work, frugality and sheer determination, Sidney had collected enough money to purchase a forty-acre farm in Vineyard for $260 on October 3, 1887. Soon, he had the land under cultivation and was enjoying more success than he had realized in Kentucky, though not by much. He tried, but had been unable, to procure full-time assistance with his farming. Facing sixty years of age in 1897, he and Phoebe decided that adopting a healthy young boy was a feasible measure to ensure continuity on the farm over the next decade.

Sidney had about ten more years before he would be too old to perform the chores himself, which would give him plenty of time to mold a young boy to his specifications. Taking in an orphaned teen would only give Sidney about five years of decent help before the kid moved out on his own, so that was not an option. However, if he and Phoebe took in a toddler or a boy in early childhood, they would have help around the farm until their respective deaths.

Sometime before 1900, Sidney and Phoebe Barger visited the orphanage where Charlie tarried, and he appeared to be the perfect candidate to help them attain their laborious farming ambitions. The Bargers did not immediately adopt Charlie, perhaps out of concern over the Staffelbach name. After all, there was no telling if the quiet, four-year-old possessed violent tendencies or had a disagreeable temperament, so holding off for a time seemed reasonable. One result of this decision, however, was that by the time the Bargers did adopt Charlie and changed his name to Barger, he knew that he was a Staffelbach by birth.

Charlie is found using the name "Denver Staffelback" and residing in the Barger household in Vineyard, Missouri, when the 1900 census was enumerated. The Bargers formally adopted him soon thereafter. There is no indication from Charlie's recollections or family sources that the Bargers ever physically abused him. It was clear from the outset, however, that Charlie was there to work on the family farm—nothing more—and, in that sense, he would be considered mistreated, even abused, by today's standards.

Charlie's childhood was not a typically happy one under his care from the Bargers. Birthdays, Christmases and other holidays never brought gifts and were rarely observed. As soon as Charlie was old enough to do chores, he worked six days a week caring for the animals, tending the fields, erecting and mending fences, chopping wood, and completing whatever other tasks were required, no matter how substantial or minuscule. It is unknown if he ever attended church.

Hunting was commonplace in rural communities such as Vineyard, and it stands to reason that Sidney would have taught young Charlie how to handle a rifle at an early age. The ability Charlie displayed on the rifle range upon entering the military indicates that he had already mastered the fundamentals of marksmanship, such as sight alignment, sight picture, breath control and trigger squeeze. Once in combat, he rarely missed.

In 1901, Charlie was seven years old. Unbeknownst to him, his mother, Cora, had settled in the little town of Waco, Missouri, in Jasper County, one county to the west of where Charlie lived with the Bargers. Cora, now going by Mabel, an alias, was working in retail, according to her niece. Charlie, of course, knew nothing about his mother. Still living with and working for the Bargers, he was oblivious as to the whereabouts of his birth family. Likewise, Cora had no knowledge that her son was in such close proximity to her home.

That same year, 1901, the Bargers sold their Vineyard farm for $800, but remained in the community for two more years before departing Missouri for Fayetteville, Arkansas. Charlie completed the fourth grade in Stotts City before departing for Arkansas. That move, unfortunately, marked the end of his formal education. At the tender age of nine, he was now considered by his parents to be old enough to assume more responsibility around the house.

The exact years of Sidney and Phoebe's deaths are unknown; however, they passed away sometime before 1910. Tragically, Charlie had become orphaned for the second time in his young life. He had lost contact with his birth parents at a critical early age, and now he had lost his adoptive parents. He was all alone in the world and on his own. Life for Charlie would henceforth be an uphill struggle.

The Bargers may not have had much, but they had some assets—a home, several acres of land, and, of course, material possessions. Charlie, the rightful heir to their estate, received nothing, and it is presumed that everything went to Sidney's niece, Nancy (Bybee) Miller. Although Charlie didn't name Nancy as his next of kin when he enlisted in the Army, they remained in close contact and visited frequently until his death.

Charlie ventured out and became a full-time farm laborer, residing with anyone who would accept his services for room and board and a small salary. Drifting eastward, he departed Fayetteville and settled for a time in North Township, Arkansas, situated about two miles southwest of Wirth. Notably, his own path at this juncture was not unlike that of his mother, who was sent away from home at a young age to settle a debt of her father's.

In North Township, Charlie was taken in by Joseph Lee and Mary (Hurst) Weaver, who often accepted orphaned children into their home and employed them as laborers and domestics. Joseph was born in Arkansas in 1870, and married Mary in 1892, when she was 24. They never had children of their own, and never formally adopted the children that they took in, but, according to newspaper accounts, the couple regarded the children they took in as their own. In fact, two of these children, Marie "Maggie" Fletcher and Clyde Armstrong, would assume the Weaver surname.[149]

By 1910, Joseph and Mary Weaver moved 13 miles south to Hardy, Arkansas, but Charlie remained in North Township where he found employed as a hired man for Claus and Margit Holm, who were both German immigrants. In 1911, the same year his father would have met his death in prison, Charlie returned to Vineyard, Missouri, in Lawrence County, presumably to seek out his adoptive mother's cousin, Sarah (West) McFeron. Sarah's mother, Nancy, was the same Nancy who prompted the Bargers to move to Vineyard.[150]

Sarah had married Henry Spencer McFeron in Lawrence County on October 2, 1867. He had served his country during the Civil War, having enlisted on May 5, 1864, with Company B, 47th Regiment, Iowa Volunteer Infantry. After his discharge on September 20, 1864, he was proud to say that he "killed or harmed no man." Politically, he was an avowed Socialist.[151]

After their marriage, Henry and Sarah lived the first year in Newton County, Missouri. In their second year, they moved to Vineyard where Henry purchased about 100 acres of farmland. When he purchased this land, which he dubbed "Pleasant Hill Farm," it was only partially improved, but over time he put up good buildings and made it one of the best kept farms in Vineyard. He also added forty acres to the original farm. The entire place was rich, tillable land, except some twenty-five acres, which was wood land. Henry had always made a business of general mixed farming and stock-raising.[152]

Henry and Sarah had raised three daughters: Frances, Mertie and Lizzie. Although Henry had retired from active farming in 1906, he had retained ownership of his farm with plenty of work still to be done. Fortunately, he continued to be strong and healthy, and had managed to maintain the farm with the help of his wife and youngest daughter, Lizzie.[153]

The last thing Henry needed in 1911 was another mouth to feed, but he consented to Sarah's appeal to take Charlie into their home—providing that Charlie was willing to work for his keep. Charlie proved to be a grateful teenager who worked hard for Henry. It held a lot of weight with Henry to learn that Charlie was not lazy and not seeking charity. Henry came to understand that the boy was simply down on his luck and needed a place to stay.

Charlie and Henry developed a good rapport, and when Charlie enlisted in the Army he cited Henry as his adoptive uncle and next-of-kin. Charlie soon moved away from the McFeron's home and reverted to working for room and board, but he came and went from staying at their home through the years leading up to the war. The reasons for why he didn't stay there the whole time are not known. Perhaps he felt he was intruding, perhaps Henry could not afford to keep him, perhaps something better came along.

During that time, Charlie earned about $20 a month—or about $475 today. With those meager wages, he would never own property, and based upon statements he made in 1920 to a reporter with the *Plain Dealer* of Cleveland, Ohio, owning property was his goal in life.[154] Without an education beyond the fourth grade, he was qualified to do little else.

Charlie would tell his Army buddies that before the war he often had to hunt for food if he wanted to eat. Author A.M. Haswell provides in his book, *The Ozark Region: Its History and Its People, Volume 1,* a glimpse of the game situation and terrain in and about Vineyard, Missouri, around the time that Charlie would have arrived back from his time spent in Arkansas. Large game was scare during those years, Haswell tells us in his book, so we can surmise that Charlie would have caught small game, such as rabbits, squirrels and foul. Minute chiggers and ticks were ferocious, making the incessant mosquitoes seem innocuous in comparison. As Charlie made his way through the trees and brush, all nature must have seemed hostile.[155]

Upon turning eighteen in 1912, Charlie appeared destined to be no more than a poor dirt-farmer, toiling on land owned by others for wages that never seemed to be enough to make ends meet. In these years, blacks and Indians usually got the most labor-intensive and lowest paid jobs. But Lawrence County, with a population of 26,500 that year, had less than 100 Black residents and only one Indian. This gave opportunities to Whites, such as Charlie Barger, who were at the bottom of the socio-economic rung, to earn their way by taking on the tough, filthy, low-paying jobs.[156] Indeed, with a paltry education and no real roots, Charlie's future looked bleak. The only constants in his life, it seemed, were hard work, poverty and loneliness.

For seven years, Charlie worked harder than he had ever worked in his life. In the fertile soil of Lawrence County, he planted, raised, and harvested the ordinary staples, such as corn, potatoes, wheat, oats and hay, and oftentimes broomcorn, tobacco and vegetables. He also planted fruit trees, such as apples, pears, peaches and various small fruits. Strawberries were particularly plentiful in Lawrence County, and brought in a better profit than other produce when sent to St. Louis and Kansas City.[157]

Farmhands never lived in the main houses of the farms where they worked, but rather in a small shack, converted shed, or an occasional barn. Amenities would have been primitive, and baths and/or showers were rarely provided for common laborers. This meant that Charlie would have probably bathed in Spring River, which cuts across Vineyard.[158] Coincidentally, Spring River also ran through the town of Waco, Missouri, and right next to his mother's house.

Without the luxury of warm water, farmhands would forego bathing during winter months, but would generally clean up enough so as not to be offensive around decent folk. As for material possessions, Charlie owned a rifle and perhaps he had a change of clothing or two, but that's about it. He was too poor to own transportation, such as a horse, bicycle or car, and without transportation, he would have had to walk countless miles down the gravel and macadam country roads, seeking out anyone who needed plowing, hoeing, mulching and planting.

The community was close before the war, and people were aware of each other throughout northwest Lawrence County. As Charlie traveled around, he would encounter people with whom he had grown up and went to school with. He saw that they were purchasing their own farms or branching out in other vocations that, due to his limited education, he would not have an opportunity to compete in. His experience in menial jobs brought him to understand the value of a good education.

One native of Lawrence County that Charlie became reacquainted with was Oren Clinton Sharon. Oren and Charlie had been friends in grade school, but, unlike Charlie who only went through the fourth grade, Oren went on to complete two years of high school. Now Oren was married to his childhood sweetheart, Sallie Thomas, and owned a profitable farm. In 1916, he hired Charlie to work for him on his farm in Vineyard.

Farmland prices at that time varied around Lawrence County, generally according to location and improvements. Cultivated land could be purchased for $35 to $75 an acre, and unimproved land from $25 to $30.[159] If Charlie could just save enough money to purchase twenty acres, he could cultivate the land, plant an orchard, grow strawberries, and, perhaps, raise a few cows and chickens. The possibilities were endless.

Charlie had no family structure, no sense of direction, and no means of lifting himself higher in the social strata, but with world events beginning to stir in a big way, social mobility was about to change. He did not realize it at the time, but fate intervened in his favor when on April 6, 1917, the United States entered World War I.

Charlie was indifferent to the war being waged in Europe, and to the events leading up to the United States' involvement in that war. He didn't read newspapers and had no time for town gossip, so what little he heard about the war went in one ear and out the other. And then one day, Oren told him he had to register for the draft. President Woodrow Wilson issued a proclamation under the Selective Service Act that all males between the ages of 21 and 30 had to report to their nearest polling place on June 5, 1917, or face up to a year in prison. Administration was entrusted to local boards composed of leading civilians in each community, which would issue draft calls in order of numbers drawn in a national lottery.[160]

On June 5, 1917, Charlie caught a ride with Oren to downtown Stotts City to register for the draft and to submit to a medical examination by the local physician. According to the U.S. Army Medical Department, "the character of the examination varied with different boards and also at different periods of mobilization with changing orders from time to time relative to the standards for rejection and classification."[161] Both Charlie and Oren easily passed the exam, but Oren would never be called to serve.

On his draft registration card, Charlie was described as medium height and build, with blue eyes and brown hair. The unsteady signature evidences his meager formal education, and his physical description gives no hint of how powerful he had become. There was also no indication that this unimposing farmhand would exhibit a courage rarely witnessed in our nation's military history.

Michel Staffelbach
Credit: George W. Grokett IV

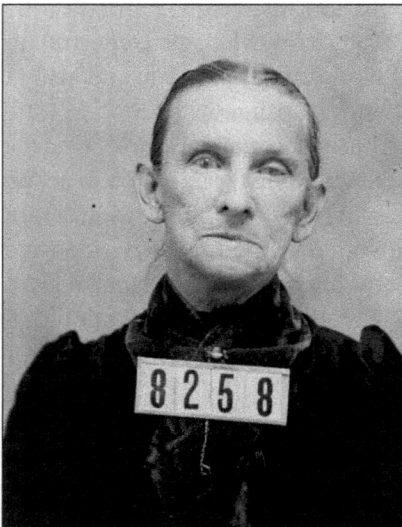

Nancy Staffelbach
*Credit: kansasmemory.org, Kansas State
Historical Society*

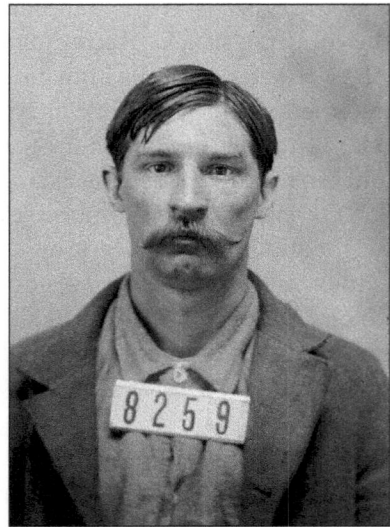

George Staffelbach
*Credit: kansasmemory.org, Kansas State
Historical Society*

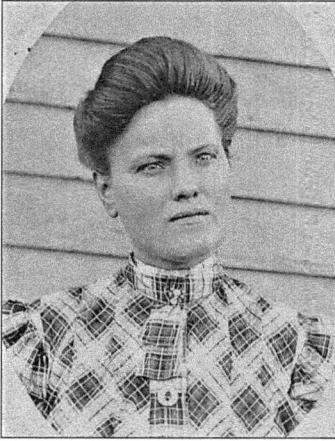

Cora (Lake) Staffelbach
Credit: June Buccina

Ed Staffelbach
Credit: St. Louis Republic,
19 Sep 1897

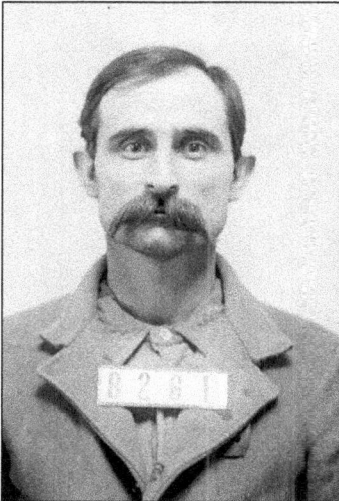

Mike Staffelbach
Credit: kansasmemory.org, Kansas
State Historical Society

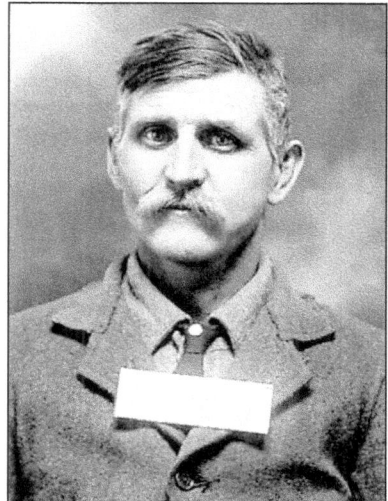

Charles Wilson
Credit: kansasmemory.org, Kansas State
Historical Society

Sidney and Phoebe Barger
Credit: Joe and Euleta Barger

Charlie Barger (1902)
Credit: Joe and Euleta Barger

Stotts City School Building
Credit: Charles Stearns

The McFerons: Lizzie, Henry, Mertie, Sarah and Ellen
Credit: Springfield, MO, Interstate Historical Society

Chapter Four

INDUCTION AND TRAINING

In March 1918, officials in Washington, DC, directed local draft boards to mobilize 2,500 men from Colorado, Kansas and Missouri to bolster the 89th Division for deployment overseas. At the time that Charlie received his draft notice, he was employed with the Coglizer Tent & Awning Company in Joplin, Missouri, which is still in operation today. He reported for enlistment in the National Army at Mt. Vernon, Missouri, on April 1, and departed the following day by train for Fort Riley, Kansas.

Fort Riley is a United States Army installation located along the Kansas River, between the Kansas cities of Junction City and Manhattan. During World War I, a cantonment named Camp Funston was built five miles east of the permanent post, thereby becoming one of sixteen divisional cantonment training camps for the National Army. The National Army, formed from ex-Regular Army troops, and augmented by units of the National Guard and a large draft of able-bodied men, combined conscript and volunteer forces to fight in the war.[162]

The 89th was the first division to train at Camp Funston, and was composed primarily of men from Arizona, Colorado, Kansas, Missouri, Nebraska, New Mexico and South Dakota. An estimated 2,800 to 4,000 buildings were erected to accommodate more than 40,000 soldiers, and appeared more like a city than a military installation.[163] To avoid congestion and best handle the huge influx of new draftees, many detention camps were built on Camp Funston wherein recruits were initially processed, screened and trained. Each detention camp, or depot brigade, could accommodate about 3,000 men at a time and had separate and distinct unit organizations. Once the draftees passed initial processing and screening, they were rudimentarily trained in military customs, courtesies and drills before transferring to their permanent division, regiment and company. This process took two weeks.[164]

The terms officer and enlisted require further explanation for those unfamiliar with military rank structure. Officers, even during World War I, were generally, but not always, college educated. They were commissioned, meaning they were trained by the military in leadership and management, and given a specialty mission or assignment in the military to function as a manager over the enlisted troops.

Commissioned officers are lieutenants, captains, majors, colonels, and generals, and may be designated to serve as commanders. In the Army, the term commander is not a rank; rather, it is a term applied to the officer in charge of a unit. Consequently, there are division commanders, brigade commanders, regimental commanders, battalion commanders, company commanders, and platoon commanders.

Enlisted troops join the Armed Forces and are not commissioned. Enlisted ranks include privates, corporals, and sergeants. Corporals and all grades of sergeant are called non-commissioned officers, as they obtain their position of authority by promotion through the enlisted ranks.

When Charlie stepped from the train at Camp Funston, he would have met a stern-looking officer, wielding a swagger stick. The division commander specifically ordered that company-grade officers meet the new recruits to deliver a short narration about what to expect in the weeks ahead. The swagger sticks were required by the division commander to be carried by all officers to instill a sense of authority, but veteran drill sergeants often wisecracked that it only served to give the officers something to do with their hands.[165]

When the officer completed his speech, a "guide" would have assigned Charlie to the 23rd Company, 164th Depot Brigade, and would have then led him and many others to their designated barracks. These two-story buildings were 43 x 140 feet, and the guide would have made it a point to tell the recruits that they were new and clean, and were expected to stay that way. A kitchen, a mess hall, a company commander's office, several supply rooms, and squad rooms to accommodate 150 men were all located inside these buildings.

Lieutenant Orris R. Jones, who transitioned through the 164th Depot Brigade during the same timeframe as Charlie, felt it amusing to watch the long line of draftees, of every description, size and nationality, filing in, later to become individual units in the great National Army. He recalled that from Kansas came many cowboys, wearing high-heeled boots, chaps, cowboy hats, and knotted red handkerchiefs around their necks. He said they looked as if they had just stepped from a Frederick Remington painting. One draftee, without baggage and minus a hat, even had a huge checkerboard strapped to his back![166]

No incoming recruit would have been permitted to set foot inside the barracks until he had discarded his civilian clothes and taken a shower in one of the detached lavatories. Most of the civilian clothing was sent to the destitute in Belgium, but Charlie's duds were so worn that they were tossed in a trash bin.[167] He was probably relieved to exchange his old farm clothes for a brand-new uniform, for now he was ostensibly in the same social class as every other private in his outfit.

Immediately after showering, cultures were taken for contagious and infectious diseases. Just a month earlier, in fact, some of the first reported American cases of what came to be known as the worldwide influenza epidemic were reported at Camp Funston, so such precautions were quite prudent.[168] The recruits then underwent a brief but strenuous physical examination, which included a psychiatric evaluation, during which time keen emphasis was placed on the proper completion of service records to cut down on training delays.

Still nude from his shower, Charlie would have filed down a narrow passageway, designated by a sign bearing the name of his native state, and collected his uniform, cafeteria style. By order of the division commander, company commanders were required to supervise the recruits as they were fitted with shoes—a task generally assigned to a noncommissioned officer at other installations. Infantrymen, after all, traveled everywhere on foot, and the division commander believed that podiatry was vital to the organization's success in combat.[169]

Prior to departing the Processing Center, Charlie would have also been issued two blankets, a mess kit, and a straw-filled bed sack. Upon finally entering the barracks, coffee and sandwiches would have been waiting, and after a small meal he would have located his assigned room. Unlike Army barracks during World War II and later, which were open-bay and housed 40 or more soldiers, the barracks at Camp Funston during World War I had smaller rooms that were shared by six men. Inside the room would have been a vacant steel-spring cot where Charlie would have arranged his bed sack and blankets. For the typical recruit, it would have been a long, exhausting day, and it is likely that Charlie would have instantly fallen asleep.[170]

Lieutenant Colonel George H. English, Jr., Adjutant of the 177th Brigade, 89th Division, and official 89th Division historian, writes: "He [the recruit] arose the next morning to begin a routine of days so full of duties that one recruit expressed his feelings by saying plaintively that Sunday in the Army was just like Monday on the farm! Elementary military instruction began immediately, and an early hour of his first morning in camp usually found the recruit lined up with others learning to fall in in double ranks, to stand at attention and to execute squads right and left. Very soon his company marched away to the hospital to receive the first 'shot in the arm' and to be vaccinated."[171]

Respiratory diseases were of particular concern; pneumonia and spinal meningitis contributed to most deaths by disease in the 89th Division during the Great War. Colonel John L. Shepard, the division surgeon, implemented several novel methods which proved so successful that they were afterwards adopted throughout the Army. The men, for example, were required to keep windows and ceiling ventilators in their cramped sleeping quarters open during the night, and officers inspected routinely to ensure compliance; shelter tent halves were stretched so as to partition off each bunk slightly from ones neighbor, thus minimizing the effect of coughing as a disseminator of disease; the floors were washed daily with disinfectants; and every utensil used at the table was sterilized after each meal with scalding water.[172]

The first week in the Army was designed to break the men down, to dispel their individuality and instill what is called a "military mindset." They were constantly ridiculed, told they were inept, issued ridiculous orders, and humiliated beyond anything they would ever tolerate in civilian life. In other words, they were socially broken. If they made it through that phase of training, their drill sergeant would gradually build them up; encourage them to succeed; to forget about personal gain; and to focus on what benefited the unit. They ultimately become institutionalized, not unlike a prisoner in a penitentiary.

Charlie's day would begin with breakfast, after which there would be a brief interlude to "police" the camp. Then the workday would commence in earnest, with 14 half-hour training periods, which included calisthenics, lectures, marching, and drill, drill, and more drill.[173] Due to the nature of the Great War, Basic Military Training was accelerated, but no less rigorous than any other era. During that time, Charlie would have learned the value of teamwork, and those assigned to his company would have formed a close-knit military bond.

Today, Charlie's time with the 164th Depot Brigade would be considered Basic Military Training, and what followed would equate to Advanced Individual Training. Most recruits sought any military occupational specialty other than infantry, but that required special qualifications or education, which most farm workers lacked. Men like Charlie were suited for nothing else.

Having completed the fundamentals of soldiering on April 24, 1918, Charlie was assigned, in ascending order, to Company L, 3rd Infantry Battalion, 354th Infantry Regiment, 177th Infantry Brigade, 89th Infantry Division. Each division had two brigades assigned, the 89th Division having the 177th and 178th Brigades. To each brigade there were assigned two regiments. The 177th Brigade had the 353rd and 354th Infantry Regiments, and the 178th Brigade had the 355th and 356th Regiments. Each regiment had three battalions assigned, and each battalion was comprised of four companies. Companies are designated by letters, "A" through "M" (excluding "J" to avoid confusion with "I"), and each company includes four platoons.

The 89th Division also had three machine gun battalions assigned, the 340th, 341st and 342nd. They would provide sustained, fully automatic machine gun fire to defend against enemy infantry attacks. Machine guns had a fearsome reputation during the war—and for good reason—but it was the artillery units that caused the greatest number of casualties.

The division's 164th Field Artillery Brigade included four subunits: the 340th Field Artillery Regiment (75-mm guns); the 341st Field Artillery Regiment (75-mm guns); the 342nd Field Artillery Regiment (155-mm guns); and the 314th Trench-Mortar Battery. These artillery regiments would launch barrages to disrupt enemy units before an assault, inflict heavy casualties upon advancing enemy troops, stymie enemy reinforcements from advancing with their infantry, and fire in advance of its own infantry as they moved forward in combat. The 314th Trench-Mortar Battery would employ portable mortars in forward positions, such as trenches, to shoot projectiles at a high trajectory over a short range.[174]

The 89th Division also had a complement of support units with various combat functions. A headquarters troop, unrelated to the division commander's staff, would provide such functions as liaison, security, and labor-related details. The 314th Field Signal Battalion would provide communications and information systems support for the division. And the 314th Engineer Troops Regiment would build and repair roads and bridges, erect buildings, remove land mines, provide clean water, construct and remove barbed wire, and perform other construction-related projects, as needed.[175]

Major General Leonard Wood, the division commander, was a magnanimous officer, revered by his officers and men. He began his career as a physician in 1884, and two years later took a position as a contract surgeon for the Army at Fort Huachuca, Arizona. Later that year, 1886, he participated in the last campaign against Geronimo, and earned the Medal of Honor for carrying dispatches 100 miles through hostile territory, and commanding an infantry detachment in hand-to-hand combat against the Apache.[176]

Wood served as personal physician to Presidents Grover Cleveland and William McKinley, and became a close friend to Theodore Roosevelt.[177] Wood and Roosevelt formed the legendary Rough Riders upon the outbreak of the Spanish-American War. Wood led his brigade—which included the Rough Riders—to victory at Kettle Hill and San Juan Heights. He went on to serve as Military Governor of Santiago, and then Cuba.[178]

In 1903, Wood was assigned to the Philippines where he commanded the Philippines division. The following year, he was promoted to major general and became commander of the Department of the East, which encompassed the entire Pacific Theater of Operations.[179] During his time in the

Philippines, Wood came to befriend a fellow who would one day become President of the United States: William Howard Taft. Taft succeeded Theodore Roosevelt as President, and in 1910, Taft appointed Wood as Army Chief of Staff.[180]

As Chief of Staff, Wood implemented several programs. For example, the forerunner of the Reserve Officer Training Corps (ROTC) program, and the Preparedness Movement, a campaign for universal military training and wartime conscription. The Preparedness Movement plan was scrapped in favor of the Selective Service System shortly before World War I. Wood also developed the Mobile Army, a vital component of the modern battlefield, which laid the groundwork for American success in the Great War.[181]

As a vociferous advocate of the Preparedness Movement, led by Republicans, Wood fell out of favor with newly elected Democratic President Woodrow Wilson. In 1914, Wilson selected General William Wotherspoon to replace Wood. When the United States declared war against Germany on April 6, 1917, Republicans recommended Wood to be the U.S. field commander in Europe, but Wilson did not favor the recommendation. Deferring to the President's design and opposition to Wood, Secretary of War Newton Baker appointed Major General John J. Pershing to that position.[182]

At the time, Wood outranked Pershing by thirteen years—Wood was promoted to major general in the Regular Army on August 8, 1903, and Pershing's date of rank was September 25, 1916. The ultimate decisions in these matters, however, sat with the President, and President Wilson's politics trumped Wood's seniority.

Although bypassed as field commander of American Expeditionary Forces in Europe, Wood may have anticipated deployment to France to command an Army unit commensurate with his rank and expertise. Instead, he was sent to Camp Funston and charged with training the 89th Division. To his credit—and to the benefit of those assigned to the division—he took this assignment quite seriously and performed his duties with distinction.

Meanwhile, all division commanders were required to rotate to Europe for a short time to tour the front lines and visit American training camps. Wood departed for France in November 1917, and in his absence, Brigadier General Frank L. Winn assumed command of the 89th Division.

On January 27, 1918, Wood was visiting the French-occupied front with a party of twenty or thirty American and French officers. They were watching the firing of a trench mortar at a training camp when the premature detonation of a shell burst the gun. Two French officers on either side of Wood were killed instantly, as were five privates. Seven splinters penetrated Wood's right arm, one lodging on the main nerve and causing a slight paralysis, which soon disappeared. His escape with comparatively slight wounds was miraculous.[183]

Wood was hospitalized for a week in Paris, and convalesced at Pershing's personal quarters in Chaumont, France, where he made a speedy recovery. On April 12, 1918, Wood returned to Camp Funston and resumed command of the 89th Division, giving him just enough time to prepare the division for what they would encounter overseas. This was certainly a daunting challenge for Wood, for during his absence, troops assigned to the division had been removed and placed for use in other units. Now he had to simultaneously bring the 89th back up to division strength while ensuring the training they received was adequate for overseas deployment the following month.[184]

"Large contingents of men equipped and partially trained in Camp Funston, were sent to fill deficiencies in other divisions which were supposed to be destined for earlier service overseas than we were," explained George English. "Thus contingents were sent to Camp Kearney, others to Camp Doniphan for the 35th Division, and finally, in the late winter and early spring [1918] large quotas of men were sent directly overseas to serve as replacements for divisions already engaged or about to be engaged with the enemy. Many of these men were assigned to the 3rd and 4th Divisions, and participated in the fighting of the spring and summer of 1918 at Château-Thierry and along the Vesle.

"As a result of these transfers the division was much depleted on the return of General Wood on April 12th, 1918. Replacements soon began to flow in. Some of them were partially trained men from Camp Grant. Early in May a large contingent of newly drafted men reported in numbers sufficient to fill all vacancies. These men were received within two weeks of the departure of the division for overseas, and those weeks were crowded weeks for them."[185]

Wood ordered that the men under his command drill hard, and he had them hiking up and down the precipitous bluffs and ridges almost daily. Those who had trouble maintaining the demanding pace were assisted and encouraged by their fellow recruits. The general also commanded the men to play energetic athletic games, citing that such activities "made giants out of weaklings in no time."[186]

Wood was not just a tough taskmaster; he took care of his troops. At one point, the interurban electric line between Junction City and Manhattan, which passed through Camp Funston, was in such disrepair that there were frequent wrecks. The general threatened to keep his troops from patronizing the rail system until repairs were made, and the situation was resolved forthwith. Another time, merchants at Junction City and

Manhattan were overcharging soldiers, so he advised the merchants that one more reported incident would result in those towns being off limits to his troops. That did the trick![187]

The war in Europe was unlike any war ever fought up to that time, for technological advances and the advent of nearly impermeable defensive barriers stymied infantry units on both sides. Artillery, machine guns, small arms and barbed wire barriers forced the belligerent parties into trenches early in the war and commanders on either side failed to puzzle out a way to make advancements without suffering severe casualties.

The Allied and Axis trenches, which stretched along the entire Western Front, between Switzerland and the North Sea, were considered impassable by both sides and, thus, could not be flanked. Anyone caught between the trenches, commonly known as "No Man's Land," were likely killed. For this reason, the Western Front in 1914, hopelessly deadlocked, closely resembled the Western Front in 1918, when Charlie enlisted in the Army. General Wood, in seeking a way to break the deadlock, looked to experts from many different disciplines to diversify the training of his men.

Training for May 1918, would have been intense, while Charlie participated in numerous trench exercises at the Carpenter Hill trench system and Smoky Hill Flats, both designed to prepare the 89th Division for trench warfare. At Carpenter Hill, unit elements, such as fire teams, squads and platoons, practiced relieving other elements at night; trench orders would have been issued for the attack and defense of the "battlefield"; defense plans would have been devised to thwart enemy attacks and prevent penetration of the American lines; and these conditions would have then been simulated and the plans put into effect.[188]

General Wood solicited the assistance of foreign officers to share their experiences, provide specialized training, and develop training scenarios to enhance the division's proficiency. Three British officers gave special attention to machine gunnery, gas warfare and bayonet training; five French officers were on hand to supervise training in artillery, field maneuvers, automatic rifles, bombs and liaison; and one Canadian officer arrived to instruct the 89th Division's mortar platoons.[189]

"Assisted by these officers, an elaborate system of trenches was laid out and constructed by the troops on Carpenter Hill," English reveals. "The system covered an area about a thousand yards square and comprised three lines of trenches with communicating trenches, dugouts, wire entanglements and machine gun emplacements."[190]

Progressing to training at Smoky Hill Flats, some five miles from Camp Funston, Charlie would have received instruction in varied forms of modern warfare. This instruction was conducted by the Division School of Arms, under the command of Major E.A. Keyes, and aided by the aforementioned foreign officers. At Smoky Hill Flats, a more elaborate system of trenches was constructed or indicated than that at Carpenter Hill, and larger problems of trench warfare were worked out.[191]

Troops lined up at the west gate of Camp Funston every morning before sunup and marched to Smoky Hill Flats. Work began at 8:45 in the morning and ended at 4:30 in the afternoon. With the return march, entrance to camp was made under cover of darkness. During the workday, Charlie would have undergone bayonet training, grenade throwing, automatic rifle practice, and trench and combat formations—all in unbroken succession.[192]

In the official 89th Division history, George English reveals that on nearby Republican Flats there existed an enormous target range with 300 targets. Soldiers could shoot at targets that were 100-, 200-, or 300-yards away at that range. For those soldiers who displayed particularly good marksmanship skills, there was a smaller range set aside on the reservation where ranges of 500- and 600-yards could be practiced. On both ranges, no one was permitted to fire their M1917 Enfield rifle until he had preliminary instruction in sighting, aiming, nomenclature and loading. During the course of fire, each soldier received individual instruction.[193]

Trench warfare resulted in new infantry weapons being developed, and the men detailed to handle them had to be trained as specialists. These specialists included hand grenadiers, rifle grenadiers, automatic rifle crews, and riflemen. American infantry companies were now organized on a basis of these specialists.[194]

Each of the company's four platoons had one lieutenant, serving as platoon commander, and one sergeant, serving as an assistant to the platoon commander. Each platoon was divided into four sections of specialists. The 1st Section, consisting of hand- and rifle-grenadiers, was led by a sergeant and had assigned 22 men; the 2nd and 3rd Sections were riflemen, led by corporals, and had assigned 12 men each; and the 4th Section, equipped with Chauchat automatic rifles, was led by a sergeant and had assigned 11 men.[195]

Charlie qualified as an expert marksman, so when men were selected for specialized training, according to their fitness, he was designated a Chauchat gunner. The *Manual of the Automatic Rifle (Chauchat)*, published in 1918, states: "All members of the Automatic Rifle Section must be healthy, robust men. No other type will be able to carry the loads and meet the demands that will be made upon them. They must be intelligent and must be expert shots. Otherwise, the great fire power [sic] which is put in their hands will be wasted."[196]

The Chauchat was the first mass-produced automatic rifle, which, at twenty pounds, was light enough to be carried on combat patrols. Being an automatic rifle, it filled the gap between bolt action rifles and the heavier machine guns. For the reader, unfamiliar with firearms, the bolt action rifles were single-shot, cable of firing 10-30 rounds per minute, and were standard issue to infantrymen during the war. Machine guns, such as the widely used M1914 Hotchkiss, could fire 450 rounds per minute, but its recoil was supported by a fixed mount, and due to its weight of 54 pounds, it was typically set up in a stationary position during combat.[197]

There were two versions of the Chauchat during World War I, the M1915 and M1918. They were virtually identical, except for the ammunition used. The M1915 used the French 8mm Lebel cartridge, a term used to distinguish the French rifle cartridge from other 8mm rifle cartridges. The M1918 used the American-made .30-06, the "30" referring to the caliber and the "06" referring to the year the cartridge was adopted—1906.[198]

The M1915 was designed to use 8mm Lebel ammunition, which typically operated the weapon free of ammunition-related issues. The M1918, however, was adapted to fire the more powerful .30-06 cartridge, and these cartridges tended to overpressure the system, causing the weapon to jam due to overheating.[199] During training in the United States, the troublesome M1918 was used exclusively, and, thus, many American troops formed a negative impression of the Chauchat.

Automatic rifles, such as the Chauchat, were supported by the gunner's body and carried during assaults against the enemy. When operating optimally, the Chauchat could fire 240 rounds per minute and had a range of 2,000 meters. During WWI, soldiers with the infantry used this weapon under all circumstances. The weapon was particularly ideal where intense infantry fire of short duration, or limited bursts of infantry fire, was required.[200]

It was alluded to earlier that a platoon's 4th Section included automatic rifle squads. The sergeant assigned to the section commanded two squads, each led by a corporal, and there were two rifle teams per squad. Each rifle team consisted of a Chauchat gunner, who served as the team commander, and two privates, one serving as an assistant gunner/ammunition carrier, and the other as an additional ammunition carrier.[201]

Chauchat rifle teams all received the same instruction so that they could fill in if the gunner was killed or wounded. Every member of the Section would undergo four phases of instruction with the Chauchat: (1) Individual Training; (2) Rifle Team Training; (3) Squad Training; and (4) Section Training.[202]

Charlie would have been taught two firing positions with the Chauchat: prone and marching fire. In the prone position, he would have been instructed to position his body on the ground as nearly as possible in prolongation of the line of sight. His assistant gunner/ammunition carrier would have been positioned next to Charlie, on his right. The additional ammunition carrier would be on the ground, aligned five yards to Charlie's right or left.[203]

During marching fire, Charlie would have, of course, assumed a standing position. By hanging the weapon's sling over a shoulder hook, located on the upper left side of his Y-strap, the Chauchat could easily be fired while marching forward. Y-straps were used to support the weight of equipment on a soldier's cartridge belt.[204]

Charlie would have grasped the Chauchat's carrying handle with his left hand and the pistol grip with his right; the butt of the Chauchat would have been positioned against the front of his right hip. When firing, he would have exerted a downward and outward pressure, and his body would be bent well forward from the waist. The assistant gunner/ammunition carrier would have marched from a position to Charlie's right rear, his left hand on Charlie's right shoulder. The additional ammunition carrier would have marched in alignment with Charlie, five paces to his right or left.[205]

The duties of the Rifle Team were the same in the prone and marching fire positions. Charlie's job was to direct fire on the target. The assistant gunner would watch for signals from the Squad Leader to commence or cease firing, and then communicate this to Charlie by tapping him twice on the shoulder. The additional ammunition carrier would act as a scout, pointing out targets of opportunity for Charlie and protecting the Rifle Team with his Enfield rifle when the Chauchat was out of action.[206]

Chauchat gunners had to be right-handed, because the magazine, open on the right side, had to be monitored by the assistant gunner and quickly exchanged with a loaded magazine when empty. When the assistant gunner would see that the magazine was empty, he would notify Charlie by calling out, "Magazine!" Charlie would pull the operating handle back to cock the Chauchat, at the same time turning the barrel slightly to the left without lowering it from his shoulder. He would then press forward on the magazine catch with his left thumb, releasing the empty magazine. The assistant gunner would then remove the empty magazine with his left hand and insert a loaded magazine with his right.[207]

Charlie would have carried about four magazines in reserve, but the standard combat load was twenty magazines; ten carried in a magazine canister by the assistant gunner and ten carried in a magazine canister by the additional ammunition carrier. Each magazine, fully loaded with 20 rounds, weighed about two pounds. When the assistant gunner's magazine canister was empty, he would exchange it with the additional ammunition carrier's canister. It was the additional ammunition carrier's job to reload empty magazines and exchange empty magazine canisters with the squad leader.[208]

In training, and in combat, the Chauchat gunner to the Squad Leader's right would fire first. Just before the gunner's magazine was empty, the assistant gunner would give the signal to the Rifle Team on the left to commence firing, and then the process would repeat itself. This ensured that consistent suppressive fire was focused on the enemy.[209]

One can begin to see how critical the assistant gunner was to the gunner, and how they would have grown to depend on one another on the battlefield. Charlie's assistant gunner was an affable and carefree Colorado cowboy named Jesse Nathaniel Funk, who very well may have been the closest friend that Charlie ever had.

Jess was born on August 20, 1888, in New Hampton, Missouri, a sickly child who suffered with several bouts of pneumonia. A doctor warned Jess' father, Martin Funk, that his son's condition could develop into tuberculosis. Certain that conditions in Colorado would benefit Jess, Martin purchased a ranch in Calhan, Colorado, in 1899, and moved his family there the following year. By then, Jess, 11, had quit school to work exclusively on the family ranch.[210]

"Well," Jess reflected, in an interview published in the *Denver Post* in 1919, "my father had the right idea, and he kept me out in the open. When I was 14 years old I punched cattle all summer, and that helped a lot. This sunshine surely can do wonders for a fellow, and the first thing I knew I was strong and husky, again. Well, I stayed with the cattle business, and I'm mighty glad of it."[211]

"Jess was never afraid of anything," recalled Martin Funk in the same newspaper story. "He was the most fearless lad I have ever seen. And I'll give his mother credit for his bravery. I believe the mother is responsible for the bravery or lack of bravery of any child. He had a pony of his own when he became able to ride one, and when 10 and 11 years of age he would go out on dark nights and round up a cow or two that was missing.

"He worked for me on our ranch until seventeen years of age, when he started to ride the range for a large cattle outfit. This outfit had an outlaw horse, known as 'Black Bill,' which all of the other cowboys were afraid to ride and which caused the injury of a number of those who had tried to master him. There was a big turnout of cowboys and other interested [folks] when the attempt to ride 'Black Bill' by Jess was made. Jess was thrown a couple of times, but he stuck to the job until he had completely mastered the wild animal. The horse was a beauty and for several months ridden only by my boy.

"Jess remained with me on the ranch for several years and then engaged in the livestock business, with headquarters at Calhan. In 1912, he was sent on a business trip to South America by Murdo McKenzie, the big Colorado cattleman. On his return, he went to Canada and remained in that country one year.

"An accident, which he had in Canada, again proved his bravery. He was alone when thrown from his horse, thirty-five miles from town. A broken collarbone and other severe bruises were the result of the fall. Despite these injuries and the great pain he suffered, Jess, after a hard struggle, climbed on his horse and rode the thirty-five miles to the nearest town and doctor."[212]

Jess returned to Calhan and engaged in the livestock business for a couple of years. During this time, on February 3, 1915, he married Anna Louise Phillips, a teacher who quit her job that month to settle down as a wife and mother. They went on to have a son named Frank Martin Funk in January 1917, but Anne soon grew tired of Jess' carefree ways and their marriage turned acrimonious. Certain that a short separation would benefit them, Jess ventured to Portland, Oregon, to work as a cowboy with his uncle and aunt, James William and Margaret (Funk) Sevier, who owned a stockyard and cattle business.[213]

A few months later, Jess received a draft notice, but returned to Colorado so he could enlist in his home state. He resided on the Holt Ranch, near Colorado Springs, until entering military service on April 27, 1918. At that time, he underwent the same processing and training as Charlie. "We didn't get any of that intensive training that a lot of fellows had gone thru," Jess recalled, "and we were just as glad of it."[214]

On May 10-11, 1918, divisional maneuvers were conducted. The entire force at Camp Funston hiked out to the range for battle practice, all organizations and branches working collectively, as they would in actual combat. The first day was spent working out battle problems in the field, and that night the division was entrenched at Camp Funston, as though they were at the front in France. The following morning, specific units attacked a theoretical enemy, and then the exercise culminated. Critique and analysis would have followed.[215]

There was also a gashouse built in which the men, after having been drilled in the use of their gas masks, were required to endure a long period of contact with deadly gases. According to George English, this served to demonstrate the protection these gas masks afforded, but was also designed to give the men confidence in them.[216]

It was learned in early May 1918, that the 89th Division would depart Camp Funston for overseas later that month. General Wood personally inspected the troops and equipment, ensuring there were no last-minute glitches. On May 21, the first units of the division departed Camp Funston en route to Camp Mills, on Long Island, New York.[217] Charlie's company departed Camp Funston before daybreak on May 27, and arrived at Camp Mills three days later.[218]

In an unexpected turn of events, General Wood was relieved as Commander of the 89th Division on the eve of embarkation, and replaced by General Winn. Few ever learned the reason Wood was ordered to remain stateside, and there is no revelation in the 89th Division history, but it stemmed from Wood's criticism of Pershing's wartime strategy and tactics while he was convalescing in France. Pershing took offense to Wood's comments, and pressed Secretary of War Newton Baker to relieve Wood of his command.[219]

Judging by documented accounts, most officers and men assigned to the 89th Division were quite upset over the sudden removal of their illustrious commander. Although General Wood did not lead them into combat, it was his experience, his training, his discipline, and his foresight that propelled the 89th to distinction on the battlefield. Charlie certainly would have benefited from the general's leadership in the intense, realistic training he received. Such intense training likely would have even been the experience Charlie drew on, later, to save his own life.

Most elements of the 89th Division set sail for Europe from New York Harbor; but not Charlie's unit. On the evening of June 3, 1918—his twenty-fourth birthday—177th Infantry Brigade headquarters, the 354th Infantry Regiment, and the 341st Machine Gun Battalion, proceeded via train to Montreal, Canada, from where they would depart the following day. It was not at all unusual for large units, such as the 89th Division, to be apportioned for the voyage across the Atlantic and then reassembled in England.[220]

By the end of June, Charlie would set foot in France, coincidentally arriving at Le Havre, the same port where his Staffelbach ancestors departed for America eighty-three years earlier. He had never been told about his connection to his grandfather, Michel, or his Staffelbach ancestors, nor would he in his entire life ever learn about them. Charlie's great-grandparents, Georg and Louise Staffelbach, enjoyed substantial means, good social standing and a promising future. They would encourage their children to take advantage of the opportunities that America had to offer, and all their sons, except Charlie's grandfather, grew up to become successful in many respectable pursuits.

Charlie was separated from the rich heritage of his Grandfather Staffelbach's ancestry by rude beginnings. Born into his grandmother's den of iniquity, the crimes of Charlie's father and grandmother catapulted him into an orphanage at a young age, where all ties with his roots were severed. By the time he was a teenager, he was on his own, seeking his own way in life with no family to support him in any way. Ironically, he lived not far from his mother and maternal grandmother in rural Missouri, but he might as well have lived in another universe, as neither knew of the other's whereabouts.

Charlie would vaguely remember his father, George, and his grandmother, Nancy Staffelbach, both of whom died in prison for committing murder. Completely unknown to Charlie was his grandfather, Michel, who had become estranged from Nancy and the children years before Charlie was born. Having a connection to Michel might have given Charlie entrance to the rich heritage of the Staffelbach family, but that was not to be.

Taking a look at the Staffelbach line of Charlie's family, we find many heartwarming stories and a rich background that Charlie was never privy to. Comparing his life path to that of his Grandfather Staffelbach's family yields an interesting perspective, leaving the reader to ponder where young Charlie's path in life might have traveled, if only . . .

Chapter Five

ROOTS

Much of what is known about the Staffelbach family before they immigrated to America comes from a family chronicle maintained by Charlie's great-great-great-great-great-grandfather, Hans Peter Staffelbach, and a 1936 book by Georg Staffelbach and Dora F. Rittmeyer titled *Hans Peter Staffelbach: Goldschmied in Sursee, 1657-1736*. As the title suggests, Hans Peter is the principal subject of the Staffelbach/Ritter book, and he is famous even today as founder of an illustrious goldsmith dynasty that culminated with Charlie's immigrant ancestor, Georg Staffelbach.

Hans Peter was born on April 28, 1657, in Sursee, Switzerland, in the canton of Lucerne, a region which assumed German customs, language and traditions. He spent his formative years in Sursee at a time when it was an art-oriented community that offered enormous opportunity to an aspiring young artist. Sculptors carved beautiful altars, pulpits and choir stalls, and goldsmiths inlaid them for use in the local church. Indeed, arts and crafts flourished, and by the time Hans Peter was a teenager, Sursee boasted no less than twelve artists, stained glass makers, sculptors and goldsmiths.[221]

Hans Peter served with the Papal Swiss Guard between 1675 and 1683. Many of the archival records during that period have been lost, but it is known that he used his eight-year enlistment in the Papal Swiss Guard to hone his artistic skills. His influences were Gian Lorenzo Bernini, the Italian artist and architect, and Giovanni Giardini, the silversmith and founder of the Apostolic Palace Room under Pope Innocent XI.[222]

One can see Bernini's inspiration, Giardini's style, and evidence of Baroque architecture in two copper engravings created by Hans Peter in 1714. Art critics point to the relaxed, playful ornaments, which were less cluttered than earlier masters. Moreover, his drawings were beautiful, correctly proportioned, and represented his own unique style.[223]

In November 1704, Hans Peter was commissioned to create a monstrance for St. Urban's Abbey in the municipality of Pfaffnau. The result was a beautiful showpiece, which, in 1706, led to orders from neighboring parishes. Having earned a good reputation in the goldsmith business, orders for his work poured in and he was soon at the height of his artistic creativity. During his lifetime, he was the highest paid artisan in Switzerland, and his work graced the Vatican and court of Louis XIV of France.[224]

Hans Peter also earned the confidence and respect of the community through the years and held a plethora of civic offices. The town's aristocracy even bestowed upon him the title of "Lord." More than a century after his death on February 12, 1736, Hans Peter's American progenies erected a monument in his honor, which is still proudly displayed in Sursee today. Even two hundred years after his death there was a commemorative exhibition of his stunning relics in Switzerland, thereby indicating that his legacy will continue well into the future. Today, Hans Peter's artifacts are highly coveted throughout Europe and his name ranks among the greatest goldsmiths in Swiss history.[225]

Forty-three years after the death of Hans Peter, Georg Staffelbach, Charlie's great-grandfather, was born in Sursee on January 1, 1779. In about 1805, Georg, then 25, married Louise Ellen Göldlin. Aside from her birth in Sursee in September 1787, nothing has been discovered about her parentage or background. In the years that followed their marriage, Georg and Louise had sixteen children, all born in Sursee: Alois, Xavier, Rosa, Balthasar, Louisa, twins Maria Christina Josepha and Maria Josepha Carolina, Elisa, Frances, Bertha, Nanette, Josepha, Joseph, Michel (Charlie's grandfather), Henry, and Louis.

Georg became a goldsmith under the able tutelage of his father and was skilled in forming metal through filing, soldering, sawing, forging, casting and polishing. He was not a member of the aristocracy, nor was he classified as poor, but times were still challenging for the Staffelbachs under Napoleon. As a boy, Georg and his father traveled to France, Germany and Italy to sell their merchandise, for international trade had become vital to the family's livelihood. Now, however, Swiss citizens were subjected to strict international customs and high tariffs.[226]

In 1806, Napoleon established the Continental System, whereby France and its allies were forbidden to trade with Britain. Isolating Britain meant that Georg was unable to obtain raw materials, such as gold and other precious metals needed to maintain a striving business.[227] Aside from the traditional goblets, platters, and ceremonial or religious items, which made his forefathers such noteworthy figures in the metallurgic arts, he made decorative and serviceable utensils. Rising prices of precious metal during the French Revolution, however, curtailed the making of such items to a large degree, and by the end of the war Georg was near bankruptcy.[228]

Napoleon's stronghold on Switzerland had diminished by 1813, thereby leaving the country susceptible to attack by warring nations seeking to expand their territorial horizons. In December 1813, Austrian troops—with support from some Swiss factions—crossed the Swiss border without opposition and served as an occupying force. By the end of the year, the Act of Mediation, which had established the Swiss Confederation under Napoleon, had been completely abolished, and the Swiss Diet met to replace the constitution. Napoleon's subsequent defeat at the Battle of Waterloo in June 1815, marked the end of his regime.[229]

Between September 1814 and June 1815, ambassadors from several European states convened in Vienna, Austria, to establish a long-term post-French Revolution peace plan. The Congress of Vienna, as it was called, ordered Austrian troops removed from Switzerland, reestablished Swiss independence, and recognized permanent Swiss neutrality. This also set into motion Switzerland's eventual return to the same exclusive and oppressive upper-class system as the people had suffered under before the French Revolution.[230]

A lot of this had to do with creation of the Holy Alliance by the monarchist powers of Russia, Austria and Prussia in 1815. Switzerland became a member of the Alliance shortly after its inception. The problem with the Holy Alliance in Switzerland was that it overpowered all liberal institutions, and that interfered with the equal rights of most its citizens.[231]

Dr. Ignaz Paul Vital Troxler and Dr. Kaspar Köpfli, two liberal-minded physicians who strongly supported the basic freedoms under the short-lived Helvetic Republic (1798–1803) and Napoleon's reign, opposed restoration of the conservative government. They circulated a petition calling for a liberal constitution, which resulted in them being jailed in Lucerne for more than a month. Still, these men continued to advocate liberal ideas ... ideas that were embraced by Georg Staffelbach.[232]

Gottfried Duden, a German immigrant and author, who resided for a time in the United States, returned to Germany and penned a book titled *Bericht über eine Reise nach den westlichen Staaten Nordamerika's*. Therein, he described in great detail the exquisiteness of the relatively new state of Missouri, formed in 1821 in the United States.[233] Only 1,500 copies of the first edition of Duden's report were published, but it spread like wildfire! Family and friends passed it around; portions were read at meetings and immigration societies; and copies may have even been left behind for others who were considering immigrating to the United States.[234]

One of the men encouraged by this report to immigrate to the United States was Dr. Kasper Köpfli, who continued to push for liberal reforms. He and his small party arrived in St. Louis, Missouri, in July 1831, and then ventured a few miles east and settled in Madison County, Illinois. Dr. Köpfli purchased several hundred acres of nearly barren prairie land and envisioned a vibrant Swiss colony. Through letters home, he encouraged further immigration by painting a life of beauty, tranquility and boundless opportunity. His correspondence, however, concealed the hardships of prairie life.[235]

In 1834, Georg Staffelbach visited New Switzerland, Illinois, which today is the city of Highland. He wanted to determine firsthand whether immigration was right for his family, and by the time he returned to Sursee later that year, he felt that it was. In March 1835, he departed Sursee with his sizable family and about fifty others, most of whom he persuaded to immigrate with him. They traveled to Le Havre, France, to board the ship *Salem,* and disembarked in New Orleans, Louisiana, on May 23, 1835. The following month they arrived in their new community.

In *Journey to New Switzerland,* authors John C. Abbott and Raymond J. Spahn point out that the liberal Swiss immigrants traveling to Highland were not typical of immigrants at the time. They were prosperous and well-educated, had a clear view as to what they hoped to accomplish in the United States, and had the financial means to carry out their plans. "While their objectives were primarily political, members of the party were highly sensible to economic and social considerations," write Abbott and Spahn.[236]

Georg built a log cabin that was ample size for his large family. Cast iron stoves were expensive and difficult to haul over the rough terrain, so heating, cooking and baking was done on a large fireplace. The family's meals typically consisted of cornbread, bacon, rabbit and venison. Deer at that time were so numerous that the meat could be bought for less than one cent per pound in wintertime.[237]

In Sursee, Georg was a successful goldsmith and merchant, but there was little use for an artistic goldsmith in such a primitive expanse of land on which he now found himself. He might have been a merchant in some other capacity, of course, for there were a number of businesses cropping up, but instead of sticking to what he knew, he decided to become a full-fledged farmer.

On August 12, 1836, Georg purchased forty acres of farmland for $50, and on September 10, he purchased another forty acres on adjacent property for the same amount. Being a sober, industrious and resourceful man, he was convinced that he could prosper ... and he was right. The climate was perfect for farming, and the soil on Georg's property was rich alluvial, a variation unsurpassed by any in the world for inexhaustible fertility.

With his sons, Georg planted corn, wheat, oats, barley, rye, buckwheat and a variety of fruit trees, to include apples, peaches and pears.[238] During harvest season, his marketing prowess paid off. Not only did he transport goods to markets in St. Louis and Chicago, like most farmers, but he also took advantage of the proximity of the Mississippi River to sell his produce to river towns as far south as New Orleans. The first few years in Illinois were so profitable, in fact, that Georg purchased an additional eighty acres of farmland on January 1, 1840, therein doubling his spread. Now, aside from the wheat, corn and potatoes he had been growing, he purchased dairy cows, hogs, sheep and chickens, and profited from homemade Swiss cheese, pork, mutton and poultry.

Georg's wife, Louise, died in January 1853, and for the remainder of his life, he was cared for by his unmarried daughter, Eliza. He passed away in his Highland home on September 21, 1872, at the age of ninety-three.

Through the years, Georg provided well for his family, and in death he left for them his small fortune, fertile farmland, and a birthright that has been cherished by many and tainted by few. Unfortunately, it is those few, including Charlie's grandfather, Michel, that leave a mark on his legacy. However, the stories of how his sons, Xavier, Joseph and Henry found their way to tremendous success might have lifted Charlie to a different path had he known about them, and been given the opportunity to become inspired by his own family legacy.

Xavier remained in New Orleans, Louisiana, where he married Bertha Simon around 1837. They had a daughter, Emilie, and two sons, Albert and Edward. Gold was discovered at Sutter's Mill in California in 1848, and the following year Xavier became one of the 300,000 people to flood into the future state. The Staffelbachs left New Orleans and sailed around the Horn of South America on a ship skippered by Captain Filimon Julius "Louis" Traung. They disembarked in San Francisco and then settled in Sacramento.

Xavier was not a miner, and never would be, but he had his father's business sense. He purchased a hotel in Sacramento, and purchased another hotel when he moved to San Francisco in the mid-1850s. Later, he opened a barbershop with his sons, and dabbled in real estate on the side. When he passed away on February 1, 1868, in San Francisco, he was a wealthy man.

Xavier's daughter, Emilie, married Louis Traung, the ship captain who brought the family to California years earlier. They had five children, the most notable being their twin sons, Charles and Louis. Intelligent and industrious, Charles and Louis established a multi-million-dollar lithograph empire bearing their surname, with offices in San Francisco, Seattle and New York. Charles also served for many years as the California State Athletic Commissioner and as a member of the Board of Police Commissioners in San Francisco.

Georg Staffelbach's son, Joseph, married Priscilla Foster on October 2, 1845, in McDonough County, Illinois, and fathered six children. The reader may recall from the first chapter that Charlie's grandfather, Michel, joined Joseph in the confection industry in St. Louis, Missouri, about 1847. This successful venture gave him the means to delve into farming.

On September 28, 1853, Joseph purchased 220 acres of premium farmland for the sum of $3,200 on the outskirts of Rockingham, Iowa. This property was situated right along the Mississippi River, where he established a riverboat landing. Shipping wheat and grain via riverboat up and down the Mississippi, his farming business proved so prosperous that he left the confection industry in 1859 to pursue farming full-time. When Joseph retired from farming in the late 1870s, his estate, by today's standards, was valued at more than $250,000.

All of Joseph and Priscilla's children did well in life, but their son, William, was particularly noteworthy. At the age of twenty, he began teaching school in Davenport, and three years later he decided to enter the legal profession. After graduating from Iowa State University in 1878, he purchased 480 acres in Wellington, Kansas, and opened a law office. Through the years, he held positions as City Clerk, City Attorney and Probate Judge.

Georg Staffelbach's son, Henry, purchased eighty acres just outside of Highland in 1847, five years before his marriage to Rebecca Kile. During the 1870s, he moved to Saline, Illinois, and toward the end of his life he settled in St. Louis, Missouri. According to Dr. Elmer H. Staffelbach, Henry's grandson, he was "a man of down-to-earth Swiss honesty and father in hard work." This hard work paid off, as he left an estate worth $7,000, or nearly $190,000 today. This, of course, paved the way for his children to succeed in life.

Dr. Elmer Staffelbach, the son of Henry's son, William, was a remarkable man and venerated educator. Having earned his Ph.D. at Stanford University in 1926, he became Dean of the School of Education and Professor of Education at San Jose State College in California. He also authored a number of textbooks, and the popular Long Rifle Series, a fictional trilogy about the exploits of a young man named Pierre, set in the 1830s and '40s.

During World War II, Elmer was commissioned a captain in the U.S. Army Air Corps and assumed duties as Academic Director of Heavy and Medium Bombardment Training in Orlando, Florida. Later, when his immediate supervisor was transferred to the Pentagon to organize a Sea and Rescue program, he arranged for Elmer to join him. In that capacity, Elmer had the opportunity to serve in Europe, Africa, the Mediterranean, and the Pacific, where he identified search and rescue deficiencies and presented solutions to the Pentagon and the Theater Air Commanders. Elmer was discharged after the war with the rank of lieutenant colonel and returned to his position at San Jose State. Today, the University's AFROTC Detachment is named in his honor.

In stark contrast to his ancestors' affluent lifestyle, Charlie had known only poverty in small neighborhoods in middle America. Of course, his standard of living had been raised since he had joined the Army. He didn't have to worry about being laid off, or where he would sleep at night, or where his next meal would come from. Best of all, now he had friends unlike any he had ever met in civilian life. Within a year's time, his horizons would be expanded considerably, by traveling outside his rural Missouri community to see the world.

Though Charlie never had the opportunity for a decent education, never inherited or acquired land, and financial security eluded him throughout his life, he still proved to have a strain of the Staffelbach spirit in him. Soon to be on the continent inhabited by his forefathers, and in the same port where they embarked on their journey to the New World, Charlie would, by the time he departed Europe, have earned recognition from military leaders, kings, and political dignitaries, including the President of the United States of America.

Chapter Six

OVER THERE

The New York Port of Embarkation (NYPOE) was an Army command responsible for the movement of troops and supplies from the United States to overseas commands.[239] The NYPOE had facilities in New York and New Jersey, and subports in other cities under its direct command. These subports were at Boston, Baltimore and Philadelphia, and the Canadian ports of Halifax, Montreal and St. John's, Newfoundland.

Upon arrival in Montreal on June 4, 1918, 177th Infantry Brigade headquarters, the 354th Infantry Regiment, and the 341st Machine Gun Battalion boarded the Australian troop transport *Ascanius*. The following day they began their three-day trek down the St. Lawrence River to Halifax, Nova Scotia. After an overnight stay in Halifax, the *Ascanius* left port at three o'clock on the afternoon of June 9 and headed out to open sea.[240]

We get information about this journey from histories that were written by officers assigned to the 354th Infantry Regiment and 89th Division. The twelve-day voyage to England was quite uncomfortable for the troops, who were generally restricted to side-by-side bunks in very cramped quarters. There were also boat drills, several unfounded reports of enemy U-boats, and a fair share of seasickness as the ship zigzagged across the Atlantic. Finally, in the early morning hours of June 21, the *Ascanius* made its way up the River Thames to Tibury, England, seventeen miles east of London.[241]

Charlie would have disembarked in Tibury and marched to a nearby train depot where a representative of King George V made a brief speech.[242] Upon completion of the speech, each soldier was handed a small card, signed by the King, which read: "Soldiers of the United States, the people of the British Isles welcome you on your way to take your stand beside the Armies of many Nations now fighting in the Old World the great battle for human freedom. The Allies will gain new heart & spirit in your company. I wish that I could shake the hand of each one of you & bid you God speed on your mission."[243]

Charlie would have then boarded a boxcar bound for Winchester. During the 100-mile westerly trip, he would have experienced a warm welcome, with the windows open and people cheerfully waving to the Americans all along the way. He would have looked out over beautiful scenery, oddly clad Brits, and bustling cities, and may have been in awe of the landscape, which was a far cry from Vineyard, Missouri. Traveling to Europe would likely never have been in his wildest dreams; yet, here he was seeing new and exciting places, and going to war for something that he didn't completely understand.

That afternoon, Charlie's regiment marched east through Winchester to rendezvous with other units of the 89th Division at an American rest camp called Winnall Down. This camp, situated near Winchester Cathedral, was surrounded with barbed wire entanglements and was nothing like Camp Funston. The makeshift accommodations were substandard, most troops slept on the ground, the grub was terrible and in short supply, and, for June, the weather was cold, particularly at night. As for Winnall Down being a rest camp, that term was a misnomer, for Charlie's outfit spent four busy days drilling and training.[244]

The 354th Infantry Regiment departed the Port of Southampton about dusk on June 25, 1918. Charlie would have boarded one of several long, slender speedboats used to cross the English Channel. The men were packed into cabins like sardines, making sleep impossible, and many of those whose stomachs did not betray them during the long trip across the Atlantic were now subjected to seasickness. Submarine chasers enveloped the ship, and when night fell, blinker signals sent messages between the vessels in rapid succession, warning of U-boats lurking nearby.[245]

Charles Dienst writes in *History of the 353rd Infantry Regiment* that several times over the course of the evening, speedboats invoked sharp turns, zigzagged, briefly turned back, and then turned again toward France. As the voyage progressed, bursts of flames from the sub-chasers could be seen at regular intervals, followed by the thunderous boom of naval guns. The sub-chasers were obviously targeting enemy U-boats, and they did a splendid job protecting the combat-bound troops. Finally, at about 3:00 a.m., on June 26, 1918, Charlie's regiment arrived in Le Havre, France, where they stayed for two days in a British rest camp on the outskirts of the city.[246]

Living conditions at the rest camp at Le Havre were similar to that in Winchester, as the compound was lined with barbed wire entanglements, and they slept on the bare ground. However, the men were not permitted to leave the premises and the amenities were appalling. For whatever it was worth, they did have an opportunity to write home. They could not include where they were, their organization, troop numbers and movements, the morale and physical condition of Americans or Allies, or details regarding supplies. "What was there that could be safely said!" exclaimed Charles Dienst.[247]

On the morning of June 28, a mess sergeant prepared a cold lunch to be carried and consumed by the soldiers as they resumed their trek to the front. By nightfall, Charlie's company marched to a blacked-out railroad yard to board an unlighted train. The black-out conditions were precautions taken "out of deference to the not infrequent German air raids," explains George English.[248]

The boxcars into which the enlisted men boarded were known as "hommes 40-chevaux 8," as they were designed to accommodate forty men or eight horses. In Charlie's group, thirty-six men with full equipment would have been crowded into the boxcar, leaving no room to sit or lie down comfortably.[249] Officers traveled in third-class French coaches.[250]

The trip, which should have taken about 12 hours, was prolonged until the evening of June 29, at which time the 354th Infantry Regiment arrived in Rimaucourt. A number of men, who likely included Charlie, found a barn filled with animals in which to bed down for the night. Many complained about the stench. Living in a barn at frequent intervals, however, would not have been an anomaly for Charlie, so it is likely that he simply claimed a piece of real estate and caught some shuteye.

The following morning, troops assigned to the 89th Division dispersed to various towns and villages where they resided over the next five weeks while undergoing training at the Fourth Training Area in Reynel, France. Reynel is situated in the Haute-Marne countryside, about 19 miles northeast of Chaumont and about the same distance southwest of Neufchâteau. Company L, 354th Infantry Regiment, to which Charlie was assigned, lodged in Busson, about 2.4 miles northeast of Reynel.[251]

Charlie would have slept in a hay loft or a barn, under the same roof with horses, cows, pigs and chickens.[252] The water in Busson was contaminated, so he would have had to chlorinate it before using it for drinking purposes. At night, Charlie would have been able to hear the explosive artillery fire that had become a way of life for the villagers, as Axis and Allied forces thrashed it out around Château-Thierry.[253]

Not one able-bodied French male could be found in the town, and women, having performed all chores over the past four years, appeared prematurely aged, bent and frail. Morale among the beleaguered villagers did not exist, as they had endured much through years of war. The Americans were seen by many as a glimmer of hope, but the Yanks would be hard-pressed to find any inhabitant within these villages who felt the United States could have any real impact on the war. In fact, the French, and, to a degree, the Brits, sensed that the war was lost.[254]

Those who underwent training in Reynel agreed that it was the most strenuous program to date. In Charlie's case, it must have been like going through infantry training all over again, except this time he would have spent a significant amount of time in practice trenches where daily war games provided the most realistic combat training short of actual combat. This included constructing and repairing entanglements, executing trench raids, and defending against counterattacks.[255]

Alongside of the schools of the line were the schools for specialists, and Charlie would have attended Automatic Rifle School during this time. His company was issued sixteen M1915 Chauchats, which proved to be more reliable than the M1918 he used while training at Camp Funston, but there were still problems. For one, the weapon used a lot of ammo in a very short period. Then there were the flimsy crescent-shaped magazines, which were made of very thin metal and easily damaged in a combat.

In trench warfare, the Chauchat's open magazines would quickly accumulate dirt and mud, thus clogging the system and preventing the ammunition from feeding into the chamber. Another magazine-related problem was that the first round would often fail to feed into the chamber. Gunners, such as Charlie, would have become accustomed to loading eighteen or nineteen rounds instead of the maximum twenty, as this would relax the tension on the magazine spring enough to feed properly.[256]

The Chauchat also tended to seize up due to overheating when more than 200 rounds were fired in rapid succession. In these instances, the barrel sleeve would remain in the retracted position for about ten minutes before the Chauchat cooled down and the weapon was functional again. Army manuals recommended firing short bursts to alleviate the problem, but in the heat of combat, that was not always feasible.[257]

There may have been instances in combat where Charlie cursed his Chauchat, but for the most part we can assume that he accepted it for what it was. He would have adjusted to the weapon's violent recoil, learned that the sights made the Chauchat shoot systematically too low and to the right, and he would have made on-the-spot adjustments, as needed.[258]

At Camp Funston, Charlie would have heard horrific tales of troops being mowed down by machine gun fire, and that was a real concern to all ground-pounders, as there appeared to be no defense against such a rapid-fire weapon. At Reynel, however, the training staff revealed lessons learned from the American 1st and 2nd Divisions at Château-Thierry and Soissons that was helpful to the soldiers in going forward. It had been standard practice up to that time for infantry troops to advance just a yard between men, which led to heavy casualties. Now, however, there was a new tactic.[259]

"More important even than target practice was the training given in the new method of platoon attack," explains English. "This instruction showed the platoon leader how to scatter out his platoon in two lines twenty or thirty yards apart, with the men six or seven yards from each other in each line. Troops were taught that the machine gun which held up their advance must be taken by flanking, and not by a frontal attack."[260]

There were two day-long reprieves during training at Reynel, the first being on the Fourth of July. Charlie's company celebrated America's independence with a field day that would have included races, baseball, and a large picnic for the edification of the French villagers. Similar activities occurred on July 14, to commemorate the fall of the Bastille in 1789.[261]

The 89th Division also adopted a unit insignia while training at Reynel, which consisted of the letter "W" enclosed in a circle. "The official explanation of its meaning made at the time is that it designates the 'Middle West' division, as the central letter can in one aspect be read as an M and in another as a W," English elucidated.[262]

The 89th Division soon came to be known as the "Rolling W," although in inner circles, and with many Midwestern newsmen, they were called the "Fighting Farmers."[263] Breaking down unit designations even further, subunits of the 89th colored the center of the patch. For example, the 177th Infantry Brigade was light blue; the 178th Infantry Brigade was navy blue; the 164th Field Artillery Brigade was red; etc.[264]

At the onset of hostilities in 1914, the Germans made appreciable advances against French forces on the Western Front. The French checked the German push near St. Mihiel and prevented a debouching movement on its flanks during the First Battle of the Marne (September 5-12, 1914). The Germans, however, captured the commune of St. Mihiel and seized the railway lines from Verdun to Commercy, and from Toul to Nancy.[265] St. Mihiel is situated in the Lorraine region, which maintains nearly half of France's border with Germany, and also borders Belgium and Luxembourg.

The numerical strength of the French Army was not sufficient to push the Germans out of St. Mihiel without weakening the French lines elsewhere, and the Germans did not have the resources to push further into French-held territory. Consequently, the French and German armies settled into a protracted stalemate in what was known as the St. Mihiel salient.[266]

In military terms, a salient is a battlefield extension that projects into enemy territory.[267] During World War I, salients were usually formed when a broad, frontal attack was made, and units in the center of the attacking force progressed farther than units on its flanks, forming somewhat of a triangular shape protruding into enemy territory. At the apex of the salient, the center forces would set up their defensive line.

The Woëvre Plain, which separates the Metz ridges from the line of heights along the Meuse River, formed the base of the triangular-shaped St. Mihiel salient. The boundaries of this salient stretched west to east, from the village of Fresnes-en-Woëvre to the township of Pont-à-Mousson, a

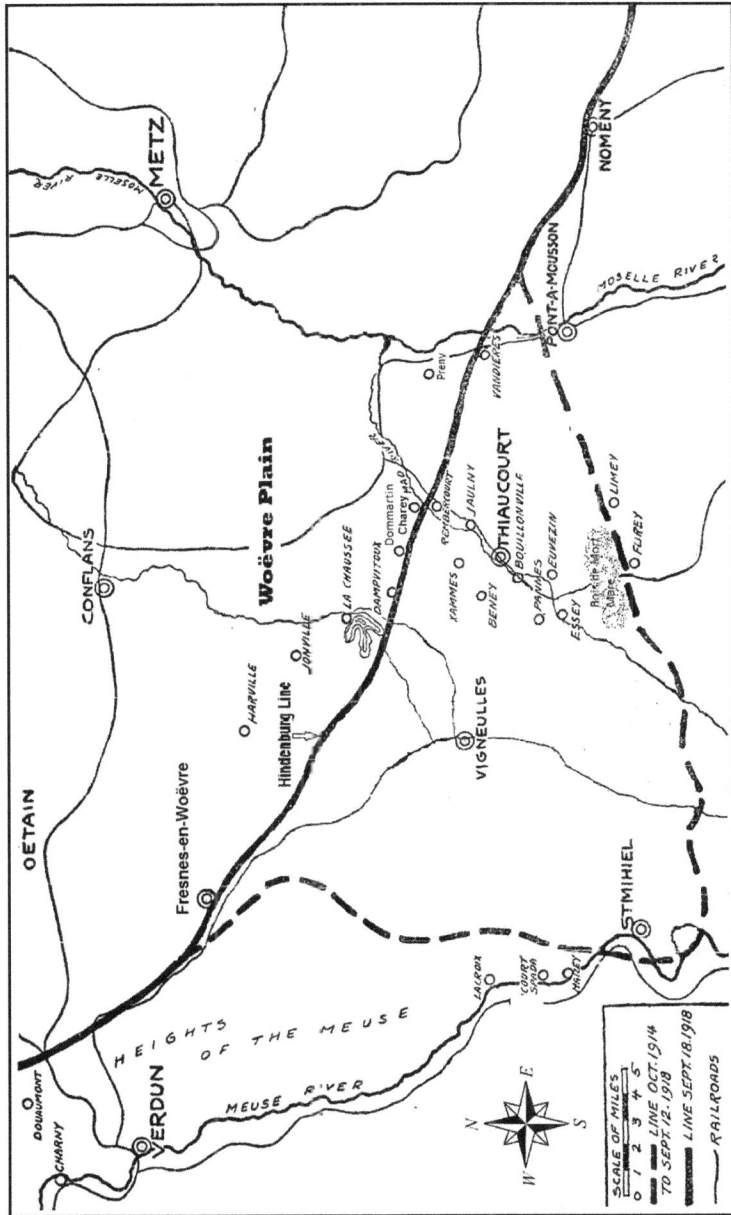

THE ST. MIHIEL SALIENT

Credit: Adapted from a map in *World's War Events, Volume III, by Francis J. Reynolds and Allen L. Churchill, New York, NY: P.F. Collier & Son Company, 1919, p. 257.*

distance of 26 miles. St. Mihiel, located at the apex of the salient, is situated 19 miles south of Fresnes-en-Woëvre and 25 miles west of Pont-à-Mousson.[268]

As training for the 89th Division was winding down in Reynel, the American 82nd Division and French 154th Division were pummeling it out with the Germans near Flirey, France. Flirey is situated 15 miles east of St. Mihiel, in a direct line between St. Mihiel and Pont-à-Mousson. After four years of stagnation in the St. Mihiel salient, Flirey was considered a relatively "stabilized and quiet" sector for the troops, a place where American divisions could gain experience in trench warfare preparatory to engaging in all-out combat.[269]

Once the 89th Division completed its training at Reynel, it would relieve the 82nd Division near Flirey. The 89th Division expected Flirey to be a manageable theatre in which to conduct military operations, one that would prepare them for more intense battles in the future. However, for Charlie and the others assigned to the 89th, Flirey would prove to be anything but stabilized and quiet.[270]

Fighting around Flirey had at one time been fierce, but it had calmed considerably by the time the 82nd Division assumed control of the sector in June 1918. In the weeks since, the 82nd dispatched nightly fighting patrols and occasional offensive raids into No Man's Land, just north of Flirey, with the express purpose of causing loss and damage to the enemy. This goal was accomplished by ambushing the enemy's patrols and working parties, or by raiding his frontline posts or trenches.[271] Using the intelligence garnered by each side in these nightly excursions, American and German forces would launch a general exchange of artillery fire each morning at daybreak.

One of the weapons most feared by Allied and Axis forces during World War I was chemical warfare. Contrary to the prevailing myth that the Germans were the first to use gas during the war, it was the French who attacked German forces with toxic gas in August 1914. This act was in clear violation of the 1899 Hague "Declaration Concerning Asphyxiating Gases," and the 1907 Hague "Convention on Land Warfare," both of which prohibited the use of "poison or poisoned weapons."[272]

After the French used toxic gas, the Germans saw no reason to refrain from using their own chemical weapons. Less than two months later, in October 1914, the Germans fired 3,000 shrapnel irritant shells on British and Indian forces near Neuve-Chapelle in Northern France. Subsequently, the use of chemical agents escalated, with the Brits, French and Germans producing deadlier gases and more effective delivery systems over the course of the war.[273]

In 1915, the Germans began using chlorine, the first lethal gas used up to that time. Initially, chlorine had the desired effect, but it emitted a yellowish-green vapor, which was easy to detect, and simply covering one's nose and mouth with a damp cloth neutralized the effects. By the end of the year, the Germans began using phosgene, the single-most chemical killing agent of the war. Postwar analysis indicates that phosgene accounted for 85 percent of the 100,000 deaths from chemical weapons, with another 1.3 million nonfatal casualties.[274]

Phosgene, like chlorine, had its drawbacks. It was detectable by its distinct "moldy hay" odor, giving troops time to don their gas masks; it was lightweight, and therefore dissipated rapidly; and it took at least 24 hours to manifest, which meant that troops could continue to fight well into the following day. The Germans overcame many of these issues by combining phosgene and chlorine, as the heavier chlorine supplied the necessary vapor to carry the denser phosgene.[275]

In May 1916, the Germans introduced diphosgene, an effective lung irritant and choking gas. As poisonous as phosgene, and sometimes considered more toxic, diphosgene was developed because the vapors could destroy the gas mask filters in use at the time. Diphosgene also lingered in the environment longer than phosgene. Eventually, the Germans released combinations of diphosgene, which compelled Allied troops to remove their masks, and phosgene, which resulted in a high casualty rate.[276]

By 1917, advances, such as gas masks and chemical warfare training, made phosgene and most other gases all but obsolete. That July, however, the Germans used mustard gas against Canadian troops near Ypres, Belgium. Mustard gas was the most widely reported and, perhaps, the most incapacitating gas of the First World War. It was distinguished by the serious blisters it caused within hours after exposure, both internally and externally. Once in the soil, it remained active for several days, weeks, or even months, depending on weather conditions.[277] By the time the Americans entered the fray in Europe, mustard gas was the prevalent chemical used.[278]

The Germans carried out gas attacks by gas waves or artillery shells. To initiate a gas wave, German soldiers would carry heavy pressurized cylinders containing liquefied gas across No Man's Land, and, with a favorable wind, they would release the gas into frontline trenches. Gas waves were more efficient than artillery shells, but they required special apparatus, trained personnel, and could be used only under favorable atmospheric conditions.[279] This was an ongoing problem for the Germans, as the prevailing winds on the Western Front blew from west to east, which meant that the Allies more frequently had favorable conditions for chemical warfare.[280]

The German gas attacks with artillery shells aimed to neutralize Allied units, and, if possible, to kill and wound their soldiers. The shells could be used for a variety of purposes, including counter-battery fire against artillery emplacements, shelling a wooded area in which Allied troops were located, or bombarding strong points. These gas shells might also target a village in the rear, or flank positions where the Allies could organize a counterattack.[281]

German artillery shells containing chemical agents were marked with colored crosses, not so much to designate the chemical contained therein, as the area of the body or organs affected. Generally speaking, White Cross shells contained chemical irritants, affecting the eyes and mucous membranes; Green Cross shells contained pulmonary agents, affecting the lungs; Blue Cross shells contained chemicals affecting the upper respiratory tract; and Yellow Cross shells contained chemicals affecting exposed surfaces of the body.[282]

Even though the United States never used chemical weapons of its own manufacture in World War I, America's entry into the war allowed the Allies to increase mustard gas production.[283] Prior to September 1917, the back and forth exchange of chemical weapons between the Allies and Axis powers was just about equal, but after that time the Allies mounted more gas attacks than did the Germans.[284] Germany could no longer afford to produce chemical weapons on such a large scale, so they relied heavily upon their chemical stockpiles and used them discerningly, but aggressively.

The first American division to travel to France was the 1st Division, commanded by Major General Robert Lee Bullard. In late January 1918, the 1st Division took over the Ansauville sector of the St. Mihiel Salient, which was situated midway between St. Mihiel and Pont-à-Mousson. On February 1, the Germans fired 25 phosgene or diphosgene shells just east of the American's 1st Division's sector, and the 1st Division's artillery brigade responded with 80 cyanogen chloride and phosgene shells. This was the first reported use of chemicals by and against troops of the American Expeditionary Forces.[285]

The popular belief is that the Germans used gas against the Americans, and the Americas were nothing more than helpless victims. Not true. The U.S. 1st Division had been given a daily allotment of cyanogen chloride and phosgene gas shells, and had begun to fire them fiercely at the Germans. In fact, between February 1 and April 4, 1918, the 1st Division's artillery brigade fired gas shells at the Germans on 39 of the 64 days that they occupied the Ansauville sector.[286]

Gas was used reciprocally by the Germans, French, Brits, Canadians and Americans on the Western Front for the remainder of the war. Had the war lasted another year, the United States intended to use Lewisite, a blister agent and lung irritant already being manufactured for wartime use in Ohio. The crux of the matter is that all major powers who were signatories of the 1899 Hague "Declaration Concerning Asphyxiating Gases" and/or the 1907 Hague "Convention on Land Warfare," were guilty of war crimes—and that included the United States.[287]

The American 82nd Division artillery brigade, near Flirey, was not allotted gas shells with which to fire upon the Germans, but they had attached to their unit the 1st Gas Regiment.* This regiment was equipped with Stokes mortars, which fired smoke, poison gas, and thermite (incendiary) rounds. On the night of June 18, 1918, soldiers assigned to this regiment launched a gas mission against the Germans, and followed up with a second gas attack on July 8. A third gas attack was projected to take place a week later, but the wind direction changed, and they had to hold off to prevent becoming subjected to their own chemical weapons.[288]

Finally, at 3:00 a.m., on August 3, 1918, the 1st Gas Regiment launched their third gas attack against the Germans, followed up by heavy French artillery fire thirty minutes later. The Germans suffered six dead and over 40 hospitalized. In a small-scale retaliatory strike that took place on the following day, enemy artillery fire killed 20 U.S. soldiers and wounded 45. That was just the beginning. The 89th Division would soon feel the brunt of the Germans' reprisal, enduring a gas attack on a scale seldom suffered by a U.S. division during the Great War.[289]

---

* The 1st Gas Regiment was formerly the 30th Engineer Regiment (Gas and Flame), but was re-designated on July 13, 1918.

Chapter Seven

THE TRENCH SYSTEM

After the United States declared war against Germany in April 1917, General Pershing commissioned a group of officers from his Operations staff to study the proper tactical organization for the U.S. Army. The result was a document that later came to be known as "The General Organization Project." Adopted in a joint conference with the War Department Committee, then in France, the advice laid out in this Project guided the American Expeditionary Force's organization throughout the war and outlined a million-man field army, comprising five corps of 30 divisions.[290]

In forwarding the General Organization Project to the War Department for approval, Pershing stated: "It is evident that a force of about 1,000,000 is the smallest unit which in modern war will be a complete, well-balanced, and independent fighting organization. However, it must be equally clear that the adoption of this size force as a basis of study should not be construed as representing the maximum force which should be sent to or which will be needed in France. It is taken as the force which may be expected to reach France in time for an offensive in 1918, and as a unit and basis of organization. Plans for the future should be based, especially in reference to the manufacture of artillery, aviation, and other material, on three times this force, i.e., at least 3,000,000 men."[291]

To maintain divisional effectiveness, the General Organization Project brought each division to a strength of 25,484 men, about twice the size of British, French and other Allied divisions. Increasing both the number and the size of rifle companies within the divisions accounted for more than three-quarters of this expansion.* The project added one company to each of the division's twelve rifle battalions and increased the

---

* Rifle companies, battalions, regiments, etc., simply refers to infantry troops armed with rifles. While all infantry units are typically armed with rifled weapons, the term is used to denote units that differentiate them from other infantry units.

size of the rifle company by fifty men, bringing the total rifle company strength to 256 men.[292]

The command structure and unit strength during the war was fluid. The 89th Division, for example, was commanded by one major general, and, when fully manned, consisted of 991 officers and 27,114 enlisted men. The division's two brigades, each under the command of a brigadier general, would have had a total strength of about 13,000 men. The division's four regiments—two assigned to each brigade—would each fall under the command of a full colonel.[293]

The regiment's three battalions, each commanded by a major or lieutenant colonel, had assigned to it four companies, each commanded by a captain. The reader may recall that there are four platoons assigned to a company, and to each platoon there would be one lieutenant, serving as platoon commander. To each platoon there would be assigned 57 enlisted men.[294]

Contrary to popular belief, trenches during the First World War were not just a couple of long, narrow ditches opposite each other where soldiers were ordered to go "over the top" towards the enemy, risking massive losses.* In fact, once defensive lines were established, a complex system of trenches were dug both laterally and in depth in order to hold their respective terrain. Soldiers settled into and occupied the trenches in these defensive lines for more than four years. A basic understanding detailing a frontline trench system will be helpful to the reader as we move forward with Charlie's story.

During the first months of the war, the Germans dug in first, so they seized most of the high ground. In typical German efficiency, their fortifications were superior, often with running water, electricity, toilets and concrete walkways. They were even known to have bunkers several stories deep.[295]

The Allies, on the other hand, who established their lines immediately opposite the German lines, had no running water, no electricity, no toilets and no concrete walkways. And, they were forced to inhabit trenches that were just a couple of feet above sea level. Consequently, their trenches were frequently filled with mud and water.[296]

The German's frontline position might be anywhere between 50 yards to a mile across No Man's Land—the deadly stretch of terrain between Allied and German trenches. To stymie an enemy advance, the Allies erected six-foot posts and set up a belt of barbed wire that spanned the entire front, from the North Sea to the Swiss border, a distance of some 475

---

* "Over the top" was a phrase that came into use during WWI and referenced troops climbing over the top of their trenches to attack the enemy across No Man's Land.

miles. The Germans, along their own front, had also erected a barbed wire belt to protect *their* lines.[297]

U.S. regimental headquarters would be established in a sizeable building in a nearby French village some distance behind No Man's Land. Fanned out between regimental headquarters and No Man's Land would be three basic lines of defense. The amount of terrain a regiment occupied varied significantly, but, keep in mind, it would have had to be large enough to accommodate more than 3,800 troops.[298]

Each line of defense would include a network of lateral, horizontal, and oblique trenches with very specific purposes. In order to maintain some perspective on the general layout of a regimental sector, the typical command structure, and the purpose of each line of defense, it is fitting to explain the sector configuration from the third line to the first, rather than vice versa.[299]

The third line of defense would be occupied by one of the regiment's three battalions, and was generally situated in close proximity to the French village occupied by regimental headquarters. The third line was commonly known as the Reserve Line, as it was used to give troops a break from the first two lines of defense. During this break, however, they were responsible with serving a back-up role in the event the front lines were being overrun.[300]

While the third line consisted of only one battalion, the first and second lines were occupied by two battalions. It was not set up, however, so that one of these two battalions occupied the first line and the other battalion occupied the second line; instead, the two battalions shared both the first and second lines, each half of the lines under the leadership of their own battalion's commander. Remember, the amount of terrain occupied by a regiment varied significantly, and so it goes with each line of defense. In the case of Flirey, for example, each of the three lines of defense were spread out about two-and-a-half miles apart.[301]

Furthermore, both battalions, sharing the first and second lines, would each have four companies under them. Two of the companies from each battalion would occupy the second line, and the other two companies from each battalion would be dispersed along the first line and beyond, into No Man's Land. Each battalion would have had over 500 men in the first line of defense, and there would be even more in the second line.[302]

The first line of defense, known as the Firing Line, was the most susceptible to enemy attack upon the regimental sector proper. If it appeared that the first line of defense was at risk of being overrun, the battalion's companies in the second line could respond to prevent that from happening. If, however, the first line *was* overrun, and seized or occupied

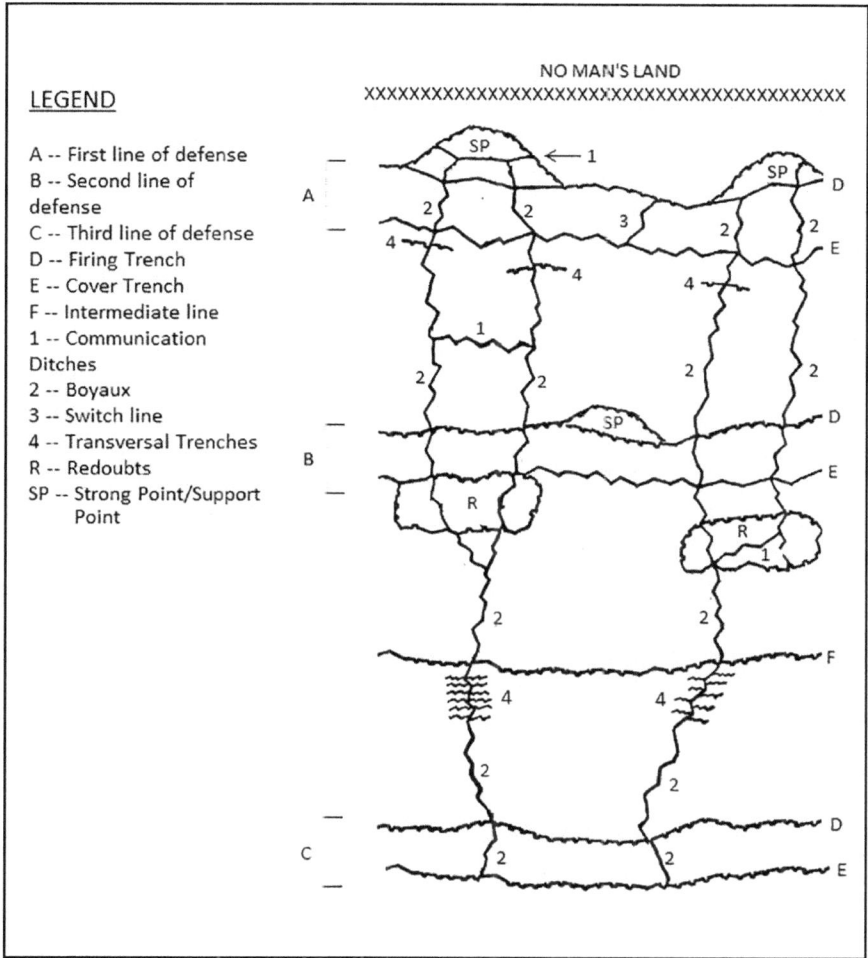

LEGEND

A -- First line of defense
B -- Second line of defense
C -- Third line of defense
D -- Firing Trench
E -- Cover Trench
F -- Intermediate line
1 -- Communication Ditches
2 -- Boyaux
3 -- Switch line
4 -- Transversal Trenches
R -- Redoubts
SP -- Strong Point/Support Point

TRENCH SYSTEM MODEL

Credit: Adapted from a diagram in Tactics and Duties for Trench Fighting *by Georges Bertrand and Oscar N. Solbert, G.P Putnam's Sons, NY, 1918.*

by the enemy, those American soldiers not captured or killed could retreat to the second line of defense and aid the second line in staging a possible counterattack to recover the first line.[303]

The second line of defense, known as the Support Line, was the regiment's main defensive line. This line would have the largest concentration of defending forces, which, in addition to the 500-plus troops from the two aforementioned companies, would include plenty of battalion support and reserve troops dispersed throughout. The fighting positions and enemy obstacles in the second line had to be as nearly impregnable as possible. This concept is called defense in depth.[304]

Although the enemy may find it easy to breach the U.S. forces' weaker-defended front line, as the enemy advanced to the second line, they would encounter stiffer resistance and the enemy's flanks would become vulnerable. If the advance were to stall, the attackers would risk being enveloped by the U.S. forces' strong second-line reinforcements. Regimental troops falling back would have the opportunity to exact a devastating toll on the advancing enemy, all the while avoiding the danger of being overrun or outflanked. Delaying the enemy advance mitigates the attacker's advantage of surprise, while giving regimental forces time to establish a defensive line and prepare for a counterattack.[305]

The regimental commander was in charge of all forces under his command in all three lines of defense, to include battalions, companies, platoons, and other miscellaneous units. Nothing precluded him from visiting troops in any of the three lines of defense in his sector at any time he desired. Moreover, he could issue orders directly to any of his subordinate commanders, individual officers, or enlisted men, but regimental commanders would generally adhere to the chain of command. That is to say, he would issue orders to his battalion commanders, who, in turn, would issue orders to their respective company commanders.

Battalion commanders would establish their headquarters in redoubts at varying distances behind the second line of defense. These redoubts were defensive strongholds, completely enclosed and organized for all-around defense. In plain English, they were independent fortifications within the regimental sector and, for that reason, they were considered the last line of serious resistance.[306]

Every post of command (P.C.), which would be referred to as a command post in modern-day lingo, was linked to the other commands by telephone wires, so that each commander could immediately communicate with his superiors and subordinates, or follow and direct every move under him. Therefore, it was essential that these commanders maintain close liaison with their respective headquarters. For this reason, battalion and company commanders, regardless of which line they were currently occupying, would seldom venture outside of their areas of responsibility, unless directed to do so by the regimental commander.[307]

Each company had its own headquarters. Company headquarters in the first line of defense had both an administrative and tactical function. Administrative functions included preparing daily duty schedules, assigning Officers of the Watch, completing and submitting daily reports, and providing written reports to the battalion commander. Tactical functions were to assist the company commander in handling his company in action, sending orders to platoons, receiving orders from and sending information to the battalion commander, and maintaining contact with neighboring units.[308]

Combat action could be initiated at any level of command, right down to the individual soldier, without coordination or approval from a commanding officer. The commanding officer of the area under attack would coordinate and direct a counterattack, as necessary, and relay to his commanding officer via telephone or runner, essential information that may have an immediate and significant effect on current operations. If warranted, reinforcements could be dispatched from the first-, second-, or third-line companies.[309]

Each of the three lines of defense would include a firing trench and a cover trench, both parallel with the front. Firing trenches were the forward-most trenches in any of the three lines of defense wherein troops were posted to defend that particular line. The firing trench in the first line of defense was continuously, though lightly manned, as it was the most susceptible to enemy attack. At night, one sentinel would be posted about every 10 yards along the first firing trench; during the day, only enough sentinels would be posted so that all parts of No Man's Land could be observed.[310]

Cover trenches would be situated about 30- to 40-feet behind a firing trench, and their main purpose was to shelter troops from observation and shell fire. Troops occupying cover trenches generally used them for communicating purposes, for lateral movements of troops, for liaison between neighboring units, and for shelter where men who were not posted in the firing trenches could rest. These cover trenches were not generally used for defense, but troops therein could respond if necessary to reinforce the firing trench, and to counterattack the firing trench if it were to fall into enemy hands.[311]

The regimental sector would include a series of strong points, boyaux and communication ditches, switch lines, and transversal trenches. Each of these features were vital for traveling from one trench to another, or for defending the regimental sector in the event of an attack.[312]

Strong points on a battlefield are strategic positions often situated on a high place, such as a hill. In the first line of defense, these strong points were referred to as support points, as they were not as well established, fortified or defended. Strong points in the second and third lines of defense were fewer and farther apart than in the first line, as they would not be as exposed to hostile attacks. Strong points in the second line would be connected by support trenches, forming a Center of Resistance.[313] Each Center of Resistance would include a defense force of troops, would be strongly protected with barbed wire and sandbag revetments, and would be well-supplied with ammunition, food, and water, to enable the soldiers to withstand heavy attacks.[314]

Because these strong points were sited at higher elevations, they were used to provide overhead covering fire for the trenches they defended during an attack. They also maintained a good amount of ammunition and other supplies to be sent to the firing trenches, when needed. It was a general rule that if the enemy were to overrun a firing trench, the soldiers occupying the strong points were to hold out until the last man was killed.[315]

Boyaux and communication ditches were a series of narrow and deep trenches dug in depth and laterally, respectively. Boyaux were essentially trenches used by troops to travel back and forth between the first line of defense and the third line of defense. Specifically, they were of vital importance to the various lines in enabling rapid movement of ammunition, supplies and reinforcements.[316]

The number of boyaux was not fixed, as was that of the other lines. There would typically be so many boyaux in each regimental sector that they were given names, complete with signs, posted similar to those for a city street. Communication ditches, which ran lateral to the firing trenches, were simply designed to travel from one boyaux to another.[317]

During an attack, all boyaux were used for movement of troops from rear to front. Though not typically used as a firing trench, they could be used to provide flanking fire if the necessity arose. Boyaux could also serve as a base for a counterattack if an adjoining boyaux were to fall into enemy hands.[318]

Lines oblique to the front, which connected firing lines and cover lines, were called switch lines, presumably adopting the name from their similarity to railroad switch lines. Switch lines were situated at strategic points where the enemy might overrun the sector, leaving the flanks exposed. The switch line, like the boyaux, would act as a firing trench in such instances.[319]

Transversal trenches were usually constructed between the first and second lines of defense, and between the second and third lines of defense. These transversal trenches stretched short distances parallel to the front. They were designated for special purposes, such as: for depots that stored equipment and supplies; for machine gun disposal; to serve as observation posts within sector lines; and for troop protection during artillery attacks.[320] In the first line of defense, transversal trenches also served as posts of command for company commanders in charge of support points.[321]

Between the second and third lines of defense there may be an intermediate trench line. Intermediate trench lines served as a base of departure for counterattacks, and could be used as a new first-line position, if needed. Behind the intermediate trench line, there would be a series of transversal trenches, leading off both sides of a central boyaux, wherein two waves of companies would be dispersed.[322]

Trenches were typically about seven-feet deep, about six-feet wide, and constructed in zigzag patterns to minimize casualties and structural damage if attacked by enemy forces or hit by artillery. The general idea was that the trenches were to be narrow and deep to prevent observation by the enemy, and to present a small target for high-angle enemy fire to the Allied soldiers occupying them.[323]

Inside all main trenches, wire mesh and wooden frames lined the walls to prevent them from collapsing. Sandbags were stacked above the trenches on both sides to absorb bullets and shrapnel, and to impede rainwater from flowing into the trench. Wooden planking, or duckboards, were also put in place to prevent men from standing in water. During heavy rains, however, the duckboards would often become submerged, and this led to a debilitating ailment known as "trench foot."[324]

Firing trenches would have fire steps, which were cut into the side of the trench wall facing the enemy. From these steps, the soldier could peer over the top and take aim at his target. In the cover trenches, there would be "funk holes" burrowed into the wall for sleeping or resting, but in these firing trenches, the troops would typically sleep on the fire steps.[325]

Extending into No Man's Land, there would be three types of advance posts (the Germans had a similar setup): listening, observation and combat posts. Advance posts would have provided excellent service to a regiment if not too numerous. If there were too many, the advance posts would be tempting targets for snipers, combat patrols or hostile raids.[326]

Listening posts extended into No Man's Land from appendages along the firing trench, and were furnished with microphones for the purpose of picking up the enemy's field telephone or radio messages. Observation posts would have been used to watch enemy movements, to warn of approaching soldiers, or to direct artillery fire. And combat posts would have been established along the barbed wire belt for use by machine gunners or automatic riflemen.[327]

This large area of activity was more or less useless if it could be seen by the enemy and subjected to heavy artillery fire, so camouflage would be extensively employed against both ground and aerial observation for the active trenches. However, the Allies also designed inactive trenches to draw fire from the enemy. These were called dummy trenches, which included dummy figures and weapons. Enemy airmen, out on reconnaissance patrols, believing they had discovered a viable Allied target, would signal their nearest artillery battery to unleash a storm of shells upon these unoccupied trenches. The ploy would typically go undetected until a great waste of valuable ammunition was expended.[328]

One more aspect of trench warfare, which has been mentioned several times but not expounded upon, was the control of artillery in the trenches. The division's field artillery brigade would fall under the command of a brigadier general; its three field artillery regiments would be under the command of an artillery colonel; and a captain would command the field artillery brigade's trench mortar battery.

Field artillery regiments would not be assigned to specific infantry regiments, but would work in cooperation with infantry regiment commanders to support the infantry regiment's position. Subunits assigned to these field artillery regiments would be divvied out where they were needed at the time, depending upon the importance of the ground or the tactical situation.[329]

Broadly speaking, artillery targets could be broken down into two categories: (1) targets of opportunity, and (2) planned targets. An example of a target of opportunity would be when a reconnaissance plane spots a target worth attacking. Planned targets might consist of a specified sector identified as a viable target, or scheduled as part of an offensive operation.

Artillery units would typically deploy roughly one-third of their maximum range, behind the frontline troops. Weaponry varied between divisions. In the case of the 89th Division, two of its three field artillery regiments were equipped with French-made 75mm guns, and the other field artillery regiment was issued 155mm Howitzers, known as Schneiders'. The 75mm guns had a maximum firing range of 7,500 yards, and the Howitzers had a maximum firing range of 12,400 yards. All artillery guns used by the Americans during the war could potentially engage any target within their range.[330]

Terrain would be a key factor when establishing an artillery position, as artillery units would need to avoid areas that were visible to the enemy. Moreover, reasonable proximity to roads and railroad tracks would have been a consideration due to the need for ammunition resupply. The 89th Division had assigned to it the 314th Ammunition Train to resupply its artillery units, which included four motor companies and one wagon company. Distributed among the motor companies were 22 ammunition trucks and 16 caissons with their full quota of horses. The wagon company drew 33 combat wagons and two-wheeled vehicles to which a caisson could be attached, plus 150 mules.[331]

Because artillery units were rarely in the line of sight of their targets, forward-positioned artillery observers would be posted in No Man's Land to identify specific enemy hotspots and to dispatch coordinate corrections, as necessary. Artillery units also answered barrages against hostile attacks, launched targeted surprise fire on enemy forces detected in No Man's Land, and, at night, inflicted harassing fire against supply parties and their routes.[332]

Trench mortar batteries operated separately from field artillery regiments, as they had a distinctly autonomous mission. The number of trench mortar personnel and weapons allotted to an infantry's regimental sector was ambiguous, depending upon the tactical situation or activity of the enemy. If a trench mortar detachment was assigned to an infantry regiment, they would be distributed at each of the regiment's centers of resistance and placed under operational command of the infantry battalion commander in that sector.[333]

The 89th Division's trench mortar battery was equipped with Stokes mortars, a British weapon issued to American trench mortar batteries during the war. The Stokes mortar was a smooth-bore, muzzle-loading weapon, designed for high angles of fire. Although called a three-inch mortar, its bore was actually 3.2 inches, or 88mm.[334] One potential problem with the Stokes mortar was the recoil, which was, according to the official Army Handbook, "exceptionally severe, because the barrel is only about 3 times the weight of the projectile, instead of about one hundred times the weight as in artillery. Unless the legs are properly set up they are liable to injury."[335]

Trench mortars had to be perfectly concealed and used with extreme caution, as they almost always drew concentrated enemy artillery fire. Nonetheless, they were remarkably efficient. They could be used to destroy enemy positions that the heavier artillery units could not reach, could be employed in preparation for an offensive against the enemy's first line of defense, or could be used for reply fire against enemy trench mortars.[336]

Such was the trench system in which Charlie would find himself up to the time of the St. Mihiel offensive. Fortunately for Charlie, who was assigned to the 3rd Battalion of the 354th Regiment, it was the 1st Battalion of the 354th Regiment that was assigned to relieve units of the 82nd Division in the front lines near Flirey. Had Charlie's battalion moved to the front first, he may have been just another obscure soldier forgotten by history, for what followed was nothing short of horrific!

Chapter Eight

FROM THE SHADOWS OF DEATH

"Relieve the Advance Battalion of the 82nd Division and hold that position to the death unless withdrawal is ordered by the Army Commander."[337] General Winn received these powerful orders from General Pershing's headquarters in Chaumont, just before the 89th Division began its relief of the 82nd in the Lucey Sector on August 4, 1918.*

As commander of the 89th Division, Winn disseminated General Pershing's orders "to hold that position to the death" to his battalion commanders, which included Major Nathan C. Shiverick. Shiverick was a West Point graduate (1908) and a veteran of the border war with Mexico. He had assumed command of the 1st Battalion, 354th Infantry Regiment, under Winn, on August 7, 1918. That same day, Shiverick had established his post of command in a ravine behind the second line of defense in the Bois de Hazelle, a little more than a half-mile southwest of the ruined and largely deserted village of Flirey. "Bois," in French, means "woods," and in nearly every instance, the wooded area is named for the closest town or village.[338]

Even before Shiverick moved into the line with his 1st Battalion, intelligence reports indicated that the Germans were preparing a large-scale retaliatory counterattack for the gas attack launched at the Germans by the U. S. 1st Gas Regiment on August 3. Senior U.S. military officers assigned to the 82nd Division were privy to these intelligence reports, but, unthinkably, no one saw fit to warn Winn or his staff in the 89th Division as the first four brigades moved into the line.[339]

German gas shells began to fall at 10:30 p.m. on August 7. For some unknown reason, there was a break in the shelling about midnight, but when it resumed about 1:00 a.m., on August 8, it continued relentlessly for two solid hours. The shelling fell principally in the vicinity of Shiverick's post of command in the Bois de Hazelle, although, to the west, the 1st

---

* The Lucey sector, like the Ansaville sector, encompassed the entire area occupied by a division. The sector took its name from the village where division headquarters were established.

Battalion, 355th Infantry Regiment, also took quite a beating. It is estimated that 9,000 to 10,000 artillery shells were fired over a four-hour period, about 95 percent of which contained mustard gas and phosgene interspersed with high explosives.[340]

At the onset, Shiverick's men donned their British-made Small Box Respirators (SBR). These British-made respirators replaced the French-made gas masks after American troops lost faith in them. The British SBR was, in fact, a better mask, yet it contained an uncomfortable mouthpiece and had constricting nose clips, which resulted in troop exhaustion after six or seven hours of continuous use.[341] Although everyone assigned to the 89th Division received the prescribed gas training, no one was instructed in the use of the SBR—a shortfall leveled directly upon those in command at the Fourth Training Area in Reynel.

And there were other problems, too.

In the late 1950's, Army historian Rexmond C. Cochrane wrote a series of studies on gas warfare in World War I. He contends that frontline troops had no real understanding of what they were up against. Some Blue Cross gases containing diphosgene were unquestionably included in the bombardment, as the cases of coughing and vomiting indicate, even though all the duds and shell fragments found later were Yellow Cross, which always contained the toxic, blistering mustard gas.[342]

A heavy mist kept the gaseous contaminants on the ground throughout the night and into the next day. The unsuspecting troops, believing that the danger had passed, removed their protective gear and began moving about, inadvertently disturbing the contaminants and suffering the effects! Gas officers and NCOs, who were assigned to the Lucey sector, were vital during gas attacks, for they could properly assess the situation, assist those unfamiliar with the SBR, and would have been able to recognize that the poisonous gas had not dissipated overnight. However, the Gas officers were unavailable to help; they were engaged in unrelated duties in the rear areas. Tragically, mismanagement of this situation by the higher-ups cheated these troops of the expertise of the Gas officers who would have prevented scores of casualties.[343]

Perhaps the greatest blunder, however, was the 89th's refusal to evacuate for fear of violating Pershing's order to "hold that position to the death." There were established procedures in place regarding gas attacks, including preventive measures and evacuation to fallback positions, but in this case, these procedures were not followed. Rexmond Cochrane reveals that the 89th Division received no instructions about moving out of a mustard-gassed area, or about alternative positions.[344]

When the gas threat had not subsided by the evening of August 8, General Winn assembled his staff and instructed his brigade commanders to evacuate their men from the contaminated areas posthaste. However,

Colonel John C.H. Lee, his Chief of Staff, warned against doing that. Inconceivably, Lee advised the general to keep his frontline forces in position, as the whole plan of defense depended upon it. He even argued that additional troops should be sent *into* the contaminated areas to prevent being overrun by the Germans! Lee reminded Winn that evacuating his forward troops without consulting the Army commander would open him to criticism and possible removal from command.[345]

That settled it; they weren't going anywhere.[346]

This blunder would fall squarely on Winn, for he was the division commander, but Lee was at least equally culpable. It would seem a matter of common sense that the Germans would never enter an area they knew to be contaminated by gas; Americans defending such an untenable area would seem pointless. However, American troops were still new to gas warfare as well as German strategy and tactics in 1918, and this unchartered territory may explain, albeit not excuse, Lee's absurd recommendation.

Perhaps historian Max Hastings said it best when he noted that "Lee was regarded even by his colleagues as vain, self-indulgent and undisciplined."[347] Lee was a West Point graduate (1909) and trained as a military engineer. Much like Dwight D. Eisenhower, he showed great administrative promise and quickly rose through the ranks. He had been General Wood's aide de camp before deploying overseas, and then became the youngest divisional chief of staff during World War I, which came with a promotion to full colonel. After the war, he would remain in the Army, and during World War II, he would rise to the rank of lieutenant general.

The conduct of the men who served under Winn and Lee " ... was an example of courage and steadfastness deserving the highest praise and the spirit of the troops was further indicated by the fact that they requested to remain in the line and finish their tour of duty when relief was proposed." This quote, which is derived from General Order No. 75, Headquarters, 89th Division, was justifiable in praising the courage and resolve of the officers and enlisted men, as they did perform heroically ... but at what cost?[348] A report drafted on August 18, 1918, placed the total number of casualties for the 89th Division during that first night in combat at 590, including 43 deaths. The majority of those casualties were from the 1st Battalion, 354th Infantry Regiment (214 wounded and 1 death), and the 1st Battalion, 355th Infantry Regiment (324 wounded and 39 deaths).[349]

"Their suffering seemed to be greater, judging from the groans to be heard all over the woods, than any other suffering from wounds witnessed by me later," recalled Major (Dr.) Reginald H. Meade, Chief Medical Officer for the 354th Infantry Regiment's Medical Corps. He had visited the field hospital to which the casualties of the 89th had been removed. All the cots were filled, and men were lying about on the ground.[350]

Mustard gas, Meade said, was the most effective of all enemy gases, as it could be absorbed through the skin, respiratory system, genital tract, and eyes, and it also affected various organs. Although not considered as fatal as some other types, it produced the greatest number of casualties. Meade, himself, would suffer a gas attack at St. Mihiel on September 26, which would force his early return to the United States, his subsequent discharge from the Army, and his untimely death in 1922, at the age of fifty.[351]

A couple of days earlier, on August 6, 1918, Company L, 354th Infantry Regiment, to which Charlie was assigned, boarded a train in Reynel, France, and then took a series of truck rides bound for Bruley, about 53 miles northeast of Reynel and 13 miles due south of Flirey.[352] Packed into the truck with some thirty-five others, complete with full combat gear at the peak of summer, the trip for Charlie and the others would have been miserable! It may have crossed many of the soldier's minds that the American Expeditionary Forces didn't know how to manage travel, even to the point of where a soldier might enjoy just a little elbow room. Was it that any degree of comfort, any break from training, any gesture of kindness, would somehow diminish their combat edge?

About midnight on August 7, 1918, Charlie and the rest of his company would have arrived in Bruley, where they would enjoy a fifteen-hour respite before resuming the 10-mile trip north to Minorville. John H. Bratt, a Health Economics Scientist from North Carolina, authored a biographical account about his grandfather, Martin Verhage, who served with Company I, 354th Infantry Regiment, during World War I. Many of Verhage's experiences paralleled Charlie's, since they were both in the 3rd Battalion of the 354th Infantry Regiment. Bratt provides some insight into the battalion's jaunt north to Minorville on the afternoon of August 8, 1918.

"At 4 PM," Bratt writes, "the entire 3rd Battalion (including Companies I, K, L and M) boarded a narrow-gauge train for the trip to the front lines. These little trains were used extensively by both German and Allied armies as a means to transport soldiers, equipment and supplies; engineer troops had developed extensive networks of tracks between front lines and rear supply areas.

"Fifty soldiers crowded onto each flatcar for the ten-mile ride, and during the trip they soon saw more evidence of the battles between French and German troops that had been fought over this land in 1914-1915: old abandoned trenches and barbed wire entanglements, dummy artillery pieces, desolate fields, destroyed buildings and groups of wooden crosses marking gravesites. And then, rounding a curve, the train suddenly brought the soldiers of the 3rd Battalion face to face with the results of the German gas attack of the previous night."[353]

Charlie would have witnessed absolute pandemonium as he looked from the train window. Medics, nurses, and countless others, were scurrying about to care for the soldiers that had been affected by gas. Many of the victims were lying on the ground with their eyes covered to protect them from the light, and many others were vomiting and begging for relief.[354] Among the victims was Major Shiverick, who was blinded for eleven days and eventually evacuated back to the United States. At the time of his death from an automobile accident in 1932, he was serving as a full colonel in the Army Reserve.[355]

Jess Funk, Charlie's assistant gunner, revealed after the war that he and Charlie were more eager than ever to do their part. "Now that we had been taken to where the fighting was," Jess stated, "we wanted to get into it."[356] Charlie and Jess, like most infantrymen witnessing such carnage for the first time, were faced with the sudden realization that combat was not at all what they envisioned. Rather than infantry fighting infantry, frontline soldiers had to contend with artillery fire, to which they couldn't retaliate, and mustard gas, the most horrific weapon imaginable! The horror of seeing their own men writhing in agony, spread across the field that day, likely drove Charlie and Jess to a strong desire for retaliation. Their opportunities for retaliation lay just ahead.

On the evening of August 12, 1918, the 354th Infantry Regiment—minus the depleted 1st Battalion—marched north to Noviant, and during the evening, the 2nd and 3rd Battalions assumed positions in the first and second lines of defense in the vicinity of Flirey. The first line of defense bordered the southern edge of a heavily wooded area known as the Bois de Mort Mare. The regiment's second line of defense was situated south of the main road, known today as D958, connecting the villages of Beaumont, Flirey and Limey. The third line of defense assumed a staggered route to the north of the villages of Grosrouvres and Noviant.[357]

For the first two nights in Noviant, regimental headquarters were attacked with artillery fire, albeit without damage until the evening of August 14. That night, enemy artillery rounds hit the adjacent building and the regimental staff suddenly grew suspicious. The Germans were obviously privy to where their facilities were situated, and even tapped into their lines of communication. The church pastor was the obvious culprit, but there was also a watchmaker, and probably a myriad of others, spying for the enemy.[358]

Second Lieutenant John F. McGrath, official historian for the 354th Infantry Regiment, who was assigned to Company C, describes the trench system inhabited by regimental forces during this time. "The trench system at Flirey was an irregular dilapidated system of ditches and holes which had stood since the early days of the war in 1914," he writes. "This having been a quiet sector for over three years, the opposing forces had surged back and forth over an area of about a kilometer in local attacks and raids. As a result, 'No Man's Land' consisted of a complicated network of old abandoned trenches, and there were enough deserted dugouts between the lines to house a battalion in their murky depths. Innumerable barriers of barbed wire were all that served to block many trenches running directly from the German line into our own, and there were several communicating boyaus [sic] with no barriers at all."[359]

Charlie was initially assigned to one of two combat groups in a platoon in the second line of defense. Combat groups defended support points, strong points and centers of resistance, along any one of the three lines of defense. These groups were equipped with rifles, Chauchat automatic rifles, rifle grenades, hand grenades, and, on rare occasions, machine guns. Riflemen and grenadiers assigned to a combat group provided close defense and ensured that there was no interference with the Chauchat gunner's flanking fire.[360]

It was determined by military tacticians that two Chauchats, properly supported, could, by its flanking fire, effectively defend 200 yards of line and repulse the most determined assault.[361] It would not be Charlie's job to defend his own combat group; he and his combat group were there to defend the combat groups to their left and right flanks. Those combat groups, in turn, would defend his combat group in the event of an attack. Charlie's Chauchat team would have occupied one of many well-camouflaged automatic weapon emplacements behind the firing trench so that his flanking fire would not interfere with the remainder of the combat group in the event that they had to repel an assault.[362]

John Bratt writes that the men assigned to the 3rd Battalion "spent their time digging trenches, fortifying the network of dugouts and shelters, stringing barbed wire and observing the daily dogfights overhead and the nightly artillery exchanges."[363] During the first week, days in the trenches were generally quiet, but false gas alarms could be heard almost every hour throughout the night. There was little shelter from the elements and the landscape around Flirey consisted of dead and obliterated trees, destroyed buildings, and pockmarked terrain from four long years of artillery attacks.

On August 19, 1918, 89th Division headquarters issued Field Order No. 6, directing its subordinate units to assume new positions of resistance less than two miles below the original line, where the gas attack took place. This move was decided upon after Pershing's headquarters conducted an investigation of the German gas attack on August 7. The original line was determined to be uninhabitable and the trenches therein were said to be "gas traps."[364]

A move was made preparatory to the St. Mihiel offensive, scheduled for September, to bring U.S. troops under complete American command and control. Since arriving in the Lucey Sector on August 4, the 89th Division was assigned under the French 32nd Army Corps, commanded by French Major General Fenelon F.G. Passaga. On August 20, however, command of the 89th Division passed to the American IX Army Corps.[365]

That same day, August 20, Charlie's company rotated to the first line of defense, situated in the woods north of Flirey. George English describes No Man's Land in front of the trenches of Flirey as one of "whiteness and desolation." In some of the ruins, the cellars had been strengthened with beams and girders, and several groups of men were always sheltered there. Beyond that was the powerful German defensive line—the Bois de Mort Mare. The Bois de Mort Mare, which lay wholly within the sector in front of the 89th Division's position, was the most formidable German defensive position on the entire southern line of the St. Mihiel salient.[366]

All that Charlie would have been able to see from his frontline position was a confusion of wire and gnarled trees.[367] Hardship, austerity and misery were conditions all too familiar to Charlie in his young life, but nothing he went through up to this point could have prepared him for the horrific, primitive existence in which he now found himself. Men were infected with head and body lice, and slugs, horned beetles and frogs were in abundance. Add to that the appalling stench from latrines, disinfectants, cigarette smoke, body odor, and remnants of poisonous gas from chemical attacks. But, worst of all, was the sight and smell of death—death from artillery barrages, death from sniper fire, death from disease. Neither side could emerge from the safety of their trenches to retrieve and bury their dead, so the putrid smell of rotting flesh was ever-present.

Almost every doughboy who served on the front lines during World War I would agree that rats—some the size of cats—were particularly reviled. They would eat the flesh of dead soldiers, spread disease, contaminate food, and were seemingly everywhere. Soldiers couldn't even sleep without rats crawling over them. One doughboy, Private William Langstaff, commented in a letter to his parents that trench rats "really bothered us more than the Fritzes did."[368]

Prior to sending out a patrol, battalion headquarters would coordinate with the artillery liaison officer to shell the enemy's barbed wire entanglements in the area to be penetrated; this move would help prevent friendly artillery fire where friendly patrols were lurking. Just a few hundred yards north of the first line of defense's firing trench, on the southern edge of the Bois de Mort Mare, were the German frontline trenches. During the night, the Americans and Germans routinely crossed into No Man's Land to attack advanced posts or support points, to reconnoiter enemy lines to determine if they had cut passages in his barbed wire belt preparatory to an attack, to examine their own barbed wire entanglements, to gain information about the enemy and his defenses, and, if possible, to take prisoners.[369]

It is well documented that Charlie often volunteered for fighting patrols. He first volunteered for a venture into No Man's Land in August 1918, during that initial eight-day excursion to the first line of defense. The patrols to which he was assigned would have been armed and equipped according to the mission to be accomplished. He would have been mandated to leave everything behind which might furnish information to the enemy if captured, such as regimental insignia and distinctive markings, letters, sketches, etc. In short, everything except his dog tag.[370]

It was particularly necessary for fighting patrols to get into position before the enemy's patrols got into their position; that is, as early as possible in the evening, at points between the lines where the enemy was known to pass.[371] These fighting patrols would provide flank protection to reconnaissance patrols by shutting off all avenues of approach from the enemy. Reconnaissance patrols would sneak into enemy lines looking for weak spots, strengths, and the natural layout of the land. Their findings would be reported back to regimental headquarters, and then sent up the chain of command where follow-up operations were considered.[372]

The greatest danger Charlie and his fighting patrol would face during this time would be strong enemy patrols.[373] One can only imagine what Charlie felt when he first engaged the enemy, but we know these were not optimal circumstances. From what we know of the conditions of these patrols, we can assume that Charlie was tired and hungry, and beads of perspiration probably trickled down his forehead. His visibility would have been limited, obstructed by the thick growth all around him. Dry twigs, when broken, would resonate through the woods like a firecracker.

Charlie and Jess' opportunity for retaliation on the enemy was upon them now. In an instant, gunfire would erupt, and Charlie's patrol would attack the Germans swiftly and violently with Chauchat and rifle fire. Hand grenades would add to the pandemonium.[374] The distinctive whiz of bullets would fill the air, and everyone would be trying to communicate all at once. Charlie's adrenaline would have been peaked, but he would have had to keep his mind clear and focused on his job.

The rounds in Charlie's Chauchat magazine would have been expended much faster than he remembered during training, and a five-minute firefight may have seemed like an hour. The engagement would be at once exhilarating and terrifying. After the battle, when the adrenaline wore off, Charlie would have felt more drained than ever before. Every soldier reacts differently to combat, but they adapt better with every subsequent engagement. Charlie, it seems, adapted to combat better than most.

If, instead of a group of enemy soldiers, Charlie's fighting patrol happened upon a single German soldier, they would attempt to capture him without weapons fire so as not to alert other enemy forces in the area. Prisoners would be escorted back to American lines, and any enemy soldiers killed during the engagement would be stripped of their uniform insignias and their papers.[375]

On the other hand, the fighting patrols to which Charlie was assigned were duty-bound to leave none of their soldiers with the enemy—neither prisoner, nor any wounded or dead. If one of their soldiers was in danger, every member of the fighting patrol was obligated to help him escape. If escape was impossible, the honor of the soldier demanded that he should refuse to make any statement to the enemy, whatever it may be, so as not to betray his comrades.[376]

Charlie learned that the enemy had cut, tunneled, wired and built until he had made the Bois de Mort Mare nearly impregnable. In its strong dugouts, large numbers of German soldiers could be held, ready to repel an attack. In the more established dugouts, further back, the Germans lived in comparative safety and moderate comfort, complete with running water, but many of the dugouts closer to the front were old, caved in, and lightly held by the enemy, or only visited by their patrols.[377]

Charlie recalled one instance where his own patrol happened upon a German patrol. A firefight ensued, forcing the enemy to retreat into a small dugout. With complete disregard for his own safety, Charlie darted forward and entered the dugout alone, emerging a few minutes later with two German officers and seven enlisted men.[378] It is regrettable that additional details are not available regarding these lesser acts of heroism, but Charlie was not one to brag.

During the time that Charlie spent in the front lines in August 1918, he earned a reputation for having extraordinary control of his nerves. It was also during this time that he killed his first enemy soldier. Charlie never revealed what he felt about killing his first enemy soldier, or all the soldiers he killed thereafter. Generally, the first instinct is self-preservation: kill or be killed.

Audie Murphy, the most-decorated combat soldier in World War II, whose pre-war hardships closely parallel Charlie's, recalled his first combat kills. Two Italian officers rode up on horseback, and when they noticed Audie, they turned and hurried away. Audie dropped to one knee and fired two shots, killing both men instantly. In his autobiography, *To Hell and Back,* Audie writes: "I feel no qualms; no pride; no remorse. There is only a weary indifference that will follow me throughout the war."[379]

Charlie seemingly shared Audie's viewpoint, and, like Audie, he learned early on how to suppress his emotions. At some point, Charlie had to reflect upon killing another human being, and, based on accounts of many other soldiers, Charlie probably, like them, rationalized that he was just doing his job. Given his later feats of heroism, one can only wonder whether his motive was more of concern for his fellow soldiers than for himself.

On August 27, 1918, Charlie was promoted to private first class. This would be the first and only promotion given to a remarkable soldier who demonstrated leadership in combat on a daily basis. Was this due to Colonel Conrad S. Babcock, who would assume command of the 354th Infantry Regiment in September, and who perceived Charlie as unintelligent? We will never know. Certainly, the evidence of Charlie's brave and accomplished acts merited further advancement.

The following day, August 28, Charlie's company retired to the Bois de Réhanne, a wooded area, about two-and-a-half miles southwest of Minorville. That night, he and his fellow soldiers were treated to an unexpected pyrotechnics display. The Bois de Réhanne was used by various units of the 89th Division for rest and refitting after strenuous periods of duty on the front lines.[380] "These woods were far enough behind the front lines to be reasonably safe, but still were within range of German artillery," writes John Bratt. "Approximately two miles south of the Bois de Réhanne was a small patch of woods that the Americans used as an ammunition dump."[381]

The ammunition dump contained vast quantities of pyrotechnics, rockets, flares, light bombs, and the like, which the French left behind in the trenches over the course of the war. They were deemed useless for combat, but were considered adequate for training purposes. Colonel James H. Reeves, temporary commander of the 177th Brigade, decided to have each man in the trenches fire off three pieces from this stockpile just after supper on August 30, and advised adjacent units to pay no attention to rocket signals from his sector. They didn't, but the Germans did.[382]

Concerned that this exhibition was preparatory to another offensive strike, German artillery batteries retaliated. They released a barrage in front of their own lines and No Man's Land. Suddenly, a series of long-distance artillery shells hit the ammunition dump and set off a firework display that everyone in the vicinity would remember. No casualties were inflicted, but it was spectacular! Charlie would have had a front row seat to the illuminated sky.[383]

Just after midnight on September 1, 1918, Charlie's battalion was ordered to Corniéville, a village about 11 miles southwest of Minorville. Not surprisingly, transport trucks failed to arrive, so the battalion was forced to embark on a four-hour hike with just one 15-minute break. When they arrived at Corniéville at 4:30 a.m., the men were exhausted and sought out the nearest barns in which to get some sleep.[384]

Upon awakening around noon, Charlie would have assembled in one of several long lines to receive that month's pay, which was doled out in French francs. Quite a few men frittered away their money on women and alcohol. Charlie would never acquire a taste for liquor; as for women, we don't know. Whatever Charlie did with his money, certainly, he, like the others, must have been glad to get paid, finally!

The 354th Regiment had by this time evolved into a cohesive, experienced, fighting unit that would distinguish themselves repeatedly before cessation of hostilities. On September 5, Charlie's battalion returned to Noviant, and the following day he resumed his station in the trenches near Flirey.[385] From that time until the St. Mihiel offensive commenced on September 12, the 177th Brigade, to which Charlie was assigned, was under continuous artillery fire, making it the longest American unit to remain engaged in continuous trench warfare without relief during World War I.[386] This experience could only go to their advantage in advancing their combat goals during their time on the front lines.

On September 6, Major General William M. Wright assumed command of the 89th Division, and General Winn assumed command of the 177th Brigade.[387] The following day, Colonel Conrad S. Babcock, who was commander pro tempore of the 353rd, replaced Colonel Americus Mitchell as commander of the 354th Infantry Regiment, in which Charlie served. Mitchell felt justifiably slighted, as he was given just two hours' notice that he was losing his command.[388]

Mitchell, a West Point graduate (1895), served during the Spanish-American War, Philippine Insurrection, and skirmish with Mexico, earning the reputation for being a fine administrative officer. In August 1917, when the 354th Infantry Regiment was formed, he was designated its first commander and rapidly earned the respect of his men, even though he could be a little quirky. At one point, he court-martialed a mule and sentenced it to five days' extra duty for kicking a slat out of its stall. Another time, he denied himself breakfast for oversleeping.[389] Here the reader can get a glimpse of what kind of commander Charlie was serving under when Mitchell was in charge of the 354th.

The 354th arranged a send-off dinner to honor Mitchell's devotion, efficiency and father-like qualities, but he begged off. Therefore, the dinner was made to welcome the incoming commander, Colonel Babcock, who could have cared less. No sooner had the banquet room been cleared than Babcock summoned his battalion commanders, regimental surgeon, and personnel (G-1), intelligence (G-2), operations (G-3) and logistics (G-4) officers, to lay out his plans for the 354th in the weeks ahead.[390]

Colonel Babcock, the son of Medal of Honor recipient John B. Babcock, came from the 353rd Infantry Regiment to the 354th with an interesting history. By April 1918, the Germans had pushed to within 40 miles of Paris, and the U.S. 1st Division was ordered to the outskirts of the small village of Cantigny to bolster the exhausted French 1st Army. At the time, Babcock was serving as commander of the 28th Infantry Regiment, 1st Division; Major General Charles P. Summerall commanded the 1st Division.

During the Battle of Soissons in July 1918, Summerall ordered Babcock to send his men in frontal attacks against enemy machine guns defending Cantigny. Babcock, an austere but efficient Regular Army officer, knew that complying with the general's order would result in the death of almost every man in the assault unit, so he audaciously refused to use that tactic. Instead, he used an alternate strategy to attack the town, and within 45 minutes, the 28th Infantry Regiment captured Cantigny, along with 250 German soldiers. The regiment was thereafter named the "Black Lions of Cantigny."[391]

Summerall was not impressed. For failing to carry out his orders, he relieved Babcock of his command, and now Babcock, coming in to command the 354th, was understandably disgruntled. Babcock relished his time as temporary commander of the 353rd Infantry Regiment, a unit in which he was extraordinarily proud, but he was not at all impressed with the 354th. Ironically, it wouldn't be until the last days of the war when he truly came to appreciate the regiment's heroic conduct.

To Babcock's credit, however, he brought with him a wealth of experience. Charlie might have expected to undergo more of the mundane close-order drills and parade ground work when not on the front lines, but instead, Babcock ordered his battalion commanders to conduct field maneuvers to better prepare them for battle. He even added compass navigation to the schedule.[392]

Under Babcock's personal tutelage, regimental units were also drilled in the new "diamond" attack formation.[393] "This consisted of each battalion being formed in two lines, two companies in each line, each company in two waves, distance between battalions being 1,000 meters," explains Charles Dienst. "Depth of each battalion was between 600 and 800 meters."[394]

The 89th Division held the front line until September 11, 1918, the eve of the St. Mihiel offensive. At that time, the 42nd Division relieved the 89th from the sector between Sèicheprey and Lucey, and the 2nd Division relieved the 89th's eastern line. In the late afternoon of September 11, 1918, under a heavy blanket of rain, Colonel Babcock ordered the beleaguered 1st Battalion, 354th Infantry Regiment, to proceed to Limey to serve as a reserve unit for the 177th Brigade. The rest of the regiment drew back to act as division reserve. The stage was now set for the first offensive action in which the 89th Division would participate in its entirety.[395]

Major General Leonard Wood
Credit: Bibliothèque Nationale de France

General John J. Pershing
Credit: National Archives

Major General William Wright
Credit: "The World's Work," September 1918.

Brigadier General Frank Winn
*Credit: Regimental History, 341st Field
Artillery, 89th Division*

Nathan C. Shiverick
*Credit: The Howitzer, U.S.
Military Academy, 1908*

Col. Conrad S. Babcock
Credit: Library of Congress

89th Division Gas Casualties
Credit: History of the 89th Division, U.S.A, George English, 1920

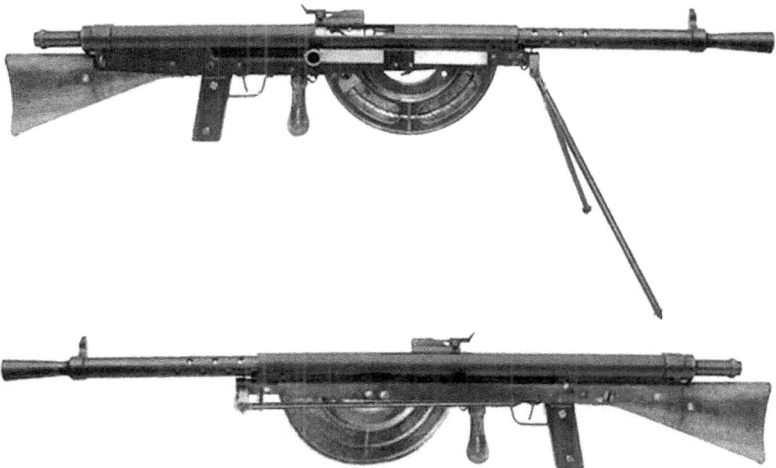

M1915 Chauchat
Credit: Vern Bryant,
www.germandaggers.com

Chapter Nine

THE SAINT MIHIEL SALIENT

Russia entered WWI in 1914, declaring war on Germany. By 1916, after some successes and some losses, the Russian government began to encounter civilian protests against the war. As a result, the Russian government, on their own and without the Allies being on board, attempted to get a peaceful settlement to the war, in 1917. This independent move on the part of the Russians would prove to be beneficial to the Germans.

On December 16, 1917, Russia signed a preliminary armistice with Germany, which allowed the Germans to transfer a number of divisions to the Western Front. In the spring of 1918, the Germans used their improved position on the Western Front with bolstered armies to launch the first of five massive offensives against Paris and the Channel Ports of France. These offensives pushed nearly 60 miles westward, marking the deepest advance by either side since 1914. In fact, the Germans came within shelling distance of Paris, and very nearly succeeded in forcing a breakthrough of French and British lines.[396]

To enable the Allies to better respond to each German Advance, on March 26, 1918, the Allies agreed to a unified command under French Marshal Ferdinand Foch, giving him coordinating authority over all Allied forces. American divisions also began to play an increasing role, achieving their first victory in the Battle of Cantigny in May 1918, and another at Château-Thierry that July. By then, the tide had turned against the Germans and placed them on the defensive.[397]

Recall that a salient (a battlefield extension that projects into enemy territory) had been formed within French borders back in 1914, by the German Army, who had penetrated France and established a front line. From that front line, a lead number of German troops pushed further into Allied territory than units on its flanks, forming a substantial triangular-shaped extension penetrating Allied territory. At the apex of one such penetration was the French city of St. Mihiel, and the German-held territory within that triangular-shaped extension became known as the St. Mihiel salient.

Now, four years later, during the early summer months of 1918, General Pershing, who headed up the American Expeditionary Forces (AEF), wanted to launch an American offensive to eliminate the St. Mihiel salient. Such an effort, requiring the Americans to drive the Germans back to the Hindenburg Line, would be large-scale. But, the destruction of German positions in the triangular-shaped salient, which extended out several miles from the Hindenburg Line, would give the Americans an advantage: they could fight the Germans along a more controllable straight line. By the end of August, Foch decided that he had viable reserve forces at his disposal and gave Pershing the go-ahead to launch his offensive during the month of September.

The Germans had three defensive zones, or positions, within the St. Mihiel salient. The first position was the front line, stretching several miles south, from Fresnes-en-Woëvre to St. Mihiel, and several miles east, from St. Mihiel to Pont-à-Mousson. This German position was well-organized, with a dense network of wire. It also had deep, well-constructed trenches, outpost positions, and numerous concrete dugouts and machine gun emplacements. The second position lay from two-and-a-half to five miles to the rear of the first position, and generally parallel to it. It was also well-protected by wire, but had few trenches. Across the base of the salient was the third defensive position, which formed a part of Germany's great defensive system, popularly called the Hindenburg Line.[398]

Although it had not been entirely completed, this third defensive position had a good system of wire entanglements and numerous concrete strong points. Pershing's original plan had called for overtaking the first two positions, penetrating the Hindenburg Line, and then seizing the heavily fortified city of Metz, the entrance to and exit from western Germany. On September 2, 1918, however, he decided that taking the German city of Metz would require such a massive operation that it would unduly deplete his forces. Therefore, he abandoned that part of the plan.[399]

Heading up this St. Mihiel operation, General Pershing would be in command of four Army Corps, with some French units immersed therein. The 89th Division, under which Charlie was serving, fell under the command of IV Corps, which included the U.S. 42nd and 1st Divisions, with the U.S. 3rd Division in reserve. Also at Pershing's disposal were various French artillery units, elements of the French Independent Air Force, and a compliment of British air squadrons.[400]

Pershing's plan, as finally approved, provided for penetration of the German's first and second positions. After those positions were overtaken by the Allies, the Allies would continue pushing forward toward the Hindenburg Line where Pershing would establish a defensive line. Once that objective was achieved, he would shift most of his divisions northwest, to positions between the Meuse River and Argonne Forest. If a breakthrough in the Meuse-Argonne region was successful, the Germans could feasibly have their forces in such disarray that it could bring about the end of the war.[401]

German reconnaissance by aircraft and balloons, and from nightly raids, left no doubt in their minds that the Americans were about to attack on a large scale. While a surprise attack would have been ideal for the Allies to perpetrate onto the enemy, the element of surprise was impossible. Remember, the Germans held the salient for four long years, and, due to the close proximity of the two enemies to each other, separated only by a No Man's Land, the Germans, from their high, advantageous positions, could observe the American buildup.[402]

The Germans may have held superior positions; however, they lacked sufficient manpower, firepower and effective leadership along the St. Mihiel salient to launch a counterattack against the Americans.[403] Therefore, German Lieutenant General Georg Fuchs, commander of Army Detachment C, decided upon a piecemeal withdrawal of German troops from the salient, leaving behind enough men to fool the Americans as to how strong the German force was.* But his main goal was to reposition Detachment C to the area behind the Hindenburg Line.[404]

Based upon intelligence reports, General Fuchs believed that the Allies would not launch the St. Mihiel offensive until September 15; so, he planned his measured withdrawal to begin on September 8. Even before the Americans began their offensive, Fuchs reasoned, he would begin to move his troops to defend the Hindenburg Line and, thereby, fortify the city of Metz. However, the Germans miscalculated the timing of the American offensive.[405]

The Americans, it turns out, had in fact scheduled commencement of the St. Mihiel offensive for September 12, 1918. This left the Germans completely off guard when the Americans attacked, and they would consequently suffer significant casualties.[406] Colonel Babcock, Charlie's regimental commander, would later recall that the fleeing enemy went so far as to abandon food (still warm), clothing, equipment, important documents, money, and even their high-bred horses.[407]

It may help the reader to reiterate where Charlie fit into the scheme of things as we progress. In ascending order, he was assigned to Company L, 3rd Battalion, 354th Infantry Regiment, 177th Brigade, 89th Division, IV Corps, First Army. The reader may also recall that Colonel Babcock was Charlie's regimental commander, General Winn his brigade commander, and General Wright his division commander.

---

* Detachment C were the troops occupying the St. Mihiel salient.

"In a battle there is no time to inquire into the identity or motives of persons who create panic, disorganization or surrender. It is the duty of every officer and soldier to kill on the spot any person who in a fight urges or advises anyone to surrender or to stop fighting. It makes no difference whether the person is a stranger or a friend, or whether he is an officer or a private."[408] This terse warning in General Order Number 5, dated September 5, 1918, was delivered to the Allied soldiers, who were anticipating an all-out frontal assault on the Germans, and assumed the Germans would be standing their ground, ready to fight back. Tensions were understandably high as D-day and H-hour approached—terms first coined for this operation. Higher headquarters understood this tension and, therefore, warned American troops against fleeing or displaying cowardly conduct.*

George English writes about the night of September 11-12. "All seemed confusion and disorder," he recalled. "There was no thrill for the coming conflict, no pomp and circumstance whatever as the tired troops plowed their way through the mud to their allotted positions or huddled in their trenches vainly trying to keep dry and to snatch a little rest." Conditions were, in fact, dismal, cold and rainy. The trenches were filled with water and mud, and the roads were slippery and congested with moving troops, guns and supply trains.[409]

Sometime after nightfall on September 11, 1918, and before the St. Mihiel offensive began at 1:00 a.m., on September 12, Charlie volunteered to join a raiding party, probably to get out of the trenches, which were filled knee-deep with water. Raiding parties were routine patrols involving small-scale operations, conducted almost nightly. Their mission was to inflict loss and damage upon the enemy by engaging the enemy's patrols and working parties, or by raiding his short trenches, listening posts, or frontline trenches. Prior to an offensive, the magnitude of the St. Mihiel offensive, these raiding parties would be used to soften German strong points.[410]

Raiding parties consisted of two separate groups. The first group, which executed the raid, was to accomplish any particular destruction they were assigned, and to capture prisoners. The second group was the flank group, which protected the first group by shutting off all avenues of approach from the enemy. Mission orders would be precise and relevant to the specific patrol in order to minimize losses. Order details included the hour of departure and return; and, each patrol would be briefed on supply routes, road junctions, etc. Word, of course, would be disseminated along the line to the Allied soldiers in the trenches, alerting them that a patrol

---

* D-day is the day on which an important operation is to begin; H-hour is the time of day at which an attack, landing, or other military operation is scheduled to begin.

was out in front, along with other necessary information about the patrol to avert friendly fire.[411]

The target of Charlie's raiding party was an enemy strong point in the Bois de Mort Mare. His patrol had to penetrate this enemy strong point, get behind it, and ultimately take out its machine gun nests. Hand grenadiers, supported by a Chauchat gunner, were used to carry out concentrated surprise fire. Except for one small, but gut-wrenching glitch, the mission was a success. Immediately after the raid, the raiding party returned to their own lines where riflemen stood ready to receive them.

Upon reaching the safety of the firing trench, the lieutenant in command of the raiding party suddenly realized that one man was missing. Distressed, the lieutenant assembled his men around him and called for a volunteer to locate and rescue the missing man. It is likely that the lieutenant did not expect a volunteer to step forward, because of the high risks of this mission.

At this point, the Germans were still guarding their posts. The corridor through No Man's Land, across which the volunteer soldier would have to pass, was not only flanked by enemy snipers; directly ahead were a series of German machine gun nests. Any indication to a German soldier that an Allied soldier had penetrated their lines would call for a sweeping rain of bullets on the volunteer rescuer's position.[412]

Compounding the danger of such an undertaking was the fact that the enemy was on high alert. The Germans were not only alert to any small raids such as this, but also alert to the massive activity preparing for the offensive all along the front lines. It was not a matter of *if* the volunteer soldier would encounter enemy machine gun, mortar and sniper fire, it was a matter of *when* he would encounter it … and if he could survive it.

And, of course, the Americans were also on high alert. The night before, on September 10, Chester A. Beggs of Company F became a casualty of friendly fire. Beggs had taken part in a patrol mission wherein German artillery fire was encountered. He was struck twice by fragments of shrapnel, one piece tearing away part of his left shoulder, and another carrying away two fingers of his left hand. Beggs was ordered to return to the American trenches to have his wounds treated by a surgeon.[413]

As Beggs approached the American trenches, he was "challenged" by an Allied sentry, a soldier whose duty it was to stand guard against enemies trying to infiltrate the American camp. A "challenge" is a method for the sentry to determine if an approaching entity is friendly or hostile. It usually involves a test question and a password answer to which a friendly force would know the correct response. The noise of the bombardment, however, was so great that, tragically, Beggs did not hear the challenge, or the sentry did not hear the response. The sentry, who could not see Beggs in the darkness, must have thought he was a German, and fired into the darkness, killing Beggs instantly.[414]

So, the lieutenant, when asking for a volunteer that night to go back into the raiding area to rescue the missing soldier, knew of the danger involved, and was fully aware that he was asking for a volunteer to risk his life. In fact, all soldiers were aware of the danger of such a mission for which the lieutenant was seeking someone to step up. As the lieutenant stood there waiting for a response, only one of his soldiers courageously stepped up to accept the mission. That soldier was Charlie Barger.

Charlie's weapon of choice for this mission was a sawed-off shotgun; such guns were then filtering into the division's inventory. The sawed-off shotgun, in combat, had a daunting psychological effect upon the enemy.[415] The German government, in fact, declared that any Allied troops found in possession of a shotgun would face immediate execution.[416] These shotguns, or "trench guns" as they were called, were pump action, where the finger-grip could be pumped back and forth to fire a shell, with a new shell descending into the chamber; they had short barrels, and had a magazine capacity of six rounds that fired 00 buckshot.[417]

Most troops assigned to the 89th Division were farmers, like Charlie, so they were quite comfortable with shotguns. They liked that this weapon had no trigger disconnector, so that shells could be fired in rapid succession simply by working the slide if the trigger was held down. Also, when fighting within a trench, the shotgun's shorter size made it possible to turn rapidly and fire in both directions along the trench axis.[418]

As Charlie embarked upon his rescue, he would have slipped into the darkness, and would have stealthily blended in with the terrain as he slowly wormed his way forward. The enemy would have heard an occasional twig snap or brush rustling in the distance, and would have responded with a couple of trench mortars or several bursts of machine gun or rifle fire. Charlie would have to stop, wait for the activity to subside, and then resume his zigzag trek forward. Subsequent bursts would have had him repeating this cautious approach a number of times.

When close enough to the enemy's machine gun nests, Charlie would have crawled along on the ground, creeping from position to position until he discovered the emplacement in which the captured soldier was being held. In that particular machine gun nest, it has been reported, five German soldiers were posted, and it wasn't long before they noticed Charlie. Charlie recalled that the machine gunner fired upon his position, but failed to hit him.

Charlie may have crawled outside the machine gunner's field of fire, or maybe he was just lucky; he stormed the position under heavy fire without being hit. In the process, he fired several rounds from his shotgun, wounding three German soldiers and compelling the other two to surrender. Shortly after midnight, on September 12, Charlie was back behind his own lines with the missing American soldier, five German prisoners, and two enemy machine guns.

Colonel Babcock should have submitted Charlie for a decoration for this heroic act, but he didn't. He had made it clear when he assumed command that in his mind there was nothing a soldier could do that would be considered above and beyond ordinary duty. The paltry number of decorations he submitted on behalf of his officers and men prior to November 1, 1918, solidifies that mindset.

Of the three Medals of Honor Babcock recommended that were ultimately approved, two were earned on October 31, and one the following day; of the forty Distinguished Service Crosses approved, only six were submitted for action before November 1. Fortunately, Charlie's heroic feat was mentioned in a dispatch from Colonel Babcock's headquarters to division headquarters, and soon after the Armistice was signed, Marshal Foch presented Charlie with his first Croix de Guerre (Cross of War) with Palm.*

General Winn, commanding the 177th Infantry Brigade of the 89th Division, to which the 353rd and 354th Infantry Regiments were subcomponents, selected the 353rd to spearhead the attack when the St. Mihiel offensive commenced. The 1st Battalion of the 354th, which suffered such tremendous losses during the gas attack on August 7, had since been replenished and was selected to serve as brigade reserve. The 2nd and 3rd Battalions of the 354th, the latter battalion to which Charlie was assigned, would be held in division reserve and would remain entrenched around Flirey until later in the day.[419]

At 12:55 on the morning of September 12, 1918, a single artillery shell whined across the sky and into the German lines. Five minutes later, the hills and valleys burst into cascades of flame. The Allied offensive of the St. Mihiel salient had begun. According to John McGrath, historian for the 354th Infantry Regiment, men assigned to the 354th Infantry Regiment, 89th Division, watched the artillery barrage for a short time, and then slept until a little before 5:00 a.m.[420]

"After four hours' artillery preparation the seven American divisions in the front line advanced at 5 A.M. on September 12th, assisted by a limited number of tanks, manned partly by Americans and partly by the French," General Pershing writes. "These divisions, accompanied by groups of wire cutters and others armed with Bangalore torpedoes, went through the

---

*   The Croix de Guerre, or War Cross, may either be awarded as an individual or unit award to those soldiers who distinguish themselves by acts of heroism involving combat with the enemy.

successive bands of barbed wire that protected the enemy front line and support trenches in irresistible waves on schedule time, breaking down all defense of an enemy demoralized by the great volume of our artillery fire and our sudden appearance out of the fog."[421]

The 353rd Infantry Regiment, 89th Division, advanced that morning, closely following an artillery barrage as it penetrated the German frontline positions in its sector. At 10:30 a.m., the 3rd Battalion of the 354th Infantry Regiment, which included Charlie, was ordered to provide additional support to the 353rd. The 353rd was then making rapid headway against the disorganized Germans, far exceeding the schedule set by General Wright and General Winn.[422] By 1:00 p.m., in fact, Winn's 177th Brigade, which included the 353rd and 354th Infantry Regiments, was three miles beyond where they were supposed to be in the execution of the Allied military plan.[423]

There were many acts of valor performed by men of the 89th Division that day, but one feat as told by George English, is particularly worthy of mention. Second Lieutenant John Hunter Wickersham of Company H, 353rd Infantry Regiment, was advancing with his platoon when he was severely wounded in four places by the bursting of a high explosive shell. Before receiving any aid for himself, he dressed the wounds of his orderly, who was wounded at the same time.[424]

Although weakened by loss of blood, Lieutenant Wickersham led his platoon forward. His right hand and arm being disabled by wounds, he continued to fire his revolver with his left hand until exhausted by loss of blood. When he became unconscious, he was endeavoring to tie his pistol halyard around his right arm as a ligature to stop the bleeding. He fell and died from his wounds before aid could be administered, and was posthumously awarded the Medal of Honor.[425]

All frontline troops assigned to the 89th Division achieved their first objectives. For the division's 353rd and 354th Infantry Regiments, this first objective was to reach the heights south of Bouillonville. The 353rd was the first to arrive, and its regimental commander ordered his patrols to push vigorously to capture the village.[426] Lieutenant Colonel Fred W. Boschen, with a few men, entered Bouillonville and returned with several hundred prisoners, mostly sanitary troops who had been cut off by Allied artillery fire and were waiting to surrender to *someone.*[427]

The greatest prisoner roundup of the day, however, belonged to Sergeant Harry J. Adams of Company K, 353rd Infantry Regiment, who would earn the Distinguished Service Cross for his actions and become a legendary figure in 89th Division history. Adams saw a German soldier in Bouillonville run into a house. He followed in time to see the soldier disappear into an opening in the hillside behind the house, and learned afterwards that this opening led to a large dugout. With just two shots left in his pistol, he fired in the door to the dugout and called for the occupants to surrender.[428]

"Soon they began to pour out," writes George English, "more and more and more, until the astonished sergeant found himself the sole custodian of approximately three hundred prisoners, including seven officers, one of whom was a [German] Lieutenant Colonel. Coolly assembling them under the menace of his empty pistol, he convoyed them safely to the rear...."[429]

By mid-afternoon on September 12, the 354th Infantry Regiment, which had been trailing behind the 353rd, and to which Charlie was assigned, had also reached the heights south of Bouillonville and began to set up camp. The original plan had called for the regiment to bivouac there, but, due to the Germans' rapid retreat, plans had changed. Now the 89th Division was to push the enemy back to the Hindenburg Line; an objective which Pershing's other divisions had already achieved in their assigned sectors.[430]

When General Wright, commander of the 89th Division, discovered that his regiments had stopped in Bouillonville under the division's original orders, he ordered them to immediately resume their advance. Following the new orders, the regiment advanced, but they didn't get much further by nightfall. John McGrath describes the two-and-a-half-mile march from Bouillonville to Beney, the regiment's destination, as a "slow dogged walk that always characterized the advance of the Americans. Fingers were numb, faces dirty and unshaven, stomachs pinched, but the enemy were ahead, some-where the other side of that high ground...."[431] The 354th Infantry Regiment rendezvoused in its entirety on the night of September 12, 1918, near a demolished railroad bridge in Bouillonville, where they bivouacked that evening.[432]

"Not a hostile shot was thrown against us the night through," recalled McGrath. "The enemy was too busy collecting his wits and burning the towns he had to abandon. For miles along, the high ridge to the left of us, flames threw themselves against the sky, —eloquent proof of the panic into which we had thrown our foe."[433] At the first hint of dawn, on the morning of Friday, September 13, 1918, the 354th Infantry Regiment resumed its advance along the roads and across the open fields.

The war to destroy German positions in the salient had obliterated the terrain between Bouillonville and Beney; this left Colonel Babcock's men generally exposed to artillery fire. Consequently, a lone, low-flying German reconnaissance aircraft located Babcock's regiment, and shortly thereafter, German artillery fire commenced. Although the 354th Infantry Regiment incurred some casualties during the artillery attack, as they were exposed on the open slopes, Company L, to which Charlie was assigned, did not suffer any losses during that time.[434]

"Fortunately," writes English, "the weather, which seemed to have been ordered to suit the American forces, again changed, so clouds and gusts of rain hindered somewhat the enemy's observation and concealed the [89th Division's] movements."[435]

The village of Beney was located five miles south of the Hindenburg Line. After the 354th Infantry Regiment reached Beney, Charlie and the others assigned to the 3rd Battalion continued to the Bois de Beney, a wooded area a mile or more north of the village.* There, Company L, which included Charlie, was ordered to dig foxholes and string barbed wire. Charlie had been in the line long enough to know that they weren't going anywhere anytime soon, and he was right.

Beney is the village where Colonel Babcock decided to establish 354th Regiment headquarters. Before personally entering this village, he sent an advance detail to select a good location for his headquarters, and ordered that telephone lines be established with 177th Brigade headquarters and his three subordinate battalions. Babcock also directed the detail to put into service a regimental observation post, which they did, positioning it upon the rooftop of a German bowling alley.[436]

When Babcock arrived in Beney, he surveyed the forward lines from this regimental observation post. About a mile-and-a-half to the northeast was the German-occupied village of Xammes, which was two-and-a-half miles south of the Hindenburg Line. Babcock decided that the bowling alley location for the observation point would be too exposed to enemy artillery fire and would put his observers at undue risk. So, he ordered the observation post to be moved to the attic of a nearby stone house. This stone house had a hole in its upper walls, apparently from an artillery shell, which was ideally situated for an observing aperture.[437]

"That night," writes McGrath, "a shell tore a passage through [the] bowling alley large enough for the passage of a tank. The colonel's advice [to relocate the observation post] had been most wise."[438]

Charlie's battalion was not prepared for the challenges that would test their survival over the next couple of days. "When we jumped off toward Beney," recalled Jess Funk (Charlie's buddy), "we had to throw away all our equipment and dug in with our bare hands."[439]

"This was a most trying period," added English. "In the first place, all the men were tired after the long stay in the trenches and the rapid advance in the battle. Supplies of all kinds were slow in getting up and there was many an empty stomach. The labor was arduous and had to be done at

---

* West of Beney was another patch of woods, also called the Bois de Beney, but the two woods were detached by a series of farms.

night, and all night, while in the daytime little genuine rest could be had by men lying in cramped positions in their little fox-holes, subjected all day long to galling and well-regulated artillery fire."[440]

Jess recalled that Charlie sat in stoic silence as their fellow soldiers complained about the lack of food, shelter and the most basic creature comforts. Charlie had experienced much deprivation from the time he was a young teenager, when Sidney and Phoebe Barger passed away, to the age of 23, when he joined the Army. During those coming-of-age years, Charlie was on his own for meeting all his needs; he suffered days without food, and even longer periods without adequate shelter. He knew from his experiences that if he didn't work, he didn't eat, period. He was never afforded the luxury of complaining about it. One can only imagine how strange it must have seemed to him to hear the guys around him complaining. Charlie's Army buddies, including Jess, who had always had family or friends to turn to in difficult times, probably found, in turn, Charlie's silence to be disconcerting and difficult to understand.

Once the 89th Division was in its designated sector, its mission was to establish defenses and proactively reconnoiter the enemy's defenses to determine their strength along the Hindenburg Line.[441] On the evening of September 13, Charlie would have heard enemy artillery fire in the background, and the occasional rattle of German small arms fire.

"After toiling upward from the dark valleys," writes George English, "a scene of rare and terrible beauty greeted the soldier on the heights. For, far to the southwest, in the angle of the old St. Mihiel salient, now no more a salient, blazed hundreds of fires. They were from military stores and supplies, barracks and even villages which the defeated enemy had sought to destroy to prevent their falling into the hands of the victors."[442]

By dawn on September 14, Charlie, and every other man assigned to Company L, inhabited a small, muddy foxhole, below ground level, which provided some degree of shelter from the elements. However, just as they were getting settled, orders came down that they had to change their position—a few yards forward one night, and a few yards back the night after. "...these changes were needed to adjust the American positions to the German Hindenburg Line less than a mile north, and also to accommodate the departure of several divisions which were withdrawn and sent to the Meuse-Argonne area," explains John Bratt.[443]

To the frontline doughboys it didn't matter; they were convinced that higher headquarters were set on making their lives miserable, and that gave them yet another reason to gripe.

In an unusual wartime occurrence, both the 177th and 178th Brigades of the 89th Division decided to establish their headquarters in the same village—the village of Beney. With the division's two brigade headquarters now in Beney, Colonel Babcock was induced to relocate his 354th Infantry regimental headquarters to a little house on the south edge of the village. Although it wasn't much of a regimental headquarters, there existed a nearby cellar that was lined with sandbags, giving those assigned there a sense of security during artillery attacks.[444]

By noon on September 14, hunger was a real issue, and it didn't help that constant complaining kept rations at the forefront of everyone's mind. In fact, throughout the war, armies on both sides were stymied by logistical difficulties; in this instance artillery and food supplies were left behind on the muddy roads. Relief finally arrived later that afternoon when the Red Cross and Salvation Army braved enemy fire to provide to the troops food, shaves, and other amenities.[445] What in the civilian sector might be considered small gestures of kindness, soon forgotten, to the typical doughboy, such benevolence was indeed a magnificent gift.

"Then they couldn't get rations up to us," Jess disclosed to his father, "and at last the Salvation Army sent us word that there was hot chocolate and cookies for us, and cigarettes. Well, Dad, when they handed me that stuff, it just got to me, and I just broke down and cried. Honest, I did, and I'm not ashamed of it."[446]

That civilians would risk their lives to help those in need, just out of the kindness of their hearts, overwhelmed many otherwise hardened combatants. Charlie, who was likely as grateful as Jess and the others, probably couldn't understand why organizations such as the Knights of Columbus, Red Cross and Salvation Army took such risks. No one he met had ever been so generous and selfless without expecting something in return. It must have been heartwarming to see a glimmer of humanity amid all this death and destruction.

Unfortunately, it didn't last long.

"Although Beney was not within six or seven miles of the enemy light artillery," Colonel Babcock would later write, "the little village received a daily pounding, and fragments from the shells bursting on the hard street or stone walls wounded or killed many men, some of whom had no business in the village. A woman of the Red Cross came into the village and set up a hot chocolate stand. Of course that brought in a crowd of soldiers, and an enemy shell got several of them belonging to the 355th Infantry (on our left) before this kind but perilous enterprise was stopped."[447]

Death was ubiquitous. German corpses, during the St. Mihiel offensive, could be found thickly strewn on the hillsides and roads, over which the German Army had attempted to flee. There were also many loaded wagons with horses lying dead in their harnesses, twisted into grotesque shapes by the fearful artillery explosions. It was almost impossible for night patrols to avoid treading upon these ghastly obstacles, and no one who witnessed these battlefield horrors would ever forget them.[448]

Seeing one of their own wounded was a particularly sobering reminder to everyone in the outfit that life was precarious; that they were at war, living every moment on the edge of life and death. On September 15, 1918, Private Louis Raymond Strayhorn, a 24-year-old native of Benton, Missouri, was severely wounded, becoming Company L's first battle casualty. He remained in a field hospital until early December, and was awarded 60 percent disability upon being discharged on February 14, 1919. (He went on to marry Edyth E. Williams that September, but the marriage produced no children. Strayhorn reached his 81st year before he passed away in Missouri on April 16, 1975.)

Although artillery support had failed to arrive until six days after commencement of the St. Mihiel offensive, food was filtering in much sooner. John McGrath recalled, "The food situation improved daily, the rolling kitchens were less than 300 yards behind the foremost lines, so close that they were constantly harassed by machine gun and one pounder fire. It was a hobby of the Commanding Officer [Babcock] to see that the men got hot food, and not only our own men, but any who happened past. A hungry Doughboy was just as hungry if he belonged to one regiment as to another."[449]

The St. Mihiel offensive culminated in a successful Allied victory on September 16, 1918, the Americans having effectively broken the four-year-long deadlock by eliminating the entire salient. The goal had been to push the Germans back behind the Hindenburg Line, and that had been accomplished. Now the Germans were on one side of the Hindenburg Line and the Americans were on the other side. They opposed each other along a straight line and the salient was no more. The stage was now set for the Meuse-Argonne offensive, which would be launched on September 26, 1918.

With their victory over the German-held St. Mihiel salient, the course of the war for the Americans changed suddenly and dramatically, as it was no longer a war of attrition, but one of eventual decisive victory in favor of the Allies. The soldiers could feel the change. After four long years, these weary soldiers had finally broken free of trenches! And being no longer confined to the trenches, they knew they were overtaking the enemy. "The Allies found they had a formidable army to aid them," General Pershing stated, "and the enemy learned finally that he had one to recon with."[450]

The 89th Division played no small part in the success of the St. Mihiel offensive, accomplishing a great deal more than was expected. The division had reduced the Bois de Mort Mare without the assistance of the 2nd and 42nd Divisions, and had assisted these divisions in capturing the villages of

Euvezin, Bouillonville, Xammes and Beney.[451] "The division had been given a task that was believed to be beyond its powers and had accomplished it," George English proudly declared.[452]

Casualties inflicted upon the troops of the 89th Division were determined to be comparatively light, especially when considering the territory recovered and the results it achieved during the campaign: 14 officers and 177 enlisted men killed in action, 41 officers and 892 enlisted men wounded, and 60 enlisted men reported missing. These figures were reported by Lieutenant Horace R. Palmer, who penned a lengthy newspaper article about the 89th Division's combat history in June 1919.[453]

As for the enemy, the two German divisions opposing the U.S. 89th Division suffered approximately 300 officers and enlisted men killed in action, and had 2,287 troops taken as prisoners of war. The number of casualties from the two German divisions is unclear, but they were enough to render the enemy in that sector incapable of further immediate service.[454]

In addition to those enemy soldiers killed, wounded and captured, the 89th Division seized from the Germans a large number of arms, ammunition and equipment. This included 72 cannons, 95 machine guns, some 1,000 rifles, and enormous quantities of artillery and small arms ammunition, grenades, clothing and blankets, engineer's stores, and other equipment. Several locomotives and many railroad cars were also seized.[455]

It is important to iterate that, while the St. Mihiel salient had been eliminated, the war in that region was still ongoing, and minor shifts in position, calculated skirmishes, and combat operations would continue in the weeks ahead. Four German divisions now occupied the Hindenburg Line, opposite the U.S. 89th Division. Their advance positions were lightly held by scattered combat groups, and a main line of resistance existed a bit further back.[456]

To their credit, the Germans selected defensive positions on reverse slopes and built phenomenal concrete dugouts and emplacements. In addition, their flanks were well-protected by natural obstacles. However, their trench systems remained unfinished, their exposed rear positions were not organized, and those positions in the concealed woods had only been partially prepared for defense.[457]

The 354th Infantry Regiment, to which Charlie was assigned, remained in and around Beney until September 17, on which date it advanced nearly two miles northeast to Xammes. Xammes had been used as a German supply depot, and Colonel Babcock discovered an abandoned German officer's club in which to reestablish his regimental headquarters. Babcock's battalions were posted in trenches stretching from the village outskirts to the Hindenburg Line, about two-and-a-half miles to the northeast.[458]

In Xammes, John McGrath recalled finding rooms full of rare engineering instruments and materials, cellars full of wine and Schnapps, and warehouses full of sauerkraut, potatoes, jam, hard bread, hay, corn and oats. German artillery batteries did not want the Americans to have these supplies, so they persistently bombarded the village in an effort to destroy them. Each night, the Germans bombed the area until the Beney-Xammes road was twisted, torn, upheaved, and nearly impassable.[459]

Although shellfire during that time was quite heavy, for the most part, soldiers could sense which shells would fall close to their position and which ones they didn't have to worry about. They also knew by this time that barring a direct hit, the trenches they occupied afforded reasonable protection. McGrath writes that all men assigned to the 354th quickly became acclimated to enemy shellfire, and cites an amusing example.[460]

"Standing behind the P.C.," McGrath writes, "we were watching a Doughboy washing his underwear near the pump about 100 yards away when, with a rush of air a shell burnt its way along and exploded about 20 yards from the man. He looked up at it when it exploded (without harming him luckily) but simply continued to rinse his clothing as the shell smoke blew over him."[461]

Since being assigned to the trenches north of Xammes, Charlie and the others in Company L wallowed in unimaginable filth in their shallow trenches, all the while enduring bitter cold and hunger. Seeking to do anything but sit around waiting to be hit by artillery fire, Charlie, a Chauchat gunner, volunteered for Colonel Babcock's newly formed regimental patrol group, or "shock group," as they were now known. To Charlie's chagrin, Chauchat gunners were considered too vital to the unit, and his request was declined. Charlie did, however, continue to participate in fighting patrols and raids where Chauchat gunners were needed.

The 354th's regimental shock group initially consisted of one officer and 60 enlisted volunteers, drawn from the entire regiment. Some days later, however, the shock group swelled to 110 men who "made nightly expeditions up to and along the enemy lines for over a week, one-third going out each night," Babcock explains in his memoirs. "The group lived in Bouillonville with the rear echelon of the regimental headquarters, where they could get three hot meals daily. We all might sleep two nights out of three and a day's sleep after the night patrol."[462]

Charlie remained in the Xammes sector until September 24, on which day Company L of the 354th Infantry Regiment withdrew to Bouillonville for food, a bath, and clean clothing. That same morning, an enemy reconnaissance plane was brought down intact by an American pursuit plane outside of Xammes. Members of the 354th detained the pilot and observer, and escorted them to regimental headquarters for interrogation.

Their maps revealed that they knew the precise location of the 354th's headquarters element, and, more surprisingly, details of their trench system, which was plotted from aerial photographs.[463]

Army chemical warfare historian Rexmond C. Cochrane reveals that the constant movement of troops in and out of the American line increased enemy fears that another attack was imminent. The Germans still believed that Pershing's objective was the city of Metz. In their nervousness, therefore, the Germans stepped up their gas and high explosive artillery fire night after night, filling the sky with "flares, rockets, and lights of all kinds."[464]

"The artillery of the 89th found itself unable to return the enemy's gas fire," writes Cochrane. "Furnished with quantities of gas shells for the operation of 12 September, which had not been used, the [89th Division's] 164th FA [Field Artillery] Brigade had 'no information as to the contents of these shells or their tactical use,' and the division gas officer, called into an artillery conference, 'told them practically everything I knew on the subject, which wasn't very much.' As a result, the [164th] brigade fired little gas, and at no time more than 200 gas shells on any one day."[465]

The day after Company L left Xammes for Bouillonville, the Germans attacked Xammes. Just after midnight on September 25, 1918, German artillery shells destroyed the 354th headquarters building in Xammes, one blast catapulting an American runner through the door astride a chair. For two hours thereafter, enemy artillery bombarded the village with mustard gas, and the Allied troops therein held their position with gas masks on, hoping the shelling would cease. Ultimately, lower Xammes became untenable and the headquarters element was forced to evacuate to Bouillonville.[466] Amazingly, Charlie, away from Xammes for rest and recuperation (R&R), had dodged yet another "bullet"!

Postwar intelligence reports suggest that 11,116 high explosive shells fell within the 89th Division's sector between September 14 and September 30, 1918. Rexmond Cochrane, in his study, contends that that count should be doubled, as there were nine barrages or bombardments in a three-day period in which the 356th Infantry Regiment did not file a report.[467]

"It is probable that gas shells totaled at least 1,000," Cochrane writes. "G-3 [Operations] records for those two weeks [following the St. Mihiel offensive] show 48 killed, 310 wounded, 76 gassed, and 18 men missing, with casualties omitted on three days. Medical Department records suggest that the killed and wounded figures may be approximately correct, but gas casualties were more nearly 224 than 76."[468]

"What's a man to do? The gas is sure to get you. They say you can recognize it by its color, but it always comes at night when you can't see it. Then they say one can tell it by its smell, yet one whiff will kill you. There's no chance for a man."[469] This quote comes from Lieutenant Marion W. Page, a medical officer serving with the 354th Infantry Regiment.

Thus far, Charlie had avoided direct contact with mustard gas. The 89th Division would now move to a new front where they would begin clearing what today is an all-but-forgotten German stronghold in and around the Bois de Bantheville, a comparatively small affair in comparison to the St. Mihiel offensive. But for members of the 89th Division, the Bois de Bantheville would come to rank as one of their most spirited engagements. It would be there where Charlie would earn the Medal of Honor.[470]

Chapter Ten

THE BOIS DE BANTHEVILLE

On September 16, 1918, immediately upon culmination of the St. Mihiel offensive, General Pershing directed his attention to the Meuse-Argonne region. The easternmost tip of the Meuse-Argonne jump-off line, or line of departure, was approximately 27 miles northwest of the line held by the 89th Division in the St. Mihiel region, and extended 30 miles westward. Pershing's objective would be to reach Sedan, which was about 45 miles north of the Meuse-Argonne jump-off line.

Pershing needed to cut the German's principal rail supply line going into Sedan, which enabled the Germans to maintain a strong system of field fortifications throughout the region. To sever this artery would render the German positions to the west and northwest of Sedan untenable. The Germans had gone to great lengths, however, to protect this supply line, and any effort to destroy it would be a formidable challenge.[471]

For this offensive, Pershing rushed American divisions up from southern training areas; hurried others down from the north, where they had been fighting alongside British troops in Flanders and with the French at Château-Thierry; and he swung some of his divisions away from the St. Mihiel operation. Supporting the Americans, to the west, would be the French Fourth Army.[472]

The original American plan, if the reader recalls, was for the St. Mihiel offensive to continue after reaching the Hindenburg Line and seize the city of Metz. This written plan was purposely permitted to fall into German hands; the plan, however, unbeknownst to the Germans, had been abandoned by the Americans by then. The German High Command, therefore, still expecting the Americans to break through the Hindenburg Line and attack Metz, dedicated six divisions to Metz's defense. German troops were now diverted from the Meuse-Argonne region, which is precisely what Pershing wanted![473]

Artillery barrages would be standard attacks that preceded all major offensives. Such barrages were designed to destroy strong points and clear enemy territory through which friendly forces would be advancing. At precisely 11:00 p.m., on September 25, 1918, and continuing for six hours thereafter, General Pershing would execute a series of artillery barrages on two different fronts: (1) along the jump-off (departure) line in the Meuse-Argonne region as an attack to soften the enemy's frontline; and (2) along the Hindenburg Line, in the St. Mihiel region, as a diversionary operation.

The artillery barrage in the Meuse-Argonne region was designed to soften German frontline defensive positions prior to the Americans advancing en masse toward the enemy front lines on the morning of September 26.* This target was Pershing's true objective. The artillery barrage in the St. Mihiel region would be comparable in intensity to the barrage on Meuse-Argonne; however, it would have a different function. While these barrages would target German strong points, they would not be followed up by troops advancing across the Hindenburg Line. Instead, the barrages would serve as a diversionary ploy to continue to confuse the enemy as to where the Americans intended to launch their actual offensive.

The 89th Division would be among those divisions who, for now, stayed behind, along the Hindenburg Line in the St. Mihiel region, to distract the Germans. Continuing to hold the same ground that they had occupied at the end of the St. Mihiel offensive, the 89th would reinforce the German expectation that seizing the city of Metz was the American goal.[474] To discuss implementing a diversionary raid along the Hindenburg Line, beyond the 89th Division's frontline outposts, General Wright's Chief of Staff, Colonel John C.H. Lee, met with Colonel Babcock a few days before the Meuse-Argonne offensive commenced.[475]

Lee called upon Babcock to use his specially trained 354th Infantry Regiment shock group, which fell under the 89th Division, to raid areas and distract the Germans in the St. Mihiel region.[476] Such shock groups could be considered a forerunner to the modern-day Special Forces, although their preparation and training dwarfed in comparison. Since its inception, Babcock's regimental shock group had performed nightly raids against enemy strong points with stunning results and minimal losses. Lieutenant Marshall P. Wilder, of Company H, 354th Infantry Regiment, who commanded the regimental shock group, had earned the respect and confidence of Colonel Babcock, and was thereby charged with carrying out this important assignment.

The 89th Division held advanced outposts in the northern edge of a wooded area known as the Bois de Charey, three-and-a-half miles northeast of Beney. This is where the division organized its main line of resistance along the Hindenburg Line, in the St. Mihiel region. One-and-a-half miles

---

* During the Meuse-Argonne campaign, Americans would oppose up to 44 German divisions, although most of those were at half-strength or less.

east of the Bois de Charey was the village of Charey, a stronghold still occupied by the Germans. After discussing the matter with Lieutenant Wilder, Colonel Babcock selected Charey as the shock group's objective for the morning of September 26.[477]

"Opposite the right of our line [in the Bois de Charey] and about 300 yards' northeast of it was a bluff, sixty or eighty feet high, which formed the southern end of what was called the plateau of Grande Fontaine," explained Babcock. "At the top of this bluff the Germans had their outpost line covering the approach to Charey, about 1,100 yards to the northeast. Wilder's patrols had reconnoitered this area several times and were familiar with the terrain between our lines and the enemy.

"Wilder was directed to move his party after dark on the twenty-fifth and before 11:00 p.m. to this bluff, to remain there all night, and at 5:30 a.m. the next morning to advance up the bluff, attack the German outpost and drive them into Charey. Having accomplished this, he was to fire a Very light signal, which would be repeated by the C.O. [commanding officer], First Battalion and by regimental headquarters, notifying the artillery to stop firing over the entire division front."[478]

Named for Edward Wilson Very (1847-1910), "Very pistols" were flare guns that were used for many years prior to WWI, and they reportedly "kicked like a mule" when fired. These pistols fired "Very flares," more commonly known as "Very lights," which could be used as signal flares or for nighttime illumination. Very lights would deploy little parachutes, of paper or silk, which would hold the flare over the battlefield for 15- to 25-seconds.[479]

Very lights, when used as signals, came in red, white and green, and would be fired skyward in three-flare combinations, such as two green flares and one white flare; two green flares and one red flare; or any one of a number of variations. These combinations had specific meanings and were changed from week to week, or from night to night, keeping the enemy off guard as to what three combinations of signals were being used.[480]

Very lights, when used for illumination, emanated a yellow smoke that remained airborne long enough to illuminate the Allied barbed wire belt, through which the Germans may be penetrating. There were also firework-like flares, which were described as "caterpillars of flame that crawl and zigzag between heaven and earth for from 20- to 25-seconds." These were designed to signal Allied troops miles away that the unit firing the flare was about to be overrun.[481]

Ahead of the diversionary attacks along the Hindenburg Line on the morning of September 26, Charlie and the others in his unit were placed on alert and told to be prepared for "any emergency." Up until this time, the soldiers had been told nothing about the Meuse-Argonne offensive, and only enough about the diversionary attacks in the St. Mihiel region to prevent friendly fire incidents.

However, being told to be on the alert, soldiers from the 89th Division sensed that something was up, and whenever something was up, rumors ran rampant. By the afternoon of September 25, American troops in the St. Mihiel region were certain that they would be called upon to storm the Hindenburg Line with the intention of taking the city of Metz. Some doughboys were even concerned that the Germans were about to launch a counteroffensive against them.[482]

The reason that soldiers not involved in the action were told nothing about the Meuse-Argonne offensive, or that the attacks and raids in the St. Mihiel region were only diversionary, was because Pershing believed this secrecy to be critical in carrying out his plan. He did not want to take any chances of a doughboy, such as Charlie, being captured by the Germans and revealing any details of what the Americans were up to. Keeping the target from the Germans of where the actual offensive was to take place (in the Meuse-Argonne region) was crucial to the plan's success.[483]

On the evening of September 25, 1918, General Pershing's plan was firmly in place, and at 11:00 p.m., artillery fire erupted along both battle-fronts— the Meuse-Argonne and St. Mihiel regions. Throughout the ensuing six-hour period, events unfolded in accordance with Pershing's orders.

Troops assigned to the 89th Division, having been placed on alert, were not surprised by the artillery barrage taking place along the Hindenburg Line, but they still didn't know Pershing's intentions. Company L, to which Charlie was assigned, was still bivouacked in Bouillonville, more than five miles southwest of the Hindenburg Line when the artillery barrage commenced. Therefore, those assigned to Company L could only hear the artillery barrage nearest to their them, and remained oblivious to the fact that Pershing was pulling off the huge offensive in the Meuse-Argonne region more than 35 miles away.

It was a crisp September evening, and a heavy, damp mist hung white and low over Bouillonville. Charlie would have spent the hours listening to others swap stories in a high-bank dugout in a railroad cut, for sleep was impossible. Troops assigned to the 89th Division anxiously awaited orders to pierce the Hindenburg Line and then fulfill their role in what they believed was a renewed offensive, but no such orders arrived.

Division, brigade and regimental commanders, including those of the 89th, knew, of course, of Pershing's plan, and therefore never ordered their troops into action along the Hindenburg Line. Battalion, company and platoon commanders would not order their men into combat unless they had a specific mission, or they were attacked by the enemy. In the end, nothing occurred along the Hindenburg Line other than the artillery barrage and scattered diversionary skirmishes.[484]

As the sun ascended above the horizon, the barrages in both the Meuse-Argonne and St. Mihiel regions continued with unabated fury. The Germans, understandably uneasy, sent reconnaissance planes over the American lines to assess the situation. American machine gun fire and anti-aircraft artillery erupted to destroy the aircraft, and some German planes were shot down. Those German airmen that returned safely to their aerodromes delivered conflicting, albeit chilling reports as to the Americans' apparent intentions. Some claimed that a renewed offensive along the Hindenburg Line was in progress, while others insisted that a massive frontal assault was occurring in the Meuse-Argonne region. All the German airmen agreed that whatever the target, something big was in the works.[485]

Wilder and his shock group, of course, were briefed about the American artillery barrage, and had traversed the plateau of Grande Fontaine in the St. Mihiel region. They were now situated on the bluff, which formed the southern edge of the plateau, and were not far from Charey. Their only resistance came from German machine gun crews that had moved forward to escape the American barrage.[486]

At one point, however, the American shock group was caught under such heavy enemy machine gun fire that the success of the raid was in jeopardy. Wilder took personal charge of one platoon, whose leader had become a casualty, and stormed the hostile German strong point. He succeeded in clearing the strong point, with heavy casualties to the enemy, and the remaining Germans retreated. For this heroic feat, Wilder would receive the Distinguished Service Cross.[487]

Wilder and his men waited until 5:30 a.m., as instructed, and then took the town of Charey with little opposition. Recall earlier that Wilder was to fire a Very light, to be repeated on down the line, to signal the artillery to stop firing. Once that occurred, Wilder and his shock group returned to their lines with a number of prisoners. They had suffered just two casualties during the operation, and for Wilder's "repeated good work during such raids," he was promoted to captain.[488]

By the time the Germans realized the Meuse-Argonne region was the Americans' actual objective, the American diversionary strategy proved successful and Pershing's forces had a foothold in the Meuse-Argonne region.[489] In response to the American offensive, the Germans robbed every reserve division on the Western Front and hurried them to bolster the badly broken defensive line along the Meuse-Argonne front. Their communications and transportation system were of vital strategic military importance, which meant that the Germans had to hold this line at all costs.

They had the resolve and held the natural military strength of the terrain, but they did not have the critical numbers necessary to defend against the powerful American Army.[490]

The Meuse-Argonne offensive would evolve into the largest and deadliest American operation of the war. American presence on the Western Front had now broken the four-year stalemate that had German and Allied forces confined to trenches. Marshal Foch intended to exploit the recent American successes with other offensives along the entire Western Front by using forces from France, Britain, Belgium, and several other countries. If successful, the German Army would be divided, which would ultimately lead to their defeat.[491]

On the same morning on which the Meuse-Argonne offensive commenced, September 26, Charlie's company departed Bouillonville and moved into the third-line trenches near Xammes, opposite the Hindenburg Line. The following day, Company L advanced to the first-line trenches, north and west of Xammes, where they would remain for three days. By this time, everyone in the 89th Division knew that American forces had broken through the Meuse-Argonne line, and at night they could hear the rumbling of artillery fire in the distance.

During the last week of September, there were five gas attacks perpetrated against the Americans in the sector held by the 89th Division. Although there was no count of shells made, the division suffered about 100 gas casualties. Fortunately for Charlie, the company to which he was assigned, Company L, was not affected.[492]

The newly assigned gas officer, Captain Hugh A. Rowan, was incensed upon learning that his officers and NCOs were not notified until 24 hours after these gas attacks, and that they were assigned unrelated duties in the rear, just as they had been the previous month. Rowan visited General Wright to push for immediate procedural changes, to which the general readily concurred.[493]

Rexmond Cochrane writes that on September 28, 1918, General Order Number 76 "spelled out the AEF General Orders of 27 May by emphasizing that every regimental and battalion gas officers and NCOs in the 89th Division were henceforth to be relieved of all other duties. The new order also set up a system of gas alarms for all troop areas, forbade the repeating of gas alarms from neighboring units, and ordered daily inspection of gas masks and daily gas mask drill, including wearing the mask a half hour once each week while performing normal duties."[494]

Assigned to Company L was a tall, slender, second lieutenant named John M. Millis, Charlie's platoon commander, who was born in Boyd County, Kentucky, on January 20, 1893. Most enlisted men referred to him as "Buck," for he was as ordinary as a buck private, sleeping in the same small lean-to tents and consuming the same terrible rations. Everyone knew that if they had any trouble they could go to Millis and speak freely, Charlie included. In the coming days, Millis would not only demonstrate his courage in combat, but also the high regard he had for his subordinate soldiers.

On September 29, Company L was relieved from the first-line trenches to assume positions in the second line of defense. During that transition, an officer returned from patrol in No Man's Land and reported that he had encountered heavy enemy machine gun fire, which forced him to leave behind a wounded enlisted man. Lieutenant Millis, with Corporal Charles S. Morrison, who volunteered to go along, set out to retrieve the wounded soldier from enemy territory.[495]

Millis and Morrison proceeded over rough and broken ground to a point 400 yards beyond the company's outposts where they exchanged fire with the enemy. Learning that the enlisted man was about 100 yards beyond that, Morrison followed Millis into the open terrain, still under heavy enemy machine gun fire. Unfortunately, when they located the wounded soldier, he was dead. Making their way back to their outpost, they continued to engage the enemy, one of whom they killed.[496] Millis and Morrison were awarded the Distinguished Service Cross for their actions that day, and Millis' credibility with the enlisted men soared!

Charles Morrison was another interesting fellow, possessing more military experience than most men in his company. Born in St. Louis, Missouri, on March 16, 1888, his civilian vocation was that of a shoemaker. In 1907, he enlisted as a private in Company A, 5th Cavalry, and two years later embarked on a one-year military assignment in Hawaii. Upon returning stateside in 1910, he accepted a discharge and returned to St. Louis, where, a few months later, he married Agnes Marchwinski. They had two children.

Morrison went on to serve as a stable sergeant with Headquarters Company, 1st Infantry Regiment, Missouri National Guard, which was mustered into Federal service in June 1916. He deployed to Laredo, Texas, and remained on duty along the Mexican border until his discharge that September. Between that time and the time that he was drafted for service in World War I, he worked as a watchman at the Union Station in St. Louis.

Morrison was slightly wounded in action on October 18, 1918, but he survived the war. After being discharged on June 3, 1919, he returned to St. Louis and resumed his prewar vocation of making shoes. For the remainder of his life, he suffered from exposure to mustard gas, and contracted lobar pneumonia. He passed away in St. Louis on December 16, 1923, at the age of 35. Morrison, Millis, Jess Funk and Charlie Barger were the only men from Company L to earn America's top two decorations during the war.

On September 30, 1918, and into the following day, the 353rd Infantry Regiment, 89th Division, relieved Charlie's regiment, the 354th, from the town and trenches of Xammes. Troops assigned to the 354th subsequently embarked on a four-mile march, led by Colonel Babcock, to Pannes, where they were afforded two days to relax and clean up, away from the front lines. After that time, the 354th Infantry Regiment returned to the Bois de Beney where, during the day, the men could circulate freely due to the shelter of the woods. At night, however, the main arteries of circulation were pounded by enemy artillery at irregular intervals, and every depression was full of mustard gas.[497]

The 354th Infantry Regiment's historian, John McGrath, recalled that Colonel Babcock arranged a little entertainment for his troops by ordering the regimental band up to the lines to give the boys a concert. Around dusk, on the evening of October 4, the woods echoed to the strains of the regimental march, and Babcock's men were nearly as astonished as the enemy. In fact, many of the men assigned to the 354th believed that the war was over. "It was probably the most unusual stunt of the war," writes McGrath, "and the very audacity of it carried it off, for not a shell was fired at them. The boys were immeasurably cheered by it."[498]

Little activity occurred within the sector held by the 89th Division during its remaining time in the St. Mihiel region. Finally, between October 7-9, the division was relieved by the battle-weary 37th Division, which had just arrived from the Meuse-Argonne region. During its time on the Meuse-Argonne battlefront, the 37th's objective was to capture the town of Montfaucon, situated about 43 miles north of St. Mihiel, and 20 miles north of Verdun.[499]

The 37th Division made valiant efforts to advance to Montfaucon in the days after the Meuse-Argonne offensive began, but the division was repeatedly driven back by heavy artillery shelling. Consequently, the U.S. divisions west and east of the 37th were forced to withdraw from the territory they had captured. On October 1, 1918, the 32nd Division relieved the 37th in the Meuse-Argonne region, and the 37th Division set out to relieve the 89th in the St. Mihiel region. By that time, the St. Mihiel region was considered a quiet sector.[500]

After being relieved by the 37th Division, the 89th Division assembled near Commercy, a town located 10 miles south of the city of St. Mihiel, and completely away from the front lines. According to George English, the 89th had by then been in the line or in battle continuously for two months and a day, perhaps the longest period of uninterrupted conflict which any American division was called upon to endure.[501]

On October 10, members of the 89th Division departed Commercy and traveled via truck 40 miles north to the village of Brocourt-en-Argonne, situated 11 miles west of Verdun. Charlie would have settled with his company into a barracks in Brocourt where, that day, the 354th Infantry Regiment, 89th Division, was to begin three weeks of well-earned rest. The 89th was now in the Meuse-Argonne region, and would remain in the region until after the war, but at this point they were still some miles south of where the fighting was taking place.[502]

The move to the Meuse-Argonne region was so rapid that the 89th Division left behind its slow-moving, horse-drawn 164th Field Artillery. This was not uncommon during the war. In many instances, artillery units were detached from their own divisions and linked up with nearby infantry units. Thus separated, they did not rejoin their own divisions until after the Armistice.[503]

On October 12, the 89th Division, still "resting," was reassigned to V Corps and began to receive fresh troops from the 86th Division. The first units of the 86th had embarked for overseas on September 8, 1918, and the last units of this division would not arrive in France until October 28. It was decided by Pershing's staff to split up the 86th to replenish other divisions, such as the 89th, to bring it back up to war strength prior to resuming combat operations.[504]

On the evening of October 12, while Charlie and fellow troops members assigned to the 354th Infantry Regiment, 89th Division, were in their bunks and glad not to be outside in the pouring rain, an orderly entered the barracks with orders to prepare to move out at 7:00 the following morning. At that time, the regiment departed Brocourt and began its 15-mile trek northward to Éclisfontaine, where it would fall in behind the 32nd Division for the purpose of eventually replacing it along the Meuse-Argonne front. Charlie could have had no idea that he would be marching through the wildest, muddiest countryside imaginable! Chilly autumn rain plagued the entire excursion, and his regiment was forced to march single file all the way, bridging deserted trenches and cutting through barbed wire. That night, they either camped out or were billeted in the town through which they passed.[505]

In transit, abysmal road jams caused the regiment's kitchens to become separated, so Charlie and the other men in his unit endured hunger along with exhaustion. The hike resumed the following morning, October 14. "On the roadsides we passed walking wounded cases," writes John McGrath, "hobbling to the hospitals in the rear, and they dropped hints to us as to the ferocity of the fighting in the woods ahead."[506]

That afternoon, Charlie's regiment reached Éclisfontaine, which had been captured from the Germans but a day or so prior. The men assigned to the 354th Infantry Regiment pitched their shelter halves in well camouflaged spots, carpeted the mud with branches, and tried to ease the

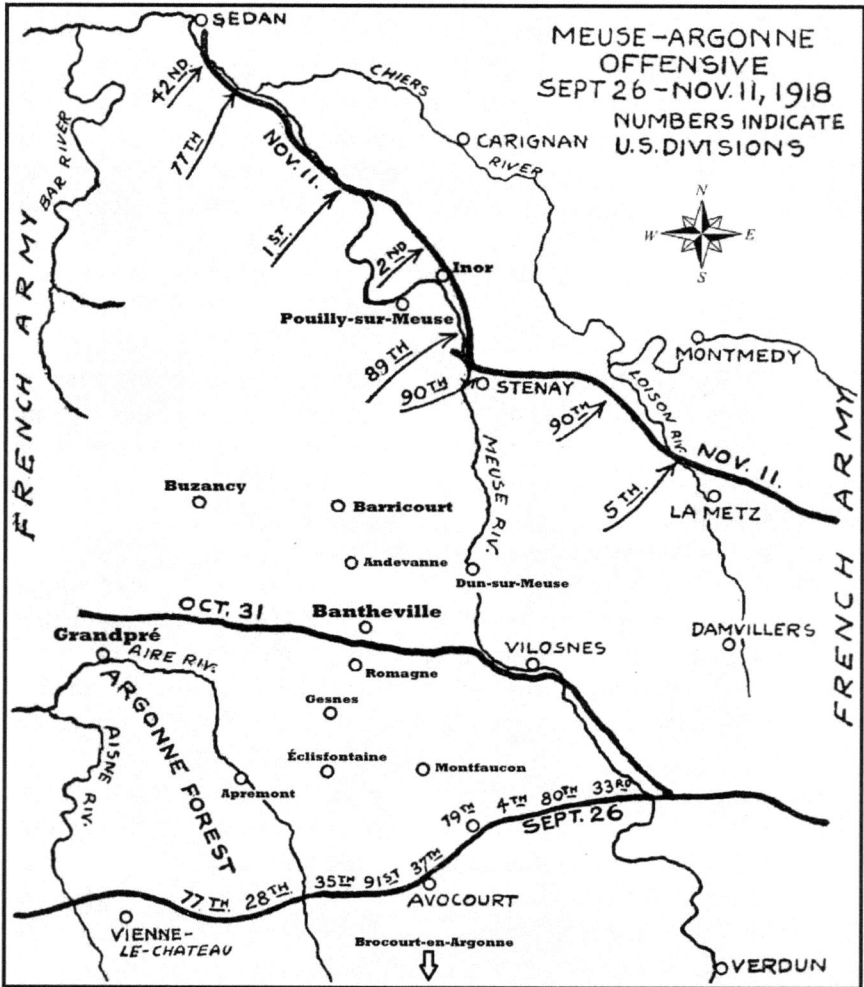

THE MEUSE-ARGONNE REGION

Credit: Adapted from a map by P.F. Collier. <u>Collier's New Encyclopedia</u>, *vol. 10, 1921, p. 433.*

discomfort a bit. According to McGrath, they billeted in the mud with barbed wire for a pillow.[507]

"Some kitchens had arrived and conditions were better," reveals McGrath. "We were held constantly at the alert, expecting the order to advance any hour. Equipment was renewed, daily drills held in the attack formation and exercises in passing through woods to a given point by compass at night. Now and then a stray shell exploded harmlessly nearby, otherwise there were no untoward incidents. Burying parties interred many horses [that] German machine gunners killed in the battle a few days previously."[508]

The 354th Infantry Regiment would remain in Éclisfontaine until the evening of October 19, when the entire 89th Division would advance five miles north to relieve the 32nd Division in the Bantheville sector.[509] The 32nd's front line consisted of a five-mile northerly arc, west-to-east, between the villages of Landres-et-St. Georges and Bantheville. The Bois de Bantheville and, to the immediate southwest, the Bois de Romagne, lay between these villages.

Charlie's layover in Éclisfontaine, between October 14-19, was spent training, refitting, and participating in regular reconnaissance patrols to scattered positions held by the 32nd.[510] During that interim, a report from 32nd Division headquarters was sent to General Wright, informing him that the Germans had been driven out of the Bois de Bantheville and only "mopping up" was required.[511] In military terms, mopping up is an operation following a battle or campaign to root out remaining enemy forces or installations.[512]

Having no reason to believe that the report he received from 32nd Division headquarters would be inaccurate, General Wright directed the 178th Brigade, 89th Division, to have the Bois de Bantheville mopped up by the end of the day on October 20. After the Germans were completely eradicated from the woods, Wright would have the 178th fall back to division reserve, and the 177th Brigade, to which Charlie was assigned, would take over the division front. The 177th Brigade would then serve as the 89th Division's assault brigade in a renewed general assault all along the Meuse-Argonne front. This renewed assault would commence on November 1, 1918, in a massive, collective, effort to seize the German's railroad supply routes leading into Sedan.[513]

On the evening of October 19, the 89th Division was sent in, as planned, to relieve the 32nd Division. The 354th Infantry Regiment, which included Charlie, was specifically assigned to a subdivision of the Bantheville sector held by the 127th Infantry Regiment, 32nd Division. Colonel Babcock, commander of the 354th Infantry Regiment, ordered his 2nd Battalion to take up a position on the southern edge of the Bois de Bantheville; he ordered his 3rd Battalion, which included Charlie, to establish a nearby support line; and, he placed his 1st Battalion in reserve.[514]

When troops assigned to the 178th Brigade, 89th Division, moved up to relieve frontline troops of the 32nd Division, they found large numbers of enemy troops still present in scattered groups, and others were constantly entering by infiltration.[515] The report General Wright had received from the 32nd Division was wrong! The area had *not* been cleared of enemy troops.

Consequently, the 178th Brigade, 89th Division, would not have the Bois de Bantheville mopped up by the evening of October 20, as General Wright ordered, or even by midnight on the 21st.[516] In fact, the woods would not be cleared until the evening of October 22, when Charlie and his fellow soldiers from the 177th Brigade, 89th Division, moved up to relieve the 178th.[517]

John McGrath describes how the men in the 354th Infantry Regiment, 89th Division, dug in industriously, but many made the fatal mistake of considering cover the same as protection. "They feel as safe under a blanket spread across the top of their funk holes as though under 30 feet of concrete," he writes. Artillery fire after midnight hit Company L particularly hard, killing Sergeant James N. Ramsey, Private First Class Bernard R. Piepmeyer, and Private Claude Pyles. Six more men from Charlie's company were wounded before daybreak, making this a very costly lesson indeed.[518]

When Colonel Babcock, commander of the 354th Infantry Regiment, awoke on the morning of October 20, he was absolutely appalled at the situation. "After we took over this area," he writes in his memoirs, "we found the unburied dead of the 32nd Division everywhere; and on our left in the area of the 42nd Division, I saw dead Germans lying at the very entrance to the P.C. [post of command] of some organization occupying a dugout on the Tuilerie farm. It may be unfair to criticize these organizations [regiments, brigades and companies] for failing to bury the dead of both sides, but it is difficult to understand why the American dead, well behind the front, and the German dead, at the door of a dugout could not have been buried. In the 354th Infantry, the Chaplains and the Band performed these sad but necessary duties most efficiently."[519]

Up to the time that the 89th Division assumed its position in the front lines of the Meuse-Argonne region on October 20, the Americans had been making steady progress, but at this stage of the offensive, it was by no means a success. The Germans would fight, and fight hard, until the last hours of the war. In fact, Charlie's division would see its heaviest fighting in the days ahead. The Germans may have been retreating, but they were not whipped, and they continued to hit the Americans with artillery fire at every opportunity.

On October 22, 1918, the 177th Brigade, 89th Division, to which Charlie was assigned, advanced through a heavy enemy artillery barrage to relieve the 178th Brigade in the 89th Division's frontline positions. About 750 German artillery shells were reported, principally in the central and southern portions of the woods, since enemy forces still held parts of the northern sector. It was estimated that 30 percent of these shells contained Blue, Green, and Yellow Cross gases.[520] It was immediately evident to those assigned to the 177th Brigade that even then mopping-up operation was not complete.

The 353rd Infantry Regiment, 89th Division, which was under direct German artillery and gas fire, had a particularly tough time combating enemy forces during this relief, prompting Colonel Reeve, the regimental commander, to take personal charge. Using his 1st Battalion, Reeves went through, cleaned out that area of the woods still occupied by the Germans, and rescued some elements of the 356th that had been cut off. In the process, however, he lost 11 men killed and 24 wounded.[521]

General Winn, Commanding the 177th Brigade, 89th Division, was particularly concerned over the shelling, and sent a message to General Wright, which stated: "I have already reported the gassing of the Bois de Bantheville. The matter is a serious one. Gas extends over a wide area. Division should determine whether or not the situation justifies giving up extensive areas. I have directed organizations to change positions but remain in the general locality. It is a difficult and perplexing question, in view of the past experiences of the division."[522]

General Wright advised Winn to hold on to the Bois de Bantheville, as these woods were of great importance for the renewed general assault all along the Meuse-Argonne front, scheduled for November 1, 1918. Wright suggested that there had to be places unaffected by gas where the men could establish a defensive line. Rexmond Cochrane writes that it is not known if the Germans had hoped to retake the Bois de Bantheville, or if they simply wanted to delay as long as possible an advance above the woods, but it was certain that the enemy's high-explosives and gas fire on the central part of the forest was intended to cut off American troops and force them to withdraw.[523]

By daybreak on October 23, 1918, the 354th Infantry Regiment held the 89th Division's western front line, and the 353rd held the division's eastern front line. To the 354th's left, just south of the village of Landres-et-St. Georges, was the 42nd Division; to the 353rd's right, north of the village of Bantheville, was the 90th Division. During the push northward, the 90th Division advanced alongside the divisions to its left and right, as anticipated, but the 42nd Division was stymied by a German strong point at Landres-et-St. Georges. Therefore, the 42nd Division's easternmost line, where it merged with the 354th Infantry Regiment, 89th Division, was less advanced.[524]

From October 23 to November 1, 1918, the mission of the 353rd and 354th Infantry Regiment was to hold the 89th Division's front line, patrol for enemy activity, and prepare for the renewed general assault along the Meuse-Argonne front. The 354th, to which Charlie was assigned, had the additional mission of organizing its positions once the 42nd Division broke through Landres-et-St. Georges. It was imperative that every division along the Meuse-Argonne front be prepared to advance in unison on November 1, if that phase of the offensive was to prove successful.[525]

"As soon as our positions of the whole forest was secure," writes George English, "the enemy inaugurated a campaign of harassment that made the holding of the position one of severe hardship. Continuous shelling of the position was coupled with airplane raids upon the troops in the edge of the woods. Worst of all was the establishment of gassed areas extending across the central portion of the forest, which maintained by an almost uninterrupted bombardment for days with the gas shells."[526]

The 89th Division's experience with enemy aircraft generally consisted of reconnaissance flights, which were followed up by artillery attacks. On October 23, however, frontline troops occupying regimental outposts were subjected to relentless strafing by Baron Manfred von Richthofen's celebrated Flying Circus.[527] To this day, von Richthofen is known as the Red Baron, as his aircraft were painted red instead of the typical green of the day. The pilots in his squadron were so good that their aerobatics were circus-like; hence the nickname. They were the most feared German air unit of the war, and many Allied pilots fled when they saw their distinctive red planes.

The trees in the Bois de Bantheville by that time had lost most of their leaves, allowing the Flying Circus to fire their machine guns up and down the line at the semi-exposed Americans positioned at the edge of the woods. When the German airmen expended their ammunition, they would return to their own lines, reload, and return to resume their attack on the Americans.[528] The Americans, defending their front lines, had no choice but to be where they were, as they could neither advance nor retreat.[529]

On the night of October 24, 1918, and into the morning of the 25th, the Germans fired 1,100 high-explosive and Blue Cross shells on positions held by the 42nd and 89th Divisions. These positions included the Bois de Bantheville, Bois de Romagne, and the densely wooded Côté de Châtillon.[530] During this barrage, the 2nd Battalion, 354th Infantry Regiment, 89th Division, lost 250 men and six officers, killed and wounded. One shell fell amid Charlie's company, in the 3rd Battalion's sector, hitting a hut wherein Corporal Clarence J. Brock and Bugler Edgar McCann were sleeping. Brock was killed and McCann was severely wounded.[531]

The 2nd Battalion, 354th Infantry Regiment, which had been holding the 354th's front line, was effectively depleted during this overnight barrage, and Colonel Babcock moved the 1st Battalion up to replace it. Due to poisonous gas lingering in the area, however, he requested authorization from General Winn to move his forces back. Winn, fearful of Pershing's wrath, refused Babcock's request, but permitted him to move his 3rd Battalion, which included Charlie, south of the Romagne-Sommerance Road.[532] The 3rd Battalion was not on the front lines anyway.

Opposing the 89th Division was the German 13th Division, which was working at a furious pace to fortify its own positions with an enormous shortage of personnel. The 13th had been in continuous combat since October 1, and had just 569 effective men remaining in its three frontline regiments, exclusive of their machine gun and mortar units. Behind the front lines, this German division had 1,367 recruits, of which only 120 could be used in the near future due to their supportive roles, lack of training, or injury or illness.[533]

Although the 13th Division was in no condition to drive the 89th Division out of the Bois de Bantheville with its infantry, its artillery continued to bombard the Americans with high-explosives and gas shells. The 89th Division had little artillery support at the time, forcing them to endure the German artillery attacks with no means of retaliation.[534]

After the 354th Infantry Regiment was shelled again on the night of October 25-26, Colonel Babcock asked General Winn to permit him to pull his forces back from the front line, citing that they were being pounded by artillery and gas on a nightly basis. "I have investigated the outpost line in the Bois de Bantheville and find even the high ground shelled strongly with gas," Babcock writes, "and numerous men stationed there were more or less affected. From my experience in the gas today and from the number of working parties, ammunition carriers, engineers and others found in the gassed area, and food details going up to the 353rd infantry, it is very possible that there will be many more gas casualties during the next 24 hours. The woods seemed to be saturated with gas and the sunshine is bringing it out over a vast area."[535]

Winn courageously, albeit reluctantly, took a chance at being rebuked by General Pershing and authorized Babcock to reduce the number of frontline companies to two. Babcock immediately withdrew the 1st Battalion from the front lines. In its place, he had Company G take up an advance position in the northernmost part of the Bois de Romagne, and had Company H occupy the western portion of the Bois de Bantheville. These companies, he decided, would maintain strong outposts and machine gun positions, capable of holding the front line.[536]

Sometime between October 25 and October 27, Charlie and Jess suffered the effects of poisonous gas, on a much larger scale than casual contact. Although not subjected to direct shelling, they were introduced into the heavily saturated woods where decontamination had not taken place. Their respective families remain convinced that their untimely deaths were due in some part to gas exposure during the war. In Charlie's case, the Veterans Administration repeatedly denied his claims for compensation, maintaining that there was no evidence of exposure. Following his death, however, an autopsy revealed that Charlie had in fact been gassed during the war.

"The lungs are rather subcrepitant* throughout," the Medical Examiner notes in Charlie's autopsy report. "On section thru the lower lobes of both lungs they are moderately congested and hemorrhagic. One or two dense fibrosis adhesions are present between the visceral and parietal pleura on the right side, and one small thin band is present on the left side. A small healed tubercle is also present in the lower portion of the upper left lobe of the lung which measures 1 cm. in diameter."[537]

On October 28, 1918, and again the following evening, Colonel Babcock sent platoons from companies of his support and reserve battalions to relieve platoons from companies that had been in or were positioned on the front lines. On the evening of the 29th, Company L dispatched a 42-man platoon to relieve a platoon in Company C, which was then under heavy artillery fire.[538] One shell hit a dead tree and exploded about five feet in front of Jess Funk. He felt a terrible pain in his left foot, and his first thought was that it had been severed, but when he looked down, the foot was still there. Jess grabbed ahold of his foot, wiggled it around a bit, and decided that he was all right, so he turned his attention to the wounded men around him.[539]

Private Louis Golden, also from Company L, was lying on the ground screaming, having had an eye put out and his nose blown off. Jess rushed over to administer first aid, and was momentarily joined by Private Thomas Sweeney of Company M. Upon applying bandages to Golden's wounds, Jess and Sweeney were detailed by a sergeant to help other wounded troops back to the dressing station.[540]

When the sergeant realized that Jess had been wounded, he ordered him to the first aid station for treatment. "That little hole in my leg didn't amount to shucks," Jess later remarked, downplaying its severity. "They put some iodine on it and it felt fine."[541] Actually, the medical officer treating Jess had him hospitalized, but released him the following day, after Jess insisted upon returning to his Chauchat team at the front.[542]

---

* Crepitant denotes a fine bubbling noise produced by air entering fluid in lung tissue; heard in pneumonia and in certain other conditions. Subcrepitant would indicate that Charlie's lungs were partially affected by this affliction.

Many of Charlie and Jess' exploits are not recorded in the unit's history, but to those who served with them, their repetitive feats of bravery were very well-known. Colonel Babcock, who would soon praise Charlie's heroic actions, would also remark that he was so "underdeveloped mentally" that he had no real concept of fear. That was an unfair statement, and one that still upsets the family to this day. The Medal of Honor rolls are filled with heroes from all walks of life, all educational levels, all shapes and sizes. Their common bond: fearlessness in combat.

"Then there was Charlie Barger," Jess Funk recalled. "He came from down at Stotts City, Missouri, and he'd never had much of a chance in life. He was an automatic Chauchat gunner; I was his carrier, and I used to write his letters for him and I got to know him pretty well. He was scared, too—just as badly scared as any of us, but he had the grit to put it all behind him, and what was more, he'd force it down so far that he could cheer up the other fellows. Believe me, he sure had grit, and I'm proud to have been the running mate of a man that had as much fight in him as he had.

"But don't think we weren't scared, because we were! I remember one fellow in our company who would just lie and quiver and shake when the firing started, but when the signal came for him to go over the top, he was right there. To my mind, he was one of the bravest fellows in the company. When a man can realize that he's liable to be killed any minute, and can force down his fear and make a good fight, he's a brave man in my estimation. And every time I saw that fellow quivering and shaking, it used to give me new heart, because I knew that here was a good example to follow, that here was a man who was brave clear thru and that as long as I could keep up with him, I'd be doing my part."[543]

General Winn estimated that the 354th Infantry Regiment lost 28 killed, 105 wounded, and 211 gassed between October 19 and 29; the 353rd lost 52 killed, 265 wounded, and 38 gassed; and the 341st Machine Gun Battalion, which served with them, suffered 11 killed, 66 wounded and 15 gassed. "Notwithstanding the losses [791 officers and men] on account of shells and gas, the morale and spirits of the men remain fine," Winn concluded in his report.[544]

On the night of October 29-30, the German 88th Division relieved the German 13th Division, which was positioned opposite the U.S. 89th Division. The 88th had met the 89th Division once before, in the St. Mihiel region, and was considered a high-rated division, fully capable of battle. Throughout the night, the Germans maintained harassing artillery fire on the 89th Division's frontline troops, firing 600 high-explosive and 130 Blue Cross rounds upon the Americans. This artillery fire encompassed the northernmost sector of the Bois de Bantheville, and traversed all the way down to the Romagne-Sommerance road. Special emphasis was placed on the north and west edges of the Bois de Bantheville, and the vicinity of Robinette Farm where batteries of the 89th Division were situated.[545]

Everything that Charlie had learned about combat up to this time— every bit of training, every single experience, every patrol in which he had participated, everything he heard from others during their combat exploits—had come down to the last two weeks of the Meuse-Argonne offensive. His unit having been held in reserve, occupying secondary lines, or simply enduring endless artillery barrages, was now a thing of the past. Company L, the 177th Brigade, the 354th Infantry Regiment, and Charlie himself, would go on the offensive, and would stay on the offensive until the Armistice on November 11. Charlie proved to be up to the challenge, and what follows is the stuff of legend.

Chapter Eleven

BRAVEST OF THE BRAVE

In two short months, Charlie Barger had evolved into the consummate soldier, perfectly adapting to the rigors of military life and exhibiting repetitive bravery which often went unnoticed to those outside his platoon. Heroism, of course, has many tiers, and Charlie had by this time nearly run the gamut, whether formally recognized or not. Now would come the supreme challenge, which would set him apart from the pantheon of heroes in the American Expeditionary Forces and propel him into the ranks of the bravest of the brave, the recipients of the Medal of Honor.

The German 13th Division held the sector opposite American 89th Division outposts until the night of October 29-30, 1918. During their time in the Bantheville sector, this German division organized its positions in a series of staggered machine gun nests, concentrated in strength in the neighborhood of La Dhuy Farm.[546] La Dhuy Farm was a German strong point and consisted of several stone buildings situated along a road that was, and is, the main route between the villages of Landres-et-St. Georges and Bantheville. Today, the stretch of road that passes by La Dhuy Farm is designated D24.

German forces along the front had been withdrawing for several days prior to the end of October, yet on the night of October 29, the German 88th Division moved up to relieve the 13th Division. German morale had generally plummeted by this time, but not within their highly rated 88th. Even though there were some older replacements within its ranks, most were young, vigorous, aggressive soldiers, prepared to slug it out with American forces. To make matters worse for the American 89th Division, the German 13th Division did not immediately withdraw, but spent the next couple of days assuming support positions for the 88th. This meant that the 13th Division could provide immediate backup for the 88th Division when the Americans launched their renewed general assault on November 1.[547]

The 354th Infantry Regiment, to which Charlie was assigned, carried on active patrolling during this time with a view to determining the enemy's

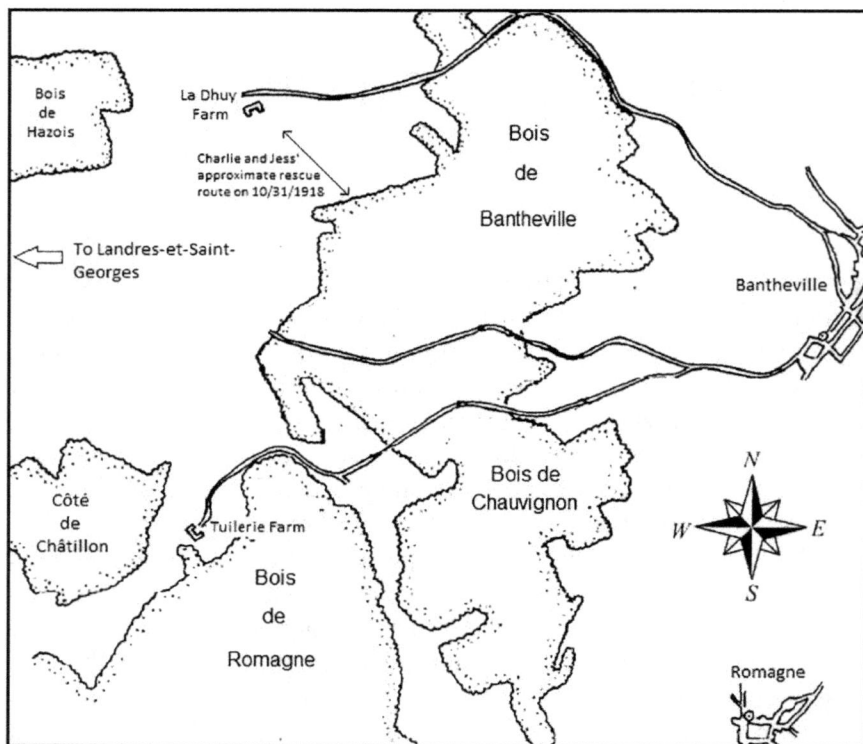

Bois
de
Hazois

La Dhuy
Farm

Charlie and Jess'
approximate rescue
route on 10/31/1918

To Landres-et-Saint-
Georges

Bois
de
Bantheville

Bantheville

Côté
de
Châtillon

Tuilerie Farm

Bois
de
Chauvignon

N
W   E
S

Bois
de
Romagne

Romagne

THE BANTHEVILLE SECTOR

Credit: Adapted from a map in The 89th Division in the Bois de Bantheville, October 1918, *by Rexmond C. Cochrane. U.S. Army Chemical Corps Historical Office, Office of the Chief Chemical Officer, Washington, DC, Study No. 18, June 1960.*

strength and possible intentions.[548] It was apparent to these patrols that the Germans considered this front vital to their line of defense and intended to hold it for as long as possible. Once this line was breached, the Germans would fall back upon their main line of defense along the rugged crest of the Bois d'Andevanne and in the formidable Bois de Barricourt.[549]

The 354th Infantry Regiment held a one-mile line, southwest to northeast, from the easternmost edge of the Côté de Châtillon through several hundred yards of the Bois de Bantheville. The regiment's left flank, positioned north of the Bois de Romagne, was almost totally exposed, while more than half of the regiment's right flank was concealed in the Bois de Bantheville. North of the line, on the right flank, was open ground, sloping gently to a long valley, in effect a glacis, beyond which was road D24 and La Dhuy Farm.[550]

On the afternoon of October 30, the company to which Charlie was assigned, Company L, was positioned on the 354th Infantry Regiment's right flank. From Company L's vantage point, they could see a German observation balloon to the north, near Rémonville, which was being used to monitor the American's 89th Division's movements and to direct artillery fire on the 89th's forward positions. Observation balloons were typically positioned beyond the range of artillery and other weapons fire, making fighter aircraft the only feasible means of destroying them.

One might think that such a large object, hovering high in the air, would be an easy target for fighter aircraft to destroy, but balloons were defended by anti-aircraft fire and fighter aircraft. If an attack appeared probable or imminent, ground crews would rapidly lower the oval-shaped balloons to the ground, where the attacking fighter would be susceptible to machine gun and small arms fire. These balloons were, in fact, such formidable targets that most, but not all, American pilots avoided them.

At 4:35 p.m., on October 30, a lone Spad XIII fighter aircraft, piloted by an American, destroyed a German fighter plane near Saint-Juvin, about six miles southwest of Rémonville. Immediately thereafter, the Spad pilot noticed the observation balloon, which had been monitoring the 89th Division's movements and was still hovering overhead near Rémonville. When the German ground crew assigned to the observation balloon noticed the American aviator making a beeline in their direction, they worked furiously to haul the balloon down.[551]

German anti-aircraft fire erupted all around the Spad as the American aviator came within range of the balloon's defending guns, but the pilot remained undeterred. The balloon was nearly on the ground when the pilot turned sharply, dived, and fired several long bursts from his 11mm Vickers machine guns, which had special incendiary bullets that were ideal for destroying enemy balloons. From Company L's vantage point, along the north edge of the Bois de Bantheville, Charlie and his fellow soldiers could have witnessed the balloon being destroyed, and the pall of black smoke and flames ascending into the heavens. The men assigned to Charlie's company and regiment would never know the historical significance of this engagement, as it the last aerial victory secured by the American Ace of Aces, Eddie Rickenbacker.[552]

For several days prior to October 30, enemy activity along the front above the Bois de Bantheville had been negligible.[553] From the air, American reconnaissance pilots would have observed all the activity occurring near La Dhuy Farm, as the German 88th Division relieved the German 13th Division. Evidently, these reconnaissance pilots mistook this relief as the Germans withdrawing, for a report was received at 89th Division headquarters around dusk on the 30th that the enemy had completely withdrawn from La Dhuy Farm and the surrounding area.[554]

Foot soldiers, assigned to the 353rd and 354th Infantry Regiments, 89th Division, engaging in reconnaissance patrols, repudiated the Air Service's report. Their patrols revealed that German machine gun crews were discovered all along the front, holding the enemy's position "in force and with determination." Throughout the day of October 30, the brigade also saw an increase in harassing enemy artillery fire, as 460 high-explosive and 420 Blue Cross shells were fired in and around the Bois de Bantheville. Throughout the night of October 30-31, light and heavy German artillery guns fired 500 high-explosive and 290 Blue Cross rounds into the Bois de Bantheville, the ravine on the east side of the woods, and the roads used by the Americans.[555]

"In the last order to its artillery," writes Rexmond Cochrane, "as it waited relief after thirty full days in the line, the [German] 13th Division ordered annihilation fire at 0710 on the 31st [of October] across the top of the Bois de Bantheville [towards the 177th Brigade, 89th Division] by both its light and heavy guns, assisted by the 41st Division artillery on its right. During the day targets in Bantheville woods and as far south as Robinette Farm (Transvaal Farm) were kept under harassment, with 810 HE and 150 blue cross shells allotted for the period."[556]

Colonel Babcock knew that any impediment to the 354th Infantry Regiment's advance could keep the 89th Division from progressing in unison with its neighboring divisions when, on November 1, the American general assault upon the Germans would commence. If a delay occurred to the 354th, the enemy could flank regimental lines and destroy Babcock's regiment. To determine precisely what his troops were up against, he made the difficult decision to dispatch two daylight patrols from the 3rd Battalion to reconnoiter the open terrain between the regimental line and road D24.

First Lieutenant Ernest G. Rowell of Company I, and Second Lieutenant John Millis, Charlie's platoon commander of Company L, led their respective patrols from the sheltered woods. Each patrol consisted of 25 enlisted men, which included four noncommissioned officers, appropriately dispersed to minimize casualties if attacked by enemy artillery shell or machine gun fire. Crouching down, and occasionally low-crawling across the muddy terrain, they traversed the high open ground, and then descended into the glacis beyond. Although they proceeded slowly and cautiously, the Germans spotted the patrols and quickly deployed several machine gun squads and a complement of riflemen.[557]

The initial three-second bursts from the machine guns caught the patrols completely by surprise. Millis and Rowell were severely wounded in the first moments of the attack and could not retreat, but they ordered their troops to withdraw immediately and by any means possible. Machine gun fire was deafening as all semblance of military order vanished. It would be ludicrous for the Americans to advance and further, and extremely difficult for them to withdraw.[558]

Those unable to make it out of the field in the first minutes of the initial attack—and not so severely wounded that they could not escape—inched their way back into the woods. Enemy machine gunners, who could oversee the entire expanse wherein the 354th's patrols were spread out, scanned the terrain for any movement whatsoever. An occasional burst from one of the machine guns let the Americans know that one of their own had been spotted. Millis and Rowell were likely by now coming to terms with the realization that rescue was impossible and that the odds of their own survival were practically nil.

Sergeant Charles F. Kelly, of Company L, eventually made his way back to 354th headquarters to inform Colonel Babcock that Millis and Rowell were alive, but added that they were severely wounded and openly exposed to enemy machine gun fire.[559] Babcock had a difficult decision to make about whether to order any of his soldiers to undertake the mission to rescue Millis and Rowell. The thought of those two brave officers alone in that field with no hope of survival was likely gut-wrenching, even to Babcock, who was known as an emotionless commander that had witnessed death in many forms during his time in uniform.

Any soldiers undertaking such a mission would have to run more than 500 yards through No Man's Land under the most intense barrage of machine gun and rifle fire imaginable. If they reached one of the officers, they would have to load him onto a stretcher while in a stationary position as every enemy gun was trained directly on them. Then, if they made it that far, they would have to run 500 yards back through the same hail of bullets at a much slower pace while virtually erect. To retrieve the other officer, they would have to repeat this process. After careful consideration, Colonel Babcock decided against ordering his men to rescue Millis and Rowell, for that would be tantamount to murder.

Charlie, standing nearby, overheard Kelly reporting Millis and Rowell's predicament. Charlie's respect for and appreciation of Lieutenant Millis was particularly warm. Millis treated Charlie better than any officer he had come across since entering the military and he was not about to leave him out there to die. "Lieutenant John Millis of Kentucky was one of the wounded officers," Charlie would tell a reporter upon returning to Missouri. "As soon as I heard who was out there, I volunteered to go, because all the men loved Lieutenant Millis, and I would have done anything for him."[560]

"Grab a stretcher and we'll bring the lieutenant in!" Charlie called to Jess as he tossed him a Red Cross brassard.[561]

In donning those brassards, Charlie and Jess were ostensibly under protection of Article 9 of the Geneva Convention of July 6, 1906, which states: "The personnel engaged exclusively in the collection, transport, and treatment of the wounded and the sick, as well as in the administration of medical units and establishments, and the Chaplains attached to armies, shall be respected and protected under all circumstances. If they fall into the hands of the enemy they shall not be treated as prisoners of war."[562]

Contrary to popular belief, stretcher bearers were authorized to be armed "for the protection of themselves and their patients," and Charlie and Jess would undertake this mission with pistols strapped to their hip.[563] But here's the glitch: regimental stretcher bearers were not exclusively engaged in care of the wounded, which meant they were not entitled to protection under the Geneva Convention. They were not even entitled to wear the Red Cross brassard.

Charlie and Jess knew that they, as infantrymen, were not under protection of the Geneva Convention, and they also knew that the Germans would ignore the brassards anyhow. Nonetheless, anything they could do to increase the dismal odds of survival for Millis and Rowell was worth a shot.

Colonel Babcock was not warm to Charlie's idea. "Barger," Babcock exclaimed, "you haven't one chance in 5,000 of making that trip! I'm not going to stop you from trying, but I want you to understand that this is entirely a voluntary proposition. That applies to Funk, too."[564]

"Well, Colonel, I'll take the chance," Charlie responded. "Funk said he would, too."[565]

Babcock, in absolute awe of their courage, shook their hands and wished them luck. As they departed camp, lugging the stretcher, Jess casually asked Charlie, "How's your nerves?"[566]

"Nerves, hell," he responded, "I ain't got any."[567]

"He sure was calm," Jess revealed to his father after the war. "That fellow sure had the stuff in him, Dad! He sure was game!"[568]

It was about 10:00 a.m., when Charlie and Jess emerged from the woods and started across the open field, crouching down and zigzagging to avoid becoming an easy target. Almost immediately, there was an initial rat-tat-tat from the enemy's machine guns. Troops assigned to the 354th Infantry Regiment, posted at the edge of the woods, momentarily glanced up, and then did a double-take. No one witnessing Charlie and Jess' heroic feats that day could believe the audacity of these two men!

Suddenly, the distinct sound of uninterrupted machine gun and rifle fire echoed across the open terrain, compelling the American soldiers to inch toward the wooded perimeter to see firsthand what was happening. At first, the onlooking soldiers stood in stunned silence, but as Charlie and Jess progressed under firing German guns, their comrades began to hoot and holler, cheering them on as fans would cheer a major-league football player running the length of the field to score the winning touchdown.

American retaliatory fire to provide cover for Charlie and Jess would have placed them in danger of crossfire, and would have been a waste of ammunition. In fact, small arms fire would have fallen short of the German machine gun emplacements, and the 354h Infantry Regiment's Vickers machine guns, with an effective range of 2,187 yards, would have no effect upon the enemy's machine gun fortifications. The use of artillery was also out of the question. The 155mm Howitzers were not designed for pinpoint accuracy, and never used for individual rescue operations. The 75mm artillery guns and three-inch Stokes mortars, by this time in the war, used high-explosive shells exclusively, which burst above the ground and would likely have killed Charlie, Jess, Millis and Rowell.

"Dad, I was scared," Jess confessed. "Those darned machine-gun bullets were just singing songs around us and I figured every minute they were going to get us. You bet I was scared!"[569]

Jess had every reason to be.

In his memoirs, Colonel Babcock provided an accurate depiction of the psychological effect of machine gun fire: "In some respects the machine gun bullets were, to us, the most terrifying. The bullets, following one another in thousands of files, sounded to me like giant shears cutting a mile-wide sheet of tin. Although these bullets were clearing the trees under which we waited 'H' hour, it really took quite a bit of mental effort to stand up; it was hard to believe those bullets weren't flying right past one's head."[570]

Of course, in Charlie and Jess's case, the bullets *were* flying right past their heads!

George English adds: "This weapon, firing small arms ammunition, had more than fifty times the firepower of the rifle. A handful of machine guns, distributed over a given front and manned by very few men, was capable of delivering as great a volume of fire as a whole regiment of infantry armed with the rifle; and furthermore, the gun being mounted on a fixed base, this fire could be kept low and thus be made more effective against masses of troops."[571]

In the case of Charlie and Jess, the Germans weren't up against "masses of troops." They weren't even up against adversaries that were about to fight back. Their target was two American soldiers, lugging a cumbersome stretcher across an open, muddy, shell-pocked field, completely exposed and defenseless against weapons that were known to rip men apart in a fraction of a second ... and in broad daylight no less! It was a proverbial turkey shoot and the odds were stacked against Charlie and Jess a thousand-fold.

"We hadn't gone twenty yards before the Jerries opened up on us," explained Charlie. "The air seemed to be full of machine gun bullets. Then the rifles opened up. The noise was deafening. We took up a run and zigzagged, but the fire stayed right with us. A bullet spun my helmet halfway around and I felt one tear through my first aid packet. One whanged into my pistol, and another slapped me across the kneecap and I nearly went down. Jess was getting every bit as much as I was.

"We made it to the patrol, found them [Millis and Rowell] less than a hundred yards from a nest of four machine guns, the guns from all the nests firing directly at us. We started to pick up Lieutenant Millis, but he ordered us to take Lieutenant Rowell, another officer, who had been severely wounded."*

Charlie and Jess relocated Millis to a place of relative safety, and then reentered the line of enemy fire, which was ongoing. Crouching down, they traversed the field forward and oblique of Millis' position, all the while dodging craters left by artillery shells. The fervent rifle and machine gun fire ripped through the air with such intensity that the battlefield around them was a tumultuous scene filled with ricocheting bullets and unadulterated pandemonium. Making matters worse, the German force was no flimflam unit, but a crack machine gun outfit with years of combat experience. Charlie and Jess' survival was not simply a matter of skill, but that of exceptional courage and the grace of a merciful God.

"We placed Lieutenant Rowell on the stretcher and made the trip back," Charlie stated.[572]

"All the time I was figuring that if I could just get hit a little bit—you know, shot somewhere so that it would stop me from getting back in again!"

---

* For refusing evacuation and ordering his men to return without him when he was severely wounded, Millis would receive an oak leaf cluster to his Distinguished Service Cross.

Jess admitted. "But shucks, not one of 'em touched us, and we just kept zigzagging on, and every once in a while, Charlie would say something funny or stop and cuss a sniper, and I just couldn't help but keep up with the procession."[573]

"We arrived completely winded and with our clothing shot to rags," Charlie stated, "but we were not injured. Men in the trenches took the stretcher and we flopped to the ground."[574]

Upon catching their breath, they started out again, both men dashing into the open to face the hail of bullets from machine guns and automatic rifles.[575] This time they knew what they were up against and that the odds of survival had deteriorated dramatically. The only thing they had going for them was adrenalin, for the Germans were more prepared than ever to stop them dead in their tracks.

Nearly every able-bodied man assigned to the 354th had by now occupied the wooded perimeter, seeking to observe the most heroic feat they had ever witnessed. Officers and men pushed forward for a better view; others craned their necks around taller men to catch intermittent glimpses of Charlie and Jess. Every millisecond they expected one or both to be killed, but held their breath and offered silent prayers that their mission would somehow succeed.

Lieutenant Millis, not expecting Charlie and Jess to return, had since crawled thirty yards away from enemy lines to a large shell hole in the ground, which he decided to use for cover until he was rested enough to continue his trek out of the open field. When he reached the hole, however, he fell in and couldn't get out due to seven bullet wounds in one leg, which was broken, and two bullet wounds in the other. It was indeed a frustrating impasse!

"Here he was, with his leg broken, laying out there in a shell-hole and with not a chance for life, it seemed," Jess recalled. "But when we came up to him, he didn't have a word to say about what a tough time he'd had, or the danger that he'd been in. He just made some gritty, joking remark about having crawled into the shell-hole and not being able to get out again."[576]

Charlie lowered himself into the hole, hunkered beside the lieutenant, and directly assessed his injuries. He was in terrible condition. "You can't make it back," Millis protested, and then insisted that Charlie leave him there.

"We did it before," Charlie reasoned, and without another word he heaved the lieutenant over his shoulder and lifted him from the hole. Jess moved up to help load Millis onto the stretcher, and they immediately started back across the open field and into another hail of bullets.

"The stretcher was hit several times and I saw bullets slash open the seat of Jesse's pants," Charlie confirmed. "A bullet cut the canvas under the lieutenant from side to side, but he was not hit."[577]

"Time after time when we were coming back with Lieutenant Millis the machine gun bullets were hitting pretty close to us," Jess stated. "[Charlie would] say something that would take my whole mind off of the danger, and would help us to get along a lot faster. We had 500 yards to go, and two or three times the bullets hit the stretcher we were carrying—and two or three times it looked like we weren't going to get in at all. But Charlie always had something to say that would keep us plugging on, and it sure helped a lot. Now, that's real bravery! Here he was, in constant danger of his life, but he didn't forget there were others in the same fix, and it was mighty keen cutting on his part to play the game the way he did."

From the beginning, Charlie and Jess were subconsciously aware that their mud-caked boots slowed their progress, and in the wetter areas they could feel the suction as they lifted their boots to take their next step. At least once on the return trip with Lieutenant Millis, Jess stumbled and lost his grip on the handles of the stretcher, but Charlie forged ahead, dragging the wounded lieutenant several yards until his partner could regain control of his end.[578] Finally, they turned into a wooded area below their own company, having saved Millis from certain death.

But they weren't quite finished.

"Well," stated Jess, "on the way back we saw another fellow crawling around out there and we thought it would be mighty low and mean to leave him out there. But right then we was awful busy. The snipers and the machine guns were banging away at us and I remember the lieutenant saying: 'Boys, never shoot at a wounded man.'* We promised we wouldn't and we managed to lug him back. Then we got to thinking about that other fellow out there, and we figured it wouldn't be right to leave him, so we started back again."[579]

That man was Private Philip B. Montoya. Montoya was born in 1889 in Las Vegas, New Mexico, to Santiago and Estafana Montoya, and had two older brothers, Ramon and Edward. After his father died, Montoya followed Edward in the printing business, and later ventured to Stockton, California, where he worked as a farm laborer for Tony Soares on Roberts Island. By 1918, Montoya relocated to Denver, Colorado, where, in March, he was drafted into the Army. His brother, Edward, would later state that Philip always wanted to be a soldier, even when they played with wooden guns as children.

Now Montoya was lying in that open field and fighting for his life. The rain of bullets continued until Charlie and Jess reached the wounded private, and then there was complete silence. "The German machine guns ceased firing and the machine gunners stood up and watched us," Charlie

---

*   Millis was referring to shooting at a German soldier who was wounded and defenseless on the battlefield.

disclosed. "It was not an act of goodwill; they just couldn't understand why we hadn't been killed long before."[580]

Charlie, possessing nerves of steel, surprised even Jess when he sat down the stretcher and walked within spitting distance of the nearest machine gun. He warned the gunners that he'd be back in a day or two to "blast 'em out of there," and then returned to rescue Montoya. It didn't matter whether the German understood him; he meant what he said and their fate was sealed.[581]

"He [Montoya] was about thirty yards from a German machine gun when we got to him," Jess acknowledged. "He was actually crawling <u>toward</u> German lines. It was kind of hot there then. Well, we gathered this fellow up and started back with him. We'd gone a hundred yards when one machine gun bullet got him just above the heart, and then another went thru his head, about six inches from my stomach. Gosh, it scared me! But Charlie just looked over his shoulder and said some fool thing, and everything was all right again.

"Well, we were pretty badly shaken up after we got back. We realized we'd been plumb next door to death! I don't know about Charlie, but I sure got as weak as a cat. So the new lieutenant who'd been sent in to relieve Lieutenant Millis said we could have time off from all duties and get some sleep. That sure was nice of him, because we were kind of shaky."[582]

At a train station in St. Louis, Missouri, after the war, a reporter asked Charlie how he felt after the incident. "Well," Charlie replied, "it was just like stepping off this train. I wasn't worried at all during the forty-five minutes it took to bring the officers in, but I sure was worried afterwards, when I got to thinking about it."[583]

Montoya had been wounded five times during the ordeal, and his misfortune continued even after the medics dressed his wounds. Stretcher bearers loaded him into an ambulance, and just as the vehicle sped away from the aid station, an artillery shell exploded directly in front of it. The driver, who may have been killed in the blast, veered off the road and crashed into a tree. Montoya was killed instantly.

Montoya is not named in regimental or division histories, other than being killed in action, but the fact that he was crawling toward the enemy indicates that, despite his wounds, he was seeking to take out a machine gun nest. There were countless men who were never recognized for such heroic feats, so this was not an anomaly. It is enigmatic, however, that he was never mentioned when details of Charlie and Jess' heroism emerged, and his rescue was even excluded from their Medal of Honor citations. Perhaps this was because he died in the ambulance accident; perhaps it was because he was an enlisted man.

When Montoya's death reached his mother, she was devastated. It was later learned that his brother, Edward, was just ten miles from where Philip was killed. Montoya was buried in France until April 1922, and then his remains were returned to New Mexico via the funeral ship *Cantigna*. He is interred in the Santa Fe National Cemetery in Santa Fe, New Mexico.

Unbeknownst to Charlie and Jess, Private William Hillery, a runner assigned to Company L, who had been wounded while on patrol with Lieutenant Millis, and Privates Ernest C. Bork and Pete Collins, of Company I, had also been cut off by machine gun fire. As the day waned on, the Germans demanded that they surrender, but they refused. Digging in with their mess kits, they remained in No Man's Land until dusk, and then managed to return to friendly lines.

Charlie and Jess were under the impression that Lieutenant Rowell succumbed to his wounds, but he was very much alive. After the war, he returned to New Hampshire, married twice, and had a daughter named Natalie from his second marriage. He became an insurance agent and broker, eventually making his way to Glendale, California. He died in San Bernardino County on April 13, 1963, at the age of sixty-nine.

Although the 354th Infantry Regiment's daylight patrols had been stopped far short of their objective, the intelligence they gathered was indispensable. Rowell's patrol had found hollows west of La Dhuy Farm that were full of gas—the probable reason that the regiment had not encountered German troops that far north.[584] The 354th would completely bypass those areas the following morning.

The daylight patrols were also credited with determining enemy strength and fighting positions, which would expedite the regiment's advance. Colonel Babcock stated in his memoirs that the enemy was "holding their rear with hundreds of light and heavy machine guns and relatively small forces of infantry, and about half as much artillery as we had."[585] Millis, Rowell, and their men, had indeed fulfilled their mission, but Charlie still had one bit of unfinished business to complete before moving on from the Bantheville sector.

Chapter Twelve

VICTORY!

On the morning of November 1, 1918, intense preparation for the renewed American advance charged the atmosphere. At daybreak, the fight would break out all along the Meuse-Argonne front. Brigades, regiments, battalions and companies sparked last-minute adjustments in the line. Headquarters elements were rife with activity. Combat patrols increased. Commanders ordered their men to assemble their equipment. Then, at precisely 3:30 a.m., the thundering artillery barrage that preceded every American advance filled the air with chunks of earth and whistling metal. Over the next two hours, the Americans launched almost 60,000 high-explosive shells to destroy and soften German frontline positions in the Meuse-Argonne region.[586]

Amid all of this excitement, Charlie was preoccupied with some unfinished business he had to take care of. During the rescue of Private Montoya on the previous day, Charlie had told the German machine gunners firing at him that he'd return to "blast 'em out of there," and he had every intention of keeping that promise. But first, he had to secure authorization to carry out this mission from his company commander.

Being a Chauchat gunner, Charlie's request to his company commander to go back and destroy the German nest might have been declined; Chauchat gunners, after all, were critical to the advance. However, every enemy outpost destroyed prior to H-hour (set for 5:30 a.m.) would facilitate the regiment's advance. Based upon this higher goal, Charlie built the case to his company commander that taking out "his" enemy nest would also go to support the regimental advance.

First Lieutenant Vernon E. Bates, then commanding Company L, was the company's last remaining officer; all others had been killed, wounded or hospitalized by November 1. Bates was receptive to Charlie's proposal, as there were several other fighting patrols venturing into No Man's Land at the time with the express purpose of causing loss and damage to the enemy's outposts. These patrols were, of course, armed and authorized to attack specific targets and targets of opportunity.[587] Charlie was permitted to go forward with his plan.

At Charlie's request, Bates also authorized Jess Funk to accompany Charlie to serve as his assistant gunner/ammunition carrier. By this time, Charlie and Jess had formed a particularly close bond. They were comparably courageous, although Jess, by his own admission, did not take many of the same risks that Charlie had taken. He did, however, come to trust Charlie's approach and ability in combat, and they worked exceptionally well together.

Sometime between 4:30 and 5:00 a.m., Charlie and Jess crossed into No Man's Land, braving explosions from American artillery shells, and approached the area where they knew the enemy machine gun nest to be. "Private Barger and another soldier [Funk] crawled around the German machine gun nest and opened fire from the rear with an automatic rifle, advancing as they fired, and capturing the entire crews and guns of the nest, consisting of 12 men and six guns," reveals Charlie's citation for the Croix de Guerre with bronze palm.

Charlie and Jess began to return to their lines right about H-hour, just as American artillery units proceeded to fire white phosphorus shells into No Man's Land. These white phosphorous shells created a non-toxic smokescreen wall, which would allow the Americans to advance across the field undetected. However, these shells also produced an initial explosion, capable of killing soldiers on the battlefield who were in close proximity.[588] Charlie, Jess, and their prisoners were right in the midst of it all!

The barrage of white phosphorous shelling into No Man's Land kept Colonel Babcock's units from advancing until ten minutes after H-hour. This delay was certainly frustrating to Babcock, as he made an extraordinarily optimistic wager that within fifteen minutes of H-hour the 354th Infantry Regiment would have taken enemy prisoners. He had just about given up hope when, at precisely 5:40 a.m., there appeared out of the smoke and fog Charlie and Jess with a dozen prisoners in tow![589] Babcock had won his bet, against all odds, that his unit would capture prisoners within the first 15 minutes of H-hour, and with five minutes to spare!

The white phosphorous shelling had since ceased, but the smokescreen remained, permitting American divisions all along the Meuse-Argonne front to advance across No Man's Land in unison. The 354th Infantry Regiment was represented by Companies C and D of the 1st Battalion, which pushed forward under the protection of machine guns and a rolling artillery barrage.[590] In a scenario characteristic of Hollywood, the men of Company D advanced toward enemy lines through the smokescreen and fog, chomping on cigars, which were purchased from the YMCA by two of their officers sometime earlier.[591]

One could only imagine the eeriness experienced by the German soldiers as 200 ghostly forms emerged from the fog, with bayonets affixed and cigars clenched tightly between their teeth![592] According to George English, many enemy soldiers surrendered upon seeing the frightening apparitions, and even more retreated. The 89th Division's numerical superiority may have also been a factor, as the division started out that morning with 12,000 riflemen, and German riflemen numbered just 2,300.[593]

"Almost immediately after the jump-off," writes English, "the assault companies of the 3rd Battalion, 353rd Infantry, were met by withering machine gun fire from the woods north of Bois de Bantheville, which delayed the advance and caused severe casualties. First Lieutenant Harold A. Furlong, arming himself with a rifle, went ahead of his line, crossing an open space several hundred yards wide and attained a position on the flank and to the rear of the enemy's machine guns. From this point he closed in on them, and one by one silenced their fire, killing a number of the machine gunners himself by his fire and driving twenty of them as prisoners into our lines. For this deed, he was awarded the Medal of Honor."[594]

The reader may recall that General Pershing's objective for the Meuse-Argonne offensive was to seize the city of Sedan, the hub of Germany's regional supply route, which lay 35 miles from the Bois de Bantheville.[595] Taking control of this particular supply route, a 40-miles line extending southeast to northwest between the French cities of Carignan, Sedan and Charleville-Mézières, would almost certainly result in the defeat of half of the German Army.[596] Sedan, however, would never be reached, as the American Army would defeat the Germans at the halfway point, just after crossing the Meuse River.

The 89th Division would cross the Meuse at Pouilly, about eighteen miles north of the Bois de Bantheville jump-off line. Towards pursuing that objective, General Pershing ordered the 89th to take the heights of Barricourt by midnight on November 1. These heights were about 1,000 yards south of, and overlooking, the village of Barricourt.[597]

Between the Bois de Bantheville and the heights of Barricourt were a series of German strong points through which the 89th Division would have to pass. Chief among them were the Bois d'Andevanne and the village of Rémonville. Most enemy artillery fire that targeted the division over the past week had originated from these two strong points, so the Americans were certain that they would face tough resistance in those sectors.[598]

The 89th Division's clash against German forces defending the perimeter of the Bois d'Andevanne was indeed brutal, leaving the surrounding battlefield littered with casualties from both sides. Once the division breached this German perimeter, however, the enemy all but abandoned the Bois d'Andevanne, and the 89th Division cleared the

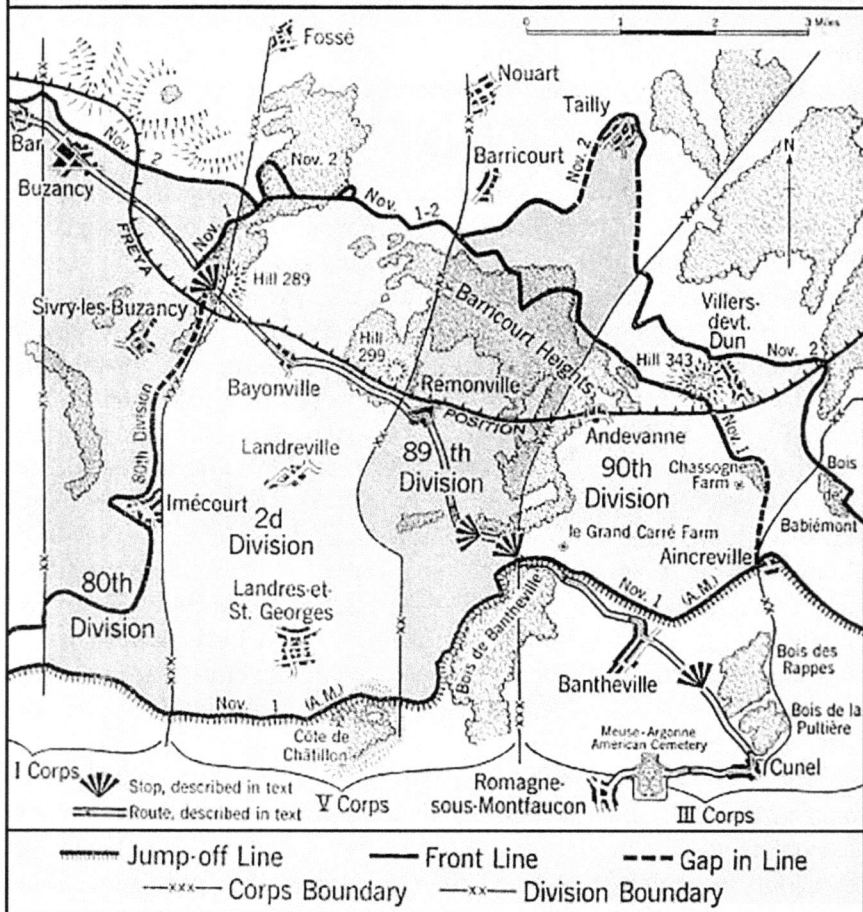

GROUND GAINED NEAR BARRICOURT HEIGHTS,
NOVEMBER 1-2, 1918

Credit: American Battle Monuments Commission. 2d Division, Summary of Operations in the World War. *Washington, DC: U.S. Government Printing Office, 1944.*

woods of enemy forces with little resistance. Now, the division's 353rd and 354th Infantry Regiments pressed forward to the strongly fortified town of Rémonville where each clump of trees along the town's approaches had German machine gun nests, and hastily assembled enemy barricades lined the streets.[599]

To minimize casualties and avoid serious opposition as they approached Rémonville, the 354th Infantry Regiment continued to follow the rolling barrage from its own artillery. "Instead of indulging in street fighting in Rémonville, as invited by the Germans with their heavily barricaded streets," writes John McGrath, "the troops simply passed around and behind the town, cutting its defenders from their retreat and capturing nearly 100 men."[600]

The 354th Regimental history asserts that during the battle of Rémonville there were too many acts of valor to mention. That is true, but there is one extraordinary feat that is particularly noteworthy. On November 1, Company D was stopped by bursts of fire from a nest of six enemy machine guns. Sergeant Arthur Joseph Forrest, a 23-year-old professional baseball player from Hannibal, Missouri, worked his way to a point within fifty yards of the machine gun nest without being discovered. He then single-handedly charged the nest, therein driving the enemy out and scattering them in a disorderly fashion. This heroic action protected the advance platoon from annihilating fire, permitted Company D to resume its advance, and earned Forrest the Medal of Honor.[601]

Once Rémonville had been effectively neutralized, the 354th Infantry Regiment moved on to the Bois de Barricourt. This was no simple feat, as the men had to traverse 800 meters across open terrain to secure a ridge opposite the enemy's line of defense. The 354th reached the ridge at 10:55 a.m., and overtook the German position shortly after noon—right on schedule. At this point, the 354th's 3rd Battalion, to which Charlie was assigned, took the regiment's lead from the 1st Battalion, as ordered, to make the final push to the heights of Barricourt.[602]

The heights of Barricourt were a series of hills running from Les Tuilleries Farm, along the northern edge of the Bois de Barricourt, to some high ground called La Polarde, about 1,000 yards south of the village of Barricourt.[603] These heights were considered by the Germans to be one of the most vital points in the whole German line of the Meuse-Argonne region. It was realized by American operational planners that if the heights of Barricourt were taken, the enemy could be driven beyond the Meuse River with relative ease.[604]

It was on that first day of November that Captain (later Major) Hugh M. Pinkerton, a distinguished attorney before and after the war, took command of the 3rd Battalion, 354th Infantry Regiment. He formed several combat groups to attack and destroy German outposts to facilitate the regiment's eventual advance on the heights of Barricourt. Commanding one such combat group was Lieutenant Bates from Company L, who selected Charlie, Jess, and 12 others to accompany him. Bates led his group into the dense woods, preceded by a thin line of scouts, when suddenly the group was pinned down by machine gun fire.[605]

The exchange of weapons fire was deafening, with the rhythmic rat-tat-tat of German machine guns, and the Americans retaliating with rifles, grenades, and, of course, Charlie's Chauchat. Bates managed to assemble his men and edge his way out of the line of fire, but was wounded in the process. Nonetheless, he showed skill and bravery in handling his men, and by his example, he inspired them to resist until dark. At that time, Bates' combat group, aided by a dense fog, extricated themselves and returned to their own lines with their dead and wounded.[606]

Lieutenant Bates' family received notification that he died of disease on November 1, but, to the family's utter delight, that report turned out to be false. Three weeks later, his family learned that he had been severely wounded in action, but was hospitalized in France where his wounds were being treated.[607] He would recover from his wounds, return home, and become an insurance agent. Bates passed away in Manhattan, Kansas, on October 5, 1976, at the age of 87.

Wounded and removed from his command, Lieutenant Bates left Company L without an officer. Now, command of the company fell to an enlisted man, First Sergeant Vernon J. Tuley. Fortunately, Tuley proved to be the right man for the job, and he expertly guided Company L as they slugged it out for control of the heights.[608] Fighting was brutal, with the Germans occupying strongly defended trenches and dugouts, and employing snipers in treetops. Some enemy machine gunners were even chained to their posts and left behind in a forlorn hope of staying the American advance! These enemy soldiers dutifully continued to fire until surrounded, captured or killed.

The woods through which the 354th Infantry Regiment had to pass was so thick that some companies on the 3rd Battalion became disoriented and wandered into American artillery fire.[609] The regimental history does not indicate if, or how many, casualties occurred as a result of this snafu, but it does state that Colonel Babcock responded and personally assisted Captain Pinkerton in reorganizing his men. Pinkerton subsequently led the 3rd Battalion through a dense set of woods, and then several hundred yards beyond, to reach the slopes on the hills northwest and southeast of Barricourt.[610]

It had been a long, hard day for the 354th, but by dusk on November 1, the heights of Barricourt had been captured, hours before the midnight deadline set by the commander.[611] To say that capturing the heights was important to the overall campaign would be an understatement. When Marshal Foch learned the news, he reportedly leapt up from his chair and exclaimed, "The war is finished!"[612] He realized that the Americans were now on a steady march towards victory and nothing could stop them.

But there was still more fighting to be done. That evening, November 1, Charlie and Jess settled into a large crater, which had been made that day in the wet, heavy soil by American artillery fire. Colonel Babcock described one such crater as follows: "This shell hole was, in the center, about six feet deep with a diameter of perhaps twelve feet, and had been made, probably, by one of our big 8-inch guns or mortars."[613]

Major Howard B. Stivers, who preceded Captain Pinkerton as commander of the 3rd Battalion, was still in the Bois de Bantheville when he was told to have his men leave behind their heavy packs for the November 1 assault. Stivers, however, took this order a step further and directed his men to leave behind their bedrolls and mess kits. Therefore, during the night of November 1-2, Charlie and the others assigned to his brigade consumed what was left of their rations using their filthy fingers. Even worse, they had no protection from the foggy mist, which transitioned into a cold rain, and any appreciable sleep on the cold wet ground was impossible.[614]

Prior to departing on the morning of November 2, Colonel Babcock explained to his battalion commanders that a rolling artillery barrage was to commence at 5:30 a.m. Ten minutes later, the 2nd Battalion would set out from behind but at the same rate as the barrage. The 3rd Battalion, under Captain Pinkerton, would trail in support of the 2nd Battalion at 1,200 yards, and the 1st Battalion, held in reserve, would follow the 3rd Battalion at about the same distance.[615]

The November 2nd artillery barrage commenced as scheduled, but just 22 of the 608 artillery guns that had paved the way for the 177th Brigade on November 1 were able to move its weapons forward during the night. Consequently, the American barrage was so weak that those assigned to the 2nd Brigade, 354th Infantry Regiment, did not recognize it as a barrage, and therefore did not advance; neither did the lead battalions assigned to the 2nd Division, to the 354th's left, or the 353rd Infantry Regiment, to the 354th's right.[616] The regiment's push to the Tailly-Nouart line, about a mile north of Barricourt township, was not off to a good start!

General Winn, commander of the 177th Infantry Brigade, assembled a couple of his staff officers and met with Colonel Babcock and Babcock's three brigade commanders in a crater where Captain Pinkerton had established his post of command. While the officers were conferring, an enemy reconnaissance plane discovered their position and artillery shells were soon exploding within yards of the crater. Babcock persuaded Winn to depart the area for his own safety, and once Winn was out of sight, Babcock started for a wooded area to the south.[617]

"Before I had taken a dozen steps the enemy fired their battery salvo," Babcock remembered. "The four shells just cleared the big hole, and not one of them missed me by twenty feet. Fortunately the ground was wet, heavy and free of stones; those four shells burst simultaneously, showered me with dirt, scared me almost to death, but I was unhurt. Before another salvo could arrive, all but Pinkerton and his staff had evacuated his P.C., and the enemy observers seeing the running figures of men probably decided the hole was empty; they ceased firing on it."[618]

Before General Winn evacuated the crater, he decided not to immediately proceed with the scheduled advance, for without adequate artillery support it was deemed too dangerous. Another American artillery barrage was ordered for 10:00 a.m., but when it proved as ineffective as the first, Winn determined that he could not wait any longer. The entire American line in the Meuse-Argonne region hinged on all divisions advancing at approximately the same rate. He ordered his regiments to break through the Barricourt sector using trench mortars, machine guns, Chauchats and rifles, irrespective of Allied artillery support.[619]

The U.S. 177th Brigade did not launch its attack from the northern edge of the Bois de Barricourt until 12:55 p.m., on November 2, due to the 353rd Infantry Regiment taking two hours to reform its ranks. At that time, the brigade's 353rd and 354th Infantry Regiments commenced their advance simultaneously, under cover of a two-minute machine gun barrage, and against a strong line of German machine gun nests.[620] The 354th was stopped almost immediately, and American soldiers assigned to the 353rd, who initially stepped out of the woods, were either killed or wounded by German machine gun fire.[621]

Throughout the day, the 353rd Infantry Regiment progressed, but slowly, as German forces fervently defended their position with artillery and machine guns. It wasn't until early evening when the 353rd reached Tailly, one-and-three-quarter miles northwest of Barricourt.[622] The 354th Infantry Regiment was unable to advance until darkness set in, and then used patrols to infiltrate enemy positions. Finally, after midnight, a patrol from Company B reached Nouart, just over a mile north of Barricourt. By this time, the Germans were retreating toward the Meuse River en masse due to the collective efforts of American divisions all along the line.[623]

The 89th Division had done its job, and done it well, but casualties for the 353rd and 354th Infantry Regiments for November 1-2 were significant. The 353rd suffered the loss of 56 men who were killed in action, 18 more who would die later of their wounds, and 220 whose wounds were not

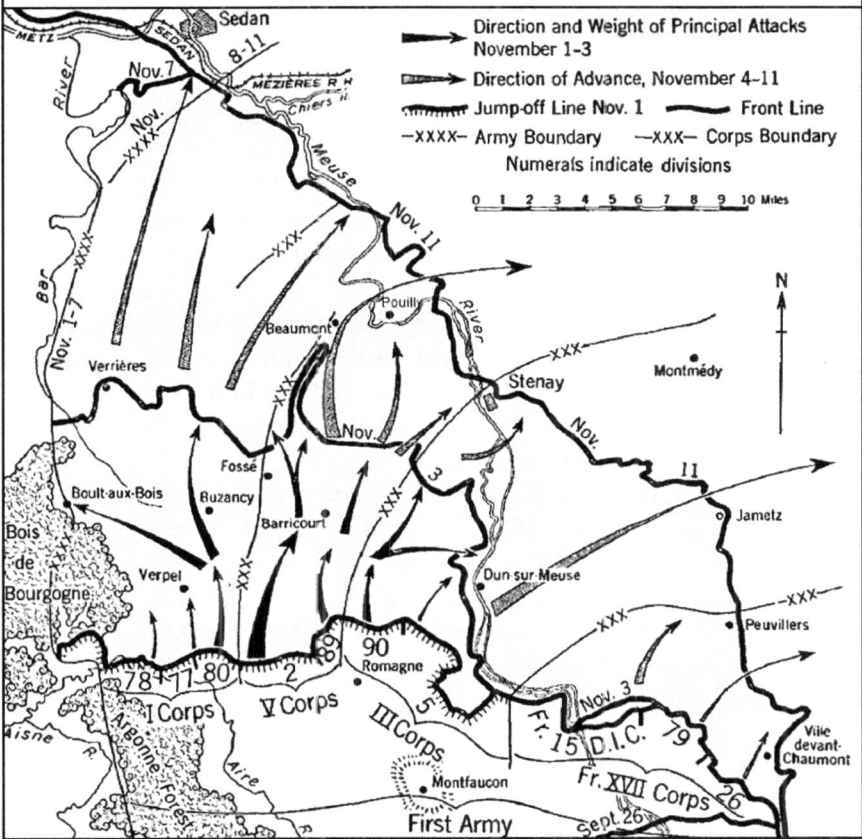

OPERATIONS OF THE FIRST ARMY
NOVEMBER 1-11, 1918

Credit: American Battle Monuments Commission. 2d Division, Summary of Operations in the World War. Washington, DC: U.S. Government Printing Office, 1944.

fatal. The 354th registered 108 men killed in action, 32 more who would eventually die of their wounds, and 320 whose wounds were not fatal. To their credit, the 89th Division's combat activities from November 3, 1918, to the end of the war, was little more than a mop-up effort.[624]

The 89th Division's 355th and 356th Infantry Regiments relieved the 353rd and 354th Infantry Regiments before daybreak on November 3. During this changeover, Charlie and Jess happened upon a mixed group of sergeants, corporals and privates from the 356th Infantry Regiment who had become lost and disoriented. Some weeks earlier, a special effort was made to secure extra compasses for infantrymen, and all troops had been instructed in their use.[625] Ironically, Jess, who retained one of these compasses, somehow found himself in command of the lost men, many of whom outranked him.[626]

Employing his compass, Jess led the lost group forward to their assigned sector, encountering enemy troops with some degree of frequency all along the way. During these encounters, the men of the 356th rushed for cover, but not Charlie. With Jess by his side, he went to work with his Chauchat and decimated the German aggressors.[627]

Eventually, Charlie, Jess, and the others, arrived at an area where a stronghold could be established. As the men of the 356th Infantry Regiment built defensive fighting positions, more enemy soldiers attacked at sporadic intervals to kill, capture or dislodge the Americans. Charlie and Jess successfully fought them off until the 356th settled in. For their actions that evening, Charlie and Jess would receive the Croix de Guerre with bronze star.[628]

There was another incident worth noting, which occurred three-and-a-half miles north of Barricourt, near Le Champy-Bas. On November 3, the 1st Battalion, 356th Infantry Regiment, was advancing northward when it was suddenly stopped by machine gun fire from the front and left flank. Captain Marcellus H. Chiles, who had recently taken command of the battalion, picked up the rifle of a dead soldier and, calling on his men to follow, led the advance across a stream, waist deep, in the face of the machine gun fire.[629]

Upon reaching the opposite bank, Chiles was seriously wounded in the abdomen by a sniper, but before permitting himself to be evacuated, he made complete arrangements for turning over his command to the next senior officer. Chiles died shortly after reaching the hospital, but due to his inspiration and fearless leadership, the 1st Battalion reached its objective. He was posthumously awarded the Medal of Honor.[630]

Between November 3 and November 7, 1918, the 355th and 356th Infantry Regiments invoked a northeasterly wheeling action in the direction of the Meuse, advancing in the footsteps of the slowly retreating

German Army.[631] "From the passage of the lines on the position Nouart-Tailly, November 3," writes George English, "until a period of comparative stabilization had been reached along the banks of the Meuse November 7, the [89th Division] history is one of exhausting marches through mud and forest, with some bitter but not continuous fighting, and the ever-present harassing fire of the enemy artillery from across the river.[632]

"The Germans were engaged in organizing the heights beyond the river for defense. Their artillery and machine gun fire swept the entire river and dominated every possible crossing. On our side the infantry rested upon their arms, guarding the crossings, patrolling and reconnoitering the banks of the stream and preparing for the coming fight."[633]

General Wright consulted his staff and his brigade commanders, and they decided to cross the Meuse River at Pouilly.[634] On the afternoon of November 8, 1918, Colonel Robert H. Allen, commander of the 356th Infantry Regiment, received orders to send patrols across the Meuse at Pouilly to reconnoiter the opposite bank for landing places, to ascertain the enemy's positions, and to take prisoners for identification. Rafts would have been ideal, but they were not available, so several members of the regiment volunteered to swim across the river.[635]

The ice-cold Meuse was 150- to 200-feet wide, with a swift current, and the men who volunteered to cross had been in active battle and grueling marches since November 1. "A determined enemy held the opposite shore," explained English, "and they knew that if they survived the perils of the crossing they would probably have to fight upon the further shore, wet and exhausted as they would be." Of the six men who made the attempt, two failed, two succeeded, and two drowned.[636]

On November 8, Sergeant M. Waldo Hatler of Company B, and Corporal John W McAfee of Company D, were the first members of the 356th Infantry Regiment to volunteer to swim across the Meuse. Before reaching the other side, McAfee, suffering from cold and exhaustion, sank below the surface and drowned. Hatler, however, succeeded in reaching the German lines and carefully reconnoitered the enemy's positions. Upon completion, he returned with information of great value for the eventual crossing [637]

The following evening, November 9, Private First Class Harold I. Johnston and Private David B. Barkeley, both of Company A, 356th Infantry Regiment, swam the river to determine the exact location of enemy positions. They succeeded in reaching the opposite bank, despite the evident determination of the enemy to prevent them from doing so. Having obtained the needed information, they reentered the water to return. En route, Barkeley was seized with cramps and drowned. Johnston, however, made it back after a severe struggle, and upon being assisted from the water, he submitted his indispensable report. Hatler, Johnston and Barkeley earned the Medal of Honor for their heroism, and McAfee was posthumously awarded the Distinguished Service Cross.[638]

Charlie's reprieve from frontline combat between November 3 and November 10, 1918, was not pleasant by any stretch of the imagination, as the 177th Brigade, to which he was assigned, went from battling the enemy to combating hunger and the elements. John McGrath records in the 354th Regimental history that the men assigned to the 177th had insufficient rations, no opportunity to bathe, and the majority of them suffered from colds, diarrhea and other afflictions.[639]

Charlie's great-grandson, James C. Barger, inherited from his grand-mother a photo of Charlie with his platoon, which was taken a day or two after the Armistice. This picture shows Charlie to be extraordinarily gaunt, but it is also the only adult photo depicting him with a smile. One could surmise from this photo that, despite his wartime hardships, he was happier then than at any other time in his life.

During the night of November 10-11, 1918, the 356th Infantry Regiment, 89th Division, were ferried across the Meuse River on rafts. These rafts were made of pontoons captured from the enemy on another front. The 356th's 1st and 3rd Battalions crossed the Meuse River with little opposition, but the regiment's 2nd Battalion, which had been designated as the 89th Division's liaison group, crossed at a different section of the river and encountered fierce opposition.[640]

"The crossing was made in the face of most deadly machine gun and artillery fire," writes English. "The bridgehead on the enemy side had been most accurately located by the enemy and the [2nd Battalion, 356th Infantry Regiment], which had suffered already severe losses in the German counter barrage on the approach to the bridge, was here met by a withering fire of machine guns and artillery. Passing through this inferno again and again to bring his men up to their positions, Major [Mark] Hanna was killed on his third trip through the barrage. Captain Carlson took command of the [2nd Battalion], placed it in formation for the attack, and advanced. The losses were terrific."[641]

At 2:00 a.m., on November 11, the 354th Infantry Regiment, which included Charlie, began their forced march "through water and mud" along the banks of the Meuse River, en route to reinforce the 356th Infantry Regiment's frontline troops. The 354th's 1st Battalion crossed the Meuse River at Pouilly under vigorous artillery fire to relieve the 356th's depleted 2nd Battalion; the 2nd Battalion, 354th Infantry Regiment, suffered severe casualties as it advanced to relieve the 1st Battalion, 356th Infantry Regiment, near Inor; and the 3rd Battalion, 354th Infantry Regiment, to which Charlie was assigned, was preparing to cross the Meuse River to relieve the 3rd Battalion, 356th Infantry Regiment, when the war ended.[642]

The Armistice, which ended hostilities between the Germans and Allies on the Western Front, went into effect at 11 a.m., on November 11, 1918. By then, the 353rd Infantry Regiment, 89th Division, had captured the village of Stenay, formerly the headquarters of the German Crown Prince, but the 90th Division, which was to have taken the village but didn't, took credit for conquest. This would result in animosity bordering on acrimony, particularly within officer circles, but that would come later. For now, everyone was delighted that the war was finally over![643]

"The night of the 11th, bedlam broke loose," recalled John McGrath. "Every man took especial delight in having the luxury of a fire, a real fire that made heat and light, and could be seen a long ways. When the first car came along the highway with its great lights burning, the boys gave a mighty cheer at the sight for that more then even cessation of shell fire made them realize the end was at hand."[644]

The 89th Division, which had been under fire for all but eight days since August 4, had racked up several distinguished laurels. It was the first division to move from the training area to the front by truck; it was the first division to enter the line without previously being brigaded with French or British troops; it was the first division to be continuously in the front line for more than eight weeks; it was the first National Army division to participate in a major operation; and now it would be the first National Army division to enter Germany.[645]

Before the 47-day Meuse-Argonne Campaign culminated with the Armistice, 1.2 million American personnel were involved, and about 192,000 American men were killed or wounded; German forces numbered just 450,000, and their casualties were about 126,000 men killed and wounded.[646] Eighty-Ninth Division casualties, in itself, numbered 479 killed, 1,662 wounded, and 168 gassed.[647]

Following the Armistice, General Pershing established the Third Army to perform occupation duty in Germany. About a week later, the 89th Division was placed under VII Corps, Third Army. Meanwhile, General Winn replaced General Wright as commander of the 89th Division, and Brigadier General Herman Hall transferred from the 178th Brigade to command the 177th Brigade, to which Charlie was assigned. Selection to the Army of Occupation was considered an extreme honor, for only eight divisions were chosen based on their combat record, and only the 89th and 90th Divisions represented the National Army.

At this point, Charlie was on top of the world! He had earned the respect of his peers and superiors from the time he entered combat in August 1918, but after the rescue of Milis, Rowell and Montoya, he was venerated. Even Colonel Babcock changed his mind about what constituted "above and beyond the call of duty" and personally submitted Charlie and Jess for the Medal of Honor.

On November 12, 1918, the 354th Infantry Regiment moved into Cesse, France, where the first couple of days were spent burying the dead and collecting discarded equipment and ammunition. "Once more the men could bathe, shave, eat, and sleep in comfort," writes John McGrath. "New clothing was issued and the long neglected close order drill revived. We remained here till Nov. 24th when the definite order came sending us forward with the Army of Occupation.

"Under the Command of Lieut. Colonel [Joseph] Barnard in the absence of Colonel Babcock the difficulties of this forced march [175-miles with full backpacks] were over come [sic] with minimal effort. Our reception in Belgium and Luxembourg was quite friendly and the advance was uneventful except for its discomfort. The morning of Dec. 7th we crossed the border at Echternach, experiencing that longed-for thrill of placing a conqueror's foot on German soil."[648]

The 354th Infantry Regiment, to which Charlie was assigned, arrived in Waxweiler, Germany, on December 10, where the troops were billeted in the homes of local families. Colonel Babcock, who had since rejoined his regiment, was concerned for the morale of his men, for the village was isolated and had almost nothing to keep his troops entertained. "Drills, inspections and maneuvers were the order of the day," Babcock recalled. "One could have imagined we were training for a war, instead of waiting to go home."[649]

Jess Funk was promoted to corporal on November 28. He would be hospitalized between December 16 and Christmas Day, and Charlie was in the hospital from December 24 until after the first of the year. The nature of their respective ailments remains a mystery, but it is presumed that it was related to gas exposure.

On February 1, 1919, the 354th Infantry Regiment was detached from the 89th Division and assigned to the Trier sector, which was the garrison of General Pershing's advanced General Headquarters (GHQ). "They had electric lights, hot and cold shower baths, good beds, large mess halls, and near-by fine drill grounds," recalled Colonel Babcock. "In the city there were movies; and the Y.M.C.A., Red Cross, Knights of Columbus, Salvation Army and Jewish Welfare Board—all were in close competition. It was a wonderful change for my regiment, stationed in the remote little German villages."[650]

At this juncture, every effort was made to enhance troop morale. Club-houses, opened to all ranks, offered a complete entertainment schedule, with both home and professional talent on the lineup. Divisions also competed in such sporting events as football, basketball, indoor baseball, soccer, and track and field. Then, in accordance with a General Headquarters mandate, post schools were instituted, at which illiterates were taught to read and write, and an opportunity was offered for other men to obtain the rudiments of a grammar school education.[651] It is possible that Charlie participated in the course curriculum, but the likelihood also exists that he was too embarrassed or too preoccupied to take part.

Charlie's Medal of Honor recommendation was readily approved by the 89th Division commander, who forwarded it to the Board of Awards at General Headquarters in Chaumont, France. At the time, three officers (later seven) sat on the Board, which was presided over by a senior member, or president. These officers generally served in continuous combat, and most had been decorated for gallantry in action. Each member reviewed Charlie's case, and then submitted their votes to the senior member, who noted the action of the Board and forwarded their recommendation to the adjutant general for submission to General Pershing.[652]

With Pershing's endorsement, a cablegram with a citation of Charlie's heroic action was sent to the War Department in Washington, DC, for inclusion in general orders, and for official record. Although the process was quite involved, his recommendation met no opposition and was approved in December 1918. It wasn't until February 4, 1919, however, that Pershing's General Headquarters and Charlie's division commander were informed. Prior to that, there were forty-seven recipients of the Medal of Honor during the current war, and sixteen of those were deceased. Charlie and Jess were the only two from Company L, 354th Infantry Regiment, 89th Division, to be so honored.

There was an immediate press release, and local newsmen sought out those listed as next-of-kin of the heroes. One reporter tracked down Jess' wife. Recall that their marriage was not going well at the time, and she would later make a number of inflammatory statements and accusation, but at this point she responded civilly.

"Jesse always was reckless and daring," confirmed Anna Funk. "There have been many instances when he risked injury or even his life where most men would have been more careful. It is no surprise to me that he proved his courage under fire, although it is wonderful that he was not wounded. His letters have said little or nothing about these deeds of his, but recently we had official notice that he had been awarded the Distinguished Service Cross. The congressional medal award was entirely new to me until tonight."[653]

In Charlie's case, he wrote to the McFerons in Vineyard, casually mentioned saving two officers and one enlisted man, but gave no other details. The McFerons had no indication that he had already received one French Croix de Guerre, or that he had been submitted for three others. News of the Medal of Honor came as a complete surprise.

The Medal of Honor was established early in the Civil War, beginning with the Navy version in 1861, and the Army version the following year. Since it was the only decoration to recognize acts of heroism and other notable feats, it was awarded quite liberally for the remainder of the nineteenth century, and even during the first decade of the twentieth century. Then, just before World War I, a Medal of Honor Review Board struck 911 medals from the Medal of Honor Roll and established rigid standards for future awards, elevating it to a level commensurate with the Victoria Cross of Great Britain.[654]

An Act of Congress of July 9, 1918, further defined War Department requirements for the Medal of Honor, mandating that the act of valor be performed "in action involving actual conflict with an enemy" and that the soldier "distinguish himself conspicuously by gallantry and intrepidity at the risk of his life above and beyond the call of duty." Thus, the Medal of Honor became the most highly prized and most difficult to obtain of all military decorations in the world.[655]

That same year, 1918, the Distinguished Service Cross was established for heroic acts not warranting the Medal of Honor; the Distinguished Service Medal was created to recognize exceptionally meritorious service; and the Citation Star transformed into the Silver Star device (forerunner of the Silver Star Medal) for gallantry in action. Thus, the Pyramid of Honor was instituted. The lesser awards were authorized for presentation by the President, but not in the name of Congress, as with the Medal of Honor.[656]

Charlie and Jess were among seventeen newly approved recipients ordered to General Pershing's headquarters in Chaumont, France, for a spectacular presentation ceremony scheduled for 3:30 on Sunday afternoon, February 9, 1919. A great throng of American, British, French, Belgian and Italian officers and soldiers surrounded the parade grounds outside AEF headquarters to witness General Pershing bestow the medals upon the heroes. To someone with Charlie's humble background, all the pomp and circumstance had to be beyond comprehension!

From the windows of "C" Building—one of the three main structures of Damremont Barracks in which AEF headquarters was housed—a large crowd of spectators gathered to witness the event. Soon, presentation of the American flag ignited a pantheon of salutes, the band played a stirring rendition of "The Star-Spangled Banner," and the honorees marched to the center of the quadrangle. "The scene was intensely military," reported *Stars & Stripes,* "the biting air giving the movements of the Headquarters Battalion, which acted as the guard of honor, a spontaneous snap, and the snow-covered ground furnished a picturesque background."[657]

In a few minutes, General Pershing stood centered before the recipients, proper and erect, and proclaimed, "This is the highest honor an American soldier can receive for gallantry in action." Then he approached the heroes, who formed a single line, with the highest-ranking to his left. Flanking the general were two officers, one to read the individual citations, and the other to carry the medals.[658]

The medals were presented per rank. Jess was the thirteenth recipient to receive the Medal of Honor during the ceremony; Charlie was fifteenth. The frigid air caused Charlie to cough just prior to Pershing moving on to him, and archival film footage suggests that Charlie was a little nervous. Indeed, having General Pershing standing directly in front of him had to seem surreal.

The general and private stood quietly facing each other while Pershing's staff officer read Charlie's official citation: "Learning that two daylight patrols had been caught out in No Man's Land and were unable to return, PFC Barger and another stretcher bearer, upon their own initiative, made two trips 500 yards beyond our lines, under constant machine gun fire, and rescued two wounded officers."[659]

Pershing was handed another medal, pinned it above Charlie's left breast pocket, and then shook his hand while offering his personal congratulations. Charlie saluted smartly, as Pershing moved to the next man. The ceremony was brief, but impressive, and upon culmination of the formalities, Pershing circled around to the first recipient and moved down the line, speaking briefly and cordially with each one.

Well-wishers then crowded the recipients to shake hands and offer their own felicitations. General Pershing turned to one group of soldiers, who had been admiring onlookers, and remarked, "I am mighty proud of these men, and you ought to be, too."[660]

About noon the following day, in front of General Pershing's headquarters, one limousine bearing four stars, and two limousines with three stars, caught the attention of military policemen, high-ranking officers, and plain old doughboys, all of whom snapped to attention and saluted smartly. A few minutes later the vehicles drove off, not with Pershing and other generals, but with the seventeen Medal of Honor men who were en route to the general's chateau, Val des Escaliers, for a luncheon with the commander-in-chief. "Never before in the history of the American Army has such an array of stars and bars and just plain O.D. mixed in common in the dining room," revealed *Stars & Stripes*. "Take it from one of the doughboys who was there. The generals talked and exchanged jokes with the privates just as though there was no such thing as rank."[661]

Charlie had the opportunity to talk one-on-one with General Pershing, and came away with tremendous admiration for the man. According to his grandson, Joe Barger, Charlie believed that Pershing would soon forget about him, particularly since there were so many other recipients and dignitaries in the room. But this was his moment, and he cherished it forever. As Charlie sat down for a meal consisting of chicken and sweets, the generals drank a toast to the heroes. Among those present were Lieutenant Generals Hunter Liggett and Robert Bullard, Major Generals James McAndrew and Charles Summerall, and Brigadier Generals Robert C. Davis and Dennis Nolan.

General Pershing ensured that those who received the Medal of Honor were appropriately cared for, and as further reward for their heroic exploits, he personally authorized them a two-week furlough. Charlie traveled to Paris with Jess, and it would be safe to say at this point that Jess was the best friend Charlie ever had. The two men had come to understand and care for each other through the adversity of war, and the result was an ironclad friendship.

On April 23, 1919, General Pershing inspected the 89th Division in Trier and bestowed upon a number of officers and enlisted men additional decorations. The division was complimented by the general, who stated, "It will be a proud thing for you to return and say in future years that you belonged to this splendid division, whose record, for the time it was in the line, is unexcelled in the American Expeditionary Forces."[662]

That evening, General Pershing dined with a large party of officers, which included Colonel Babcock. Amid the festivities, Pershing tapped his glass to get everyone's attention, and then turned to Babcock and said, "Colonel Babcock, I want everyone here to hear this. I want to tell you that you have the finest-looking regiment I have seen in the A.E.F."[663]

In his memoirs, Colonel Babcock would write: "I had and still have a real affection for my fine regiment. I had seen them die, I had seen them tortured by horrible wounds. For weeks they had cheerfully borne the discomforts of rain, mud, cold, gas, contaminated woods—I knew they would do anything for me and the unexpected words of commendation from the Commander-in-Chief on the magnificent 354th Infantry holds a place in my military memories at the very top of the list. The next morning, in the presence of all the officers and non-commissioned officers, I told them what General Pershing had said about them. What a yell they gave!"[664]

On May 5, 1919, the 89th Division moved to Brest, France, preparatory to return to the United States. It was there on May 14, that Vice Admiral F.P. Moreau of the French Navy reviewed the 89th Division and read a letter from Premier Georges Clemenceau congratulating the division on its "brilliant conduct" during the war. Thereafter, Moreau presented General Winn with the Legion of Honor, and then lesser decorations to divisional troops, including Charlie and Jess. Charlie received the Medaille Militaire and the Croix de Guerre with two bronze palms.

The 354th Infantry Regiment embarked at the port of Brest on May 15, 1919, aboard the transport *Imperator*. This liner was turned over to the

United States by Germany under the Armistice agreement, and this was its first overseas journey under the American flag. Following her service with the U.S. Navy, *Imperator* was handed over to Britain's Cunard Line as part of war reparations, and for the final decade of her career, she sailed as the flagship RMS *Berengaria.*

The first batch of World War I Victory Medal ribbons reached Paris on May 15, just as the first ship occupied by troops of the 89th Division was ready to leave Brest. The Quartermaster Corps quickly loaded a consignment of these ribbons onto an airplane, which departed Paris at 9:00 that morning. Before the *Imperator* pulled out, the airman landed with his cargo. Thus, members of the 89th Division were the first to wear the new Allied Victory Medal ribbon back to the United States.[665]

Upon arriving at the port of debarkation in New York City on May 22, Charlie and Jess were surprised to see Lieutenant Millis, who had traveled from his home in Russell, Kentucky, to take them out on the town. "He was down at the dock to meet us," Charlie said, "and was the first person I saw whom I recognized. Who wouldn't have done it for Lieutenant Millis? There wasn't anything in the world he wouldn't have done for his men."[666]

Millis would become a bank teller in Lexington, Kentucky, would serve a term as mayor of Russell, and then win election to County Clerk in Greenup. On April 27, 1927, he married Eleanor Angeline Ramey, with whom he had four children, only two of whom survived: John, Jr., and Ruth Bantheville Millis. The Bois de Bantheville would always hold special meaning for Millis, for it was there that he almost died, and it was there that he was given a second chance at life. He passed away in Lexington, Kentucky, on June 7, 1969. An interesting side note to Millis' biography is that his sister, Ida Lee Millis, married Simeon Slavens Willis, who served as Governor of Kentucky between 1943 and 1947.

Charlie and Jess parted ways in New York, as soldiers en route to Colorado took alternate transportation home, but they would frequently talk on the phone, correspond, and meet up during various veteran's functions over the years. Jess was discharged from the Army on June 3, 1919, and returned to Colorado to a hero's welcome. He was offered a vaudeville gig, as many Medal of Honor recipients were, but few, if any, heroes accepted; the Medal of Honor, to these men, was not for sale. Jess decided instead to resume his prewar vocation as a cowboy. Though he dabbled in other ventures after the war, he primarily continued with ranching, which he thoroughly enjoyed.

Unfortunately, Jess also returned to an irate wife seeking a divorce, which turned rather bitter over the subsequent year. He eventually remarried to Christella Nielson, and they had two children, Margaret and Billy. On March 20, 1933, Jess was hospitalized in Colorado Springs and underwent surgery for appendicitis. The following evening, he died from peritonitis at the age of forty-four, and was thereafter buried in the Calhan Cemetery in Calhan, Colorado.

Colonel Babcock remained in the Army and retired in relative obscurity in 1937. Three years later, after President Franklin D. Roosevelt proclaimed the limited emergency on September 8, 1939, he tried unsuccessfully to return to uniform. As an honorary gesture, he was elevated to the retired rank of brigadier general, but his career was over. He died in 1950.

Charlie arrived in St. Louis, Missouri, with other members of the 354th Infantry Regiment, on May 30, 1919. *The St. Louis Post-Dispatch* reported: "Private Charles D. Barger of L Company, 354th, a husky, well-built soldier of 25 years, attracted much attention when he alighted from the second train by the fact that on his breast were pinned the Congressional Medal of Honor, the Medaille Militaire and the Croix de Guerre. James E. Smith, of the Mayor's Welcome Committee, shook hands with Barger and hoped he'd get married and raise a fine family of boys to enjoy their father's distinction. 'Well, now,' drawled the soldier in a pronounced 'Hoosier' accent, 'I can't say as I hope that; there might be another war, and I don't want any boys of mine to have to go through one.'

"About that time a group of Red Cross girls espied Barger, and they rushed him, shaking his hands, patting him on the back, and vowing to him, to each other and to all the world that he was 'a peach,' a 'pippin,' and 'a dear old thing,' until the hero, with his face blazing with blushes and his tongue cleaving to the roof of his mouth, broke through the charming circle and beat it back into the car, from a window of which he surveyed the still applauding throng with a speculative eye."[667]

The troops were moved that day to Forest Park, where General Wright saw Charlie standing at Westmoreland Place and King's Highway. He went over and shook hands with Charlie. "I congratulate you, young man," he said. "I don't believe there are 10 men in the Army who have what you are wearing there."[668]

General Wright, who was justifiably proud of Charlie, called him "the greatest hero of the 89th." Then, turning to the adoring bystanders, Wright remarked, "You all know about the Congressional Medal. Well, the Medaille Militaire is the last word in French decorations. Only a humble Private or a great General can wear it. When a distinguished General gets it, he wears no other decorations."[669]

Turning back to Charlie, Wright asked, "What are you going to do now?"[670]

"I'm going back to the farm, sir," Charlie replied.[671]

"Well," the general commented, "you have a priceless heritage to leave your children."[672]

Charlie was discharged from the Army on June 3, 1919, the same day as Jess. It was his twenty-fifth birthday. For a few months, everyone who was anyone in the State of Missouri wanted an opportunity to slap him on the back and shake his hand, to revel in his glory, to get a little piece of the man who earned America's highest decoration for heroism. He didn't really know what to make of it all, but, for now, he handled it fine.

As time moved on, Charlie endured severe depression and irritability, and dwelt on the loss of his friends. Today this affliction is known as post-traumatic stress disorder, or PTSD, and veterans receive help to deal with it. Back then, however, there was no recognition of the problem and no such help. Tragically, the "war to end all wars" marked the end of Charlie Barger as a fully functioning human being. Ironically, his role in combat awakened him to life as he had never before known it, and yet his wartime experiences left him without any sense of how to cope with civilian life once he returned home.

Lt. John M. Millis
Credit: Diana Childers and Bob Green

Lt. Ernest Rowell
Credit: Linda Brzezinski

Pvt. Philip Montoya
Credit: New Mexico State Archives

Charlie Barger's Squad
(Charlie, back row, third from right; Jesse Funk, back row, fourth from right)
Credit: James C. Barger and Johnny Thompson

General Pershing presenting Jesse Funk with the Medal of Honor.
Charlie is on the right.
Credit: National Archives

General Pershing presenting
Charlie with the Medal of Honor.
Credit: National Archives

Charlie Barger (front row, third from right) with General Pershing, dignitaries, and other Medal of Honor Recipients.

Credit: National Archives

Charlie Barger (third from right) during presentation of the Medaille Militaire and French Croix de Guerre with two palms.

Credit: National World War I Museum and Memorial, Kansas City, Missouri, U.S.A.

Charlie Barger following
Medal of Honor presentation.
Credit: National Archives

PFC Charles D. Barger upon return
to the United States, June 1919.
*Credit: National World War I Museum and
Memorial, Kansas City, Missouri, U.S.A.*

Chapter Thirteen

WOUNDED WARRIOR

Charlie arrived at Henry and Sarah McFeron's home in Vineyard, Missouri, on June 6, 1919, amid a throng of fanfare.* There were a lot of people, including reporters, who wanted to hear about his battlefield exploits, and while he responded to their questions responsibly, his answers were exceptionally brief. Combat for Charlie, after all, was up close and personal, and anyone not there could never comprehend the horror and devastation Charlie and his fellow combatants experienced.

The same day that Charlie arrived home, Mayor James Cowgill, of Kansas City, Missouri, sent a fellow named Charles Smith to the McFeron's farm to invite Charlie to a parade welcoming home the 356th Infantry Regiment. Charlie, hailed as "Missouri's greatest hero," graciously accepted the mayor's invitation, which included a week-long schedule of entertainment and festivities. As Cowgill's guest of honor, all of Charlie's expenses were paid.[673]

Mayor Cowgill pulled out all the stops to ensure that Charlie's stay in Kansas City was memorable, and during that time an enduring friendship was formed. He could have had no way of knowing it at the time, but accepting Cowgill's invitation would pay off a few years later when he was down on his luck.

Charlie's military occupational specialty—infantryman—did not prepare him for a suitable civilian vocation. It's difficult to imagine what might have been going through his mind as he moved suddenly from one continent to another, from the theatre of war back to the farm. Yet drifting from one place to another, working for room and board and measly wages, was about all he was qualified to do, as he had no more skilled training after the war than he had before.

Around June 20, Charlie reclaimed his job with Coglizer Tent & Awning in Joplin, but he ended up back at the McFerons' farm a month or two later. For more than a year, he worked on the McFeron farm and on

---

* Sarah was Charlie's adoptive mother's cousin.

other farms as far away as Joplin and Springfield.[674] For now, he bided his time at these menial jobs until an opportunity would arise that would give him some chance at a decent living.

On October 20, 1919, the Parent-Teacher Association at Robberson School in Springfield, Missouri, invited him to attend a short program hosted by pupils of the third and fourth grades. Charlie attended, though he didn't speak at the event. After the meeting, however, he consented to display his medals and to explain to the children what he did to earn each one.[675]

Immediately following that event, Charlie traveled to St. Louis where his former division commander, General Wright, was serving as a member of the royal entourage for King Albert of Belgium. The king was scheduled to make a brief stop at the St. Louis Club the following day to meet with members of the American Legion. General Wright knew that Charlie had been approved for the Belgian Croix de Guerre with bronze palm, and took this opportunity to have the medal presented personally to Charlie by the king. The ceremony was brief—perhaps even rushed—but it would have been memorable to anyone. Charlie was no exception.[676]

Charlie had been honored with life membership to the American Legion and Veterans of Foreign Wars, two organizations with which he remained closely affiliated. As a member of William J. Bland American Legion Post #50, named for a major in command of the 1st Battalion, 356th Infantry Regiment, 89th Division, who was killed in action on September 12, 1918, Charlie would serve as sergeant-at-arms. The company of other veterans very likely had a positive effect upon him, and he also likely enjoyed the out-of-town events, to which he was afforded free transportation, lodging, food, etc.

During a few of these functions, such as the American Legion National Convention in Cleveland, Ohio, in September 1920, Charlie had the opportunity to reunite with Jess Funk. For the first time in history, Medal of Honor recipients were brought together as guests of honor for a reunion; the idea of the Legion being to immortalize their deeds of bravery. Medals of Honor were awarded to WWI veterans as late as 2015, but in 1920, there were just 78 recipients, and only 54 were still living. Most of those recipients attended the 1920 convention.

On September 21, Charlie exited the Hollenden Hotel, where he stayed during the week and a half that he was at the convention, and noticed a fire nearby, in the rear of the Puritan Lunch restaurant. He watched as a firetruck clanked down Vincent Avenue to extinguish the blaze, and then heard an unfamiliar voice exclaim, "Gosh, I thought it was a tank!"[677]

Charlie glanced around and noticed a man with a Medal of Honor draped around his neck, this being a recent change to Army regulations to elevate the supreme medal from lesser decorations. The gentleman also noticed Charlie's Medal of Honor. "I'm from Missouri, bud, an' if that didn't make a noise like a tank runnin' up Hill 25, my name ain't Barkley!"[678]

"Missouri?" Charlie responded. "That's my state. I'm Charles D. Barger, 354th Infantry. My town's Joplin."[679]

The two men drew out their respective citation books from their pocket and each found what the other had done to earn the decoration. John Lewis Barkley, a year Charlie's junior, was born and raised in Kansas City. During the war, he served as a private first class in Company K, 4th Infantry Regiment, 3rd Infantry Division, and earned the Medal of Honor while fighting near Cunel, France, on October 7, 1918.* Crawling into an abandoned tank with a machine gun and 8,000 rounds of ammunition, he held off a regiment of enemy forces on Hill 25 for two-and-a-half hours, thereby enabling his regiment to gain and hold the hill.[680]

"Well," Charlie remarked, "I'll say you couldn't have been from anywhere else but Missouri."[681] This meeting sparked an enduring friendship, which lasted for the remainder of Charlie's life.

A few days later, on September 25, a reporter caught up with Charlie at the convention. When asked how things were going after his return home from the war, Charlie, downtrodden, expressed his discontent with farming. "But what got his goat more'n anything," claimed the newsman, "was going back to the old farm in Missouri, workin' like a mule to get out 160 acres of wheat, and then having a hailstorm come along and chop it all off before it was knee high."[682]

"Doggonedest luck," Charlie confided. "Only got two bushels to an acre, and the farmhands at $5 a day got more out of it than I did."[683]

"Then you'd be in favor of a bonus right about now?" the reporter asked, referring to government financial compensation for service during the war.[684]

"Surest thing you know, especially some plan of bonus that would be helpful to us farmers."[685]

Farming had been a booming industry during the war when the U.S. government encouraged crop production to support the war effort. The government even made it easier for farmers to acquire mortgages and take out loans for farm machinery and additional acreage. After the war, seeking to earn enough to pay their wartime mortgages and loans, farmers maintained high production levels resulting in a large surplus of wheat and other grain. Soon, supply overtook demand. Farm and crop prices plummeted, and farmers were unable to meet their financial obligations.

Some federal lawmakers tried, but failed, to pass legislation that would help the farmers. Unfortunately, Charlie's government assistance would

---

* Cunel is situated about two miles southeast of Bantheville.

never come through. Farmers began their descent into an economic depression at the end of WWI, a decade before the Great Depression hit Wall Street.

There are two versions from two family sources as to what happened next. Charlie's birth mother, Cora, told her grandniece, June Buccina, that she was working at a store in Waco, Missouri, when she looked up and saw Charlie through the window. She claimed that she recognized him immediately and exclaimed, "That's my boy!" June went on to say that Charlie received a tip that his "real" mother worked at the store, so he went to see her, but at the last minute he got cold feet and left. A couple of days later, he returned to the store, walked up to Cora, and asked if she knew who he was. "Yes," she responded. "You are my son."[686]

The other story comes from Barbara (Lake) Williams, another of Cora's grandnieces. There may have been a newsreel release of the American Legion Convention held in Cleveland, Ohio, that Charlie had attended, for Barbara states that Cora was in a movie theater in Waco when she saw footage of Charlie wearing the Medal of Honor. She immediately jumped up from her seat and exclaimed, "That's my son!" They reunited at a veteran's function in Joplin shortly thereafter.

Whichever version is accurate, Charlie and Cora came to be reunited after 22 long years of separation. After all those years of feeling abandoned, here was his mother, his flesh and blood, standing before him with an invitation to reside in her home in Twin Groves, Missouri, about two-and-a-half miles south of Waco. He readily accepted.

On August 10, 1901, Cora had married a widower named Casper Adam "Ed" Rolleg in Carthage, Missouri. He was born in Vinita, Indian Territory [Oklahoma], on July 26, 1877, to George and Alice (Crabtree) Rolleg, and worked as a miner, stonemason, and farmer at various times. After their marriage, Cora used her middle name, Victoria, and then adopted the name Mabel, probably seeking to further conceal her identity and disassociate herself from her lurid past.

Cora and Ed had no children together, but at one time she cared for the young children of her brother, Robert, after Robert's wife abandoned the family. Perhaps Robert's children called Cora "Mamie" as a variation of "Mommy." Mamie stuck, and she was called Aunt Mamie by all her young nieces. The children recalled her chewing tobacco, even in later years, and enjoyed visiting with her because she was so lively.

Charlie and Cora became quite close, and she was immediately concerned about her son's health. He appeared edgy, couldn't seem to relax, and exhibited respiratory problems that she was sure required medical attention. She would later declare, "Denver, as I always called him, was suffering from effects of gas, even when he was staying with me after the war, and frequently had hemorrhages."[687] These issues, as we shall see, exacerbated over time.

Charlie disclosed to Cora that he was very angry with the Bargers, but he didn't elaborate as to the reason. It is unlikely that Cora shared much information about Charlie's father, about her past, or about a myriad of other family secrets that she determined were better left unsaid. In fact, he went to his grave believing that his father had died when he was a child, just as the Bargers had told him, and that his mother had given him up only because she could not provide him support.

As 1920 came to a close, Charlie was restless and probably disillusioned, having failed in his first year as an independent tenant farmer. But having found his mother after all these years must have had a profound effect on him. Conceivably, a stronger link to family enabled him to go forward with a new confidence in what he could do; what he could accomplish. His options were limited, but his time in uniform had offered him an escape from an otherwise brutal, insensible world. Perhaps for this reason, he decided to cast farming aside and re-enlist in the U.S. Army.

When the National Defense Act was adopted in June 1920, the Regular Army comprised about 200,000 soldiers, or roughly two-thirds of the maximum authorized strength of 280,000 men. Both parties of the House and Senate agreed to force reduction, as there was no immediate threat to national security, but to their surprise, President Woodrow Wilson opposed such a move. Prior to World War I, the President rejected proposals to bolster the United States military, even though there was a very real threat of war, and now that the war and the threat was over, he was advocating military preparedness![688]

Congress introduced a Joint Resolution to cut the size of the Regular Army to 175,000 men, which President Wilson quickly vetoed. While the House and Senate arranged to overturn the President's veto, Charlie seized the opportunity to enter upon a three-year enlistment in the Army, commencing on January 10, 1921. With his prior training, combat experience, and medals, one may have expected him to be given a higher rank than private first class, but advancement continued to elude him.

Charlie did not have to re-attend basic military training. However, his military occupational specialty changed from infantryman to machine gunner, so he had to undergo instruction in the use of the Browning Model 1917A1 water-cooled machine gun. During training with the 89th Division, he had plenty of opportunity to fire the machine gun, but it wasn't the M1917, as that model didn't filter into the American Expeditionary Force's inventory until the last couple of months of the war. Upon completion of gunnery training, he was assigned to Company D, 38th Infantry Regiment, 3rd Division, at Camp Pike, Arkansas, eight miles northwest of Little Rock.

Camp Pike was one of the 16 divisional cantonment training camps established in 1917, after the outbreak of WWI, to train and equip the 87th Division for overseas deployment, in the same manner that Camp Funston trained and equipped the 89th Division. Once the 87th deployed to France, Camp Pike served as a replacement training facility, and then a demobilization center for troops returning stateside. In 1919, following demobilization, Camp Pike became home of the 3rd Division.

Charlie was an instant celebrity at Camp Pike. A newspaper article observed that he "wore upon his breast the most notable collection of military decorations ever worn by a member of the local garrison."[689] As a guest of honor, he attended one social function after another, including weekly luncheons sponsored by the American Legion. During one such luncheon at the Blue Dragon Cafeteria in Little Rock, Charlie even delivered a short speech.[690]

By mid-February 1921, the Senate joined Congress in overturning President Wilson's veto and directed a prompt reduction in Army strength. Meanwhile, Congress cut military funding, and installations across the nation were under consideration for closure. Camp Funston, for example, was due to close, resulting in the transfer of considerable troops and material to Camp Pike. Camp Pike was spared, for now, due to its strategic position in relation to the Mexican border.[691]

The reader may recall that after Sidney and Phoebe Barger passed away, Charlie resided with Lee and Mary (Hurst) Weaver in North Township, Arkansas. It appears that he maintained contact with the Weavers over the years, and during the time that he was stationed at Camp Pike, he visited them often. He was even there when Mary Weaver died in Hardy, Arkansas, on March 1, 1921. Her obituary went so far as to name Charlie as one of her sons.[692]

Even more notable was the whirlwind relationship that had blossomed between Charlie and Mary's niece, Audrey Ethel Hurst, who was born on June 2, 1902, in Mammoth Spring, Arkansas, to George Washington and Ollie M. (Kelley) Hurst. The day after Mary passed away, Charlie and Audrey were married in Hardy, Arkansas, and then settled into a small home in Little Rock, near the base. By all accounts, from family sources, newspaper articles, and Charlie's personnel files with the Kansas City Police Department, Audrey badgered Charlie constantly, and wouldn't stop until he lost his temper. This first marriage of Charlie's would last just five years.

At Camp Pike, much of June 1921 was centered on preparing 30 buildings and the surrounding grounds for the Arkansas National Guard Encampment, scheduled for July. Six hundred guardsmen attended a four-day school for officers, NCOs, and specialists (July 7-10), and then 1,876 officers and enlisted men participated in the encampment (July 11-July

25).[693]   Charlie would have provided instruction to machine gunners during this time, but his involvement would have been limited.

Even then, Congress had moved to skeletonize the Army. Rather than the 175,000-man force proposed earlier in the year, they decided to reduce the Army to 150,000. To facilitate the discharge of enlisted men, an amendment to the existing Army Appropriation Bill was approved. The Secretary of War was subsequently directed to grant applications for discharges, and the Army was to be cut down as soon as practicable.[694]

Charlie was one of the thousands who applied for a discharge from the Army, perhaps due to his recent marriage; maybe because the peacetime Army didn't suit him; quite possibly a combination of the two. His application was readily approved, and he was honorably discharged on July 15, 1921, just eight days before the Secretary of War ordered all discharges in the Army stopped. So many discharge applications had swamped the War Department that the Secretary of War felt it best to suspend discharges until officials had an opportunity to estimate the probable effects upon the size of the Army.[695]

Charlie returned with Audrey to his mother's home in Twin Groves, Missouri, and found employment as a miner with the High Five Mine in Waco. At the time that Charlie began working for the High Five Mine, the ground had been drained of water down to the 220-foot level, but drilling operations showed that the ore body extended at least 100 feet deeper. Mining executives were at a bypass, as this required capital and resources that the Waco-based mine simply didn't have. Fortunately, the American Zinc, Lead & Smelting Company purchased the High Five Mine on August 20, a month after Charlie was hired, and drilling operations resumed.[696]

Still restless about the direction his life was going, and unhappy with the low wages mining was bringing in, Charlie began looking elsewhere. He turned his focus to a larger city north of Joplin, to Kansas City, Missouri, for better job opportunities. He had a good connection there through Mayor Cowgill, who he had met and befriended after the war. Police work might be something his Army training would be a good fit for, and perhaps the mayor would be able to help him get a job with the Police Department.

In mid-October 1921, Charlie and Audrey left Joplin for Kansas City. He rented a small house at 5316 Oak Street in Kansas City and applied for work as a patrolman with the Kansas City Police Department. In his employment application, he cited that mining "was not payin a nuff to live on." Meanwhile, he found temporary employment in construction on a local building project, which would soon end.[697]

The commander of the Irwin Kirkwood American Legion Post in Kansas City was Robert W. Reed, who also happened to be the Assistant Managing Editor of the *Kansas City Star*. Reed, a veteran of World War I (and rising to the rank of colonel in WWII), was vehemently pro-veteran, and went out of his way to support veterans, regardless of their social or economic status.[698] Reed quickly made a friend in Charlie, and was a man that Charlie came to trust.

"It's going to be a tough winter," Charlie confided to Reed when they first met, "and I'd like to get on with the police here. I believe my record may help some."[699] Certainly, it did, and it was Mayor Cowgill's influence that led to Charlie being hired. He would start working with the department the third week in November.

Between October 30 and November 2, 1921, Charlie attended the American Legion National Convention in Kansas City, during which time they would dedicate the site for the National World War I Museum and Memorial. This convention, incidentally, coincided with the first reunion of the 89th Division, also held in Kansas City, and Charlie participated in those festivities as well.

On the morning of October 31, Charlie joined nineteen other Medal of Honor recipients around a breakfast table at the University Club, where American Legion members were staying. Robert Reed approached to interview the heroes, and noted that it was uncommonly quiet as he made his way around the breakfast table. Some were receptive to his questions; others were not. Arthur Forrest, for example, was not at all congenial when Reed asked him what he did to earn the Medal of Honor. "Darned if I remember," he tersely responded, and then stood up and impolitely walked away.[700]

When talking with Ralyn Hill, however, Reed received one of the most poignant responses ever uttered by a Medal of Honor recipient. After learning what he did to earn the medal, Hill casually remarked, "It is harder to wear than to get 'em."[701] If Charlie failed to realize that by now, it wouldn't be long before he did.

Every news article in which a recipient was mentioned indicated that he had earned the Medal of Honor. If a recipient was arrested for intoxication, domestic troubles, or even a traffic violation, the medal was invariably noted. The articles were not as defamatory as they would be today, for these men were generally revered, but no recipient wanted to bring dishonor upon the medal, and that was sometimes difficult to avoid while trying to lead a normal life.

On November 1, Vice President Calvin Coolidge and the Supreme Allied Commanders, consisting of General Pershing, Lieutenant General Baron Jacques of Belgium, General Armando Diaz of Italy, Marshal Ferdinand Foch of France, and Admiral David Beatty of Great Britain, spoke to an audience of more than 100,000. It was the only time in history that Pershing was together at the same time with his foreign counterparts.

General Pershing, like Charlie, hailed from Missouri, and while on stage, he peered into the crowd and spotted Charlie. Breaking protocol, Pershing descended the stage to greet Charlie, and the two talked for several minutes. Considering all the heroic soldiers that Pershing had met and decorated through the years, for him to pick Charlie out of an audience—Charlie, who was not an officer, but a former private first class and a common farmer—well, that was an honor Charlie never forgot. Joe Barger, Charlie's grandson, was told this story many times by his grandmother while growing up, and how Charlie always considered this to be an extreme honor. General Pershing and Charlie met again on November 11, 1921, at Arlington National Cemetery, during the dedication of the Tomb of the Unknown Soldier, and a few more times over the years.

Medal of Honor recipient M. Waldo Hatler, who served with the 356th Infantry Regiment, 89th Division, recalled that the convention was wild and extravagant in every respect. "The convention was a long series of parties, receptions, entertainment, and diversified fun," he stated. "Packards and Cadillacs accompanied by a motorcycle patrol were always at our service; and the other distinguished guests were presented to each of the Medal of Honor men in a personal greeting."[702]

Staying at the Baltimore Hotel on Baltimore Avenue, the Medal of Honor recipients participated in antics, such as turning a bull loose in the hotel lobby, playing craps games on the surrounding street corners, and tying washtubs and boilers to the street cars.[703] This and future conventions would be a welcomed escape for Charlie, even though, with his serious demeanor, it is unlikely that he participated in the shenanigans.

Charlie began working as a patrolman with the Kansas City Police Department on November 21, 1921, and was assigned to the Westport Substation. He had finally moved up from being a poor tenant farmer to a profession from which he could ultimately retire with decent benefits. In just two months, he was already making enough money to move from the small home on Oak Street to a more comfortable rental at 4112 Penn Avenue.

Charlie first made headlines as a patrolman on January 11, 1922, when he stopped to question a man carrying a basket of empty bottles at the corner of Eighteenth and Harrison. As he took the basket and lowered it to the ground to inspect its contents, the fellow pulled a revolver, opened fire, and fled the scene. Charlie drew his weapon and discharged two shots, but the suspect by that time was out of range and therefore got away. No one was injured, and the suspect was never caught.[704]

Just five days later, on the evening of January 16, Charlie was off duty and in plain clothes when John A. Dixon, a resident of Hannibal, attempted to hold him up. That didn't work out too well for the eighteen-year-old, who Charlie quickly subdued and escorted to the local jail.[705]

On February 22, 1922, Charlie and Officer Harvey Pollard were dispatched to 1724 Holly Street where two brothers were involved in bootlegging, and one was suspected of murder. When the officers entered the residence, Charlie began to search the ground floor while Pollard went to check upstairs. When Pollard reached the base of the steps, Frank and John Elliott emerged from a second-floor room, electing to shoot it out with the lawmen rather than surrendering peaceably.[706]

Catching Pollard completely off-guard, John Elliott shot him through the right forearm, causing him to drop his weapon. Quickly, clumsily, Officer Pollard picked up his pistol with his left hand and unloaded on his assailant. John Elliott was hit three times, but managed to flee the scene, leaving behind a trail of blood. The entire exchange was over in a matter of seconds.[707]

Charlie, meanwhile, rushed to Pollard's assistance, coming face-to-face with Frank Elliott, a 26-year-old laborer at the Keystone Creamery. Elliott already had his pistol aimed at Pollard and was about to squeeze the trigger when Charlie intervened. Guns drawn, Charlie and Elliott exchanged gunfire, shot-for-shot.[708]

Charlie was hit in the left wrist; Elliott was hit in the abdomen. Charlie was shot in the right arm, just below the elbow; Elliott was hit in the abdomen again. Charlie was hit in the right side of his torso; Elliott was hit in the abdomen a third time. Charlie was shot in the chest; Elliott was hit in the abdomen yet again. Charlie was struck in the side of the head; Elliott was hit in the abdomen a fifth time. Charlie, now dazed by the head wound, shot Elliott in the right leg; Elliott fired a shot that completely missed. Their bullets expended, they both collapsed to the floor.[709]

Elliott crumpled over in agonizing pain, never losing consciousness as medical personnel transported him to the Old City Hospital. Before he died the following day, he told hospital attendants that his brother had also been wounded, but had managed to escape. The deputy coroner conducted an autopsy, and his body was removed for burial in the West Lawn Cemetery on March 8.[710]

Charlie was transported to the General Hospital in Kansas City, where he underwent emergency surgery. A reporter (perhaps Robert Reed) managed his way into the recovery room to conduct an interview, therein receiving a brief response that was typical of Charlie: "A mild ruckus," he quipped, "but it seemed a little like old times."[711]

Charlie remained hospitalized for five weeks, but recovered from his injuries, at least to some degree. Already suffering the effects of mustard gas and post-traumatic stress, he now had to deal with that head injury, which caused severe migraines and affected his ability to concentrate. Over time, his physical health also began to deteriorate, but for the time being he plugged away.

Charlie's six-month probationary period with the Kansas City Police Department culminated on June 1, 1922, on which date Lieutenant C.E. Christie, commander of District 4 Station, submitted his recommendation for retention to the Board of Commissioners. "This man has the making of a good officer, is ambitious of good habits, and while at this station has shared several good arrests. I cheerfully recommend his being promoted."[712]

Charlie had been an entry-level Class C patrolman since joining the department, and was promoted to Class B patrolman effective June 1, the date of Christie's recommendation. This promotion, which came with a transfer to the District 9 station, could not have come at a better time. On June 6, 1922, Audrey gave birth to their son, Charles Denver Barger, Jr., which gave their turbulent marriage a temporary reprieve.

That September, Charlie's career was in serious jeopardy in the aftermath of two incidents where his judiciousness in the performance of his duties was called into question. The first incident occurred about 11:30 p.m., on September 4, 1922, while Charlie was engaged in a conversation with the proprietor of the Eastern Auto Livery on Prospect Avenue. He was suddenly distracted by a commotion from across the street, in front of the "Goodie Shop," where a disreputable gang of society boys, around the age of 19, often hung out.[713]

Charlie had dealt with this particular group of boys a number of times in the past and had warned them not to loiter in the area. They were known to cause problems for local businessmen, passersby, and the police, as they habitually made inappropriate remarks to women and frequently used profane language. Lieutenant Cassius M. Larrabee, commander of the District 9 station, would submit the following on Charlie's behalf after the incident: "They [the boys] all seem to think an Officer has no right to say anything to them, as their parents are all pretty well off, and they seem to think they are just a little bit better than anyone else."[714]

Charlie crossed the street to contact Merlin Sparks and Roy Thompson, two members of the gang who were fighting. Just a few feet away, three other members of the gang, Edwin LeBow, George Frye, and Wayland Franklin Sheets, were talking loudly, compelling several ladies to step off the sidewalk and go around them.

"How often must you cake-eaters be told to stop this rough stuff around this corner?"* demanded Charlie.[715]

Sparks and Thompson immediately quit fighting and said nothing, but LeBow approached Charlie and spoke to him impudently, as if trying to provoke a confrontation for the benefit of the gathering crowd. Charlie warned LeBow to shut up, as he was not directing himself to LeBow, to which LeBow replied, "Shut me up, you son-of-a-bitch!"[716]

---

* Cake-eaters is a term used to describe people who present an attitude of self-entitlement.

Charlie ignored that remark and ordered the boys to go home, as it was approaching midnight. He repeated the order at least three times, but LeBow refused to comply and continued to curse at Charlie. According to Sheets, the son of a Baptist preacher and a friend of LeBow's, Charlie "gently shoved him [LeBow] with his hand on the shoulder."[717]

LeBow told Charlie, "If you hit me, I'll have your job!" Lebow then reached for something in his right front pocket.[718]

Perceiving LeBow's action as a threat, Charlie drew his nightstick, and then struck LeBow on the calf several times. LeBow made an attempt to strike Charlie, but failed.[719]

"Take off your uniform!" Lebow shouted.[720]

Charlie swung at LeBow with his nightstick again, but this time LeBow attempted to dodge the blow, resulting in the nightstick striking LeBow in the head.[721] LeBow later recounted, "This last blow left a big scar on the top of my head, and my head was bleeding."[722]

Sheets, who offered testimony as a witness, maintained that LeBow continued to curse Charlie, calling him vulgar names, but confirmed that at no time did Charlie reciprocate.[723]

Frye approached LeBow and said, "I'll take you home," and then the two entered the Goodie Shop. A few moments later, LeBow, still defiant, emerged from the shop and demanded that Charlie arrest him. LeBow later claimed that Charlie grabbed hold of his suit and tore it in two places. "A big crowd had gathered around," LeBow stated, "among which was Ray Masters, who just came by."[724]

"What's the matter?" asked Masters.[725]

"This officer hit me over the head with a club," LeBow responded.[726]

Turning to Charlie, Masters stated, "We will get you, God damn you!"[727]

Sheets revealed in his sworn statement that LeBow continued cursing Charlie while they waited for transportation to the police station. Masters joined in, becoming so confrontational in his speech and threats that Charlie also placed him under arrest.[728] Upon arriving at the police station, LeBow was charged with disturbing the peace and Masters was booked for interfering with a police officer in the performance of his duties. LeBow's father summarily responded and posted bond for both boys.[729]

The next morning, LeBow and Masters appeared before Judge Edward J. Fleming to answer the charges leveled against them. This being a preliminary hearing, Charlie and the other witnesses were not required to be present. LeBow's version of events is provided in a sworn statement found in Charlie's police personnel records, as is Charlie's official police report and the sworn statements of Sheets, LeBow's friend, and H.J. Lederman, a bystander.

LeBow claimed that the fight between Sparks and Thompson culminated before Charlie began to cross the street, and that Charlie provoked a confrontation with him (LeBow) while LeBow was casually talking to Frye by telling them to shut up.[730]

"Go ahead and keep talking, Frye," LeBow claims to have said, "he's talking to those other fellows."[731]

"Don't get smart," Charlie allegedly responded, and then, without any further provocation, he began striking LeBow with his nightstick, all the while telling LeBow to go home and get off the corner.[732]

LeBow said that the only time he raised his hand against Charlie was to guard off one of the blows from the officer's nightstick, and insisted that Charlie continued to strike him with his club as he tried to comply with his order to leave.[733]

"I walked up as far as the Parisian Lunch, about five doors up the street south," testified Lebow, "and he kept following me and hitting me with his club on the legs and hands. Right in front of the Parisian Lunch he hit me on the head and knocked me dizzy and unconscious, and I leaned up against the side of the building, and did not know for a moment what had happened to me."[734]

LeBow told Judge Fleming that when Masters arrived, Charlie was still threatening him and hit him again with his club. "All this time this officer was talking about it and seemed very nervous," LeBow asserted.[735]

"Don't say anything to him," Masters allegedly said. "Let him alone and let him take you down and we'll get him later."[736]

"For that, you are arrested too," Charlie was said to have responded.[737]

Before the judge, LeBow said that a friend of his told him that he heard Charlie say he'd "beat them all up" if they showed up on the corner that night, and then he'd haul them down to the station. LeBow went on to tell the judge that Charlie told him that he was trying to strike him in the arm, not the head. "I told him he was 'a damned liar,' and that he tried to hit me on the head!" LeBow testified.[738]

Judge Fleming must have viewed LeBow's testimony as credible, for he dismissed the charges against LeBow and Masters, and advised LeBow to prefer charges against Charlie through the Board of Police Commissioners, if he felt it was warranted.[739] If Charlie striking LeBow over the head with his nightstick was found to be intentional, then Charlie would be fired from the department and could face assault charges.

LeBow did act upon the judge's recommendation by submitting a formal complaint against Charlie with the Board of Police Commissioners. It was LeBow's contention that Charlie struck him over the head with his nightstick intentionally. The statements submitted by Sheets and Lederman, however, completely supported Charlie's report, and even specified that the blow to LeBow's head did not appear intentional. When all was said and done, LeBow's complaint against Charlie was dropped and he was cleared of any wrongdoing. But Charlie's impression of the Board of Police Commissioners was no longer favorable, and his negativity towards them lingered.

The second incident that Charlie was involved in occurred about 1:00 p.m., on September 27, 1922, near 31st and Indiana Avenues. Details of this occurrence are rather obscure and comes primarily from a complaint by Harry Hershfield, a local jeweler. Hershfield was in the Corn Exchange Bank and noticed on the opposite corner that Charlie was involved in a scuffle with Eitel Croy, a 16-year-old high school student. At first, Hershfield believed the two were cutting up.[740]

Hershfield reported that he did not see what started the fray. But, in his complaint, Hershfield leveled the blame entirely on Charlie, who he said kicked Croy in the testicles, struck him with his nightstick, and then drew his weapon. Hershfield ran over to the scene with E.L. Perkins, a druggist, by which time other men were at the scene. The men reported that they convinced Charlie to holster his weapon.[741]

According to Hershfield, the men who responded to the incident told Charlie that if the boy had done something wrong, the thing to do was to arrest him, but not kill him. Hershfield was a close friend of Louis Oppenstein, a member of the Board of Police Commissioners, and used their association to publicly censure Charlie.[742] Nothing in Charlie's personnel file provides his side of the story.

Hershfield returned to the bank to complete his business, and Charlie followed him inside. Charlie allegedly told Hershfield that he did not think much of him. "I told him [Charlie] I did not have a gun as he had, but not to go too far with me or he would regret it, as his gun did not scare me." Hershfield then injected Oppenstein's name and threatened to tell him of the incident. Charlie made it clear to Hershfield that he didn't much care for Oppenstein, perhaps due to the incident that occurred earlier that month.[743]

Hershfield reported Charlie's comment to Captain William A. Shreeve, who would go on to serve as chief of police between 1924 and 1928. That same afternoon, Hershfield followed through with a formal written complaint to Commissioner Oppenstein. "This officers [sic] # is 558," Hershfield affirmed, "and in my opinion is not a safe man to trust with a gun. I called up Capt. Shreeve and told him of this and we will all be glad to appear against this officer if you wish."[744]

When the matter came before Acting Chief of Police Frank H. Anderson, he immediately suspended Charlie pending a formal investigation, which was justified and prudent under the circumstances. Perhaps due to Oppenstein's involvement and potential bias in the matter, Charlie felt compelled to tender his resignation on September 29. Hershfield may have been satisfied upon receipt of Oppenstein's letter advising him of Charlie's suspension and subsequent resignation, but even Oppenstein could not avert the ongoing investigation.[745]

On October 11, Chief Anderson took the peculiar step of sending a letter to Fred Croy, Eitel's father, advising him that he suspended Charlie, as per his request, and that Charlie was subsequently permitted to resign from the department. Anderson went on to write: "We are extremely sorry that your son received such treatment from a member of this department, but as we have had one other similar complaint against Officer Barger we are very glad that you brought the matter to our attention so that we could properly protect ourselves and the public against it occurring again."[746]

In early December 1922, the internal investigation into the incident with Croy culminated in Charlie's favor. On December 12, Chief Anderson handed Charlie a memorandum to deliver to Lieutenant Larrabee, merely stating: "The bearer, C.D. Barger, has been reinstated a patrolman on this department, and is assigned to duty under your command."[747]

Charlie reverted to Class C Patrolman upon his return to the department, which may have been a precautionary probationary period as a condition for reinstatement. Upon the recommendation of Lieutenant Larrabee, Charlie was again promoted to Class B Patrolman on June 16, 1923, raising his salary from $125 to $140 a month, or $1,762 and $1,974, respectively, by today's calculations. On April 22, 1924, he moved his family into a small but comfortable home at 4222 Millcreek Boulevard.

Charlie had a lot bottled up inside—his childhood, his combat experiences, his inability to adjust to civilian life—and was quietly becoming increasingly affected by mental illness. Even now, he needed counseling and rehabilitation for post-traumatic stress, which was unavailable to veterans of the Great War (or the world war after that, for that matter). Audie Murphy, the most-decorated combat soldier in World War II, would reflect, "After the war, they took Army dogs and rehabilitated them for civilian life. But they turned soldiers into civilians immediately, and let 'em sink or swim."[748] By 1926, Charlie was clearly beginning to sink.

Chapter Fourteen

BROKEN HERO

By 1926, Charlie's volatile marriage to Audrey was effectively over and they separated pending a divorce. In the divorce proceedings that August, the court decreed that Audrey would assume custody of their son, Charlie, Jr., and Charlie would have visitation rights. The court also ordered Charlie to pay $7.00 per week for his son's support and maintenance, which Charlie failed to do. He was bringing home $140 a month, and child support would have amounted to twenty percent of his paycheck.

On September 9, 1926, Charlie moved from his home on Millcreek Boulevard in Kansas City, and rented a modest domicile at 4115 Baltimore Avenue. Meanwhile, he entered a whirlwind romance with another divorcee, Ruth Irene (Bailey) Burgoon, and they were married in 1927. Ruth would turn 18 that year, and Charlie would turn 33.

Ruth was born to Elmer and Mary (Wooley) Bailey on December 4, 1909, in Tarsney, Missouri, an unincorporated community in a section of Van Buren Township, about 33 miles southeast of Kansas City. Later, the Bailey family moved to Grand River Township, in Cass County, Missouri, where Ruth met her first husband, John William Burgoon. On December 21, 1923, John and Ruth applied for and received a marriage license, even though she was fourteen and he was forty. It is likely that the couple eloped, since Ruth misrepresented her age on the marriage certificate as being older than her 14 years, and the fact that they traveled to Henry County for the nuptials. John and Ruth were married in Deepwater, Missouri, on Christmas Day.

On January 25, 1925, John and Ruth had their only son together, Joseph Elmer Burgoon, who was born in Harrisonville, Missouri. They divorced shortly thereafter, and John went on to marry Hattie May Rogers, with whom he had another son and a daughter, Donald and Hattie. John passed away in Cass County in 1938, and is buried in Peculiar, Missouri.

Charlie adopted Joe Burgoon just after he and Ruth were married. In the beginning, life was wonderful, and for the first time in his life Charlie had a good job, a supportive wife, and good friends. Bolstering their marriage even further was the birth of their daughter, Mabel Louise Barger, on April 13, 1928, in Kansas City. Mabel was the name that his mother, Cora, assumed after marrying Ed Rolleg. According to Charlie's grandson, Joe Barger, Charlie believed that Mabel was his mother's actual name and felt it appropriate to name his daughter in her honor.

Ruth began to become aware after she married Charlie that he was suppressing a lot of anger, suffering with depression and war-related nightmares, and that something was affecting his mental faculties. She was gradually learning that something wasn't quite right, but it wasn't until 1928 that he really exploded. The catalyst for what transpired could be directly traced to his previous marriage with Audrey.

Details are a little muddled, but a St. Louis court awarded Charlie full custody of his son, Charlie, Jr., shortly after his marriage to Ruth.[749] Audrey, however, continued to demand child support payments and threatened legal action to take back their son if he didn't comply. Charlie maintained that he was barely making enough to pay rent and support his present family, and that he should not have to make payments while he had custody of their son. Audrey disagreed.

In late May 1928, Audrey arrived at Charlie's house and demanded that Charlie, Jr., be turned over to her. Charlie was not at home at the time and Ruth refused to give her the boy.[750] This sparked a bitter quarrel between the two. Audrey then visited the courthouse in Kansas City to accelerate her motion for child custody and support, and added retroactive pay to the lawsuit.

On Friday, June 1, 1928, Charlie was served a summons to appear in court, and, according the *Macon* [MO] *Chronicle-Herald,* he brooded over the matter all day Saturday and into Sunday.[751] The court system at that time almost always sided with the mother, and he may have felt the case was closed the moment it was opened. His thinking may have been along the lines of: Audrey would win, he wouldn't pay, he would be sent to jail for noncompliance of the court order, and he would inevitably lose his job.

On Sunday, June 3, Charlie's 34th birthday, he arrived home from work despondent. According to Ruth, he was still grappling with his court date with Audrey and his financial woes. But, as usual, he was keeping his feelings to himself, as he fretted about the house. Meanwhile, Ruth and their infant daughter, Mabel, fell asleep.[752]

Then, later that evening, the unthinkable occurred. In the living room, Charlie drew his revolver, placed the muzzle to his chest, and pulled the trigger. The bullet entered just above the heart, nearly killing him, but he was rushed to Kansas City General Hospital where physicians worked frantically to save his life.[753]

According to Lieutenant L.A. Woodley, an investigator with the Kansas City Police Department, Charlie was in the recovery room after surgery and was just regaining consciousness when Audrey entered his recovery area screaming at him at the top of her lungs. Hospital staff summoned security and had her escorted from the premises, but she wasn't finished. She proceeded directly to Charlie's home and created such a commotion that the police were called. She was arrested for disturbing the peace.[754]

The following day, the *St. Louis Post-Dispatch* reported that Charlie had a chance for recovery. Charlie told the reporter, who had a brief opportunity to talk to him, that domestic and financial trouble caused him to attempt to take his own life. "I'm sorry I didn't do a good job of it," he added.[755]

On June 5, Audrey appeared before Judge Ira S. Gardner in the South Side Court in Kansas City to answer to the charge of disturbing the peace. Ruth and Charlie, Jr., were also present in the courtroom. Judge Gardner seemed to sympathize with Audrey, for he dismissed the charges against her, ordered that she could keep her son until that evening, and ruled that she would thereafter be granted occasional visitation.[756]

Charlie was released from the hospital after nine weeks. After some recovery time at home, he returned to work with the Kansas City Police Department and was assigned a beat along Grand Avenue. It is curious that the department retained his services after something as serious as a suicide attempt. Surely, such an act would have been seen as a telltale sign of mental instability, even in those times. Oddly, however, his pay would be cut by half, to $70 a month, which would only serve to frustrate his already volatile situation.

Meanwhile, Charlie still had to deal with Audrey, who was seeking primary custody of their son. He hired Attorney Frank E. Doyle to represent him, and racked up $74.88 in legal fees against his $70 a month salary. In court, his attempted suicide worked in Audrey's favor. Charlie lost the case. According to Charlie's police personnel records, he believed that Doyle was to blame for failing to properly represent him.[757]

On October 15, 1928, Doyle sued Charlie for nonpayment of his legal bill. Appearing before Justice of the Peace L.R. Tolivar on December 20, the Court ruled in Doyle's favor, and tacked on legal fees and court costs. The Court had now *ordered* Charlie to pay Doyle, but, still, Charlie repudiated.[758]

On February 27, 1929, the law firm Jenkins & Vance, representing Doyle, sent a letter to the Board of Police Commissioners seeking their assistance in the matter. According to attorney Chester Vance, every effort had been made to induce Charlie to settle the judgment against him, but Charlie completely refused to do so.[759] Charlie, ever defiant, still held out. Finally, for reasons unknown, on August 20, 1929, he visited Vance to arrange payments of $5.00 a month. Vance advised the Board of Police Commissioners of the arrangement, and suggested the matter be held in abeyance in order that Charlie might have the opportunity to pay the debt in increments. This time Charlie paid.[760]

On August 1, 1929, Charlie and Ruth moved to 6022 Tracy Avenue in Kansas City. Audrey had since moved 250 miles east, to St. Louis, where she rented a store at 2927 Chouteau Avenue, with intentions of opening a restaurant. Next door was a dry goods store that was owned and operated by Sam and Mary Novik, Russian immigrants who arrived in the United States around 1907. According to an article in the *St. Louis Post-Dispatch*, it was not uncommon for Charlie, Jr., to play in front of Novik's establishment while Audrey was readying her store for the grand opening.[761]

On August 9, 1929, seven-year-old Charlie, Jr., was playing on the sidewalk in front of Novik's store while 30 to 40 Missouri Pacific Railroad employees lined up to cash their paychecks. Suddenly, three masked men entered Novik's store, robbed the proprietor of $2,600, and hurried out to flee the scene. Novik grabbed a pistol from a shelf, rushed to the entrance, and opened fire.[762]

One of the bandits had a shotgun and returned fire from 100 yards away. At that moment, Charlie, Jr., ran in front of Novik, and his legs were peppered with slugs. Also injured was John C. Peckhaus, who was grazed in the head as he passed by. The robbers fled east, and then ducked around the corner where it was believed that they had a getaway car parked. They were never caught.[763]

Young Charlie's injuries were diagnosed as serious but fortunately not life-threatening, and he recovered with no permanent effect. Perhaps concerned for the safety of her son, Audrey soon abandoned her ambition to open a restaurant in St. Louis and returned to Kansas City. It wouldn't be long before she went after Charlie again for child support, but, for another year, he refused to comply with the court order.

By the summer of 1930, the Great Depression was hitting Audrey particularly hard and she renewed her effort to pursue Charlie for child support. This time, she used the same tactic as Attorney Chester Vance had used in getting Charlie to pay what he owed to Doyle; she, too, appealed to the Board of Police Commissioners. Charlie was subsequently ordered to appear before the Board on August 28, at 2 p.m., to answer to the charge of nonpayment of child support.[764]

"This [paying child support] you have failed to do," the Board maintained, "and you are hereby cited to show cause why you should not pay for the support and maintenance of this minor child under the Court's decree. The above charge against you will be heard on the date and place aforesaid, at which time you will have the right to appear, to be defended by counsel, to confront the witnesses against you and to produce witnesses in your behalf."[765]

Charlie's answer to the Board was that he could not afford $7.00 a week. The Board reduced his child support payment and ordered that he pay

Audrey $5.00 per week beginning on September 1, or be dropped from the Kansas City Police Department. Charlie began making the payments.[766] On a salary of $840 a year, Charlie was now paying $260 to Audrey, $420 for rent, and possibly still paying $60 to Doyle, leaving Charlie and Ruth with $100 a year, or little more than $8.00 a month for their food and other essentials.

In direct contrast to Charlie's everyday struggle to earn a meager living for his family, he continued to attend all-expense-paid functions, such as the elaborate annual week-long American Legion conventions. In October 1930, he and 30 other World War I Medal of Honor recipients were guests of the Legion in Boston, Massachusetts, where they were billeted in the best suites at the Commander Hotel. The highlight of the convention was a banquet held at the hotel, in which Massachusetts Governor Frank G. Allen invited President Herbert Hoover as the guest of honor. During the banquet, Charlie and the other recipients had an opportunity to meet and personally speak with the President.[767]

Around the first of the year, 1931, Audrey married Elmer Frederick Reinders, a butcher, and they made their home at 361 Pacific Avenue in Kansas City, Kansas. For those readers unfamiliar with the Kansas City metropolitan area, Kansas City, Missouri, is much larger than Kansas City, Kansas, but they're both significant cities. State Line Road defines the two state borders and splits the two cities.

Charlie, Jr., resided with his mother and her new husband, but, by court order, he would stay with his father in Missouri during the summer months. On the evening of June 3, 1931, Charlie's thirty-seventh birthday, he traveled to Audrey's house to pick up their son to take him for the summer. Details of what followed comes from a casualty report, which was generated by the Kansas City Police Department in Kansas.

When Charlie arrived at Audrey's house, she refused to permit him to take Charlie, Jr. This resulted in a volatile argument. Charlie finally grabbed his son and started to leave, ignoring Audrey's protests, and then her 19-year-old brother, Verley Hurst, intervened. A physical confrontation ensued, and culminated when Charlie picked up a meat cleaver and struck Verley over the head.[768]

Charlie departed Audrey's house with his son while neighbors called the police. Verley, who suffered a deep, five-inch cut on his scalp, was taken to the Emergency Hospital in Kansas City, Kansas, where he was treated by Dr. J.M. Rapin. Upon being released, Verley visited the Kansas City Police Department, in Kansas, and swore out a state warrant for Charlie's arrest, the charge being "Assault with the Intent to Kill."[769]

The facts were not clear to Wyandotte County, Kansas, County Attorney Fred White, who would prosecute the case. He knew that Charlie worked for the Kansas City, Missouri, Police Department, and he did not wish to embarrass the Missouri department or its officers, particularly if the charges were based solely on a family quarrel. On June 5, when the incident was divulged to Lieutenants Walter S. Goodhue and William C. Robeen of the Kansas City, Missouri, Police Department, they met with Chief Lewis M. Siegfried, of that department, and recommended that the matter be investigated.[770]

Chief Siegfried immediately suspended Charlie from the police department. A few days later, Chief Siegfried received a copy of the casualty report sent to him by Chief of Police William T. McMullen of Kansas City, Kansas. Then, on June 11, Chief Siegfried made the following recommendation to the Board of Police Commissioners, based upon the casualty report and a review of Charlie's personnel file: "This man has been in similar trouble on several previous occasions. He appears to have no self-control. I do not believe Barger is fit to be a member of this Department, and I respectfully recommend that he be dropped for the good of the service."[771]

While growing up, Charlie's second cousin, June Buccina, was very close to his mother, Cora—so much so, in fact, that June still refers to Cora as "Grandma." Though they were close, she does not remember Cora saying much of anything about Charlie. However, June's mother, Ida, did pass along some sketchy information about cousin Charlie. June could not remember the details, but she did say that Charlie had borne "a bit of a bad reputation for his behavior."[772]

The two incidents that occurred in 1922, once properly investigated, were decided in Charlie's favor, and the Board of Police Commissioners never ruled on Charlie's fate regarding the episode involving Verley. While on unpaid suspension, and receiving undue pressure from Chief Siegfried, Charlie resigned. "Gentlemen:" he wrote to the Board of Police Commissioners on June 29, "Please accept my resignation as patrolman as of June 30th, 1931."[773]

Surprising is the fact that the assault on Verley was not reported in newspapers, either in Kansas or Missouri. "The media was a lot different in those bygone days than they are now," reflects Detective (ret.) Clarence Gibson, a longtime police employee and co-founder of the Kansas City Police Historical Society. "I believe the Chief wanted to keep the assault hush-hush, and let our department deal with it. That is probably what led to him [Charlie] being forced off the job."[774]

Charlie left the police department with no financial compensation and no pension. He received no disability pay for the wounds he incurred during the scuffle with Frank Elliott in 1922. Neither did he receive recognition for his ten years of honorable service with the Kansas City

Police Department. Chief Siegfried's impulse to terminate Charlie, even before the investigation concluded, and Charlie's subsequent abrupt resignation from the police force, left Charlie with little resources to draw upon. Charlie was quietly exploding. Ahead for him were troubling events that would ultimately end in tragedy.

Within days of his resignation, Charlie was hospitalized with acute appendicitis. Following surgery and recovery, he was discharged, still carrying the burden of providing for his family during the worst economic depression this country has ever faced. In October 1931, just two weeks after being released from the hospital, Charlie was given a special night watchman's job with American Royal in Kansas City, which paid $18 a week, slightly more than what he made when he left the police department. It was decent work, and he was likely glad to have it. A week into the job, however, his firearm slipped from its holster as he went to sit down, and it discharged upon striking the floor. The bullet went through his right leg. Once again, Charlie was hospitalized ... and, again, unemployed.[775]

The same day that Charlie was wounded, his son, Joe, fell from the porch of the family home and suffered a fractured skull. He was taken to Mercy Hospital in Kansas City for treatment. Soon after returning home, Joe contracted double pneumonia, which was passed to his mother and sister. As if things weren't bad enough in the Barger household, Ruth, Joe and Mable all came down with the mumps, and Ruth, while hospitalized, was diagnosed with spinal meningitis. She was confined to an isolation ward until she fully recovered.[776]

The gunshot to Charlie's leg left him permanently disabled. He could no longer perform heavy work, and could not walk without the use of a steel leg brace and cane. Ruth tried to find gainful employment when she was released from the hospital, but was not able to withstand the rigors of hard physical exertion. And Charlie had accrued $350 in medical bills, which he was unable to pay.[777]

Charlie wasn't one to give up, though. In June 1932, he found employment as a caretaker in the shelter houses at Swope Park, at 1,805 acres, the largest park in Kansas City. However, that job lasted just two months.[778] He inevitably fell behind on child support payments to Audrey and she took him to court. He was already unable to make the $35 monthly rent payment for his home on Tracy Avenue, and furniture dealers were repossessing his unpaid household goods. The case went before Judge Thomas H. Knight of Independence, Missouri. Charlie found some good will sent his way from Judge Knight, who recognized Charlie's dire circumstances and ruled in his favor.

Charlie's misfortune soon reemerged with eviction from the house on Tracy Avenue, but his fate twisted again when a kindly landlord temporarily permitted Charlie and his family to reside rent-free at 2820 E. 60th Avenue.[779] Meanwhile, he did whatever he could to earn money, and every day was a struggle. "It's fine to have all the medals," he lamented, "but the trouble is, you can't eat them."[780]

As Charlie grew up, and as he served in the military, he was in control of his faculties, and for fifteen years thereafter, he held it together, at least for the most part. The military had lifted Charlie, given him meaning, purpose, and friendships. Earning the Medal of Honor gave him opportunities that he otherwise would never have had, and he was discharged with a promising outlook of a normal life. He met his mother for the first time; he married and had children; and he traveled to a big city where he found a respectable job as a policeman.

But, Charlie wasn't raised like many children who grew up in a family-centered environment that prepared them for normal, civilian adult life. He never had role models showing him how to build and maintain a healthy marriage, or how to deal with the pressures of society: job security, courts, political strongmen, or even how to maintain normal, healthy relationships. And now, the opportunities that looked so promising after coming home from the war had waned.

Like the courageous soldier he was, Charlie took risks in coming to the big city, taking on the role of a police officer, getting married, and having children. These risks had not, however, worked out as well as the risks he took in war. These later risks were much more complex in nature. In combat, Charlie had pushed himself beyond normal limits and became an international hero. But those heroic combat experiences did not instill upon him the patience or skills required to manage the challenges that would confront him in civilian life. Eventually, he was left emotionally and financially depleted.

In Army life, Charlie's basic needs of where to eat, where to sleep, what to wear, etc., were met, freeing him up to do what he did best: defend his buddies and pursue the enemy. In civilian life, Charlie had to figure out his role in the complex relationships of women (both in marriage and divorce), his role and responsibility as a father, and the interference of law enforcement as consequences to his behaviors, all the while trying to pursue his goal of becoming a good policeman.

The Great Depression hit nearly everybody hard, and Charlie was no exception. He could barely feed his family, keep a roof over their heads, or adequately provide for them. But he wasn't yet ready to give up. He fell back on what he knew about survival in Southern Missouri.

Charlie began raising rabbits to put meat on the table, and he planted a garden. According to Ruth, Charlie during this time had become increasingly withdrawn, tetchy, moody, sleepless and depressed, and for the first time during their marriage he exhibited intermittent bouts of hostility. Behind his cold, narrow eyes, was a tormented, depressed man, unemotional and detached.

In 1924, Congress passed the World War Adjusted Compensation Act, whereupon veterans were issued certificates of service, which were redeemable in 20 years. Each veteran was to receive one dollar for each day of domestic service, up to a maximum of $500, and $1.25 for each day of overseas service, up to a maximum of $625.[781] The stock market crash of 1929, however, propelled the United States into the Great Depression, and since then a large number of WWI veterans were out of work. In the summer of 1932, 43,000 veterans and supporters marched on Washington to demand immediate cash-payment of veteran bonuses, but they were driven out, and their shelters and belongings were burned.

In September 1932, in the wake of the Bonus Army March on Washington, DC, Robert W. Reed, Charlie's American Legion friend and staff writer for the *Kansas City Star*, published a story about the pitiful demise of Charlie's circumstances since returning home from the war. The story went nationwide, complete with a heartbreaking photo of Charlie and his family. Reed called attention to the fact that there were many veterans who had never deployed overseas, but were still receiving generous compensation by the Department of Veterans Affairs.[782]

Reed also echoed what many were saying about the United States neglecting its supreme heroes, while other countries, such as Great Britain, provided stipends to their recipients.[783] At the end of World War I, for example, those who earned the Victoria Cross received an annuity of £10, which could be increased to £50 in the event that the recipient was experiencing financial hardship. Unfortunately, Reed's proposal for compensation would not be acted upon until after Charlie's death.[784]

On March 8, 1933, in a fit of rage, Charlie beat Ruth severely, and then threatened to shoot her and himself. Fortunately, she managed to call the police, who responded immediately to their tiny home at 2641 East Sixty-First Street and took him into custody. "I guess I'm all wrong," Charlie lamented. "I think my nerves have gone to pieces. I don't want to hurt anybody. Just lock me up."[785]

Instead of taking Charlie to jail, the responding officers transported him to Kansas City General Hospital for psychiatric evaluation and treatment. Medical staff noted that he appeared detached, generally depressed, and had apparently given up on life. He was escorted to the psychiatric ward where, for two years, he remained under "observation."

When Robert Reed learned that Charlie had been institutionalized, he visited his friend, Fred Harris, who was a veteran's representative for the Department of Veterans Affairs (DVA) in Kansas City. Together, they visited Charlie in the hospital and completed the necessary documentation to apply for service-connected disability. The genesis of Charlie's present condition, they claimed, was exposure to mustard gas and "shell shock." Unfortunately for Charlie and others, the DVA compensated very few for these afflictions, often demanding more proof than a veteran could provide, or citing loopholes that would deny a veteran's claim.

In fact, Charlie could not have picked a worse time in U.S. history to apply for government assistance. Franklin D. Roosevelt campaigned for the presidency on a pledge to balance the federal budget. Six days after taking office, in March 1933, he submitted legislation to Congress which would cut $500 million from the $3.6 billion federal budget by eliminating government agencies, reducing the pay of civilian and military federal workers, and slashing veterans' benefits by 50 percent. One must wonder: Where were the politicians' loyalty to and gratitude for the soldiers that had fought so hard for the country?[786]

Roosevelt's bill, officially titled the "Act of March 20, 1933," was readily approved and signed into law. A month later, the Veterans Administration denied Charlie's application for disability benefits, citing that he didn't file his claim prior to 1925 ... the axiomatic loophole. In effect, the country to which he sacrificed so much had completely turned its back on him. "All of us who knew Charlie Barger are convinced his condition was the result of his war service," affirmed Robert Reed. "Yet the Veterans Administration at Washington refused at all times to concede that he was entitled to service-connected compensation."[787]

To their credit, Reed and Harris convinced the Veterans Administration to pay Charlie non-service-connected compensation of $30 a month for total disability, but that stopped when he was released from the hospital in the spring of 1935. According to the doctors, he was not cured, but he appeared stabilized and they had no further justification for holding him.[788]

Government funding may have also been a factor to his release at that time. Cutbacks during the Depression were widespread, particularly regarding veterans' benefits. In May 1935, President Roosevelt expressed his viewpoint when he equated veterans with every other American facing adversity. "I hold that the able-bodied citizen, because he wore a uniform and for no other reason, should be accorded no treatment different from that accorded to other citizens who did not wear a uniform during the World War," he proclaimed. "The veteran who suffers from this depression can best be aided by the rehabilitation of the country as a whole."[789]

Ruth, who had been residing with her parents in Oak Grove, Missouri, from the time that Charlie was hospitalized, visited him regularly, and she thought he was not ready to be discharged. She addressed her concerns to the medical staff, but they casually dismissed her as an overly reactive spouse. With no other recourse, she gathered her children and moved into a home Charlie rented at 4650 Heidelberg Avenue in St. Louis.

Charlie had no immediate job prospects, and therefore applied for assistance at St. Louis County Relief. Unthinkable for him to shirk his responsibility, however, Charlie would live another day to show he could still care for his family. He would take yet another job, and even buy them a piece of real estate to live on.

Chapter Fifteen

A NAME AND A CASE NUMBER

President Roosevelt, taking office on March 4, 1933, amid the Great Depression, passed an unprecedented abundance of legislation and a slew of executive orders in his first 100 days. Poverty, by now, had gripped most of the nation. Setting in motion the New Deal, his administration funded federal programs designed to spark economic recovery, spur job creation, invest in public works, and, ultimately, improve the lives of everyday Americans. Relief programs were summarily established, which included the Federal Emergency Relief Act (FERA), the Civil Works Administration (CWA), the Works Progress Administration (WPA), and the Civilian Conservation Corps (CCC). World War I veterans were not initially eligible for enrollment in the CCC, but events were already playing out that would relax the eligibility requirements.

In May 1933, two months after Roosevelt took office, veterans made a second, smaller Bonus Army march on Washington, again seeking immediate cash-payment of their Certificates of Service, which were not redeemable until 1945. Roosevelt handled this march more humanely than the Hoover Administration had handled the larger, previous one. Instead of sending the Army to disperse the marchers, he provided them with a campsite in Virginia and three meals a day.

Roosevelt also sent his wife, Eleanor, to meet with the veterans, and to listen to their concerns, many of which would have to be addressed in Congress. But what she could do for them, and did offer the Bonus Army marchers at the time, was jobs through the newly created CCC, which used unskilled laborers to conserve and develop natural resources in rural lands owned by federal, state and local governments.[790]

In 1933, when Eleanor Roosevelt met with the veterans, the CCC was providing relief for families with unmarried men between the ages of eighteen and twenty-five. Because veterans of World War I would have been above the age of 25 in 1933, they were ineligible for this program.[791] But Eleanor Roosevelt's promise to the Bonus Army marchers led to immediate expansion of the CCC, to include a quota of 25,000 World War I veterans to be used for reforestation work.[792] Veterans' applications had to be certified by the Veterans Administration, but marital status and age restrictions did not apply to them. Once the application was accepted, the veteran would be assigned to an employment camp comprised entirely of ex-veterans.[793]

On April 8, 1935, Congress approved the Emergency Relief Appropriation Act of 1935, which included continued funding for the CCC program through March 31, 1937.[794] The Director of Emergency Conservation Work summarily announced that veterans' applications would be accepted after June 5, 1935, to expand the CCC during the period of June 15 and August 31.[795] The criteria for enrollment included: (1) service in the United States armed services; (2) American citizenship; (3) physically able to perform manual labor in a work camp; and (4) unemployed and in receipt of relief from a public relief agency. Applicants also had to be prepared to fit into camp life with a group of 200 men, and give his best effort to the job.[796]

On June 6, 1935, Charlie completed the required Form P-130 for enrollment in the CCC, and his application was readily approved by the Veterans' Contingent for Emergency Conservation Work at Jefferson Barracks, Missouri. A couple of days later, he received orders to report to Army authorities at Montauk, Missouri, for an enrollment physical on the eighteenth. During the examination, First Lieutenant Austin P. Haller discovered the problem with his right leg and jotted in his notes: "...he was okay, except for a healed injury to his right leg, shattered fibula, weak ankle, and hernial protrusion of large vein through scar."[797]

The CCC approved Charlie for a job, and he would serve between June 19 and October 1, 1935. He was assigned highway beautification duties with Company 1770 in Pacific, Missouri, about 35 miles west and slightly south of St. Louis. Although he was paid $30 a month, regulations mandated that $25 automatically went to his wife and children. The government benefits for Charlie, however, were generous; the CCC provided food, clothing and barracks lodging during the work week.

Charlie held no rank or rating while working with the CCC, as he was not qualified for administrative work. He was simply designated an "enrollee," or "member." His supervisors, or leaders as they were called, consistently rated his service as satisfactory, even after he re-enrolled for three months in October 1935. Such an underrating might have been due to his physical limitations, for he had trouble walking, but otherwise he was a good worker, as confirmed by Captain Braxton L. Roberts, a Reserve Army officer with the 408th Infantry Regiment, and commander of CCC Company 1770, who recognized Charlie's contribution to the unit and rated his performance as excellent.

With the income he received from the CCC, Charlie was unable to make ends meet. Therefore, he and Ruth agreed that she should take the children and move back with her parents in Oak Grove, Missouri, about 25 miles east of Kansas City, until spring, after which time they should have enough money saved to get back together. Meanwhile, he moved from their home on Heidelberg Avenue to a small, less expensive apartment at 3918A South Grand Avenue in St. Louis, where Ruth and the children would visit him once or twice a month.

Charlie re-enrolled with the CCC for three months on January 21, 1936, and then for another six months on March 31. Meanwhile, on January 27, Congress passed the Adjusted Compensation Payment Act, authorizing the immediate payment of $2 billion in World War bonuses.[798] The twists of fate turned again in Charlie's favor when he received the lump sum payment for his Adjusted Compensation Certificate, as he was able to put $200 down on a little chicken farm, on which he would thereafter make monthly payments of $10.

Charlie's farm was located four miles southwest of Oak Grove, Missouri, near where Ruth's parents lived. It is presumed that Ruth's father, Elmer Bailey, arranged for Charlie to purchase the farm, as Charlie was working full time across the state and it would have been difficult for him to get the time off to look for a farm in Oak Grove. Once all the necessary documents were in order, Ruth likely had Charlie sign them during one of her weekend visits.

Unable to arrange a transfer before satisfying his six-month commitment with Company 1770, Charlie remained in Pacific, more than 200 miles away from his family, until July 6, 1936, leaving Ruth alone to setup and organize their new home. The following day, July 7, he had the good fortune to enroll with Company 3773 in Blue Springs, located just five miles west of Oak Grove. After initial orientation culminated on July 11, he was assigned to soil conservation.

Before beginning his new job with Company 3773, Charlie took five days of leave to settle into his house and spend some time with his family. At some point thereafter, Charlie began to grow increasingly frustrated when he had trouble settling his bills. Pressure was mounting once more, and the winds of fate were twisting again.

On October 20, 1936, Charlie suffered a serious work-related injury to his right hand, the circumstances of which are unknown. He was hospitalized overnight at Fort Leavenworth, Kansas, located 50 miles west of Blue Springs, Missouri. Upon returning to camp, he was assigned light duties as a Barracks Orderly, which it can easily be assumed that Charlie didn't much care for, but, according to First Foreman George A. Johnson, he went about his camp duties in his usual quiet and efficient manner. At home, it was another story. Ruth would later confirm that he had been irritable since being injured, even more so than the weeks preceding his breakdown in 1933.

"The battle of life grew grimmer each day for this man whose mind could not adjust itself," recalled Robert Reed. "The moment of glory left only a continuous mental disturbance which culminated in self-destruction."[799]

On Friday, November 20, 1936, Charlie returned home for the weekend and began quarreling with Ruth, who later claimed she could not recall what they argued about. The situation intensified, and in an unusual fit of rage he took her by the throat and struck her several times on the head. Their son, Joe, then eleven, tried to intervene, but Charlie picked him up and threw him on the bed where he beat him badly. Through the years, Charlie and Ruth had their share of arguments, but it had never escalated to this level of physical violence.

"I wanted to go to my folks at Oak Grove, but Charlie threatened me, so I was afraid to leave," Ruth recalled. "We stayed in the house Friday night, all day Saturday, and on Sunday morning my folks came from Oak Grove and took all of us back to Oak Grove with them. We stayed there until afternoon, and all the time Charlie quarreled with my folks. Mr. and Mrs. H.C. Goodson, my aunt and uncle, brought us back home from Oak Grove on Sunday afternoon, and then took Charlie out to the camp where he works."[800]

Ruth knew he needed help, but it was help she could not provide for him, and she needed to protect herself and her children. After Charlie assaulted her the previous Friday, she threatened to call the police; he warned her that if she did, he would kill her. In the past, when they had arguments, Charlie calmed down over time and they talked things out, but this time was different. He was in a perpetual rage and there was nothing she could say or do to calm him down.[801]

On Monday morning, November 23, Ruth visited the Veterans Administration in Kansas City and talked to Fred Harris, who knew Charlie when he resided there a few years earlier. Harris understood what Charlie was going through, but he also realized that Charlie would not voluntarily check himself into a psychiatric hospital. Therefore, he recommended to Ruth that she swear out a warrant for his arrest, and that he would then arrange to have Charlie institutionalized where, for the remainder of his life, he would be properly cared for.[802]

That same morning, Charlie resumed his duties as Barracks Orderly at Blue Springs. Section Leader Stanton R. Endsley and First Foreman Johnson, both of whom considered Charlie and exceptional worker, noticed nothing out of the ordinary through his speech or actions. It wasn't until sheriff deputies arrived at 2:00 that afternoon when they learned that Charlie had been involved in a domestic dispute over the weekend.[803]

Deputies Frank Ridenour and J.W. Byrne, acting upon a warrant signed by Justice of the Peace Joseph J. Dougherty, of Kaw Township, were led to

Captain Levy's office. They presented the warrant to Levy and explained that they were there to arrest Charlie on charges of felonious assault upon his wife. Levy ordered Charlie to be brought before him, and once the charges were read, Charlie was remanded to the custody of the deputies. At the time, he appeared calm and in control.[804]

Charlie agreed to accompany the officers to the police station, but requested that he first be permitted to change from his work clothes. The deputies agreed, and escorted him to his barracks where they waited outside his room while he went in to change. After fifteen minutes, Ridenour and Byrne became suspicious, as Charlie had not come out of his room. When they went to check on him, they discovered that he had escaped out the rear door of the barracks.[805]

The deputies rushed to Elmer Bailey's residence in Oak Grove, and then hurried Elmer to Charlie's farm to check on Ruth. She had returned to her home a short time earlier, about 3:30 p.m., and was devastated to learn that they actually had Charlie contained and then allowed him to escape. In her gut, she later reflected, she knew this was not going to end well.[806]

Ruth permitted the deputies inside the small farmhouse to search for weapons, wherein they discovered and removed a shotgun and a rifle. Then Ridenour drove Ruth to the local schoolhouse to collect Joe and Mabel before taking them all back to Elmer's house. Before leaving, Ridenour instructed them to call the station house if Charlie showed up.[807]

About 5:30 that afternoon, Charlie appeared at Elmer's house wielding a large hunting knife. He pounded on the front door and demanded to see Ruth, but Elmer just opened the door slightly, told him he didn't know where she was, and insisted that he leave.[808]

"I want to see Ruth!" Charlie demanded. "I want to cut her throat!"[809]

Elmer slammed the door as Charlie continued to shout threats and obscenities. "I'll get her yet!" he yelled. "You see this knife? I'm going home and cut my throat and set the house on fire, but if I see Ruth first, it will be too bad for her!"[810]

Charlie also warned Elmer that he would kill any deputy or other members of law enforcement who tried to stop him, and then he left the scene. Ruth's sister, who was also at the house, immediately called the Sheriff's Office, and the dispatcher called Ridenour at home.[811] Shortly thereafter, Deputies Joe Phillips and John Meany arrived at Ridenour's house, and the three lawmen hustled over to Oak Grove to contact Deputy Constable Frank J. King.

By that time, King had been contacted by Elmer Bailey twice. The first time, Elmer reported that Charlie had assaulted Ruth, that Charlie had escaped from the deputies, and asked King to be on the lookout for him. Then, after Charlie left his house—after threatening to kill Ruth—Elmer contacted King to explain what had transpired. King got into his car and traveled three or four different roads between Oak Grove and Charlie's farm, looking for Charlie, but his search was in vain.[812]

The deputies found King investigating a minor vehicle accident about 6:30 p.m., and requested that he accompany them to Charlie's house, which he did. King learned later that Charlie had bypassed the main roads and stealthily negotiated his way across a field to his home, undetected by anyone. Now he was holed up in his place, prepared to carry out his threat.[813]

When the officers arrived outside the home, the house was dark. Ridenour and Meany covered the front door, while Phillips and King made their way to the back. From inside the small house, Charlie would have heard simultaneous knocking on the front and back doors, and would have also heard the repeated demands for him to come out peaceably.[814]

Ridenour found the front door slightly ajar, but fastened with a safety chain. Soon, Phillips and King joined Ridenour and Meany in front of the house, and King suggested firing tear gas through a window. Phillips retrieved a rifle and several tear gas canisters from the trunk of King's vehicle, while the others gathered on the south side of the house to avoid being affected by the gas, themselves.[815]

A few seconds after Phillips fired a tear gas canister, the officers heard shuffling in the house, and then heard Charlie swearing and shouting that he would kill anyone he could get his hands on. Peeking under a window shade, Ridenour noticed flames inside the home. Due to the fire, Meany hollered to Ridenour, "You'd better get your car out of the way!"[816]

"My car was parked beside the house and I moved it backwards into the road, so the lights shone on the front door," stated Ridenour.[817]

Meanwhile, Meany and Phillips broke a window on the south side of the house. They were hoping that Charlie might respond to the noise, and they could grab him and pull him out the window. Instead, Charlie went to the front door, jerked it open, and ran out wielding the hunting knife in his right hand. Not only was he bleeding from the neck, but his torso, both hands, forearms, arms, neck and face were on fire![818] Charlie had indeed saturated the place with coal oil and set the house afire, just as he said he would, and he also followed through with slicing his throat.

With the knife raised above his head, Charlie ignored Ridenour's orders to stop and assume a prone position on the ground. Charlie, still walking forward, continued cursing and threatening the officers, and it appeared to King that Charlie was headed for Ridenour's car. It soon became apparent, however, that Charlie's target was Ridenour himself. Fearing for his life, the officer drew his revolver and pled with Charlie to stop.[819]

"When he got within about twelve feet from Ridenour," King recalled, "Mr. Ridenour fired into the ground, but [Charlie] did not stop. [Ridenour] fired again when [Charlie] was almost on top of him, striking him in the leg, and causing [Charlie] to fall right at [Ridenour's] feet."[820]

It is uncanny that Charlie survived the war without ever being wounded, particularly considering what he had been through, but now, as a civilian, he had just suffered his eighth bullet wound!

Responding to the gunfire, Phillips and Meany ran from the side of the house towards Ridenour, initially unaware that Charlie was still conscious, still armed, and still posing a threat. Ridenour warned the deputies that Charlie had a knife in his hand, prompting Phillips to kick Charlie's arm to dislodge it. Failing in that attempt, he kicked Charlie's hand, this time succeeding in disarming him and removing the immediate danger.[821]

Ridenour and Meany stood guard over Charlie, while Phillips and King entered the house to extinguish the flames. After putting out the fire, Ridenour and King rushed to Oak Grove to acquire an ambulance, while Philips and Meany continued to stand guard over Charlie. Upon arrival in Oak Grove, they learned that the ambulance was out on another call, so King hired a car, put a cot in it, and returned to Charlie's house to transport him to the hospital.[822]

By the time that Ridenour and King arrived back at Charlie's place, Phillips and Meany had lifted Charlie off the ground and laid him on the floor inside the house where it was warm.[823] The men loaded Charlie into the automobile and took him to the General Hospital in Kansas City, 26 miles west, where he was treated by Dr. Wallace H. Graham, a resident physician.

Dr. Graham noted two open wounds and one superficial cut, the most serious being a gaping laceration four-inches in length and one-inch deep on the left side of Charlie's neck. Although it bled profusely, no arteries were cut. Graham applied sutures to the neck wounds and a splint to the leg, where Charlie had been shot, but his real concern was the 1st-, 2nd-, and 3rd-degree burns to his face, torso and extremities.[824]

Meanwhile, Officer Ridenour returned to Elmer's home in Oak Grove to explain to Ruth that Charlie had suffered severe injuries, but she was then hiding at a neighbor's house. The following day, about noon, she arrived at the hospital and found Charlie in the shock cradle. He was listed in critical condition, with a very high temperature, and was semiconscious throughout the day, but unable to speak. The doctor explained to Ruth that Charlie's kidneys were unable to excrete fluid and his prognosis was grim.[825]

As the hours waned away, Ruth remained at Charlie's bedside, talking to him quietly and praying. It was obvious to her that he was in excruciating pain from the burns, and morphine provided little relief. How could it have come to this? It was a question for which she would never find an answer, and, according to her grandson, Joe Barger, she spent the remainder of her life feeling somehow responsible for not handling the situation better.

Doctors and other medical staff worked to save Charlie's life by administering blood transfusions and IVs to keep him hydrated, but all efforts proved futile. At 12:20 a.m., on November 25, 1936, he succumbed to his injuries. The medical examiner performing the autopsy cited the cause of death to be third-degree burns to his face and arms, omitting on the death certificate the lacerations to his throat and gunshot wound to his thigh. His death was officially ruled an accident, but newsmen labeled it a suicide.

"That the breakdown was due to his war experience, no comrade of Charles Barger would deny," Robert Reed wrote after his death. "Yet through the years every effort made by the veterans' organizations to persuade the government that sent him to war to admit responsibility for his mental condition ended in failure. There was no 'proof' in cold language that his suffering was connected with his service. Charles Barger remained a name and a case number."[826]

Charlie's funeral services were held at the George C. Carson Chapel in Independence, Missouri, at 10:30 a.m., Saturday morning, November 28. Reverend W.E. King, pastor of Maywood Baptist Church, officiated over the ceremony, hosted by the Irwin Kirkwood American Legion Post and Louis A. Craig VFW Post. The Ladies Auxiliary to the Veterans of Foreign Wars Choral Club, under direction of Ethel Lee Buxton, provided the music, and pallbearers were Harold Snell, Roy D. Rowley, W.L. Underwood, Frank B. Fisher, Jr., Ted Imes, John Gilzean, Herman Larson and Enos Truesdell.

Conspicuously missing from the procession of mourners were Congressional leaders, local politicians, and a military escort ... the last slap in the face to a selfless warrior who was ignored by the government in life and forgotten by the government in death. Among the more than six hundred attendees, however, were a considerable number of Kansas City policemen, who apparently still held Charlie in high regard.

Despite the Kansas City Police Department's failure to compensate Charlie for his service, they provided two motorcycle officers to lead the motorcade to Blue Springs Cemetery. When the motorcade reached Independence, Missouri, the Independence Police Department provided escort to their city limits, and then the Missouri State Highway Patrol took over the escort. When the procession entered Blue Springs, a patrol car detailed by County Constable Harry S. Thurman led them to the grave site. Charlie was buried with full military honors—with a color guard, firing squad, and a bugler to play "Taps." Soon, friends, family and guests left the cemetery.

No headstone was initially erected to mark Charlie's grave. Ruth didn't have the money, and evidently no one else thought of it. Then, in January 1943, she learned that the government would supply a stone free of charge, and at that time she applied for an upright marble headstone, which was delivered that June. Decades later, an effort had been made to locate the resting place of all Medal of Honor recipients, and on Memorial Day 1989, Charlie's grave site was adorned with the government-issued Medal of Honor headstone with gold lettering.

After Charlie's funeral, Ruth was left to pick up the pieces. The fire in her home left the place transiently inhabitable, and without income, she would lose it anyway. Living with her parents was an option, but that would only be temporary, for Elmer was making just $650 a year with the WPA, plus whatever he could earn from his farm. Moreover, he was still raising his preteen daughters, Thelma and Opal.

Charlie's mother, Cora, attended his funeral. While there, she expressed interest in Ruth and her children. "I would like to take Ruth and the children home with me," she stated, "but would not be able to share our household with them, because my husband is not strong, and our family income is from the WPA, which would not be enough for all of us."[827] Cora lived out her days in Twin Groves, passing away there from acute circulatory failure on May 28, 1954.

Once again, Robert Reed stepped up to the plate. Reed assembled members of his American Legion Post and organized a trust fund for Charlie's family. The American Legion's efforts were praised by both veterans and nonveterans who were disgusted with the government's failure to provide adequate compensation while Charlie was alive. By February 15, 1937, the Legion had raised $598 ($10,165 in 2017), but Ruth knew that the money would only go so far … and so did Robert Reed. There had to be a more permanent solution to her income situation.

In May 1937, Reed moved for proper legislation to "liberalize the provisions of the Medal of Honor Roll Act of April 27, 1916." Medal of Honor recipients up to that time received a special pension of $10 per month for life upon attaining the age of 65, but that didn't help Charlie, and it certainly wasn't helping Ruth. Reed believed that Medal of Honor recipients, widows, or their minor children, should receive an immediate stipend. His herculean efforts summarily caught the attention of Congressman C. Jasper Bell, who represented the Fourth District of Missouri.

Coincidentally, a similar situation was playing out in Minnesota, which gave support to Reed's proposal. The widow of George H. Mallon was living on a paltry pension of $30 a month, plus a small allowance for her two daughters. Mallon had served as a captain during World Wat I, and was twice wounded in the line of duty. He singlehandedly captured 100 German soldiers, 11 machine guns, one anti-aircraft gun, and four 155-millimeter howitzers, all the while leading his men in combat. Congressman John G. Alexander of Minnesota was working on a bill, advocating for Mallon's widow and children.

It took some time, but on February 1, 1940, the Congressional Committee on Invalid Pensions convened in Washington, DC, where two
bills, similar in purport, were submitted. Congressman Bell was ill and
convalescing at his home in Missouri, so he sent his secretary, Vernon E.
Moore, to act on his behalf. Moore introduced H.R. 3385, and Congressman
Alexander introduced H.R. 8051. Neither bill met serious opposition, and
thereafter provided immediate recompense to soldier's and their survivors
of $30 monthly.[828] This was a significant bureaucratic breakthrough. Today,
Medal of Honor recipients receive $1,330, above and beyond any military
pension or other benefit for which they may be eligible.

Ruth returned to Kansas City where she worked as a tearoom waitress
at a local department store, and then as a seamstress for a mail-order house
called National Bella Hess. She remarried four times, more out of necessity
than affection, according to her grandson, Joe Barger, and each marriage
ended in divorce. Joe stated that, as strained as his grandparent's marriage
had been, Charlie was the love of her Ruth's life, and, as such, after each
divorce she reverted to the surname Barger.

Joe Barger reported that Ruth felt responsible for the way the police
bungled Charlie's arrest. This, and the way he died, Joe claimed, really
scarred her for life. Ruth suffered several nervous breakdowns and rarely
mentioned Charlie, even to her grandchildren. She passed away in Kansas
City on January 15, 1972, and was interred in Blue Springs Cemetery.

There would be no buildings or patriotic posts named in Charlie's
honor, nor would there be memorials, tributes or other forms of recognition
for nearly 80 years. Recently, however, there has been renewed interest in
Charlie's story, and even that of the Staffelbach family, with often-erroneous
articles in books, magazines and newspapers.

On Memorial Day, 2016, VFW Post 6603 unveiled a memorial in
Charlie's honor at Blue Springs Cemetery. The impressive-size crowd that
had gathered for the event on that beautiful spring day included a number
of dignitaries and several of Charlie's descendants. The Honor Guard
presented the Colors, after which several people spoke in honor of Charlie,
including a Boy Scout. Then, a government representative described the
circumstance under which Charlie received his Medal of Honor. When the
ceremony concluded, the mournful sound of "Taps" was heard, played by
a lone bugler in the distance.

More recently, the Missouri State Museum in Jefferson City, Missouri,
set up a display in Charlie's honor to commemorate the 100th anniversary
of America's entry into World War I. During the opening-day ceremony,
Jeremy Amick, a representative of the Silver Star Families of America,
presented a Silver Star Service Banner and certificate to the Museum
Director, Tiffany Patterson, in Charlie's name, to recognize his struggle

with post-traumatic stress. This banner and certificate was turned over to Charlie's grandson, Joe, and is now in the possession of the author.

Charlie's heroism and self-sacrifice took place 100 years ago. Though not adequately compensated in life, his tragic death paved the way for better care of Medal of Honor recipients and their families, and called attention to the challenges that all veterans face after coming home from war. Great strides have been made in veteran care since the 1930s, but, as news headlines at the time of this writing reveal, much more needs to be done.

It can be said of Charlie that he came into this world similar to the way he left it—in a whirlwind of violence. Tragic though his life was in many ways, he found a niche for himself in war. And though his bravery and heroic acts never catapulted him to the status achieved by famous heroes such as Alvin York, the Medal of Honor distinguishes and forever enshrines Charlie as one of the most gallant Americans of his age.

PFC Charles D. Barger upon
enlisting in Company D, 38th Infantry
Regiment, 3rd Infantry Division,
January 1921
Credit: Joe and Euleta Barger

Sketch of Officer Charlie Barger
by Mike Theuer
Credit: Author's Collection

Cora and Ed Rolley
Credit: Chris Kraft

Elmer and Mary Bailey
Credit: Joe and Euleta Barger

Ruth (Bailey) Barger
Credit: Joe and Euleta Barger

Mayor James Cowgill
Credit: Mexico [MO] Weekly Ledger, 7 Jul 1892

Col. Robert W. Reed
Credit: Ann (Reed) Scileppi

Charlie, Mabel and
Joe Barger (1930)
Credit: Joe and Euleta Barger

Charlie and Ruth
Barger (1935)
Credit: Joe and Euleta Barger

Charlie's Original Headstone
Credit: Don Morfe

Charlie's Medal of Honor Headstone
Credit: Don Morfe

Appendix

AWARDS AND DECORATIONS

Charlie Barger's original medals were donated to the Liberty Memorial Museum in Liberty, Missouri, in 1939, where they remained on permanent display for nearly three decades. On February 14, 1967, however, a thief sawed through a barred basement window, hacked through two locked doors, and smashed glass display cases, one of which housed all of Charlie's original awards and decorations. Besides his Medal of Honor, the thief took 38 other medals, an ornate telephone that once belonged to German Chief of Staff (later President) Paul von Hindenburg, and many other items.

Charlie's medals had been in the museum for so long that no one could remember if they were engraved with Charlie's name, but in all likelihood, they weren't. Recipients at that time had to pay for their own engraving and he did not have the money. As a result, even if the medals were discovered, they would be impossible to identify as his. Even more perplexing, the medals weren't photographed or catalogued, so it was uncertain precisely what medals were on display. The Kansas City Police Department launched an investigation into the theft, and the American Legion offered a reward of $100 for information leading to the arrest and conviction of the culprit(s). Unfortunately, Charlie's medals were never recovered.

For decades, Charlie's grandson, Joe Barger, hoped to replace the Medal of Honor, but that was no easy task, even with the extraordinary efforts of Harold "Sonny" Wells of the Medal of Honor Historical Society. Wells tried for two years to cut through the red tape, but the U.S. Army Awards and Decorations Branch was not receptive to his inquiries. It appeared certain that re-issuance of the medal was an impossibility, and over time Joe Barger gave up all hope.

Then, in 2013, the author took steps on Joe's behalf, drafting letters to Senator Roy Blunt, Congresswoman Vicky Hartzler and Congressman Mike Kelley, whose collective assistance revealed the criteria for re-issuance. Official documentation was collected to establish Joe Barger as the oldest surviving grandson, plus proof that Charlie's original Medal of Honor had been stolen. Finally, after several months, the Department of the Army approved his request and the reissued Medal of Honor was received by the family on January 16, 2014.

Theft of Charlie's medals in 1967 generated another problem. Since Charlie's medals were never catalogued, it was difficult to determine his actual entitlements. There were, however, books, magazines and newspaper articles from which a tentative list could be generated, but official proof in the form of citations, certificates and order numbers were needed to establish unmitigated verification. The most controversial of Charlie's alleged entitlements was ten (10) Purple Hearts.

It is a matter of record that Charlie was never officially wounded during World War I, but sometime since Charlie's death it was said that General John J. Pershing awarded him ten Meritorious Service Citation Certificates. After the Purple Heart medal was created in February 1932, Charlie purportedly relinquished his Meritorious Service Citation Certificates for the medal, with the appropriate oak leaf clusters devices. Joe Barger understood that the Meritorious Service Citation Certificates were the result of his grandfather's voluntary participation during combat raids and patrols in which Chauchat gunners were needed.

The author's friend, Eric R. Caubarreaux, contacted Fred Borch, President of the Orders and Medals Society of America. Mr. Borch discovered four Adjutant General's Office (AGO) award cards at the National Personnel Records Center in St. Louis, Missouri, wherein most of Charlie's decorations were listed. Missing from these cards were the following decorations to which Charlie was believed to be entitled: (1) the Order of Leopold I, Belgium; (2) the Croix de Guerre with Palm, Belgium; (3) the Military Medal, Great Britain; (4) three of Charlie's four Croix de Guerres from France; and (5) the ten Meritorious Service Citation Certificates.

Mr. Borch, an undisputed expert on the Purple Heart, stated that had Charlie received 10 Meritorious Service Citation Certificates/Purple Hearts, there would have been at least a few AGO award cards in the files indicating these awards. "[I] do not believe that Barger ever got any MSCCs," writes Borch. "He certainly did not get any Purple Hearts." He adds: "Not certain where you got your information that he had 10 MSCCs—seems totally unlikely to me and the AGO award cards support that unlikelihood!"

It did not go unnoticed that several decorations to which Charlie was known to have been entitled were absent from the AGO award cards, so some question remained, even though Mr. Borch's declaration held much weight. Finally, in January 2017, a source was discovered that definitively settled the matter. *The Gleim Medal Letters*, published by the Orders and

Medals Society of America, catalogues 27 years of research by Colonel Albert F. Gleim, probably the foremost authority on America's early awards and decorations.

One section of Gleim's research deals specifically with Meritorious Service Citation Certificates, going into detail regarding distribution of these certificates (i.e., the American divisions that received the certificates, and the totals awarded to each division). Per Gleim's research, there were 4119 Meritorious Service Citation Certificates distributed during and immediately after WWI. "These certificates," writes Gleim, "issued by HQ, AEF with a Pershing signature were apparently an attempt to provide recognition for those members of the AEF in administration, staff and support roles and whose performance did not merit the award of the DSM and/or a valor decoration or gallantry citation."

On April 24, 1920, the War Department Statistics Branch, using information obtained from the AEF Adjutant General's Office Decoration Section, published in *Weekly Statistical Report No. 139*, the following allotment of Meritorious Service Citation Certificates awarded to the 89th Division: 7 to officers and 3 to enlisted men. Gleim states: "This is probably very close to a complete tabulation since the GHQ, AEF was disbanded shortly thereafter." Nine out of ten of those officers and enlisted men are specifically named in the *History of the 89th Division, U.S.A.*, by Lt. Col. George H. English, Jr. Charlie is not among them. That matter was settled.

Gleim's research also delved into foreign decorations earned by Americans during, and immediately following, World War I. For example, he provides a list of recipients of the Order of Leopold I, from a book entitled, *Memorial du Centenaire de l'Ordre de Leopold 1832-1932*. Every American recipient of the Order of Leopold I up to 1932 is depicted on this list, but, again, Charlie is not named.

When this information was presented to Charlie's grandson, Joe Barger, he responded: "While it is disappointing to find this out, it does not diminish Charlie's heroism in our eyes. It is better to be accurate than to put more on him than he was entitled to." That said, the following list of Charlie's awards and decorations are accurate, and substantiated through various sources.

OFFICIAL AWARDS AND DECORATIONS

Medal of Honor

Rank and Organization: Private First Class, U.S. Army, Company L, 354th Infantry, 89th Division. **Date and Place of Action**: Near Bois de Bantheville, France, 31 October 1918. **Authority**: General Order No. 20, War Department, 1919. **Presentation**: General John J. Pershing in Chaumont, France, on February 9, 1919. **Citation**: Learning that two daylight patrols had been caught out in No Man's Land and were unable to return, Pfc. Barger and another stretcher bearer upon their own initiative made two trips 500 yards beyond our lines, under constant machine-gun fire, and rescued two wounded officers.

World War I Victory Medal

Criteria for Award: For service between 6 April 1917 and 11 November 1918 or with either of the following expeditions: (1) American Expeditionary Forces in European Russia between 12 November 1918 and 5 August 1919; or (2) American Expeditionary Forces Siberia between 23 November 1918 and 1 April 1920. **Barger's Eligibility**: For service in the armed forces between April 6, 1917 and November 11, 1918. **Battle Clasps Earned by Barger**: (1) St. Mihiel (September 12 to 16, 1918); (2) Meuse-Argonne (October 14 to November 11, 1918); (3) Defensive Sector (for participation in the Lorraine Sector, which included the Lucey Sector, August 4 to September 11, 1918, and the Euvezin Sector, September 17 to October 7, 1918). **Authority**: War Department General Order 48, 1919.

Army of Occupation Medal, WWI

Criteria for Award: For service in Germany or Austria-Hungary between 12 November 1918 and 11 July 1923. **Barger's Eligibility:** For service with the occupation forces in Germany between December 7, 1918 and May 5, 1919. **Authority:** Act of Congress 21 November 1941, (55 Stat 781).

Medaille Militaire, France

Rank and Organization: Private First Class, U.S. Army, Company L, 354th Infantry, 89th Division. **Date and Place of Action:** Near Bois de Bantheville, France, 31 October 1918. **Authority:** French Presidential Decree, 5 May 1919. **Presentation:** Vice Admiral F.P. Moreau, Brest, France, 14 May 1919. **Citation:** In the name of the President of the Republic, The Grand Chancellor of the National Order of the Legion of Honor issued this document to Mr. Berger, Charles, of the American Army, Serial Number 2,205,271, —Private 1st Class in Company "L" of the 354th Infantry Regiment, decorated with the Military Medal by decree of 5 May 1919. Paris, the 5 May 1919. Seen, verified, sealed and stored, No. 4,954.

Croix de Guerre with Bronze Palm, WWI, France (First Award)

Rank and Organization: Private First Class, U.S. Army, Company L, 354th Infantry, 89th Division. **Date and Place of Action:** Near Bouillonville, France, 12 September 1918. **Authority:** Order number and date unknown. **Presentation:** Marshal Ferdinand Foch before February 6, 1919. **Citation:** Citation at the Army Level. Private First Class Barger, Charles, of the 354th Infantry Regiment, American, Co. "L", Serial No. 2,205,271. For an act of bravery while on the St. Mihiel front September 12, 1918. While Private Barger was out with a raiding party one of the members of the party became lost from the rest of the party. The call was made for volunteers to go far under fire of the enemy to seek the missing men. Private Barger alone volunteered to undertake the task, and ran into machine gun fire. He located the position of the German guns and opened fire with a sawed-off shotgun, wounding three and capturing five men and two guns, besides rescuing the mission member of his Company from the German machine gun Company.

Croix de Guerre with Bronze Palm, WWI, France (Second Award)

Rank and Organization: Private First Class, U.S. Army, Company L, 354th Infantry, 89th Division. **Date and Place of Action**: Near Bois de Bantheville, France, 31 October 1918. **Authority**: Order No. 16.043 "D", 13 Apr 1919. **Presentation**: Vice Admiral F.P. Moreau, Brest, France, 14 May 1919. **Citation:** Citation at the Army Level. Private First Class Barger, Charles, of the 354th Infantry Regiment, American, Co. "L", Serial No. 2,205,271. Soldier of admirable courage and dedication, has on October 31st, 1918, on learning that two day patrols were caught between American and German trenches, with the help of a soldier and under violent machine-gun-fire, on his own initiative succeeded in bringing back two officers to our lines.

Croix de Guerre with Bronze Palm, WWI, France (Third Award)

Rank and Organization: Private First Class, U.S. Army, Company L, 354th Infantry, 89th Division. **Date and Place of Action**: Near Bois de Bantheville, France, 1 November 1918. **Authority**: Order No. 16.043 "D", 13 Apr 1919. **Presentation**: Vice Admiral F.P. Moreau, Brest, France, 14 May 1919. **Citation:** Citation at the Army Level. Private First Class Barger, Charles, of the 354th Infantry Regiment, American, Co. "L", Serial No. 2,205,271. In recognition of an act of bravery on the Meuse-Argonne front on November 1, 1918, in which Private Barger's company was held up by German machine gun fire. Private Barger and another soldier crawled around the German machine gun nest and opened fire from the rear with an automatic rifle, advancing as they fired, and capturing the entire crews and guns of the nest, consisting of 12 men and six guns.

Croix de Guerre with Bronze Star, WWI, France (Fourth Award)

Rank and Organization: Private First Class, U.S. Army, Company L, 354th Infantry, 89th Division. **Date and Place of Action**: Near Barricourt, France, 2 November 1918. **Authority**: Order number and date unknown. **Presentation**: No formal Presentation. Received via registered mail in Stotts City, Missouri, 29 Jul 1919. **Synopsis:** Citation at the Regiment Level. Private First Class Barger, Charles, of the 354th Infantry Regiment, American, Co. "L", Serial No. 2,205,271. In recognition of an act of bravery on the Meuse-Argonne front on November 2, 1918, in which Private Barger defended a group from another regiment by singlehandedly fighting off repeated enemy attacks. His actions prevented the regiment from annihilation and allowed them to establish a stronghold in which they could thereafter defend themselves.

Silver Medal for Bravery, Montenegro

Rank and Organization: Private First Class, U.S. Army, Company L, 354th Infantry, 89th Division. **Date and Place of Action**: Near Bois de Bantheville, France, 31 October 1918. **Authority**: Order Number 311, dated 31 May 1919. **Presentation**: No known formal presentation. **Citation**: By the Grace of God, His Majesty, NIKOLAS I, King and Sovereign of Montenegro, Is please to confer upon Barger, Charles D., Private First Class, for military service in the War of 1914-1918, Silver medal for "Bravery".

Croix de Guerre with Bronze Palm, WWI, Belgium

Rank and Organization: Private First Class, U.S. Army, Company L 354th Infantry, 89th Division. **Date and Place of Action**: Near Bois de Bantheville, France, 31 October 1918. **Authority**: Order number and date unknown. **Presentation**: King Albert of Belgium, St. Louis, MO, 21 Oct 1919. **Citation**: In honor of the rescue work performed on October 31, 1918.

Military Medal, Great Britain

Rank and Organization: Private First Class, U.S. Army, Company L, 354th Infantry, 89th Division. **Date and Place of Action**: Near Bois de Bantheville, France, 31 October 1918. **Authority**: British War Office Bulletin WO/338, 1919. **Presentation**: No formal presentation. Received via registered mail, winter 1919. **Citation**: The following are among the decorations and medals awarded by command of His Majesty the KING at various dates to subjects of Allied Powers for distinguished services rendered during the course of the campaign: -- To be awarded the Military Medal (M.M.). 2205271 Private, 1st Class, Charles D. Barger, "L" Company, 354th Regiment.

Croce Merito di Guerra, WWI, Italy

Rank and Organization: Private First Class, U.S. Army, Company L, 354th Infantry, 89th Division. **Date and Place of Action**: Near Bois de Bantheville, France, 31 October 1918. **Authority**: Given the Royal Decree 19 January 1918, No. 205, January 19, 1918, and by the Chief of Staff, Italian Army, on December 9, 1921. Order Number of the Register of concessions 89484. **Presentation**: Received via registered mail on February 9, 1922, Kansas City, Missouri. **Citation**: Royal Italian Army, The Minister of War, Given the Royal Decree 19 January 1918, No. 205, Determines and grants Charles D. Barger, private 1st Class, Co. L., 354th Infantry, 89th Division, The Cross of Merit of War, Washington, D.C., on 9 December 1921.

War with Germany Medal, WWI, Missouri

Rank and Organization: Private First Class, U.S. Army, Company L, 354th Infantry, 89th Division. **Criteria for Award:** For service in the Armed Forces of the United States during the war with Germany, 1917-1918. **Authority**: House Bill No. 349, 50th General Assembly of the State of Missouri, February 14, 1919. **Presentation**: No known formal presentation. Received in June 1919.

Citation: In compliance with an Act of the General Assembly and on behalf of the State of Missouri, I have the honor to present you with this Medal which has been awarded you in recognition of your service as a citizen of this State in the armed forces of the United States during the war with Germany. It is intended to be to you and your posterity a token of the everlasting gratitude and appreciation of your State. Harvey C. Clark, Adjutant General.

Expert Rifleman Badge

Rank and Organization: (1) Private First Class, U.S. Army, Company L, 354th Infantry, 89th Division; (2) Private First Class, U.S. Army, Company D, 38th Infantry Regiment, 3rd Division. **Qualification Dates**: (1) May 1918, Camp Funston, Kansas; (2) Jan 1921, Camp Pike, Arkansas. **Authority**: Small Arms Firing Manual, Section 246. **Presentation**: No formal presentation. **Citation**: Not applicable. **NOTE**: During World War I, Regular Army troops received the silver oxide version, while National Army and National Guard troops received the brass version. Charlie would have worn the brass version during the war, and the silver version upon re-qualifying in 1921.

THE UNITED STATES OF AMERICA

TO ALL WHO SHALL SEE THESE PRESENTS, GREETING:
THIS IS TO CERTIFY THAT
THE PRESIDENT OF THE UNITED STATES OF AMERICA
PURSUANT TO ACT OF CONGRESS APPROVED JULY 9, 1918,
HAS AWARDED IN THE NAME OF CONGRESS TO

Charles D. Barger

THE CONGRESSIONAL MEDAL OF HONOR

FOR

VALOR

ABOVE AND BEYOND THE CALL OF DUTY IN ACTION INVOLVING
ACTUAL CONFLICT WITH AN ENEMY OF THE UNITED STATES,
*near Bois de Bantheville, France, October 31, 1918, while serving as private, first
class, Company L, 354th Infantry, 89th Division, American Expeditionary Forces.*

GIVEN UNDER MY HAND AT THE CITY OF WASHINGTON
THIS *twenty fifth* DAY OF *November* 1924.

RECORDED IN THE OFFICE OF
THE ADJUTANT GENERAL

Robert C. Davis
THE ADJUTANT GENERAL

SECRETARY OF WAR

Medal of Honor Certificate
Credit: National World War I Museum and Memorial, Kansas City, Missouri, U.S.A.

Medaille Militaire Certificate

Croix de Guerre Certificate

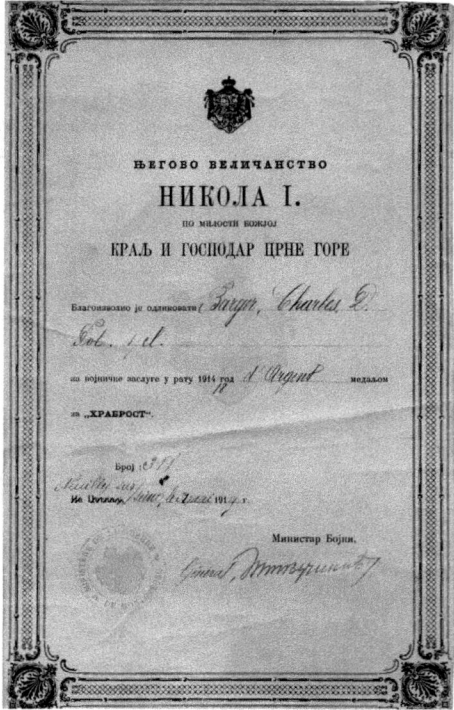

Silver Medal for Bravery Certificate

Credit: National World War I Museum and Memorial, Kansas City, Missouri, U.S.A.

Croce di Guerra Certificate

Credit: National World War I Museum and Memorial, Kansas City, Missouri, U.S.A.

Charlie's Reissued Medal of Honor
Credit: Joe and Euleta Barger

ENDNOTES

Chapter 1: "The Notorious Staffelbachs"

1. Millard, T.F. "The Stafflebacks—Rivals of the Benders." *St. Louis Republic* (St. Louis, MO), 19 Sep 1897, pp. 1 & 4.
2. Ibid.
3. Ibid.
4. Ibid.
5. "Staffelback vs. Staffelback." *Petition for Divorce.* State of Missouri, County of Lawrence, 11 Mar 1887, File #5494.
6. Ibid.
7. Millard, T.F. "The Stafflebacks—Rivals of the Benders." *St. Louis Republic* (St. Louis, MO), 19 Sep 1897, pp. 1 & 4.
8. "A Racy Divorce Case." *The Springfield Democrat* (Springfield, MO), 22 Feb 1894, p. 7.
9. Ibid.
10. Ibid.
11. Ibid.
12. Ibid.
13. "Michael Staffleback Dead." *The Jeffersonian Gazette* (Lawrence, KS), 18 May 1899, p. 6.
14. Griffin, Laurie (Lake). *Correspondence with Author,* 4-5 May 2016.
15. Ibid.
16. Ibid.
17. Ibid.
18. Kraft, Chris. *Conversation with June Buccina.* 8 Nov 2015.
19. *The Chieftain* (Mt. Vernon, MO), 21 Jun 1894, p.3.
20. *The Chieftain* (Mt. Vernon, MO), 2 Aug 1894, p.3.
21. "Mike Staffelback Talks over Crimes." *Joplin News Herald* (Joplin, MO), 9 Aug 1924, p. 2.
22. Millard, T.F. "The Stafflebacks—Rivals of the Benders." *St. Louis Republic* (St. Louis, MO), 19 Sep 1897, pp. 1 & 4.
23. Ibid.
24. Ibid.
25. Ibid.

26. Ibid.
27. Ibid.
28. Ibid.
29. Ibid.
30. Ibid.
31. Ibid.
32. "Galena's Benders." *Kansas Semi-Weekly Capital* (Topeka, KS), 17 Sep 1897, p. 2.
33. Millard, T.F. "The Stafflebacks—Rivals of the Benders." *St. Louis Republic* (St. Louis, MO), 19 Sep 1897, pp. 1 & 4.
34. Ibid.
35. Ibid.
36. Ibid.
37. Ibid.
38. Ibid.
39. Ibid.
40. Ibid.
41. Ibid.
42. Ibid.
43. Ibid.
44. Ibid.
45. Ibid.
46. Ibid.
47. Ibid.
48. Ibid.
49. Ibid.
50. Ibid.

Chapter 2: "The Murder of Frank Galbreath"

51. Ibid.
52. Ibid.
53. Ibid.
54. Ibid.
55. Ibid.
56. Ibid.
57. Ibid.
58. Ibid.
59. Ibid.
60. Ibid.
61. Ibid.
62. Ibid.
63. Ibid.
64. Ibid.
65. Ibid.
66. Ibid.
67. Ibid.

68. Ibid.
69. Ibid.
70. "Galena's Benders." *Kansas Semi-Weekly Capital* (Topeka, KS), 17 Sep 1897, p. 2.
71. "Rival of the Benders. Stafflebacks, of Galena, Accused of Many Murders." *The Kansas City Journal* (Kansas City, MO), 15 Sep 1897, p.1.
72. "A Family of Murderers." *Kansas City Star* (Kansas City, MO). 10 Mar 1909, p. 5.
73. Ibid.
74. Ibid.
75. Ibid.
76. Ibid.
77. Ibid.
78. Millard, T.F. "The Stafflebacks—Rivals of the Benders." *St. Louis Republic* (St. Louis, MO), 19 Sep 1897, pp. 1 & 4.
79. *Joplin Daily News* (Joplin, MO), 31 Jul 1897, n.p.
80. Millard, T.F. "The Stafflebacks—Rivals of the Benders." *St. Louis Republic* (St. Louis, MO), 19 Sep 1897, pp. 1 & 4.
81. Ibid.
82. Ibid.
83. "Another Murder." *The Galena Evening Times* (Galena, KS), 19 Jul 1897, p. 1.
84. "A Ghastly Find." *The Columbus Daily Advocate* (Columbus, KS), 20 Jul 1897, p. 3.
85. English Dictionary. "Coroner's jury [online]." *English Dictionary.* n.p., Dec. 2016. Web. 08 May 2017. <http://englishdictionary.education/en/coroners-jury>.
86. Millard, T.F. "The Stafflebacks—Rivals of the Benders." *St. Louis Republic* (St. Louis, MO), 19 Sep 1897, pp. 1 & 4.
87. Ibid.
88. "He was Too Slow." *Columbus Advocate* (Columbus, KS), 22 Jul 1897, p. 8.
89. Ibid.
90. "Old Nancy's Brood." *Middleton Daily Argus* (Middleton, NY), 23 Sep 1897, p. 19.
91. Ibid.
92. "He was Too Slow." *Columbus Advocate* (Columbus, KS), 22 Jul 1897, p. 8.
93. Millard, T.F. "The Stafflebacks—Rivals of the Benders." *St. Louis Republic* (St. Louis, MO), 19 Sep 1897, pp. 1 & 4.
94. *The Columbus Weekly Advocate* (Columbus, KS), 5 Aug 1897, p. 7.
95. "Galena's Benders." *Kansas Semi-Weekly Capital* (Topeka, KS), 17 Sep 1897, p. 2.
96. Ibid.
97. Ibid.
98. Ibid.
99. Ibid.
100. Ibid.
101. Ibid.
102. Ibid.

103. Ibid.
104. Ibid.
105. Millard, T.F. "Bones and Hair Found Yesterday." *St. Louis Republic* (St. Louis, MO), 17 Sep 1897, p. 1.
106. "Will the Shaft Give up its Dead." *Weir City Daily Sun* (Weir, KS), 15 Sep 1897, p. 1.
107. Millard, T.F. "The Stafflebacks—Rivals of the Benders." *St. Louis Republic* (St. Louis, MO), 19 Sep 1897, pp. 1 & 4.
108. Ibid.
109. "Will the Shaft Give up its Dead." *Weir City Daily Sun* (Weir, KS), 15 Sep 1897, p. 1.
110. *The Galena Evening Times* (Galena, KS), 2 Apr 1898.
111. Ibid.
112. "Will the Shaft Give up its Dead." *Weir City Daily Sun* (Weir, KS), 15 Sep 1897, p. 1.
113. Millard, T.F. "Bones and Hair Found Yesterday." *St. Louis Republic* (St. Louis, MO), 17 Sep 1897, p.1.
114. "No Sign of Bodies." *Belleville Telescope* (Belleville, KS), 24 Sep 1897, p. 2.
115. *Columbus Advocate* (Columbus, KS), 12 Aug 1897, p. 5.
116. "Lynchings Likely." *Independence Daily Reporter* (Independence, KS), 16 Sep 1897, p. 1.
117. Millard, T.F. "The Stafflebacks—Rivals of the Benders." *St. Louis Republic* (St. Louis, MO), 19 Sep 1897, pp. 1 & 4.
118. *Columbus Advocate* (Columbus, KS), 23 Sep 1897, p. 6.
119. "Rivals of the Benders." *Daily Tribune* (Salt Lake City, Utah), 26 Sep 1897, p. 19.
120. "The Stafflebacks Sentenced." *The St. Joseph Weekly Gazette* (St. Joseph, MO), 8 Oct 1897, p. 1.
121. *Modern Light* (Columbus, KS), 30 Sep 1897, p. 10.
122. "Are After Wilson." *St. Louis Republic* (St. Louis, MO), 22 Sep 1897, p. 8.
123. "Ed Staffleback a Maniac." *The Kansas City Journal* (Kansas City, MO), 25 Sep 1897, p. 2.
124. *The Columbus Weekly Advocate* (Columbus, KS) 30 Sep 1897, p. 8.
125. "Stafflebacks Sentenced" *The Kansas City Journal* (Kansas City, MO), 2 Oct 1897, p. 1.
126. "The Stafflebacks Sentenced." *The St. Joseph Weekly Gazette* (St. Joseph, MO), 8 Oct 1897, p. 1.
127. Ibid.
128. *The Winchester Star* (Winchester, KS), 29 Apr 1898, p. 4.
129. "First Reward in Search for Staffleback Victims." *Topeka Weekly Capitol* (Topeka, KS), 17 Sep 1897, p. 3.
130. "Leedy Believes in Hanging." *The Galena Evening Times* (Galena, KS), 11 Oct 1897, p. 1.
131. Ibid.
132. "The Benders are not in it." *Modern Light* (Columbus, KS), 16 Sep 1897, p. 1.
133. Millard, T.F. "The Stafflebacks—Rivals of the Benders." *St. Louis Republic* (St. Louis, MO), 19 Sep 1897, pp. 1 & 4.

134. "Attracted Much Attention." *Columbus Advocate* (Columbus, KS), 7 Oct 1897, p. 5.

135. Ibid.

136. Ibid.

137. Ibid.

138. Ibid.

139. "Ed Staffleback Dead." *The Columbus Weekly Advocate* (Columbus, KS), 23 Nov 1899, p. 7.

140. "Mrs. Staffelback's Burial in Joplin." *Kansas City Star* (Kansas City, MO), 12 Mar 1909, p. 3.

Chapter 3: "Alone and Forsaken"

141. Kraft, Chris. *Conversation with June Buccina.* 8 Nov 2015.

142. Ibid.

143. Ibid.

144. "Wants a Pardon." *The Columbus Daily Advocate* (Columbus, KS), 22 Jul 1898, p. 3.

145. Ibid.

146. Haswell, A.M. *Ozark Region: Its History and Its People. Volume 1: History of Lawrence County, Missouri.* Springfield, MO: Interstate Historical Society, 1917.

147. *Goodspeed's Lawrence County History.* Chicago, IL: The Goodspeed Publishing Company, 1888.

148. Haswell, A.M. *Ozark Region: Its History and Its People, Volume 1.* Springfield, MO: Interstate Historical Society, 1917.

149. "Mrs. Mary Weaver [obituary]." *Little Rock Daily News* (Little Rock, AR), 1 Mar 1921, p. 2.

150. Haswell, A.M. *Ozark Region: Its History and Its People. Volume 3: History of Lawrence* County, Missouri. Springfield, MO: Interstate Historical Society, 1917.

151. Ibid.

152. Ibid.

153. Ibid.

154. "Bullets? Pooh! But Drat That Hail in Missouri." *Plain Dealer* (Cleveland, OH), 26 Sep 1920, p. 17.

155. Haswell, A.M. *Ozark Region: Its History and Its People. Volume 1: History of Lawrence County, Missouri.* Springfield, MO: Interstate Historical Society, 1917.

156. Ibid.

157. Ibid.

158. Ibid.

159. Ibid.

160. "Text of Conscription Law Under Which Registrations are to be Made on June 5." *The Star Press* (Muncie, IN), 28 May 1917, p. 2.

161. The Medical Department of the United States Army in the World War. *Neuropsychiatry.* Washington: U.S. Government Printing Office, 1929, Vol. X, p. 158.

Chapter 4: "Induction and Training"

162. Stewart, Richard W. *American Military History, Volume I: The United States Army and Forging a Nation, 1775-1917 (Second Edition)*. Washington, DC: Center of Military History, United States Army, 2009.

163. Kansas Historical Society. "Camp Funston." Kansas State Historical Society. n.p., Nov. 2016. Web. 08 May 2017. <http://www.kshs.org/kansapedia/camp-funston/15692.>.

164. "News of Camp Funston." *The Junction City Daily Union* (Junction City, KS), 3 Apr 1918, p. 3.

165. "When General Wood Commanded the 89th; How He Put the Men in Fighting Form." *The World Herald* (Omaha, NE), May 1919, p. 7.

166. *Evening Gazette* (Xenia, OH), May 14, 1918, p. 4.

167. Ibid.

168. English, George H., Jr. *History of the 89th Division, U.S.A.* Denver, CO: Smith-Brooks Printing Company. The War Society of the 89th Division, 1920.

169. Ibid.

170. Ibid.

171. Ibid.

172. Ibid.

173. "News of Camp Funston." *The Junction City Daily Union* (Junction City, KS), 3 Apr 1918, p. 3.

174. Bertrand, Georges, and Oscar N. Solbert. *Tactics and Duties for Trench Fighting*. New York and London: Putnam's Sons, 1918.

175. English, George H., Jr. *History of the 89th Division, U.S.A.* Denver, CO: Smith-Brooks Printing Company. The War Society of the 89th Division, 1920.

176. McCallum, Jack. *Leonard Wood: Rough Rider, Surgeon, Architect of American Imperialism*. New York, NY: New York University Press, 2006.

177. Ibid.

178. "General Wood Retires from Army Service." *Salt Lake Telegram* (Salt Lake City, UT), 5 Oct 1921, p. 20.

179. "Evidence in Wood Case." *The Wichita Daily Eagle* (Wichita, KS), 28 Nov 1903, p. 1.

180. McCallum, Jack. *Leonard Wood: Rough Rider, Surgeon, Architect of American Imperialism*. New York, NY: New York University Press, 2006.

181. Ibid.

182. Ibid.

183. "Gen. Wood is Making a Rapid Recovery; Had Miraculous Escape; Seven Wounds in Arm." *The New York Times* (New York, NY), 3 Feb 1918, p. 1.

184. English, George H., Jr. *History of the 89th Division, U.S.A.* Denver, CO: Smith-Brooks Printing Company. The War Society of the 89th Division, 1920.

185. Ibid.

186. "When General Wood Commanded the 89th; How He Put the Men in Fighting Form." *The World Herald* (Omaha, NE), May 1919, p. 7.

187. Ibid.

188. Ibid.

189. Ibid.

190. English, George H., Jr. *History of the 89th Division, U.S.A.* Denver, CO: Smith-Brooks Printing Company. The War Society of the 89th Division, 1920.

191. Ibid.

192. Ibid.

193. Ibid.

194. Bertrand, Georges, and Oscar N. Solbert. *Tactics and Duties for Trench Fighting.* New York and London: Putnam's Sons, 1918.

195. Ibid.

196. *Manual of the Automatic Rifle (Chauchat).* Washington, DC: War Department, Document No.793, 29 Apr 1918.

197. Wade, Capt. Herbert Treadwell. *Handbook of Ordnance Data.* Washington, DC: U.S. Government Printing Office, 1919.

198. *Manual of the Automatic Rifle (Chauchat).* Washington, DC: War Department, Document No.793, 29 Apr 1918.

199. Ibid.

200. Ibid.

201. Bertrand, Georges, and Oscar N. Solbert. *Tactics and Duties for Trench Fighting.* New York and London: Putnam's Sons, 1918.

202. *Manual of the Automatic Rifle (Chauchat).* Washington, DC: War Department, Document No.793, 29 Apr 1918.

203. Ibid.

204. Ibid.

205. Ibid.

206. Ibid.

207. Ibid.

208. Ibid.

209. Ibid.

210. Funk, Corp. Jesse N. "Hero Funk Credits His Glorious Deeds All to Colorado." *The Denver Post* (Denver, CO), 5 Jun 1919, p. 6.

211. Ibid.

212. Frenzel, Arthur. "Jess was Brave Kid Says Proud Father of Colorado's Hero." *The Denver Post* (Denver, CO), 5 Jun 1919, p. 6.

213. Funk, Corp. Jesse N. "Hero Funk Credits His Glorious Deeds All to Colorado." *The Denver Post* (Denver, CO), 5 Jun 1919, p. 6.

214. Ibid.

215. English, George H., Jr. *History of the 89th Division, U.S.A.* Denver, CO: Smith-Brooks Printing Company. The War Society of the 89th Division, 1920.

216. Ibid.

217. Ibid.

218. McGrath, Lt. John F. *War Diary of the 354th Infantry, 89th Division.* J. Linte, Trier, GE, 1919.

219. "Everybody's Picking President Nowadays." *Star Tribune* (Minneapolis, MN), 14 Mar 1919, p. 4.

220. English, George H., Jr. *History of the 89th Division, U.S.A.* Denver, CO: Smith-Brooks Printing Company. The War Society of the 89th Division, 1920.

Chapter 5: "Roots"

221. Staffelbach, Dr. Georg, and Dora F. Rittmeyer. *Hans Peter Staffelbach, Goldschmied in Sursee, 1657-1736.* Luzern, Switzerland: E. Haag, 1936.
222. Ibid.
223. Ibid.
224. Ibid.
225. Ibid.
226. Ibid.
227. "Causes of the War of 1812. *Chicago Tribune* (Chicago, IL), 29 Mar 1896, p. 47.
228. Staffelbach, Dr. Georg, and Dora F. Rittmeyer. *Hans Peter Staffelbach, Goldschmied in Sursee, 1657-1736.* Luzern, Switzerland: E. Haag, 1936.
229. "Sketch of the History of Switzerland." *Daily National Intelligencer* (Washington, DC), 13 Nov 1833, p. 2.
230. Ibid.
231. Harper Collins Publishers. "Holy Alliance." Dictionary.com. Dictionary.com, n.d. Web. 12 Apr 2017. <http://www.dictionary.com/browse/holy-alliance>.
232. Hair, James T. *Gazetteer of Madison County.* Alton, IL: James T. Hair, 1866.
233. Duden, Gottfried. *Bericht über eine Reise nach den westlichen Staaten Nordamerika's.* Elberfeld, Germany: Gedruckt bei S. Lucas, 1829.
234. Tiling, Moritz. "The German Element in Texas 1820-1850, Chapter III." *The Houston Post* (Houston, TX), 13 Jan 1913, p. 9.
235. Hair, James T. *Gazetteer of Madison County.* Alton, IL: James T. Hair, 1866.
236. Abbott, John C. and Raymond J. Spahn. *Journey to New Switzerland.* Carbondale and Edwardsville, IL: Southern Illinois University Press, 1987.
237. Hair, James T. *Gazetteer of Madison County.* Alton, IL: James T. Hair, 1866.
238. Ibid.

Chapter 6: "Over There"

239. Dean, Charles M. "Organization at Port is Huge." *The Cincinnati Enquirer* (Cincinnati, OH), 8 Aug 1943, p. 8.
240. English, George H., Jr. *History of the 89th Division, U.S.A.* Denver, CO: Smith-Brooks Printing Company. The War Society of the 89th Division, 1920
241. (1) Ibid.; (2) McGrath, Lt. John F. *War Diary of the 354th Infantry, 89th Division.* J. Linte, Trier, GE, 1919.
242. English, George H., Jr. *History of the 89th Division, U.S.A.* Denver, CO: Smith-Brooks Printing Company. The War Society of the 89th Division, 1920.
243. King George V. *Letter to American Troops.* n.d. (1918).
244. McGrath, Lt. John F. *War Diary of the 354th Infantry, 89th Division.* J. Linte, Trier, GE, 1919.

245. Dienst, Charles Franklin. *History of the 353rd Infantry Regiment, 89th Division, National Army.* Wichita, KS: The Eagle Press, 1921.

246. Ibid.

247. Ibid.

248. (1) Ibid.; (2) English, George H., Jr. *History of the 89th Division, U.S.A.* Denver, CO: Smith-Brooks Printing Company. The War Society of the 89th Division, 1920.

249. Bratt, John. "In Grandpa Martin's Footsteps." *Howell County Mogenweb.* n.p., n.d. Web. 4 Nov. 2015. <http://www.bing.com/r?IG=91027537760B4B BCAF0EEE81AA7994A9&CID=023CD39DCB636602220BD9E1CAF367B 1&rd=1&h=wMAfwTlUhabodRpseDoigRbV8ZhLMtfvuvZW5T9ga3I&v= 1&r=http%3a%2f%2fhowell.mogenweb.org%2ffamily%2fMartin-Verhage-1. pdf&p=DevEx,5061.1>.

250. English, George H., Jr. *History of the 89th Division, U.S.A.* Denver, CO: Smith-Brooks Printing Company. The War Society of the 89th Division, 1920.

251. Ibid.

252. Ibid.

253. Dienst, Charles Franklin. *History of the 353rd Infantry Regiment, 89th Division, National Army.* Wichita, KS: The Eagle Press, 1921

254. English, George H., Jr. *History of the 89th Division, U.S.A.* Denver, CO: Smith-Brooks Printing Company. The War Society of the 89th Division, 1920.

255. Ibid.

256. *Manual of the Automatic Rifle (Chauchat).* Washington, DC: War Department, Document No.793, 29 Apr 1918.

257. Ibid.

258. Ibid.

259. English, George H., Jr. *History of the 89th Division, U.S.A.* Denver, CO: Smith-Brooks Printing Company. The War Society of the 89th Division, 1920.

260. Ibid.

261. McGrath, Lt. John F. *War Diary of the 354th Infantry, 89th Division.* J. Linte, Trier, GE, 1919.

262. English, George H., Jr. *History of the 89th Division, U.S.A.* Denver, CO: Smith-Brooks Printing Company. The War Society of the 89th Division, 1920.

263. "Knew 89th Division as Fighting Farmers." *The Walnut Valley Times* (El Dorado, KS), 26 Feb 1919, p. 2.

264. English, George H., Jr. *History of the 89th Division, U.S.A.* Denver, CO: Smith-Brooks Printing Company. The War Society of the 89th Division, 1920.

265. Ibid.

266. Conner, Brig. Gen. Fox. "Reduction of St. Mihiel Salient Accomplished by America's First Army with Immense Success." *The Oregon Daily Journal* (Portland, OR), 3 Aug 1919, p. 18.

267. "salient". Dictionary.com Unabridged. Random House, Inc. 20 Jun. 2017. <Dictionary.com http://www.dictionary.com/browse/salient>.

268. "Pershing May Plan Blow at Hun Fortress." *The Courier-Journal* (Louisville, KY), 14 Sep 1918, p.1.

269. Cochrane, Rexmond C. *89th Division Comes into the Line, August 1918.* U.S. Army Chemical Corps Historical Office, Office of the Chief Chemical Officer, Army Chemical Center, Maryland, 1958.

270. English, George H., Jr. *History of the 89th Division, U.S.A.* Denver, CO: Smith-Brooks Printing Company. The War Society of the 89th Division, 1920.

271. Taylor, Maj. John R.M. and G.H. Powell. *Infantry Journal.* Washington, DC: The United States Infantry Trust Association, Jan 1918, Vol. XIV, No. 7.

272. "Drafting War Rules." *The New York Times* (New York, NY), 30 Jan 1922, p. 10.

273. Tuorinsky, Lt. Col. Shirley. *Medal Aspects of Chemical Warfare.* Washington, DC: Office of The Surgeon General, Borden Institute, Walter Reed Army Medical Center, 2008.

274. Brooks, Peter. *A Devil's Triangle: Terrorism, Weapons of Mass Destruction, and Rogue States.* Lanham, MD: Roman & Littlefield Publishers, Inc., 2005.

275. Office of Public Health Preparedness and Response. "Facts About Phosgene." Centers for Disease Control and Prevention. Centers for Disease Control and Prevention, 12 Apr. 2013. Web. 08 May 2017. <https://emergency.cdc.gov/agent/phosgene/basics/facts.asp>.

276. Tuorinsky, Lt. Col. Shirley. *Medal Aspects of Chemical Warfare.* Washington, DC: Office of The Surgeon General, Borden Institute, Walter Reed Army Medical Center, 2008.

277. Office of Public Health Preparedness and Response. "Facts About Sulfur Mustard." Centers for Disease Control and Prevention. Centers for Disease Control and Prevention, 2 May 2013. Web. 13 Jun 2016. <https://emergency.cdc.gov/agent/sulfurmustard/basics/facts.asp>.

278. "Mustard Gas." *Great Falls Daily Tribune* (Great Falls, MT), 3 Oct 1918, p. 5.

279. Cochrane, Rexmond C. *89th Division Comes into the Line, August 1918.* U.S. Army Chemical Corps Historical Office, Office of the Chief Chemical Officer, Army Chemical Center, Maryland, 1958.

280. Lockwood, John C. (2003). "Chapter 3. The Earth's Climates". In Hewitt, C. N.; Jackson, A. V. *Handbook of Atmospheric Science: Principles and Applications.* Malden, MA: Blackwell Publishing. pp. 72–74.

281. Kleber, Brooks E. and Dale Birdsell. *The Chemical Warfare Service: Chemicals in Combat.* Washington, DC: Center of Military History, United States Army, 1990.

282. "Gas Attack to Remain, View of Chief Officer." *The Indianapolis News* (Indianapolis, IN), 27 Dec 1918, p. 10.

283. Heller, Charles E. *Chemical Warfare in World War I: The American Experience, 1917–1918.* Honolulu, HI: University Press of the Pacific, 2005.

284. Crowell, Benedict and Robert Forrest Wilson. *The Armies of Industry: Our Nation's Manufacture of Munitions for a World in Arms, 1917-1918.* New Haven, CT: Yale University Press, 1921.

285. Cochrane, Rexmond C. *The 1st Division at Ansauville, Jan-Apr 1918.* U.S. Army Chemical Corps Historical Office, Office of the Chief Chemical Officer, Army Chemical Center, Maryland, 1958.

286. Ibid.

287. Tuorinsky, Lt. Col. Shirley. *Medal Aspects of Chemical Warfare.* Washington, DC: Office of The Surgeon General, Borden Institute, Walter Reed Army Medical Center, 2008.

288. Cochrane, Rexmond C. *89th Division Comes into the Line, August 1918.* U.S. Army Chemical Corps Historical Office, Office of the Chief Chemical Officer, Army Chemical Center, Maryland, 1958.

289. Ibid.

Chapter 7: "The Trench System"

290. Stewart, Richard W. *American Military History, Volume II: The United States Army in a Global Era, 1917-2003.* Washington, DC: Center of Military History, United States Army, 2005.

291. Pershing, Gen. John J. *Final Report of Gen. John J. Pershing.* Washington, DC: Government Printing Office, 1919.

292. Stewart, Richard W. *American Military History, Volume II: The United States Army in a Global Era, 1917-2003.* Washington, DC: Center of Military History, United States Army, 2005.

293. English, George H., Jr. *History of the 89th Division, U.S.A.* Denver, CO: Smith-Brooks Printing Company. The War Society of the 89th Division, 1920.

294. Smith, J.S. *Trench Warfare: A Manual for Officers and Men.* New York, NY: E.P. Dutton & Company, 1917.

295. Reynolds, Francis J., Allen L. Churchill and Francis T. Miller. *The Story of the Great War, Volume VII.* New York, NY: P.F. Collier & Son, 1919.

296. Ibid.

297. Fussell, Paul. *The Great War and Modern Memory.* New York, NY: Oxford University Press, 1975.

298. Persons, Lt. Col. William E. and others. *Military Science and Tactics: Senior Course, Infantry, Volume 4.* University of Missouri: University Co-Operative Store, 1921.

299. Ibid.

300. Ibid.

301. Ibid.

302. Ibid.

303. Glenn, Maj. Gen. E.F. and others. *Infantry Journal.* Washington, DC: The United States Infantry Association, Jul 1917-Jun 1918, Vol. 14, p. 484.

304. Ibid.

305. Bertrand, Georges, and Oscar N. Solbert. *Tactics and Duties for Trench Fighting.* New York and London: Putnam's Sons, 1918.

306. Ibid.

307. Ibid.

308. Ibid.

309. Ibid.

310. Ibid.

311. Ibid.

312. Ibid.

313. Persons, Lt. Col. William E. and others. *Military Science and Tactics: Senior Course, Infantry, Volume 4.* University of Missouri: University Co-Operative Store, 1921.

314. Smith, J.S. *Trench Warfare: A Manual for Officers and Men.* New York, NY: E.P. Dutton & Company, 1917.

315. Ibid.

316. Taylor, Maj. John R.M. and G.H. Powell. *Infantry Journal.* Washington, DC: The United States Infantry Trust Association, Jan 1918, Vol. XIV, No. 7.

317. Bertrand, Georges, and Oscar N. Solbert. *Tactics and Duties for Trench Fighting.* New York and London: Putnam's Sons, 1918.

318. Smith, J.S. *Trench Warfare: A Manual for Officers and Men.* New York, NY: E.P. Dutton & Company, 1917.

319. Persons, Lt. Col. William E. and others. *Military Science and Tactics: Senior Course, Infantry, Volume 4.* University of Missouri: University Co-Operative Store, 1921.

320. Bertrand, Georges, and Oscar N. Solbert. *Tactics and Duties for Trench Fighting.* New York and London: Putnam's Sons, 1918.

321. Taylor, Maj. John R.M. and G.H. Powell. *Infantry Journal.* Washington, DC: The United States Infantry Trust Association, Jan 1918, Vol. XIV, No. 7.

322. Persons, Lt. Col. William E. and others. *Military Science and Tactics: Senior Course, Infantry, Volume 4.* University of Missouri: University Co-Operative Store, 1921.

323. Ibid.

324. Overbey, Diana. "Trench Construction in World War I." *Diana Overbey.* n.p., 13 Jan. 2012. Web. 27 June 2017. https://dianaoverbey.wordpress.com/2012/01/13/trench-construction-in-world-war-i/

325. Persons, Lt. Col. William E. and others. *Military Science and Tactics: Senior Course, Infantry, Volume 4.* University of Missouri: University Co-Operative Store, 1921.

326. Bertrand, Georges, and Oscar N. Solbert. *Tactics and Duties for Trench Fighting.* New York and London: Putnam's Sons, 1918.

327. Ibid.

328. "Fool the Airmen" *The Daily Republican* (Cherryvale, Kansas), 10 Nov 1914, p. 1.

329. Bertrand, Georges, and Oscar N. Solbert. *Tactics and Duties for Trench Fighting.* New York and London: Putnam's Sons, 1918.

330. English, George H., Jr. *History of the 89th Division, U.S.A.* Denver, CO: Smith-Brooks Printing Company. The War Society of the 89th Division, 1920.

331. Ibid.

332. *FM 3-09: Field Artillery Operations and Fire Support.* Washington, DC: Headquarters, Department of the Army, 4 Apr 2014.

333. Persons, Lt. Col. William E. and others. *Military Science and Tactics: Senior Course, Infantry, Volume 4.* University of Missouri: University Co-Operative Store, 1921.

334. *War Department Technical Manual 9-2005, Volume 3.* The Ordnance School, Aberdeen Proving Ground, Maryland, Dec 1942.

335. *Stokes' Trench Howitzer 3", Mark I.* Washington, DC: U.S. Army War College, Jan 1918.

336. Bertrand, Georges, and Oscar N. Solbert. *Tactics and Duties for Trench Fighting.* New York and London: Putnam's Sons, 1918.

Chapter 8: "From the Shadows of Death"

337. Cochrane, Rexmond C. *89th Division Comes into the Line, August 1918.* U.S. Army Chemical Corps Historical Office, Office of the Chief Chemical Officer, Army Chemical Center, Maryland, 1958.

338. English, George H., Jr. *History of the 89th Division, U.S.A.* Denver, CO: Smith-Brooks Printing Company. The War Society of the 89th Division, 1920.

339. Ibid.

340. Ibid.

341. Sidell, Dr. Frederick R. and Dr. David R. Franz. *Defense Against the Effects of Chemical and Biological Warfare Agents.* Washington, DC: United States. Department of the Army. Office of the Surgeon General, 1997.

342. English, George H., Jr. *History of the 89th Division, U.S.A.* Denver, CO: Smith-Brooks Printing Company. The War Society of the 89th Division, 1920.

343. Ibid.

344. Ibid.

345. Cochrane, Rexmond C. *89th Division Comes into the Line, August 1918.* U.S. Army Chemical Corps Historical Office, Office of the Chief Chemical Officer, Army Chemical Center, Maryland, 1958.

346. Ibid.

347. Hastings, Max. *Armageddon: The Battle for Germany, 1944-45.* New York, NY: Vintage Books, 2004, p. 25.

348. Palmer, Lt. H.R. "The Argonne-Meuse Battle." *The Pittsburg Morning Sun* (Pittsburg, KS), 12 Jun 1919, p. 16.

349. (1) Ibid; (2) English, George H., Jr. *History of the 89th Division, U.S.A.* Denver, CO: Smith-Brooks Printing Company. The War Society of the 89th Division, 1920.

350. "Gas Was the Most Terrible Weapon the Germans Had." *The Topeka Daily Capital* (Topeka, Kansas), 9 May 1919, p. 5.

351. Ibid.

352. McGrath, Lt. John F. *War Diary of the 354th Infantry, 89th Division.* J. Linte, Trier, GE, 1919.

353. Bratt, John. "In Grandpa Martin's Footsteps." *Howell County Mogenweb.* n.p., n.d. Web. 4 Nov. 2015. <http://www.bing.com/r?IG=91027537760B 4BBCAF0EEE81AA7994A9&CID=023CD39DCB636602220BD9E1CAF 367B1&rd=1&h=wMAfwTlUhabodRpseDoigRbV8ZhLMtfvuvZW5T9g a3I&v=1&r=http%3a%2f%2fhowell.mogenweb.org%2ffamily%2fMartin-Verhage-1.pdf&p=DevEx,5061.1>.

354. "Gas Was the Most Terrible Weapon the Germans Had." *The Topeka Daily Capital* (Topeka, Kansas), 9 May 1919, p. 5.

355. Col. Nathan C. Shiverick Fatally Injured in Crash on Way to Saratoga Races. *Democrat and Chronicle* (Rochester, NY), 19 Aug 1932, p.1.

356. Frenzel, Arthur. "Jess was Brave Kid Says Proud Father of Colorado's Hero." *The Denver Post* (Denver, CO), 5 Jun 1919, p. 6.

357. McGrath, Lt. John F. *War Diary of the 354th Infantry, 89th Division.* J. Linte, Trier, GE, 1919.

358. Ibid.

359. Ibid.

360. Persons, Lt. Col. William E. and others. *Military Science and Tactics: Senior Course, Infantry, Volume 4.* University of Missouri: University Co-Operative Store, 1921.

361. Ibid.

362. Ibid.

363. Bratt, John. "In Grandpa Martin's Footsteps." *Howell County Mogenweb.* n.p., n.d. Web. 4 Nov. 2015. <http://www.bing.com/r?IG=91027537760B 4BBCAF0EEE31AA7994A9&CID=023CD39DCB636602220BD9E1CAF 367B1&rd=1&h=wMAfwTlUhabodRpseDoigRbV8ZhLMtfvuvZW5T9g a3I&v=1&r=http%3a%2f%2fhowell.mogenweb.org%2ffamily%2fMartin-Verhage-1.pdf&p=DevEx,5061.1>.

364. Cochrane, Rexmond C. *89th Division Comes into the Line, August 1918.* U.S. Army Chemical Corps Historical Office, Office of the Chief Chemical Officer, Army Chemical Center, Maryland, 1958.

365. English, George H., Jr. *History of the 89th Division, U.S.A.* Denver, CO: Smith-Brooks Printing Company. The War Society of the 89th Division, 1920.

366. Ibid.

367. Ibid.

368. "Soldier's Letter." *The Evening Star* (Independence, KS), 7 Feb 1919, p. 2.

369. *Summary of Information, Numbers 92 to 121, Inclusive.* Second Section, General Staff, General Headquarters, American Expeditionary Forces, July 1918.

370. Ibid.

371. Ibid.

372. Bertrand, Georges, and Oscar N. Solbert. *Tactics and Duties for Trench Fighting.* New York and London: Putnam's Sons, 1918.

373. *Summary of Information, Numbers 92 to 121,* Inclusive. Second Section, General Staff, General Headquarters, American Expeditionary Forces, July 1918.

374. Ibid.

375. Ibid.

376. Ibid.

377. English, George H., Jr. *History of the 89th Division, U.S.A.* Denver, CO: Smith-Brooks Printing Company. The War Society of the 89th Division, 1920.

378. "Waco War Hero Back in Army." *Joplin Globe* (Joplin, MO), 9 Jan 1921, p. 5.

379. Murphy, Audie L. *To Hell and Back.* New York, NY: Henry Holt and Co., 1949.

380. English, George H., Jr. *History of the 89th Division, U.S.A.* Denver, CO: Smith-Brooks Printing Company. The War Society of the 89th Division, 1920.

381. Bratt, John. "In Grandpa Martin's Footsteps." *Howell County Mogenweb.* n.p., n.d. Web. 4 Nov. 2015. <http://www.bing.com/r?IG=91027537760B4B BCAF0EEE81AA7994A9&CID=023CD39DCB636602220BD9E1CAF367B 1&rd=1&h=wMAfwTlUhabodRpseDoigRbV8ZhLMtfvuvZW5T9ga3I&v= 1&r=http%3a%2f%2fhowell.mogenweb.org%2ffamily%2fMartin-Verhage-1. pdf&p=DevEx,5061.1>.

382. English, George H., Jr. *History of the 89th Division, U.S.A.* Denver, CO: Smith-Brooks Printing Company. The War Society of the 89th Division, 1920.

383. Ibid.

384. Ibid.

385. McGrath, Lt. John F. *War Diary of the 354th Infantry, 89th Division.* J. Linte, Trier, GE, 1919.

386. English, George H., Jr. *History of the 89th Division, U.S.A.* Denver, CO: Smith-Brooks Printing Company. The War Society of the 89th Division, 1920.

387. Ibid.

388. McGrath, Lt. John F. *War Diary of the 354th Infantry, 89th Division.* J. Linte, Trier, GE, 1919.

389. "Extra Duty for Mule." *Lebanon Daily Reporter* (Lebanon, IN), 12 Jun 1919, p. 8.

390. McGrath, Lt. John F. *War Diary of the 354th Infantry, 89th Division.* J. Linte, Trier, GE, 1919.

391. Ferrell, Robert H. *Reminiscences of Conrad S. Babcock: The Old U.S. Army and the New, 1898-1918.* Columbia, MO: University of Missouri Press, 2012.

392. English, George H., Jr. *History of the 89th Division, U.S.A.* Denver, CO: Smith-Brooks Printing Company. The War Society of the 89th Division, 1920.

393. Ibid.

394. Dienst, Charles Franklin. *History of the 353rd Infantry Regiment, 89th Division, National Army.* Wichita, KS: The Eagle Press, 1921.

395. English, George H., Jr. *History of the 89th Division, U.S.A.* Denver, CO: Smith-Brooks Printing Company. The War Society of the 89th Division, 1920.

Chapter 9: "The Saint Mihiel Salient"

396. Herwig, Holger H. *The First World War: Germany and Austria-Hungary, 1914–1918.* New York, NY: St. Martin's Press, 1997.
397. Koenig, Robert L. *The Fourth Horseman: One Man's Secret Mission to Wage the Great American War.* New York, NY: Public Affairs, a Member of Perseus Books Group, 2006.
398. American Battle Monuments Commission. *89th Division Summary of Operations in the World War.* Washington, DC: U.S. Government Printing Office, 1944.
399. Ibid.
400. Palmer, Lt. H.R. "Reducing the St. Mihiel Salient." *The Pittsburg Morning Sun* (Pittsburg, KS), 12 Jun 1919, p. 16.
401. Ibid.
402. Ibid.
403. Hendon, William S. *Letters from France.* Martinsville, NC: Lulu Publishing Company, 2010, p. 95.
404. Wythe, Maj. George. *A History of the 90th Division.* New York, NY: The 90th Division Association, 1920.
405. Strohn, Matthias. *World War I Companion.* Oxford, England: Osprey Publishing, 2013, p. 204.
406. Wythe, Maj. George. *A History of the 90th Division.* New York, NY: The 90th Division Association, 1920.
407. McGrath, Lt. John F. *War Diary of the 354th Infantry, 89th Division.* J. Linte, Trier, GE, 1919.
408. Dienst, Charles Franklin. *History of the 353rd Infantry Regiment, 89th Division, National Army.* Wichita, KS: The Eagle Press, 1921.
409. English, George H., Jr. *History of the 89th Division, U.S.A.* Denver, CO: Smith-Brooks Printing Company. The War Society of the 89th Division, 1920.
410. Bertrand, Georges, and Oscar N. Solbert. *Tactics and Duties for Trench Fighting.* New York and London: Putnam's Sons, 1918.
411. Ibid.
412. "U.S. Battalion Cut Off 5 Days." *The Morning News* (Danville, PA), 10 Oct 1918, p. 3.
413. "Wounded Denver Soldier Shot by His Own Sentry on Returning to Lines." *The Denver Post* (Denver, CO), 5 Jun 1919, p. 4.
414. Ibid.
415. McGrath, Lt. John F. *War Diary of the 354th Infantry, 89th Division.* J. Linte, Trier, GE, 1919.
416. "Shotguns and Reprisals." *The Atlanta Constitution* (Atlanta, GA), 2 Oct 1918, p. 8.
417. Bruce N. Canfield "Remington's Model 10: The Other Trench Gun." *American Rifleman,* November 2009, p.76.
418. "Sawed-Off Shot-Gun Played Hob With Huns, Relates Tom Marshall." *Harrisburg Telegraph* (Harrisburg, PA), 16 Nov 1918, p. 11.

419. McGrath, Lt. John F. *War Diary of the 354th Infantry, 89th Division*. J. Linte, Trier, GE, 1919.

420. Ibid.

421. English, George H., Jr. *History of the 89th Division, U.S.A.* Denver, CO: Smith-Brooks Printing Company. The War Society of the 89th Division, 1920.

422. McGrath, Lt. John F. *War Diary of the 354th Infantry, 89th Division*. J. Linte, Trier, GE, 1919.

423. Ibid.

424. English, George H., Jr. *History of the 89th Division, U.S.A.* Denver, CO: Smith-Brooks Printing Company. The War Society of the 89th Division, 1920.

425. Ibid.

426. Ibid.

427. Ibid.

428. Ibid.

429. Ibid.

430. Ibid.

431. Ibid.

432. Ibid.

433. McGrath, Lt. John F. *War Diary of the 354th Infantry, 89th Division*. J. Linte, Trier, GE, 1919.

434. Ibid.

435. Ibid.

436. Ibid.

437. Ibid.

438. Ibid.

439. "Colorado's Greatest Hero, Jess Funk, Is Home, Dodging Questions about His Deeds." *The Denver Post* (Denver, CO), 5 Jun 1919, pp. 1 & 7.

440. English, George H., Jr. *History of the 89th Division, U.S.A.* Denver, CO: Smith-Brooks Printing Company. The War Society of the 89th Division, 1920.

441. American Battle Monuments Commission. *89th Division Summary of Operations in the World War*. Washington, DC: U.S. Government Printing Office, 1944.

442. English, George H., Jr. *History of the 89th Division, U.S.A.* Denver, CO: Smith-Brooks Printing Company. The War Society of the 89th Division, 1920.

443. Bratt, John. "In Grandpa Martin's Footsteps." *Howell County Mogenweb*. n.p., n.d. Web. 4 Nov. 2015. <http://www.bing.com/r?IG=91027537760B4B BCAF0EEE81AA7994A9&CID=023CD39DCB636602220BD9E1CAF367B 1&rd=1&h=wMAfwTlUhabodRpseDoigRbV8ZhLMtfvuvZW5T9ga3I&v= 1&r=http%3a%2f%2fhowell.mogenweb.org%2ffamily%2fMartin-Verhage-1. pdf&p=DevEx,5061.1>.

444. McGrath, Lt. John F. *War Diary of the 354th Infantry, 89th Division*. J. Linte, Trier, GE, 1919.

445. English, George H., Jr. *History of the 89th Division, U.S.A.* Denver, CO: Smith-Brooks Printing Company. The War Society of the 89th Division, 1920.

446. "Colorado's Greatest Hero, Jess Funk, Is Home, Dodging Questions about His Deeds." *The Denver Post* (Denver, CO), 5 Jun 1919, pp. 1 & 7.

447. Ferrell, Robert H. *Reminiscences of Conrad S. Babcock: The Old U.S. Army and the New, 1898-1918.* Columbia, MO: University of Missouri Press, 2012.

448. English, George H., Jr. *History of the 89th Division, U.S.A.* Denver, CO: Smith-Brooks Printing Company. The War Society of the 89th Division, 1920.

449. McGrath, Lt. John F. *War Diary of the 354th Infantry, 89th Division.* J. Linte, Trier, GE, 1919.

450. Ibid.

451. Palmer, Lt. H.R. "Reducing the St. Mihiel Salient." *The Pittsburg Morning Sun* (Pittsburg, KS), 12 Jun 1919, p. 16.

452. English, George H., Jr. *History of the 89th Division, U.S.A.* Denver, CO: Smith-Brooks Printing Company. The War Society of the 89th Division, 1920.

453. Palmer, Lt. H.R. "Reducing the St. Mihiel Salient." *The Pittsburg Morning Sun* (Pittsburg, KS), 12 Jun 1919, p. 16.

454. Ibid.

455. Ibid.

456. English, George H., Jr. *History of the 89th Division, U.S.A.* Denver, CO: Smith-Brooks Printing Company. The War Society of the 89th Division, 1920.

457. Ibid.

458. McGrath, Lt. John F. *War Diary of the 354th Infantry, 89th Division.* J. Linte, Trier, GE, 1919.

459. Ibid.

460. Ibid.

461. Ibid.

462. Ferrell, Robert H. *Reminiscences of Conrad S. Babcock: The Old U.S. Army and the New, 1898-1918.* Columbia, MO: University of Missouri Press, 2012.

463. McGrath, Lt. John F. *War Diary of the 354th Infantry, 89th Division.* J. Linte, Trier, GE, 1919.

464. Cochrane, Rexmond C. *The 89th Division in the Bois de Bantheville, October 1918.* U.S. Army Chemical Corps Historical Office, Office of the Chief Chemical Officer, Washington, DC, Study No. 18, Jun 1960.

465. Ibid.

466. Ibid.

467. Ibid.

468. Ibid.

469. McGrath, Lt. John F. *War Diary of the 354th Infantry, 89th Division.* J. Linte, Trier, GE, 1919.

470. "When Kansas Doughboys of 89th Mopped Up Wood." *The Topeka Daily Capital* (Topeka, KS), 22 May 1919, p. 9.

Chapter 10: "The Bois de Bantheville"

471. American Battle Monuments Commission. *89th Division Summary of Operations in the World War.* Washington, DC: U.S. Government Printing Office, 1944.

472. Ibid.

473. Pershing, Gen. John J. *Final Report of Gen. John J. Pershing.* Washington, DC: Government Printing Office, 1919.

474. American Strategy Outwitted the Germans in the Argonne Offensive. *Lawrence Daily Journal-World* (Lawrence, KS), 26 Sep 1919, p. 2.

475. Ferrell, Robert H. *Reminiscences of Conrad S. Babcock: The Old U.S. Army and the New, 1898-1918.* Columbia, MO: University of Missouri Press, 2012.

476. Ibid.

477. American Battle Monuments Commission. *89th Division Summary of Operations in the World War.* Washington, DC: U.S. Government Printing Office, 1944.

478. Ferrell, Robert H. *Reminiscences of Conrad S. Babcock: The Old U.S. Army and the New, 1898-1918.* Columbia, MO: University of Missouri Press, 2012.

479. Stanley, A.R. "Old-Time Fourth of July Fireworks Light Our Way to Berlin." *The Des Moines Register* (Des Moines, IA), 15 Sep 1918, p. 23.

480. Ibid.

481. Ibid.

482. "American Strategy Outwitted the Germans in the Argonne Offensive." *Lawrence Daily Journal-World* (Lawrence, KS), 26 Sep 1919, p. 2.

483. Ibid.

484. Ibid.

485. Ibid.

486. McGrath, Lt. John F. *War Diary of the 354th Infantry, 89th Division.* J. Linte, Trier, GE, 1919.

487. *Citation to Accompany the Award of the Distinguished Service Cross to Captain Marshall P. Wilder.* War Department, General Orders 95 (1919).

488. McGrath, Lt. John F. *War Diary of the 354th Infantry, 89th Division.* J. Linte, Trier, GE, 1919.

489. American Strategy Outwitted the Germans in the Argonne Offensive. *Lawrence Daily Journal-World* (Lawrence, KS), 26 Sep 1919, p. 2.

490. Palmer, Lt. H.R. "The Argonne-Meuse Battle." *The Pittsburg Morning Sun* (Pittsburg, KS), 12 Jun 1919, p. 12.

491. American Battle Monuments Commission. *89th Division Summary of Operations in the World War.* Washington, DC: U.S. Government Printing Office, 1944.

492. Cochrane, Rexmond C. *89th Division Comes into the Line, August 1918.* U.S. Army Chemical Corps Historical Office, Office of the Chief Chemical Officer, Army Chemical Center, Maryland, 1958.

493. Ibid.

494. Ibid.

495. *Citation to Accompany the Award of the Distinguished Service Cross to Second Lieutenant John M. Millis.* War Department, General Orders 13 (1923).

496. Ibid.

497. McGrath, Lt. John F. *War Diary of the 354th Infantry, 89th Division.* J. Linte, Trier, GE, 1919.

498. Ibid.

499. English, George H., Jr. *History of the 89th Division, U.S.A.* Denver, CO: Smith-Brooks Printing Company. The War Society of the 89th Division, 1920.

500. Cochrane, Rexmond C *89th Division Comes into the Line, August 1918.* U.S. Army Chemical Corps Historical Office, Office of the Chief Chemical Officer, Army Chemical Center, Maryland, 1958.

501. English, George H., Jr. *History of the 89th Division, U.S.A.* Denver, CO: Smith-Brooks Printing Company. The War Society of the 89th Division, 1920.

502. Palmer, Lt. H.R. "The Argonne-Meuse Battle." *The Pittsburg Morning Sun* (Pittsburg, KS), 12 Jun 1919, p. 12.

503. Ibid.

504. Little, John G. *The Official History of the Eighty-Sixth Division.* Chicago, IL: States Publications Society, 1921.

505. McGrath, Lt. John F. *War Diary of the 354th Infantry, 89th Division.* J. Linte, Trier, GE, 1919.

506. Ibid.

507. Ibid.

508. Ibid.

509. American Battle Monuments Commission. *89th Division Summary of Operations in the World War.* Washington, DC: U.S. Government Printing Office, 1944.

510. Palmer, Lt. H.R. "The Argonne-Meuse Battle." *The Pittsburg Morning Sun* (Pittsburg, KS), 12 Jun 1919, p. 12.

511. English, George H., Jr. *History of the 89th Division, U.S.A.* Denver, CO: Smith-Brooks Printing Company. The War Society of the 89th Division, 1920.

512. "Definition of 'mopping-up operation'" *Mopping-up operation definition and meaning. Collins English Dictionary.* n.p., n.d. Web. 22 June 2017. <https://www.collinsdictionary.com/us/dictionary/english/mopping-up-operation>.

513. English, George H., Jr. *History of the 89th Division, U.S.A.* Denver, CO: Smith-Brooks Printing Company. The War Society of the 89th Division, 1920.

514. Bratt, John. "In Grandpa Martin's Footsteps." *Howell County Mogenweb.* n.p., n.d. Web. 4 Nov. 2015. <http://www.bing.com/r?IG=91027537760B4BBCAF0EEE81AA7994A9&CID=023CD39DCB636602220BD9E1CAF367B1&rd=1&h=wMAfwTlUhabodRpseDoigRbV8ZhLMtfvuvZW5T9ga3I&v=1&r=http%3a%2f%2fhowell.mogenweb.org%2ffamily%2fMartin-Verhage-1.pdf&p=DevEx,5061.1>.

515. American Battle Monuments Commission. *89th Division Summary of Operations in the World War.* Washington, DC: U.S. Government Printing Office, 1944.

516. "When Kansas Doughboys of 89th Mopped Up Wood." *The Topeka Daily Capital* (Topeka, KS), 22 May 1919, p. 9.

517. American Battle Monuments Commission. *89th Division Summary of Operations in the World War.* Washington, DC: U.S. Government Printing Office, 1944.

518. Ibid.

519. Ferrell, Robert H. *Reminiscences of Conrad S. Babcock: The Old U.S. Army and the New, 1898-1918.* Columbia, MO: University of Missouri Press, 2012.

520. Cochrane, Rexmond C. *The 89th Division in the Bois de Bantheville, October 1918.* U.S. Army Chemical Corps Historical Office, Office of the Chief Chemical Officer, Washington, DC, Study No. 18, Jun 1960.

521. English, George H., Jr. *History of the 89th Division, U.S.A.* Denver, CO: Smith-Brooks Printing Company. The War Society of the 89th Division, 1920.

522. Ibid.

523. Ibid.

524. Ibid.

525. Ibid.

526. Ibid.

527. Ibid.

528. Ibid.

529. Ibid.

530. Ibid.

531. McGrath, Lt. John F. *War Diary of the 354th Infantry, 89th Division.* J. Linte, Trier, GE, 1919.

532. Ferrell, Robert H. *Reminiscences of Conrad S. Babcock: The Old U.S. Army and the New, 1898-1918.* Columbia, MO: University of Missouri Press, 2012.

533. Cochrane, Rexmond C. *The 89th Division in the Bois de Bantheville, October 1918.* U.S. Army Chemical Corps Historical Office, Office of the Chief Chemical Officer, Washington, DC, Study No. 18, Jun 1960.

534. (1) Ibid.; (2) McGrath, Lt. John F. *War Diary of the 354th Infantry, 89th Division.* J. Linte, Trier, GE, 1919.

535. Cochrane, Rexmond C. *The 89th Division in the Bois de Bantheville, October 1918.* U.S. Army Chemical Corps Historical Office, Office of the Chief Chemical Officer, Washington, DC, Study No. 18, Jun 1960.

536. McGrath, Lt. John F. *War Diary of the 354th Infantry, 89th Division.* J. Linte, Trier, GE, 1919.

537. *Coroner's Case No. 4318.* Kansas City General Hospital, Kansas City, MO, 26 Nov 1936.

538. McGrath, Lt. John F. *War Diary of the 354th Infantry, 89th Division.* J. Linte, Trier, GE, 1919.

539. Funk, Corp. Jesse N. "Hero Funk Credits His Glorious Deeds All to Colorado." *The Denver Post* (Denver, CO), 5 Jun 1919, p. 6.

540. Ibid.

541. Ibid.

542. "Calhan Soldier Saved Comrades by Risking Life." *The Denver Post* (Denver, CO), 4 Feb 1919, p. 3.

543. Funk, Corp. Jesse N. "Hero Funk Credits His Glorious Deeds All to Colorado." *The Denver Post* (Denver, CO), 5 Jun 1919, p. 6.

544. Cochrane, Rexmond C. *The 89th Division in the Bois de Bantheville, October 1918.* U.S. Army Chemical Corps Historical Office, Office of the Chief Chemical Officer, Washington, DC, Study No. 18, Jun 1960.
545. Ibid.

Chapter 11: "Bravest of the Brave"

546. English, George H., Jr. *History of the 89th Division, U.S.A.* Denver, CO: Smith-Brooks Printing Company. The War Society of the 89th Division, 1920.
547. Cochrane, Rexmond C. *The 89th Division in the Bois de Bantheville, October 1918.* U.S. Army Chemical Corps Historical Office, Office of the Chief Chemical Officer, Washington, DC, Study No. 18, Jun 1960.
548. Ibid.
549. English, George H., Jr. *History of the 89th Division, U.S.A.* Denver, CO: Smith-Brooks Printing Company. The War Society of the 89th Division, 1920.
550. Ibid.
551. Rickenbacker, Capt. Edward V. *Fighting the Flying Circus.* Philadelphia and New York: J.B. Lippincott Company, 1919.
552. Ibid.
553. Cochrane, Rexmond C. *The 89th Division in the Bois de Bantheville, October 1918.* U.S. Army Chemical Corps Historical Office, Office of the Chief Chemical Officer, Washington, DC, Study No. 18, Jun 1960.
554. McGrath, Lt. John F. *War Diary of the 354th Infantry, 89th Division.* J. Linte, Trier, GE, 1919.
555. Cochrane, Rexmond C. *The 89th Division in the Bois de Bantheville, October 1918.* U.S. Army Chemical Corps Historical Office, Office of the Chief Chemical Officer, Washington, DC, Study No. 18, Jun 1960.
556. Ibid.
557. McGrath, Lt. John F. *War Diary of the 354th Infantry, 89th Division.* J. Linte, Trier, GE, 1919.
558. Ibid.
559. Ibid.
560. "Private Barger Tells How He Won Medal of Honor." *The St. Louis Star and Times* (St. Louis, MO), 30 May 1919, p. 3.
561. "Hero Has a Medal of Honor but No Job and Little Food." *Kansas City Star* (Kansas City, MO), 30 Aug 1932, p. 9.
562. *Geneva Convention of July 6th, 1906, Chapter III.—Personnel. Article 9.* Geneva, Switzerland, 1906.
563. *Geneva Convention of July 6th, 1906, Chapter II.—Medical Units and Establishments. Article 8, Paragraph 1.* Geneva, Switzerland, 1906.
564. "Hero Has a Medal of Honor But No Job and Little Food." *Kansas City Star* (Kansas City, MO), 30 Aug 1932, p.9.
565. Ibid.
566. "Colorado's Greatest Hero, Jess Funk, Is Home, Dodging Questions about His Deeds." *The Denver Post* (Denver, CO), 5 Jun 1919, pp. 1 & 7.

567. Ibid.
568. Ibid.
569. Ibid.
570. Ferrell, Robert H. *Reminiscences of Conrad S. Babcock: The Old U.S. Army and the New, 1898-1918.* Columbia, MO: University of Missouri Press, 2012.
571. English, George H., Jr. *History of the 89th Division, U.S.A.* Denver, CO: Smith-Brooks Printing Company. The War Society of the 89th Division, 1920.
572. "Hero Has a Medal of Honor But No Job and Little Food." *Kansas City Star* (Kansas City, MO), 30 Aug 1932, p.9.
573. "Colorado's Greatest Hero, Jess Funk, Is Home, Dodging Questions about His Deeds." *The Denver Post* (Denver, CO), 5 Jun 1919, pp. 1 & 7.
574. "Hero Has a Medal of Honor But No Job and Little Food." *Kansas City Star* (Kansas City, MO), 30 Aug 1932, p.9.
575. Ibid.
576. "Colorado's Greatest Hero, Jess Funk, Is Home, Dodging Questions about His Deeds." *The Denver Post* (Denver, CO), 5 Jun 1919, pp. 1 & 7.
577. "Hero Has a Medal of Honor But No Job and Little Food." *Kansas City Star* (Kansas City, MO), 30 Aug 1932, p.9.
578. "Calhan Soldier Saved Comrades by Risking Life." *The Denver Post* (Denver, CO), 4 Feb 1919, p. 3.
579. "Colorado's Greatest Hero, Jess Funk, Is Home, Dodging Questions about His Deeds." *The Denver Post* (Denver, CO), 5 Jun 1919, pp. 1 & 7.
580. "Hero Has a Medal of Honor But No Job and Little Food." *Kansas City Star* (Kansas City, MO), 30 Aug 1932, p.9.
581. Ibid.
582. "Colorado's Greatest Hero, Jess Funk, Is Home, Dodging Questions about His Deeds." *The Denver Post* (Denver, CO), 5 Jun 1919, pp. 1 & 7.
583. "Private Barger Tells How He Won Medal of Honor." *The St. Louis Star and Times* (St. Louis, Missouri), 30 May 1919, p. 3.
584. Cochrane, Rexmond C. *The 89th Division in the Bois de Bantheville, October 1918.* U.S. Army Chemical Corps Historical Office, Office of the Chief Chemical Officer, Washington, DC, Study No. 18, Jun 1960.
585. Ferrell, Robert H. *Reminiscences of Conrad S. Babcock: The Old U.S. Army and the New, 1898-1918.* Columbia, MO: University of Missouri Press, 2012.

Chapter 12: "Victory!"

586. "Heroes of the 89th Returning After Making a Record." *Leavenworth Post* (Leavenworth, KS), 20 May 1919, p. 6.
587. Bertrand, Georges, and Oscar N. Solbert. *Tactics and Duties for Trench Fighting.* New York and London: Putnam's Sons, 1918.
588. Cochrane, Rexmond C. *The 89th Division in the Bois de Bantheville, October 1918.* U.S. Army Chemical Corps Historical Office, Office of the Chief Chemical Officer, Washington, DC, Study No. 18, Jun 1960.

589. McGrath, Lt. John F. *War Diary of the 354th Infantry, 89th Division.* J. Linte, Trier, GE, 1919.

590. American Battle Monuments Commission. *89th Division Summary of Operations in the World War.* Washington, DC: U.S. Government Printing Office, 1944.

591. McGrath, Lt. John F. *War Diary of the 354th Infantry, 89th Division.* J. Linte, Trier, GE, 1919.

592. Ibid.

593. Cochrane, Rexmond C. *The 89th Division in the Bois de Bantheville, October 1918.* U.S. Army Chemical Corps Historical Office, Office of the Chief Chemical Officer, Washington, DC, Study No. 18, Jun 1960.

594. English, George H., Jr. *History of the 89th Division, U.S.A.* Denver, CO: Smith-Brooks Printing Company. The War Society of the 89th Division, 1920.

595. "Heroes of the 89th Returning After Making a Record." *Leavenworth Post* (Leavenworth, KS), 20 May 1919, p. 6.

596. McGrath, Lt. John F. *War Diary of the 354th Infantry, 89th Division.* J. Linte, Trier, GE, 1919.

597. English, George H., Jr. *History of the 89th Division, U.S.A.* Denver, CO: Smith-Brooks Printing Company. The War Society of the 89th Division, 1920.

598. Ibid.

599. Dienst, Charles Franklin. *History of the 353rd Infantry Regiment, 89th Division, National Army.* Wichita, KS: The Eagle Press, 1921.

600. McGrath, Lt. John F. *War Diary of the 354th Infantry, 89th Division.* J. Linte, Trier, GE, 1919.

601. English, George H., Jr. *History of the 89th Division, U.S.A.* Denver, CO: Smith-Brooks Printing Company. The War Society of the 89th Division, 1920.

602. Ibid.

603. Ferrell, Robert H. *Reminiscences of Conrad S. Babcock: The Old U.S. Army and the New, 1898-1918.* Columbia, MO: University of Missouri Press, 2012.

604. "Heroes of the 89th Returning After Making a Record." *Leavenworth Post* (Leavenworth, KS), 20 May 1919, p. 6.

605. "Lieut. Bates Was Cited." *The Junction City Daily Union* (Junction City, Kansas), 29 Jan 1919, p. 6.

606. Ibid.

607. Ibid.

608. English, George H., Jr. *History of the 89th Division, U.S.A.* Denver, CO: Smith-Brooks Printing Company. The War Society of the 89th Division, 1920.

609. McGrath, Lt. John F. *War Diary of the 354th Infantry, 89th Division.* J. Linte, Trier, GE, 1919.

610. Ibid.

611. English, George H., Jr. *History of the 89th Division, U.S.A.* Denver, CO: Smith-Brooks Printing Company. The War Society of the 89th Division, 1920.

612. Cochrane, Rexmond C. *The 89th Division in the Bois de Bantheville, October 1918*. U.S. Army Chemical Corps Historical Office, Office of the Chief Chemical Officer, Washington, DC, Study No. 18, Jun 1960.

613. Ferrell, Robert H. *Reminiscences of Conrad S. Babcock: The Old U.S. Army and the New, 1898-1918*. Columbia, MO: University of Missouri Press, 2012.

614. McGrath, Lt. John F. *War Diary of the 354th Infantry, 89th Division*. J. Linte, Trier, GE, 1919.

615. (1) Ibid; (2) English, George H., Jr. *History of the 89th Division, U.S.A.* Denver, CO: Smith-Brooks Printing Company. The War Society of the 89th Division, 1920.

616. Cochrane, Rexmond C. *The 89th Division in the Bois de Bantheville, October 1918*. U.S. Army Chemical Corps Historical Office, Office of the Chief Chemical Officer, Washington, DC, Study No. 18, Jun 1960.

617. Ferrell, Robert H. *Reminiscences of Conrad S. Babcock: The Old U.S. Army and the New, 1898-1918*. Columbia, MO: University of Missouri Press, 2012.

618. Ibid.

619. English, George H., Jr. *History of the 89th Division, U.S.A.* Denver, CO: Smith-Brooks Printing Company. The War Society of the 89th Division, 1920.

620. American Battle Monuments Commission. *89th Division Summary of Operations in the World War*. Washington, DC: U.S. Government Printing Office, 1944.

621. Bratt, John. "In Grandpa Martin's Footsteps." *Howell County Mogenweb*. n.p., n.d. Web. 4 Nov. 2015. <http://www.bing.com/r?IG=91027537760B4B BCAF0EEE81AA7994A9&CID=023CD39DCB636602220BD9E1CAF367B 1&rd=1&h=wMAfwTlUhabodRpseDoigRbV8ZhLMtfvuvZW5T9ga3I&v= 1&r=http%3a%2f%2fhowell.mogenweb.org%2ffamily%2fMartin-Verhage-1. pdf&p=DevEx,5061.1>.

622. McGrath, Lt. John F. *War Diary of the 354th Infantry, 89th Division*. J. Linte, Trier, GE, 1919.

623. Ibid.

624. American Battle Monuments Commission. *89th Division Summary of Operations in the World War*. Washington, DC: U.S. Government Printing Office, 1944.

625. English, George H., Jr. *History of the 89th Division, U.S.A.* Denver, CO: Smith-Brooks Printing Company. The War Society of the 89th Division, 1920.

626. "Exploits to Live On." *The Kansas City Times* (Kansas City, MO), 1 May 1959, p. 43.

627. Citation to accompany the award of the French Croix de Guerre with bronze star for action near Barricourt, France on 2 November 1918

628. Ibid.

629. English, George H., Jr. *History of the 89th Division, U.S.A.* Denver, CO: Smith-Brooks Printing Company. The War Society of the 89th Division, 1920.

630. Ibid.

631. Cochrane, Rexmond C. *The 89th Division in the Bois de Bantheville, October 1918*. U.S. Army Chemical Corps Historical Office, Office of the Chief Chemical Officer, Washington, DC, Study No. 18, Jun 1960.

632. English, George H., Jr. *History of the 89th Division, U.S.A.* Denver, CO: Smith-Brooks Printing Company. The War Society of the 89th Division, 1920.

633. Ibid.

634. Ibid.

635. Ibid.

636. Ibid.

637. Ibid.

638. Ibid.

639. McGrath, Lt. John F. *War Diary of the 354th Infantry, 89th Division.* J. Linte, Trier, GE, 1919.

640. English, George H., Jr. *History of the 89th Division, U.S.A.* Denver, CO: Smith-Brooks Printing Company. The War Society of the 89th Division, 1920.

641. Ibid.

642. Ibid.

643. Ibid.

644. McGrath, Lt. John F. *War Diary of the 354th Infantry, 89th Division.* J. Linte, Trier, GE, 1919.

645. "Interesting Facts About the 89th Division." *St. Louis Post-Dispatch* (St. Louis, MO), 25 May 1919, p. 49.

646. (1) Ferrell, Robert H. *America's Deadliest Battle: Meuse-Argonne, 1918.* Lawrence, KS: University Press of Kansas, 2012; (2) Rickard, J. *Meuse River-Argonne Forest Offensive, 26 September-11 November 1918*, n.p. 6 Sep 2007. Web. 10 Oct 2017. http://www.historyofwar.org/articles/battles_meuse_argonne.html; (3) *Collier's New Encyclopedia: A Loose-leaf and Self-revising Reference Work.* New York, NY: P.F. Collier, 1922, p. 209.

647. Cochrane, Rexmond C. *The 89th Division in the Bois de Bantheville, October 1918.* U.S. Army Chemical Corps Historical Office, Office of the Chief Chemical Officer, Washington, DC, Study No. 18, Jun 1960.

648. McGrath, Lt. John F. *War Diary of the 354th Infantry, 89th Division.* J. Linte, Trier, GE, 1919.

649. Bratt, John. "In Grandpa Martin's Footsteps." *Howell County Mogenweb.* n.p., n.d. Web. 4 Nov. 2015. <http://www.bing.com/r?IG=91027537760B4B BCAF0EEE81AA7994A9&CID=023CD39DCB636602220BD9E1CAF367B 1&rd=1&h=wMAfwTlUhabodRpseDoigRbV8ZhLMtfvuvZW5T9ga3I&v= 1&r=http%3a%2f%2fhowell.mogenweb.org%2ffamily%2fMartin-Verhage-1. pdf&p=DevEx,5061.1>.

650. Ibid.

651. English, George H., Jr. *History of the 89th Division, U.S.A.* Denver, CO: Smith-Brooks Printing Company. The War Society of the 89th Division, 1920.

652. Stringer, Harry R. *Heroes All!* Washington, DC: Fassett Publishing Company, 1919.

653. "Spring Soldier Wins High Medal." *Colorado Springs Gazette* (Colorado Springs, CO), 5 Feb 1919, p. 2.

654. Stringer, Harry R. *Heroes All!* Washington, DC: Fassett Publishing Company, 1919.

655. Bollmeyer, Fred J. "Welcome to Medal of Honor Men." *The American Legion 2nd National Convention: Official Program*, 1920.

656. Congressional Medal of Honor Society. "Medal of Honor." *CMOHS.org— History of the Medal of Honor*. n.p., n.d. Web. 08 May 2017. <http://www.cmohs.org/medal-history.php>.

657. "Medal of Honor Winners C-in-C's Luncheon Guests." *The Stars & Stripes*, 14 Feb 1919, Vol. 2, No. 2, p. 1.

658. Ibid.

659. *Citation to Accompany the Award of the Medal of Honor to Private First Class Charles D. Barger*. War Department General Order 20 (1919).

660. "Medal of Honor Winners C-in-C's Luncheon Guests." *The Stars & Stripes*, 14 Feb 1919, p. 1.

661. Ibid.

662. English, George H., Jr. *History of the 89th Division, U.S.A.* Denver, CO: Smith-Brooks Printing Company. The War Society of the 89th Division, 1920.

663. Ferrell, Robert H. *Reminiscences of Conrad S. Babcock: The Old U.S. Army and the New, 1898-1918*. Columbia, MO: University of Missouri Press, 2012.

664. Ibid.

665. "89th Gets Allied Ribbons by 'Plane.'" *The Stars & Stripes*, 30 May 1919, p. 1.

666. "Private Barger Tells How He Won Medal of Honor." *The St. Louis Star and Times* (St. Louis, MO), 30 May 1919, p. 3.

667. "Two Winners of Medal of Honor Arrive with 354th." *The St. Louis Star and Times* (St. Louis, MO), 30 May 1919, p. 2.

668. "Stotts City Man Greatest Hero of 89th." *The Monett Weekly Times* (Monett, MO), 27 Jun 1919, p. 3.

669. Ibid.

670. Ibid.

671. Ibid.

672. Ibid.

Chapter 13: "Wounded Warrior"

673. "Ask States Hero Here." *Kansas City Star* (Kansas City, MO), 6 Jun 1919, p. 1.

674. "Stotts City Man Greatest Hero of 89th." *The Monett Weekly Times* (Monett, MO), 27 Jun 1919, p. 3.

675. "Roberson Association Meets." *Springfield Missouri Republican* (Springfield, MO), 21 Oct 1919, p. 7.

676. "King Says he is Touched by St. Louis Reception." *St. Louis Post-Dispatch* (St. Louis, MO), 21 Oct 1919, pp. 1-2.

677. "Gosh, I Thought it was a Tank." *Plain Dealer* (Cleveland, OH), 27 Sep 1920, p. 22.

678. Ibid.

679. Ibid.

680. *Citation to Accompany the Award of the Medal of Honor to Private First Class John L. Barkley.* War Department, General Orders 44 (1919).

681. "Gosh, I Thought it was a Tank." *Plain Dealer* (Cleveland, OH), 27 Sep 1920, p. 22.

682. "Bullets? Pooh! But Drat That Hail in Missouri." *Plain Dealer* (Cleveland, OH), 26 Sep 1920, p. 17.

683. Ibid.

684. Ibid.

685. Ibid.

686. Kraft, Chris. *Conversation with June Buccina.* 8 Nov 2015.

687. "Mother Recalls Her Own Plight." *The Independence Examiner* (Independence, MO), 27 Nov 1936, n.p.

688. "The Army Reduction Veto." *New Castle Herald* (New Castle, PA), 16 Feb 1921, p. 4.

689. "Impressive Tribute Paid to Memory of Heroes Who Gave Lives in War." *Arkansas Democrat* (Little Rock, AR), 31 May 1921, p. 3.

690. "American Legion Lunch." *Daily Arkansas Gazette* (Little Rock, AR), 21 Mar 1921, p. 12.

691. "Remmel Assured of Retention of Pike." *Daily Arkansas Gazette* (Little Rock, AR), 21 Mar 1921, p. 1.

692. "Obituary: Mrs. Mary Weaver." *Little Rock Daily News* (Little Rock, AR), 1 Mar 1921, p. 2.

693. "National Guards to Hold Encampment at Camp Pike." *The Times* (Harrison, AR), n.d., n.p.

694. "House Demands Army Reductions." *The San Bernardino County Sun* (San Bernardino, CA), 7 May 1921, p. 1.

695. "Army Discharges Are Stopped by the Secretary of War." *The Oregon Daily Journal* (Portland, OR), 23 Jul 1921, p. 1.

696. "American Zinc Buys High Five at Waco." *Joplin Globe* (Joplin, MO), 21 Aug 1921, p. 7.

697. Barger, Charles D. *Employment Record.* Metropolitan Police Department, Kansas City, MO, 21 Nov 1921.

698. "Robert W. (Bob) Reed." *The Kansas City Times* (Kansas City, MO), 9 Dec 1949, p. 38.

699. "One Would be a Policeman." *Kansas City Star* (Kansas City, MO), 1 Nov 1921, p. 8.

700. Ibid.

701. "War Heroes Are Modest It's Harder to Wear Medals than Get Them, One Says." *Kansas City Star* (Kansas City, MO), 31 Oct 1921, p. 4.

702. Hatler, Margaret and Waldo. *The M. Waldo Hatler Story.* Neosho, MO: Ozarkana Book Press, 1968.

703. Ibid.

704. "Basket of Bottles Causes Shots." *Kansas City Star* (Kansas City, MO), 11 Jan 1922, p. 10.

705. "Held Up Wrong Man." *Joplin News Herald* (Joplin, MO), 16 Jan 1922, p. 1.

706. "Two K.C. Policemen Are Shot by Blacks." *Joplin Globe* (Joplin, MO), 23 Feb 1922, p. 1.

707. Ibid.

708. Ibid.

709. Ibid.

710. Ibid.

711. "Owner of 7 War Medals, Now Cop, Shot in 'Ruckus.'" *San Antonio Evening News* (San Antonio, TX), 23 Feb 1922, p. 4.

712. Christie, Lt. C.E. *Recommendation for Promotion of Officer Charles D. Barger to Board of Police Commissioners.* Kansas City, MO, 1 Jun 1922.

713. Barger, Charles D. *Miscellaneous Report, Metropolitan Police Department.* Kansas City, MO, 5 Sep 1922.

714. Larrabee, Lt. Cassius M. *Letter to Chief of Police Frank H. Anderson.* Kansas City, MO, 6 Sep 1922.

715. Sheets, Whalen F. *Statement of Witness.* Oak Grove, MO, 8 Sep 1922.

716. Barger, Charles D. *Miscellaneous Report, Metropolitan Police Department.* Kansas City, MO, 5 Sep 1922.

717. Sheets, Whalen F. *Statement of Witness.* Oak Grove, MO, 8 Sep 1922.

718. Ibid.

719. Ibid.

720. Ibid.

721. Barger, Charles D. *Miscellaneous Report, Metropolitan Police Department.* Kansas City, MO, 5 Sep 1922.

722. LeBow, Edwin M. *Complaint Against Officer Charles D. Barger.* Oak Grove, MO, 6 Sep 1922.

723. Sheets, Whalen F. *Statement of Witness.* Oak Grove, MO, 8 Sep 1922.

724. LeBow, Edwin M. *Complaint Against Officer Charles D. Barger.* Oak Grove, MO, 6 Sep 1922.

725. Ibid.

726. Ibid.

727. Barger, Charles D. *Miscellaneous Report, Metropolitan Police Department.* Kansas City, MO, 5 Sep 1922.

728. Sheets, Whalen F. *Statement of Witness.* Oak Grove, MO, 8 Sep 1922.

729. Barger, Charles D. *Miscellaneous Report, Metropolitan Police Department.* Kansas City, MO, 5 Sep 1922.

730. LeBow, Edwin M. *Complaint Against Officer Charles D. Barger.* Oak Grove, MO, 6 Sep 1922.

731. Ibid.

732. Ibid.

733. Ibid.

734. Ibid.

735. Ibid.

736. Ibid.

737. Ibid.

738. Ibid.

739. Barger, Charles D. *Miscellaneous Report, Metropolitan Police Department.* Kansas City, MO, 5 Sep 1922.
740. Hershfield, Harry A. *Letter of Complaint.* Kansas City, MO, 27 Sep 1922.
741. Ibid.
742. Ibid.
743. Ibid.
744. Ibid.
745. Oppenstein, Louis. *Letter of Response to Harry Hershfield.* Kansas City, MO, 29 Sep 1922.
746. Anderson, Chief Frank H. *Letter of Suspension of Charles D. Barger to the Board of Commissioners.* Kansas City, MO, 28 Sep 1922.
747. Anderson, Chief Frank H. *Letter of Reinstatement to Duty for Charles D. Barger.* Kansas City, MO, 12 Dec 1922.
748. Thomas, Bob. "Post-war Story Kept on Ice." *Park City Daily News* (Bowling Green, KY), 21 Nov 1960, p. 10.

Chapter 14: "Broken Hero"

749. "Mrs. Audrey Barger Free." *Kansas City Star* (Kansas City, MO), 5 Jun 1928, p. 2.
750. Ibid.
751. "Patrolman Attempts Suicide with Wife." *Macon Chronicle-Herald* (Macon, MO), 4 Jun 1928, p. 2.
752. Ibid.
753. Ibid.
754. "Mrs. Audrey Barger Free." *Kansas City Star* (Kansas City, MO), 5 Jun 1928, p. 2.
755. "War Hero Shoots Himself." *St. Louis Post-Dispatch* (St. Louis, MO), 4 Jun 1928, p. 3.
756. "Mrs. Audrey Barger Free." *Kansas City Star* (Kansas City, MO), 5 Jun 1928, p. 2.
757. Doyle vs. Barger. *Letter to the Board of Police Commissioners.* Kansas City, MO, 20 Aug 1929.
758. Tolivar, Judge L.R. *Transcript of Judgment: Doyle vs. Barger.* Kansas City, MO, 20 Dec 1928.
759. Vance, Chester D. *Correspondence Pertaining to Transcripts of Judgments Against Charles D. Barger.* Kansas City, MO, 27 Feb 1929.
760. Doyle vs. Barger. *Letter to the Board of Police Commissioners.* Kansas City, MO, 20 Aug 1929.
761. "Man and Boy Shot by Robber Firing at Store-Keeper." *St. Louis-Post-Dispatch* (St. Louis, MO), 9 Aug 1929, p. 1.
762. Ibid.
763. Ibid.
764. Board of Police Commissioners. *Failure to Pay Child Support.* Kansas City, MO, 23 Aug 1930.

765. Ibid.

766. Ibid.

767. MacDonald, A.B. "Missouri's Outstanding War Hero Braves the Peace-Time Perils of Manhattan Island." *Kansas City Star* (Kansas City, MO), 21 Dec 1930, Section C.

768. *Casualty Report*. Department of Police, Kansas City, KS, 3 Jun 1931.

769. Ibid.

770. *Investigation of Charges on State Warrant for the Arrest of Officer Charles D. Barger*. Police Department, Kansas City, MO, 5 Jun 1931.

771. Siegfried, Chief Lewis M. *Letter to the Board of Police Commissioners*. Kansas City, MO, 11 Jun 1931.

772. Kraft, Chris. *Conversation with June Buccina*. 8 Nov 2015.

773. Barger, Charles D. *Letter of Resignation from Kansas City Police Department*. Kansas City, MO, 29 Jun 1931.

774. Gibson, Det. (Ret.) Clarence. *Correspondence with Author*. 14 Mar 2016.

775. "Victim of His Own Revolver." *Kansas City Star* (Kansas City, MO), 21 Nov 1931, p. 1.

776. "Hero Has a Medal of Honor but No Job and Little Food." *Kansas City Star* (Kansas City, MO), 30 Aug 1932, p. 9.

777. Ibid.

778. Ibid.

779. Ibid.

780. "A World War Hero Dies." *The Albany Capital* (Albany, MO), 6 Apr 1933, p. 6.

781. Committee on Ways and Means. *World War Adjusted Compensation Act, Part 1*. Washington, DC: U.S. Government Printing Office, 1926.

782. "The Legion at Portland." *Kansas City Star* (Kansas City, MO), 4 Sep 1932. p.54.

783. Ibid.

784. "Victoria Cross Most Coveted." *New Castle Herald* (New Castle, PA), 6 Feb 1918, p. 7.

785. "A World War Hero Dies." *The Albany Capital* (Albany, MO), 6 Apr 1933, p. 6.

786. Kennedy, David M. *The American People in the Great Depression: Freedom from Fear, Part One*. New York, NY: Oxford University Press, 1999.

787. "Fund for Hero's Family." *Kansas City Star* (Kansas City, MO), 3 Dec 1936, p. 3.

788. Ibid.

789. Roosevelt Objections to Bonus Bill in Brief. *The Gazette and Daily* (York, PA), 23 May 1935, p. 12.

Chapter 15: "A Name and a Case Number"

790. Cooke, Blanche Wiesen. *Eleanor Roosevelt: Volume 2, The Defining Years, 1933-1938*. New York, NY: Penguin Books, 2000, pp. 44-46.

791. "28,500 Civilian Enrollees." *The Times* (Munster, IN), 13 Jun 1933, p. 3.

792. "Pick Vets Soon for Camp Work." *The Escanaba Daily Press* (Escanaba, MI), 7 Jun 1933, p. 7.

793. Ermentrout, Robert Allen. *Forgotten Men: The Civilian Conservation Corps.* Smithtown, NY: Exposition Press, 1982, p. 17.

794. Fechner, Director Robert. *Objectives and Results of the Civilian Conservation Corps Program.* Washington, DC: Civilian Conservation Corps, 1938.

795. Phillips, William J. "Veterans to Enroll in CCC." *The Springville Herald* (Springville, UT), 23 May 1935, p. 1.

796. "Want 800 Vets for C.C.C. Duty." *The Gettysburg Times* (Gettysburg, PA), 29 Jul 1935, p 1.

797. Barger, Charles D. *Record of Physical Examination—Civilian Conservation Corps.* Pacific, MO, 15 Oct 1935.

798. "Bonus Bill Becomes Law: Senate Overwhelms Veto." *The Cincinnati Enquirer* (Cincinnati, OH), 28 Jan 1936, p. 1.

799. "His Glory Dim in Death." *Kansas City Star* (Kansas City, MO), 28 Nov 1936, pp. 1 & 2.

800. Barger, Ruth L. *Statement of Witness.* Oak Grove, MO, 29 Dec 1936.

801. Ibid.

802. Ibid.

803. Levy, Capt. Jonas R. *Certificate of Investigative Findings.* CCC Company 3773, Blue Springs, MO, 20 Dec 1936.

804. Ibid.

805. Ridenour, Deputy Sheriff Frank. *Statement of Witness.* Kansas City, MO, 14 Dec 1936.

806. Barger, Ruth I *Statement of Witness.* Oak Grove, MO, 29 Dec 1936.

807. Ridenour, Deputy Sheriff Frank. *Statement of Witness.* Kansas City, MO, 14 Dec 1936.

808. Barger, Ruth I. *Statement of Witness.* Oak Grove, MO, 29 Dec 1936.

809. Ibid.

810. Ibid.

811. Ibid.

812. King, Deputy Constable Frank J. *Statement of Witness.* Oak Grove, MO, 22 Dec 1936.

813. Ridenour, Deputy Sheriff Frank. *Statement of Witness.* Kansas City, MO, 14 Dec 1936.

814. Ibid.

815. Ibid.

816. Ibid.

817. Ibid.

818. Ibid.

819. Ibid.

820. King, Deputy Constable Frank J. *Statement of Witness.* Oak Grove, MO, 22 Dec 1936.

821. Ridenour, Deputy Sheriff Frank. *Statement of Witness.* Kansas City, MO, 14 Dec 1936.

822. King, Deputy Constable Frank J. *Statement of Witness.* Oak Grove, MO, 22 Dec 1936.

823. Ibid.

824. Graham, Dr. Wallace H. *Statement of Witness.* Kansas City, MO, 17 Dec 1936.

825. Barger, Ruth I. *Statement of Witness.* Oak Grove, MO, 29 Dec 1936.

826. "His Glory Dim in Death." *Kansas City Star* (Kansas City, MO), 28 Nov 1936, pp. 1 & 2.

827. "Mother Recalls Her Own Plight." *The Independence Examiner* (Independence, MO), 27 Nov 1936, n.p.

828. Medal of Honor: Hearings before the Committee on Invalid Pensions, House of Representatives, Seventy-Sixth Congress, third session, on H.R. 3385 and H.R. 8051, bills to liberalize the provisions of the Medal of Honor Roll Act of April 27, 1916. February 1, 1940.

BIBLIOGRAPHY

Books

American Battle Monuments Commission. *89th Division Summary of Operations in the World War.* Washington, DC: U.S. Government Printing Office, 1944.

Bertrand, Georges, and Oscar N. Solbert. *Tactics and Duties for Trench Fighting.* New York and London: Putnam's Sons, 1918.

Cochrane, Rexmond C. *89th Division Comes into the Line, August 1918.* U.S. Army Chemical Corps Historical Office, Office of the Chief Chemical Officer, Army Chemical Center, Maryland, 1958.

Cochrane, Rexmond C. *The 89th Division in the Bois de Bantheville, October 1918.* U.S. Army Chemical Corps Historical Office, Office of the Chief Chemical Officer, Washington, DC, Study No. 18, Jun 1960.

Cochrane, Rexmond C. *The 1st Division at Ansauville, Jan-Apr 1918.* U.S. Army Chemical Corps Historical Office, Office of the Chief Chemical Officer, Army Chemical Center, Maryland, 1958.

Committee on Invalid Pensions. *House of Representatives Bill 3385.* Washington, DC: U.S. Government Printing Office, 1940.

Committee on Ways and Means. *World War Adjusted Compensation Act, Part 1.* Washington, DC: U.S. Government Printing Office, 1926.

Cooke, Blanche Wiesen. *Eleanor Roosevelt: Volume 2, The Defining Years, 1933-1938.* New York, NY: Penguin Books, 2000, pp. 44-46.

Crowell, Benedict and Robert Forrest Wilson. *The Armies of Industry: Our Nation's Manufacture of Munitions for a World in Arms, 1917-1918.* New Haven, CT: Yale University Press, 1921.

Dienst, Charles Franklin. *History of the 353rd Infantry Regiment, 89th Division, National Army.* Wichita, KS: The Eagle Press, 1921.

English, George H., Jr. *History of the 89th Division, U.S.A.* Denver, CO: Smith-Brooks Printing Company. The War Society of the 89th Division, 1920.

Ermentrout, Robert Allen. *Forgotten Men: The Civilian Conservation Corps*. Smithtown, NY: Exposition Press, 1982, p. 17.

Ferrell, Robert H. *America's Deadliest Battle: Meuse-Argonne, 1918*. Lawrence, KS: University Press of Kansas, 2012.

Ferrell, Robert H. *Reminiscences of Conrad S. Babcock: The Old U.S. Army and the New, 1898-1918*. Columbia, MO: University of Missouri Press, 2012.

Fussell, Paul. *The Great War and Modern Memory*. New York, NY: Oxford University Press, 1975.

Goodspeed's Lawrence County History. Chicago, IL: The Goodspeed Publishing Company, 1888.

Hair, James T. *Gazetteer of Madison County*. Alton, IL: James T. Hair, 1866.

Hastings, Max. *Armageddon: The Battle for Germany, 1944-45*. New York, NY: Vintage Books, 2004, p. 25.

Haswell, A.M. *Ozark Region: Its History and Its People. Volume 1: History of Lawrence County, Missouri*. Springfield, MO: Interstate Historical Society, 1917.

Hatler, Margaret and Waldo. *The M. Waldo Hatler Story*. Neosho, MO: Ozarkana Book Press, 1968.

Herwig, Holger H. *The First World War: Germany and Austria-Hungary, 1914–1918*. New York, NY: St. Martin's Press, 1997.

Kennedy, David M. *The American People in the Great Depression: Freedom from Fear, Part One*. New York, NY: Oxford University Press, 1999.

Kleber, Brooks E. and Dale Birdsell. *The Chemical Warfare Service: Chemicals in Combat*. Washington, DC: Center of Military History, United States Army, 1990.

Little, John G. *The Official History of the Eighty-Sixth Division*. Chicago, IL: States Publications Society, 1921.

Lockwood, John C. (2003). "Chapter 3. The Earth's Climates". In Hewitt, C. N.; Jackson, A. V. *Handbook of Atmospheric Science: Principles and Applications*. Malden, MA: Blackwell Publishing. pp. 72–74.

Manual of the Automatic Rifle (Chauchat). Washington, DC: War Department, Document No.793, 29 Apr 1918.

McGrath, Lt. John F. *War Diary of the 354th Infantry, 89th Division*. J. Linte, Trier, GE, 1919.

Murphy, Audie L. *To Hell and Back*. New York, NY: Henry Holt and Co., 1949.

Neir, Thomas J. *The Gleim Medal Letters*. Orders and Medals Society of America, 1998.

Ozark Region: Its History and Its People. Volume 3: History of Lawrence County, Missouri. Springfield, MO: Interstate Historical Society, 1917.

Pershing, Gen. John J. *Final Report of Gen. John J. Pershing*. Washington, DC: Government Printing Office, 1919.

Persons, Lt. Col. William E. and others. *Military Science and Tactics: Senior Course, Infantry, Volume 4*. University of Missouri: University Co-Operative Store, 1921.

Reynolds, Francis J., Allen L. Churchill and Francis T. Miller. *The Story of the Great War, Volume VII*. New York, NY: P.F. Collier & Son, 1919.

Rickenbacker, Capt. Edward V. *Fighting the Flying Circus*. Philadelphia and New York: J.B. Lippincott Company, 1919.

Sidell, Dr. Frederick R. and Dr. David R. Franz. *Defense Against the Effects of Chemical and Biological Warfare Agents*. Washington, DC: United States. Department of the Army. Office of the Surgeon General, 1997.

Smith, J.S. *Trench Warfare: A Manual for Officers and Men*. New York, NY: E.P. Dutton & Company, 1917.

Staffelbach, Dr. Georg, and Dora F. Rittmeyer. *Hans Peter Staffelbach, Goldschmied in Sursee, 1657-1736*. Luzern, Switzerland: E. Haag, 1936.

Stewart, Richard W. *American Military History, Volume I: The United States Army and Forging a Nation, 1775-1917 (Second Edition)*. Washington, DC: Center of Military History, United States Army. 2009.

Stewart, Richard W. *American Military History, Volume II: The United States Army in a Global Era, 1917-2003*. Washington, DC: Center of Military History, United States Army, 2005.

Stringer, Harry R. *Heroes All!* Washington, DC: Fassett Publishing Company, 1919.

Stokes' Trench Howitzer 3", Mark I. Washington, DC: U.S. Army War College, Jan 1918.

Strohn, Matthias. *World War I Companion*. Oxford, England: Osprey Publishing, 2013, p. 204.

Summary of Information, Numbers 92 to 121, Inclusive. Second Section, General Staff, General Headquarters, American Expeditionary Forces, July 1918.

Taylor, Maj. John R.M. and G.H. Powell. *Infantry Journal*. Washington, DC: The United States Infantry Trust Association, Jan 1918, Vol. XIV, No. 7.

Taylor, Telford. *The Anatomy of the Nuremberg Trials: A Personal Memoir*. New York, NY: Alfred A. Knopf, 1992.

The Medical Department of the United States Army in the World War. Neuropsychiatry. Washington: U.S. Government Printing Office, 1929, Vol. X, p. 158.

Tuorinsky, Lt. Col. Shirley. *Medal Aspects of Chemical Warfare*. Washington, DC: Office of The Surgeon General, Borden Institute, Walter Reed Army Medical Center, 2008.

Wade, Capt. Herbert Treadwell. *Handbook of Ordnance Data.* Washington, DC: U.S. Government Printing Office, 1919.

War Department Technical Manual 9-2005, Volume 3. The Ordnance School, Aberdeen Proving Ground, Maryland, Dec 1942.

Newspapers

"A Family of Murderers." *Kansas City Star* (Kansas City, MO), 10 Mar 1909, p. 5.

"A Ghastly Find." *The Columbus Daily Advocate* (Columbus, KS), 20 Jul 1897, p. 3.

"American Legion Lunch." *Daily Arkansas Gazette* (Little Rock, AR), 21 Mar 1921, p. 12.

"American Strategy Outwitted the Germans in the Argonne Offensive." *Lawrence Daily Journal-World* (Lawrence, KS), 26 Sep 1919, p. 2.

"American Zinc Buys High Five at Waco." *Joplin Globe* (Joplin, MO), 21 Aug 1921, p. 7.

"Another Murder." *The Galena Evening Times* (Galena, KS), 19 Jul 1897, p. 1.

"A Racy Divorce Case." *The Springfield Democrat* (Springfield, MO), 22 Feb 1894, p. 7.

"Are After Wilson." *St. Louis Republic* (St. Louis, MO), 22 Sep 1897, p. 8.

"Army Discharges Are Stopped by the Secretary of War." *The Oregon Daily Journal* (Portland, OR), 23 Jul 1921, p. 1.

"Ask States Hero Here." *Kansas City Star* (Kansas City, MO), 6 Jun 1919, p. 1.

"Attracted Much Attention." *Columbus Advocate* (Columbus, KS), 7 Oct 1897, p. 5.

"A World War Hero Dies." *The Albany Capital* (Albany, MO), 6 Apr 1933, p. 6.

"Basket of Bottles Causes Shots." *Kansas City Star* (Kansas City, MO), 11 Jan 1922, p. 10.

"Beginning with His Service in Indian Campaigning '80s as Sub-Altern, General Leonard Wood's Career Has Been Spectacular and Brilliant." *The Charlotte Observer* (Charlotte, NC), 5 Jul 1917, p. 2.

"Bonus Bill Becomes Law: Senate Overwhelms Veto." *Cincinnati Enquirer* (Cincinnati, OH), 28 Jan 1936, p. 1.

"Bullets? Pooh! But Drat That Hail in Missouri." *Plain Dealer* (Cleveland, OH), 26 Sep 1920, p. 17.

"Bystanders Wounded as Robber Fires at Victim." *Joplin Globe* (Joplin, MO), 10 Aug 1929, p. 3.

"Calhan Soldier Saved Comrades by Risking Life." *The Denver Post* (Denver, CO), 4 Feb 1919, p. 3.

"Causes of the War of 1812. *Chicago Tribune* (Chicago, IL), 29 Mar 1896, p. 47.

"Col. Nathan C. Shiverick Fatally Injured in Crash on Way to Saratoga Races." *Democrat and Chronicle* (Rochester, NY), 19 Aug 1932, p.1.

"Colorado's Greatest Hero. Jess Funk, Is Home, Dodging Questions about His Deeds." *The Denver Post* (Denver, CO), 5 Jun 1919, pp. 1 & 7.

Columbus Advocate (Columbus, KS), 12 Aug 1897, p. 5.

Columbus Advocate (Columbus, KS), 23 Sep 1897, p. 6.

Conner, Brig. Gen. Fox. "Reduction of St. Mihiel Salient Accomplished by America's First Army with Immense Success." *The Oregon Daily Journal* (Portland, OR), 3 Aug 1919, p. 18.

"Costly to Win a Wager." *The Kansas City Star* (Kansas City, MO), 23 Oct 1929, p. 8.

Creel, George. "Why Leonard Wood Was Not Sent to France." *Ashville Citizen-Times* (Ashville, NC), 17 Oct 1920, p. 6.

Dean, Charles M. "Organization at Port is Huge." *Cincinnati Enquirer* (Cincinnati, OH), 8 Aug 1943, p. 8.

"Drafting War Rules." *The New York Times* (New York, NY), 30 Jan 1922, p. 10.

"Ed Staffleback a Maniac." *Kansas City Journal* (Kansas City, MO), 25 Sep 1897, p. 2.

"Ed Staffleback Dead." *The Columbus Weekly Advocate* (Columbus, KS), 23 Nov 1899, p. 7.

"89th Gets Allied Ribbons by 'Plane.'" *Stars & Stripes*, 30 May 1919, Vol. 2, No. 17, p. 1.

Evening Gazette (Xenia, OH), May 14, 1918, p. 4.

"Everybody's Picking President Nowadays." *Star Tribune* (Minneapolis, MN), 14 Mar 1919, p. 4.

"Exploits to Live On." *The Kansas City Times* (Kansas City, MO), 1 May 1959, p. 43.

"Extra Duty for Mule." *Lebanon Daily Reporter* (Lebanon, IN), 12 Jun 1919, p. 8.

"Evidence in Wood Case." *The Wichita Daily Eagle* (Witchita, KS), 28 Nov 1903, p. 1.

"First Reward in Search for Staffleback Victims." *Topeka Weekly Capitol* (Topeka, KS), 17 Sep 1897, p. 3.

"Fool the Airmen." *The Daily Republican* (Cherryvale, KS), 10 Nov 1914, p. 1.

Frenzel, Arthur. "Jess was Brave Kid Says Proud Father of Colorado's Hero." *The Denver Post* (Denver, CO), 5 Jun 1919, p. 6.

"Fund for Hero's Family." *Kansas City Star* (Kansas City, MO), 3 Dec 1936, p. 3.

Funk, Corp. Jesse N. "Hero Funk Credits His Glorious Deeds All to Colorado." *The Denver Post* (Denver, MO), 5 Jun 1919, p. 6.

"Galena's Benders." *Kansas Semi-Weekly Capital* (Topeka, KS), 17 Sep 1897, p. 2.

"Gas Attack to Remain, View of Chief Officer." *The Indianapolis News* (Indianapolis, IN), 27 Dec 1918, p. 10.

"Gas Was the Most Terrible Weapon the Germans Had." *The Topeka Daily Capital* (Topeka, Kansas), 9 May 1919, p. 5.

"Gen. Wood is Making a Rapid Recovery; Had Miraculous Escape; Seven Wounds in Arm." *The New York Times* (New York, NY), 3 Feb 1918, p. 1.

"General Wood Retires from Army Service." *Salt Lake Telegram* (Salt Lake City, UT), 5 Oct 1921, p. 20.

"Gosh, I Thought it was a Tank." *Plain Dealer* (Cleveland, OH), 27 Sep 1920, p. 22.

"Grab Two Chicago Gangsters in K.C." *Jefferson City Post Tribune* (Jefferson City, MO), 12 Jun 1930, p. 3.

"Held Up Wrong Man." *Joplin News Herald* (Joplin, MO), 16 Jan 1922, p. 1.

"Heroes of the 89th Returning After Making a Record." *Leavenworth Post* (Leavenworth, KS), 20 May 1919, p. 6.

"Hero Has a Medal of Honor but No Job and Little Food." *Kansas City Star* (Kansas City, MO), 30 Aug 1932, p. 9.

"He was Too Slow." *Columbus Advocate* (Columbus, KS), 22 Jul 1897, p. 8.

"His Glory Dim in Death." *Kansas City Star* (Kansas City, MO), 28 Nov 1936, pp. 1 & 2.

"House Demands Army Reductions." *The San Bernardino County Sun* (San Bernardino, CA), 7 May 1921, p. 1.

"Impressive Tribute Paid to Memory of Heroes Who Gave Lives in War." *Arkansas Democrat* (Little Rock, AR), 31 May 1921, p. 3.

"Interesting Facts About the 89th Division." *St. Louis Post-Dispatch* (St. Louis, MO), 25 May 1919, p. 49.

Joplin Daily News (Joplin, MO), 31 Jul 1897, n.p.

"King Says he is Touched by St. Louis Reception." *St. Louis Post-Dispatch* (St. Louis, MO), 21 Oct 1919, pp. 1-2.

"Law Gains on Ray Broom." *Kansas City Star* (Kansas City, MO), 22 May 1926, p. 1.

"Law Turns on Arrestor." *Kansas City Star* (Kansas City, MO), 20 May 1925, p. 4.

"Leedy Believes in Hanging." *The Galena Evening Times* (Galena, KS), 11 Oct 1897, p. 1.

"Lieut. Bates Was Cited." *The Junction City Daily Union* (Junction City, KS), 29 Jan 1919, p. 6.

"Lynchings Likely." *Independence Daily Reporter* (Independence, KS), 16 Sep 1897, p. 1.

MacDonald, A.B. "Missouri's Outstanding War Hero Braves the Peace-Time Perils of Manhattan Island." *Kansas City Star* (Kansas City, MO), 21 Dec 1930, Section C.

"Man and Boy Shot by Robber Firing at Store-Keeper." *St. Louis Post-Dispatch* (St. Louis, MO), 9 Aug 1929, p. 1.

"Medal of Honor Winners C-in-C's Luncheon Guests." *Stars & Stripes*, 14 Feb 1919, p. 1.

"Michael Staffleback Dead." *The Jeffersonian Gazette* (Lawrence, KS), 18 May 1899, p. 6.

"Mike Staffelback Talks over Crimes." *Joplin News Herald* (Joplin, MO), 9 Aug 1924, p. 2.

Millard, T.F. "Bones and Hair Found Yesterday." *St. Louis Republic* (St. Louis, MO), 17 Sep 1897, p. 1.

Millard, T.F. "The Stafflebacks—Rivals of the Benders." *St. Louis Republic* (St. Louis, MO), 19 Sep 1897, pp. 1 & 4.

Modern Light (Columbus, KS), 30 Sep 1897, p. 10, col. 3.

"Mother Recalls Her Own Plight." *The Independence Examiner* (Independence, MO), 27 Nov 1936, n.p.

"Mrs. Audrey Barger Free." *Kansas City Star* (Kansas City, MO), 5 Jun 1928, p. 2.

"Mrs. Mary Weaver [obituary]." *Little Rock Daily News* (Little Rock, AR), 1 Mar 1921, p. 2.

"Mrs. Staffelback's Burial in Joplin." *Kansas City Star* (Kansas City, MO), 12 Mar 1909, p. 3.

"Mustard Gas." *Great Falls Daily Tribune* (Great Falls, MT), 3 Oct 1918, p. 5.

"National Guards to Hold Encampment at Camp Pike." *The Times* (Harrison, AR), n.d., n.p.

"News of Camp Funston." *The Junction City Daily Union* (Junction City, KS), 3 Apr 1918, p. 3.

"No Sign of Bodies." *Belleville Telescope* (Belleville, KS), 24 Sep 1897, p. 2.

"Obituary: Mrs. Mary Weaver." *Little Rock Daily News* (Little Rock, AR), 1 Mar 1921, p. 2.

"Old Nancy's Brood." *Middleton Daily Argus* (Middleton, NY), 23 Sep 1897, p. 19.

"One Would be a Policeman." *Kansas City Star* (Kansas City, MO), 1 Nov 1921, p. 8.

"Owner of 7 War Medals, Now Cop, Shot in 'Ruckus.'" *San Antonio Evening News* (San Antonio, TX), 23 Feb 1922, p. 4.

Palmer, Lt. H.R. "Reducing the St. Mihiel Salient." *The Pittsburg Morning Sun* (Pittsburg, KS), 12 Jun 1919, p. 16.

Palmer, Lt. H.R. "The Argonne-Meuse Battle." *The Pittsburg Morning Sun* (Pittsburg, KS), 12 Jun 1919, p. 12.

"Patrolman Attempts Suicide with Wife." *Macon Chronicle-Herald* (Macon, MO), 4 Jun 1928, p. 2.

"Pershing May Plan Blow at Hun Fortress." *The Courier-Journal* (Louisville, KY), 14 Sep 1918, p.1.

Phillips, William J. "Veterans to Enroll in CCC." *The Springville Herald* (Springville, UT), 23 May 1935, p. 1.

"Pick Vets Soon for Camp Work." *The Escanaba Daily Press* (Escanaba, MI), 7 Jun 1933, p. 7.

"Plan an Exchange for Detectives." *The Sedalia Democrat* (Sedalia, MO), 1 May 1930, p. 2.

"Played Detective to Raise Some Cash." *The Macon Republican* (Macon, MO), 26 May 1925, p. 2.

"Praise the Barger Aid." *Kansas City Star* (Kansas City, MO), 7 Dec 1936, p. 11.

"Private Barger Tells How He Won Medal of Honor." *The St. Louis Star and Times* (St. Louis, MO), 30 May 1919, p. 3.

"Radio Cuts Down Crime." *The Chillicothe Constitution Tribune* (Chillicothe, MO), 4 Feb 1932, p. 1.

"Remmel Assured of Retention of Pike." *Daily Arkansas Gazette* (Little Rock, AR), 21 Mar 1921, p. 1.

"Rivals of the Benders." *Daily Tribune* (Salt Lake City, UT), 26 Sep 1897, p. 19.

"Rival of the Benders. Stafflebacks, of Galena, Accused of Many Murders." *The Kansas City Journal* (Kansas City, MO), 15 Sep 1897, p. 1.

"Roberson Association Meets." *Springfield Missouri Republican* (Springfield, MO), 21 Oct 1919, p. 7.

"Robert W. (Bob) Reed." *The Kansas City Times* (Kansas City, MO). 9 Dec 1949, p. 38.

Roosevelt Objections to Bonus Bill in Brief. *The Gazette and Daily* (York, PA), 23 May 1935, p. 12.

"Settlement Near in Police Muddle." *The Sedalia Democrat* (Sedalia, MO), 17 Apr 1930, p. 1.

"Soldier's Letter." *The Evening Star* (Independence, KS), 7 Feb 1919, p. 2.

"Spring Soldier Wins High Medal." *Colorado Springs Gazette* (Colorado Springs, CO), 5 Feb 1919, p. 2.

"Stafflebacks Sentenced." *Kansas City Journal* (Kansas City, MO), 2 Oct 1897, p. 1.

Stanley, A.R. "Old-Time Fourth of July Fireworks Light Our Way to Berlin." *The Des Moines Register* (Des Moines, IA), 15 Sep 1918, p. 23.

"Stotts City Man Greatest Hero of 89th." *The Monett Weekly Times* (Monett, MO), 27 Jun 1919, p. 3.

"Take Police Dept. Out of Politics." *The Chillicothe Constitution Tribune* (Chillicothe, MO), 2 May 1931, p. 1.

"Text of Conscription Law Under Which Registrations are to be Made on June 5." *The Star Press* (Muncie, IN), 28 May 1917, p. 2.

"The Army Reduction Veto." *New Castle Herald* (New Castle, PA), 16 Feb 1921, p. 4.

"The Benders are not in it." *Modern Light* (Columbus, KS), 16 Sep 1897, p. 1.

The Chieftain (Mt. Vernon, MO), 21 Jun 1894, p. 3.

The Columbus Weekly Advocate (Columbus, KS), 5 Aug 1897, p. 7.

The Columbus Weekly Advocate (Columbus, KS), 30 Sep 1897, p. 8.

The Galena Evening Times (Galena, KS), 2 Apr 1898, n.p.

"The Legion at Portland." *Kansas City Star* (Kansas City, MO), 4 Sep 1932, p. 54.

"The Stafflebacks Sentenced." *The St. Joseph Weekly Gazette* (St. Joseph, MO), 8 Oct 1897, p. 1.

The Winchester Star (Winchester, KS), 29 Apr 1898, p. 4.

Thomas, Bob. "Post-war Story Kept on Ice." *Park City Daily News* (Bowling Green, KY), 21 Nov 1960, p. 10.

Tiling, Moritz. "The German Element in Texas 1820-1850, Chapter III." *Houston Post* (Houston, TX), 13 Jan 1913, p. 9.

"Two K.C. Policemen Are Shot by Blacks." *Joplin Globe* (Joplin, MO), 23 Feb 1922, p.1.

"Two Winners of Medal of Honor Arrive with 354th." *St. Louis Post-Dispatch* (St. Louis, MO), 30 May 1919, p. 2.

"Victim of His Own Revolver." *Kansas City Star* (Kansas City, MO), 21 Nov 1931, p. 1.

"Victoria Cross Most Coveted." *New Castle Herald* (New Castle, PA), 6 Feb 1918, p. 7.

"Waco War Hero Back in Army." *Joplin Globe* (Joplin, MO), 9 Jan 1921, p. 5.

"Want 800 Vets for C.C.C. Duty." *The Gettysburg Times* (Gettysburg, PA), 29 Jul 1935, p. 1.

"Wants a Pardon." *The Columbus Daily Advocate* (Columbus, KS), 22 Jul 1898, p. 3.

"War Heroes Are Modest It's Harder to Wear Medals than Get Them, One Says." *Kansas City Star* (Kansas City, MO), 31 Oct 1921, p. 4.

"War Hero is Peace Victim Lately." *The Pampa Daily News* (Pampa, TX), 13 Nov 1932, p. 5.

"War Hero Shoots Himself." *St. Louis Post-Dispatch* (St. Louis, MO), 4 Jun 1928, p. 3.

"When General Wood Commanded the 89th; How He Put the Men in Fighting Form." *The World Herald* (Omaha, NE), May 1919, p. 7.

"When Kansas Doughboys of 89th Mopped Up Wood." *The Topeka Daily Capital* (Topeka, KS), 22 May 1919, p. 9.

"Will the Shaft Give up its Dead." *Weir City Daily Sun* (Weir, KS), 15 Sep 1897, p. 1.

"Wounded Denver Soldier Shot by His Own Sentry on Returning to Lines." *The Denver Post* (Denver, CO), 5 Jun 1919, p. 4.

Internet Sources

Bratt, John. "In Grandpa Martin's Footsteps." *Howell County Mogenweb.* n.p., n.d. Web. 4 Nov. 2015. <http://www.bing.com/r?IG=9102753 7760B4BBCAF0EEE81AA7994A9&CID=023CD39DCB63660222 0BD9E1CAF367B1&rd=1&h=wMAfwTlUhabodRpseDoigRbV8Z hLMtfvuvZW5T9ga3I&v=1&r=http%3a%2f%2fhowell.mogenweb. org%2ffamily%2fMartin-Verhage-1.pdf&p=DevEx,5061.1>.

Congressional Medal of Honor Society. "Medal of Honor." *CMOHS. org—History of the Medal of Honor.* n.p., n.d. Web. 08 May 2017. <http://www.cmohs.org/medal-history.php>.

"Definition of 'mopping-up operation.'" Mopping-up operation definition and meaning. *Collins English Dictionary.* n.p., n.d. Web. 22 June 2017. <https://www.collinsdictionary.com/us/dictionary/english/ mopping-up-operation>.

English Dictionary. "Coroner's jury [online]." *English Dictionary.* n.p., Dec. 2016. Web. 08 May 2017. <http://englishdictionary.education/ en/coroners-jury>.

Harper Collins Publishers. "Holy Alliance." *Dictionary.com.* Dictionary. com, n.d. Web. 12 Apr 2017. <http://www.dictionary.com/browse/ holy-alliance>.

Kansas Historical Society. "Camp Funston." *Kansas State Historical Society.* n.p., Nov. 2016. Web. 08 May 2017. <http://www.kshs.org/ kansapedia/camp-funston/16692.>.

Office of Public Health Preparedness and Response. "Facts About Phosgene." *Centers for Disease Control and Prevention.* Centers for Disease Control and Prevention, 12 Apr. 2013. Web. 08 May 2017. <https://emergency.cdc.gov/agent/phosgene/basics/facts.asp>.

Office of Public Health Preparedness and Response. "Facts About Sulfur Mustard." *Centers for Disease Control and Prevention.* Centers for Disease Control and Prevention, 2 May 2013. Web. 13 Jun 2016. <https://emergency.cdc.gov/agent/sulfurmustard/basics/facts.asp>.

Overbey, Diana. "Trench Construction in World War I." *Diana Overbey*.
    n.p., 13 Jan. 2012. Web. 27 June 2017. https://dianaoverbey.wordpress.
    com/2012/01/13/trench-construction-in-world-war-i/.
"Salient". *Dictionary.com Unabridged*. Random House, Inc. 20 Jun. 2017.
    <Dictionary.com http://www.dictionary.com/browse/salient>.

Magazines/Pamphlets

Bollmeyer, Fred J. Welcome to Medal of Honor Men. *The American
    Legion 2nd National Convention: Official Program*, 1920.
Canfield, Bruce N. "Remington's Model 10: The Other Trench Gun."
    American Rifleman, Nov 2009, p.76.
Fechner, Director Robert. *Objectives and Results of the Civilian
    Conservation Corps Program*. Washington, DC: Civilian
    Conservation Corps, 1938.
Glenn, Maj. Gen. E.F. and others. *Infantry Journal*. Washington, DC: The
    United States Infantry Association, Jul 1917-Jun 1918, Vol. 14, p. 484.

Other Sources

Anderson, Chief Frank H. *Correspondence to Fred D. Croy*. Kansas City,
    MO, 11 Oct 1922.
Anderson, Chief Frank H. *Letter of Reinstatement to Duty for Charles D.
    Barger*. Kansas City, MO, 12 Dec 1922.
Anderson, Chief Frank H. *Letter of Suspension of Charles D. Barger to the
    Board of Commissioners*. Kansas City, MO, 28 Sep 1922.
Barger, Charles D. *Employment Record*. Metropolitan Police Department,
    Kansas City, MO, 21 Nov 1921.
Barger, Charles D. *Letter of Resignation from Kansas City Police
    Department*. Kansas City, MO, 29 Jun 1931.
Barger, Charles D. *Miscellaneous Report, Metropolitan Police Department*.
    Kansas City, MO, 5 Sep 1922.
Barger, Charles D. *Record of Physical Examination--Civilian Conservation
    Corps*. Pacific, MO, 15 Oct 1935.
Barger, Ruth I. *Statement of Witness*. Oak Grove, MO, 29 Dec 1936.
Board of Police Commissioners. *Failure to Pay Child Support*. Kansas
    City, MO, 23 Aug 1930.
Casualty Report. Department of Police, Kansas City, KS, 3 Jun 1931.
Certificate of Marriage. State of Missouri, County of Jasper, Filed for
    Record with the County Recorder on 16 Nov 1896.
Christie, Lt. C.E. *Recommendation for Promotion of Officer Charles D.
    Barger to Board of Police Commissioners*. Kansas City, MO, 1 Jun 1922.

Citation to Accompany the Award of the Distinguished Service Cross to Captain Marshall P. Wilder. War Department, General Orders 95 (1919).

Citation to Accompany the Award of the Distinguished Service Cross to Second Lieutenant John M. Millis. War Department, General Orders 13 (1923).

Citation to Accompany the Award of the Medal of Honor to Private First Class Charles D. Barger. War Department General Order 20 (1919).

Citation to Accompany the Award of the Medal of Honor to Private First Class John L. Barkley. War Department, General Orders 44 (1919).

Coroner's Case No. 4318. Kansas City General Hospital, Kansas City, MO, 25 Nov 1936.

Doyle vs. Barger. *Letter to the Board of Police Commissioners.* Kansas City, MO, 20 Aug 1929.

Drasky, 1st Lt. Stanley. *Certificate of Medical Officer.* CCC Company 3773, Blue Springs, MO, n.d. [1936].

Endsley, Section Leader Stanton H. *Statement of Witness.* CCC Company 3773, Blue Springs, MO, 22 Dec 1936.

Geneva Convention of July 6th, 1906, Chapter II.--Medical Units and Establishments. Article 8, Paragraph 1. Geneva, Switzerland, 1906.

Geneva Convention of July 6th, 1906, Chapter III.--Personnel. Article 9. Geneva, Switzerland, 1906.

Gibson, Det. (Ret.) Clarence. *Correspondence with Author.* 14 Mar 2016.

Graham, Dr. Wallace H. *Statement of Witness.* Kansas City, MO, 17 Dec 1936.

Griffin, Laurie (Lake). *Correspondence with Author.* 4-5 May 2016.

Hershfield, Harry A. *Letter of Complaint.* Kansas City, MO, 27 Sep 1922.

Investigation of Charges on State Warrant for the Arrest of Officer Charles D. Barger. Police Department, Kansas City, MO, 5 Jun 1931.

Johnson, 1st Foreman George A. *Statement of Witness.* CCC Company 3773, Blue Springs, MO, 22 Dec 1936.

King, Deputy Constable Frank J. *Statement of Witness.* Oak Grove, MO, 22 Dec 1936.

King George V. *Letter to American Troops.* n.d. (1918).

Kraft, Chris. *Conversation with June Buccina.* 8 Nov 2015.

Larrabee, Lt. Cassius M. *Letter to Chief of Police Frank H. Anderson.* Kansas City, MO, 6 Sep 1922.

LeBow, Edwin M. *Complaint Against Officer Charles D. Barger.* Oak Grove, MO, 6 Sep 1922.

Lederman, H.J. *Statement of Witness.* Oak Grove, MO, 8 Sep 1922.

Levy, Capt. Jonas R. *Certificate of Investigative Findings.* CCC Company 3773, Blue Springs, MO, 20 Dec 1936.

1900 United State Census. Delaware Township, Leavenworth County, Kansas. Sheet No. 5B, family 1, dwelling 1, line 90, 2 Jun 1900.

Oppenstein, Louis. *Letter of Response to Harry Hershfield.* Kansas City, MO, 29 Sep 1922.

Proceedings of a Board of Officers. CCC Company 3773, Blue Springs, MO, 27 Nov 1936.

Ridenour, Deputy Sheriff Frank. *Statement of Witness.* Kansas City, MO, 14 Dec 1936.

Siegfried, Chief Lewis M. *Letter to the Board of Police Commissioners.* Kansas City, MO, 11 Jun 1931.

Sheets, Whalen F. *Statement of Witness.* Oak Grove, MO, 8 Sep 1922.

Shreeve, Capt. William A. *Incident Report.* Kansas City, MO, 27 Sep 1922.

Special Order No. 252. Headquarters Missouri-Kansas District, Civilian Conservation Corps, Fort Leavenworth, KS, 27 Nov 1936.

Staffelback vs. Staffelback. *Petition for Divorce.* State of Missouri, County of Lawrence, 11 Mar 1887, File #5494.

Tolivar, Judge L.R. *Transcript of Judgment: Doyle vs. Barger.* Kansas City, MO, 20 Dec 1928.

Vance, Chester D. *Correspondence Pertaining to Transcripts of Judgments Against Charles D. Barger.* Kansas City, MO, 27 Feb 1929.